THE SPAN OF THE CROSS

Christian Religion and Society in Wales
1914–2000

D. DENSIL MORGAN

UNIVERSITY OF WALES PRESS
CARDIFF
2011

© D. Densil Morgan, 1999

First Edition 1999
Second Edition 2011

British Library Cataloguing-in-Publication Data.
A catalogue record for this book is available from the British Library.

ISBN 978-0-7083-2397-7

e-ISBN 978-0-7083-2430-1

www.uwp.co.uk

The right of D. Densil Morgan to be identified as author of this work has been asserted by him in accordance with the Copyright, Designs and Patents Act 1988.

Typeset at University of Wales Press
Printed in Wales by Dinefwr Press, Llandybïe

Y mae rhychwant y groes yn llawer mwy
Na'u Piwritaniaeth a'u Sosialaeth hwy . . .

('The span of the cross is greater by far
Than their Puritanism or their Socialism . . .')

D. Gwenallt Jones

Dedicated to

R. G. ROBERTS
JOHN RICE ROWLANDS
OLAF DAVIES

Ministers of the Word

Contents

List of illustrations

Acknowledgements

I would like to thank the following people for their help in preparing this book: my brother-in-law, Mr Huw Harries, for enlightening me on the contribution made by the Welsh regiments during the First World War and on different aspects of military history generally; the Revd Roger L. Brown who read the typescript chapters on the Church in Wales and so aided my untrained Nonconformist eye to appreciate many details pertaining to the more recent history of Welsh Anglicanism which otherwise would have escaped me; the Revd Dr Elfed ap Nefydd Roberts who performed a similar service in the sections on the Presbyterian Church of Wales and gave me the benefit of his insights into a number of ecumenical concerns as well; my colleague Dr Tony Brown of the School of English and Linguistics, University of Wales, Bangor, for sharing with me his expert knowledge of Welsh creative writing in English and for discussing some of the religious themes contained therein; Dr Ian Randall of the International Baptist Theological College in Prague for answering my enquiries about aspects of the spirituality of twentieth-century evangelicalism, and Br William Nicol of the Community of the Resurrection for his hospitality in allowing me to peruse material on Bishop Timothy Rees in the Mirfield archive. Professor A. M. Allchin read the book in its entirety and made valuable suggestions which I have tried to incorporate in the final text.

I owe a particular debt of gratitude to those students who chose to pursue postgraduate research on Welsh religious history under my supervision, namely Miss Helen Mai Owen, who shed a flood of light on the way in which secularization affected the Calvinistic Methodists during the early decades of the century, Dr Robert Pope, who has made such a signal contribution to our knowledge of the inter-relation between Nonconformity and the Labour movement, and Dr Trystan Hughes, who has unearthed so much fascinating detail relating to the history of Catholicism in twentieth-century Wales. Although he was not a student of mine, I learned an enormous amount about ecumenism from the doctoral thesis (and *viva voce*) of another Bangor researcher, the Revd Dr Noel A. Davies, whose dissertation was, alas, the last to be supervised by my erstwhile colleague and mentor, Professor R. Tudur Jones. The friendship and fellowship engendered by our collaboration (and which, happily, has now been provided with an institutional base in the Centre of Advanced Study of Religion in Wales) is something which I will treasure always. I would also like to record my thanks to Professor Gareth Lloyd Jones and colleagues in the School of Theology and Religious Studies at Bangor for their support, and to my fellow Church historian, Dr Geraint Tudur, for valuable assistance in matters photographic as well as academic!

Ms Susan Jenkins, Ms Ceinwen Jones and Ms Liz Powell at the University of Wales Press have been exceptionally helpful and efficient during the production of this study, while my wife, Ann, has displayed her usual interest and concern during the years since I have been engaged in the present venture. My thanks to her, and to our children, is, as always, immense.

It is a particular pleasure to dedicate the book to three preachers of the gospel whose ministry has meant much to me and to many others for a very long time. In honouring them, I register my appreciation for all those who (like R. S. Thomas's 'Country Clergy') have been called to proclaim the Word during this momentous century:

> . . . They left no books,
> Memorial to their lonely thought
> In grey parishes; rather they wrote
> On men's hearts and in the minds
> Of young children sublime words
> Too soon forgotten. God in his time
> Or out of time will correct this.

D. Densil Morgan
Bangor, November 1999

The extracts from the poetry of R. S. Thomas are reproduced by permission of J. M. Dent, and the extracts from the work of D. Gwenallt Jones and from 'Mewn Dau Gae' by Waldo Williams are reproduced by permission of Gomer Press.

Preface to the Second Edition (2011)

Perhaps the most graphic image of the new millennium was the destruction of the twin towers of the World Trade Center in lower Manhattan on the morning of 11 September 2001. The fact that this was seen throughout the world virtually as it happened illustrated not only the potent effectiveness of globalized technology but underscored the fact that religion, in this case as a malign force, would be a prevailing reality in the twenty-first century. It may be that the trends described in the final chapter of *The Span of the Cross* have continued unabated throughout the last decade, but religion has thrust its way from the periphery to the centre of the public imagination. Within its new context of an increased pluralism, an affirmed multiculturalism and a much more strident atheist antagonism, Christian discourse has remained a factor within post-devolution Wales.

Institutionally, Christianity has followed the trajectory traced in the chapters that follow. The two reports *Churchgoing in the UK: A Research Report from Tearfund on Church Attendance in the UK* (2007) and Blunt and Bowyer's *Presbyterian Church in Wales: Key Research Findings* (2009) charting more recent developments, along with the researches of the University of Glamorgan based sociologist Paul Chambers (*Religion, Secularization and Social Change in Wales* (2005) and 'Out of taste, out of time: the future of Nonconformist religion in Wales in the twenty first century', *Contemporary Wales* (2008), 86–100), have shown that statistical decline has continued apace and that traditional forms of religiosity, denominationally structured and theologically liberal, have suffered the most. As this is hardly unexpected, little needs to be said of it here. There are other changes within the three older traditions: Roman Catholic, Church in Wales and Nonconformist, which do invite comment, though it is beyond the mainstream denominations that the most significant developments within Welsh Christianity seem to have occurred.

The Roman Catholic Church in Wales had been spared the agony of the paedophile priest scandal which had begun to inflict itself on some English dioceses during the early 1990s and would later undermine the authority of Catholicism in Ireland, but at the turn of the millennium it registered in Wales in a spectacular way. In 1998 Fr John Lloyd, a Cardiff priest and press secretary to Archbishop John Aloysius Ward, was imprisoned for serious sexual offences against a series of young people who had been in his charge. The archbishop, who was a close confidant of Lloyd's and had known of allegations made against him, had done nothing to investigate them. Ward compounded his culpability by ordaining, also in 1998, Joseph Jordan, a known paedophile who had transferred from the jurisdiction of the diocese of Plymouth having fallen foul of the church's own child protection guidelines. Jordan's proclivities soon became known within the archdiocese of Cardiff – he was imprisoned for eight years in 2000 – while many of Ward's own priests called, unprecedentedly, for their leader to stand down. Despite failing health and a blatant loss of credibility, he refused to yield to pressure until in 2001 Pope John-Paul II personally ordered his suspension. It was the first time that such a high ranking prelate within the English and Welsh hierarchy had been forced to resign and it brought the crisis in the church into the spotlight in a glaring way. A Capuchin father who had been brought up in Wrexham and trained in Pantasaph, near Holywell, Flintshire, Ward retired ignominiously, and was bewildered, up to his death in 2007, aged 78, at the treatment that he had been meted. He felt throughout that he had done little wrong. The archdiocese of Cardiff, and the Welsh church as whole, was fortunate to have as his successor Peter Smith, a convivial chain-smoking Londoner, whose cheery demeanour masked a sharp mind, a steely determination to inculcate reform, while, as spokesman for the Catholic Bishops Conference's Department for Christian Responsibility, providing an eloquent apologetic for the Church's social teachings in the context of the new century. Although clergy numbers contracted, mass attendance declined and financial problems led to the closure of many churches, Smith's nine years in Cardiff before his translation to the archdiocese of Southwark in 2010 bound many wounds and restored a measure of confidence to his beleaguered communion.

Like the Roman Catholic Church, the Church in Wales experienced a turnover in its senior clergy over the millennium and beyond. Some thought that the integration of the Church into the Welsh mainstream, which had become patent a generation and more earlier, was in danger of being reversed. The resignation of Carl Cooper, bishop of

St Davids, 2002–8, and the untimely death of Anthony Crockett, bishop of Bangor, 2004–8, seriously depleted the Welsh-language skills of the bench of bishops, while the appointment of Dominic Walker, formerly bishop of Reading, to the see of Monmouth in 2003 and Gregory Cameron, from the International Anglican Communion's directorate of ecumenical affairs, to St Asaph in 2009, underlined what some perceived as an anglicizing trend. The tone of the church, inclusivist, socially engaged and doctrinally accommodating, has been set by Barry Morgan, bishop of Llandaff and since 2003 archbishop of Wales. Totally at home in the new, devolved Wales and a vocal advocate for further law-making powers to be granted to the National Assembly, Morgan has proved to be a skilled leader of his flock and an effective (if liberal) voice for the Christian viewpoint in the public sphere. Each of the six dioceses has undergone significant change during the last decade, with a downward trend in Easter communicant apparent throughout. The traditional pattern of parish ministry is currently being questioned while according to a recent publication, *The Church in Wales: A Small Guide to a Big Picture* (2009), the church is considering a far more flexible use of its human resources. However upbeat its posture and despite the innovative nature of the archbishop's leadership, institutionalism seems to be stifling bold creativity within the Anglican Church in Wales. There is one personality, however, from within the Church who made an enormous contribution to Christian witness generally at the beginning of the decade: it was Barry Morgan's predecessor as archbishop, Rowan Williams.

Rowan Williams had made an easy, if unexpected, transition from academia to the life of a diocesan bishop following his call, from the Lady Margaret chair of divinity in the University of Oxford, to the bishopric of Monmouth in 1992. It was by the end of the decade, though, that he had really come into his own. His election as archbishop in 1999 was greeted with extraordinary warmth by all shades of opinion, ecclesiastical and otherwise, throughout Wales. The nation realized that it had in him a person of outstanding qualities: a native-born son, a visionary, a poet, an intellectual to be sure, but one whose feeling for and commitment to the people was total – and a saint. Already an inspiring figure within the wider Anglican community, he brought the profusion of his gifts to bear on Wales. His vision for the renewal of Christian presence was seen in his 2001 paper, 'The churches of Wales and the future of Wales' (*Transactions of the Honourable Society of Cymmrodorion*, 8 (2002), 151–60) in which he called for the creation of a new language of worship, both in English and in Welsh, to convey the riches of the faith that would resonate with the deepest impulses of a globalized generation. The Anglican community worldwide realized the unique range of Williams's gifts, and it was with a sense of pride tinged with regret that in 2003 the Church in Wales yielded him to the see of Canterbury, the first Welshman ever to become leader of the Church of England. Rowan Williams remains, however, very much a son of Wales, and much more can be expected of him in the field of Welsh spirituality in the future.

For its part, Nonconformity as a religious movement was seen very clearly to be running into the sand. In 2000 a somewhat desperate last-ditch attempt to create what had been, forty years earlier, the ecumenical dream of a single Welsh Nonconformist church failed due to the noisy protestations of a phalanx of recalcitrant Independent ministers, but even more to the realization on the part of the Presbyterian Church of Wales that a putative centrally organized single Nonconformist church encompassing all the denominations would virtually bankrupt its own pension fund. Some of the key proponents of the abortive venture have since channelled their energies into doctrinal matters through the Welsh-language website *Cristionogaeth 21* ('Christianity 21') in which a reductionist theology, reminiscent of the 1960s, is once more in vogue. Trinity, incarnation, the deity of Christ and the unique authority of the Word of God are said to be incompatible with the norms of the twenty-first century world, and as such will have to be jettisoned. Such a programme will itself run into the sand, but it is indicative of the frustrations of a disillusioned generation of ministers who, at the close of their ministry, have witnessed massive and disheartening decline. Chapel closures during the decade rose to epidemic proportions, mirroring the chapel-building 'mania' of the mid-Victorian era, when it was said that one new Nonconformist chapel was being built on average every eight days. Even if both nineteenth- and twenty-first century trends sprung from sociological rather than explicitly religious causes, to see a way of life visibly disappear within a generation has been a distressing experience for many. By the end of its second decade, something of the same failure of purpose (though not necessarily doctrinal declension) seems to be characterizing Cytûn. Established in 1990 as the platform for ecumenical endeavour in Wales, Cytûn, or Churches Together in Wales, is suffering from institutional fatigue and a lack of creativity. The weaknesses of each of the three mainstream traditions since 2000, the Catholic, the Anglican and the Nonconformist, stem from their institutionalism. Those under 45 are simply not engaging with the traditional forms of religious expression, and new life, where it is to be found, exists outside the denominational structures.

If enervation is the most obvious characteristic of the older church forms, throughout the last decade newer groupings have flourished. Among the bodies listed in the Welsh Evangelical Alliance's *Church Diversity Index* (2003) are the Arabic Church in Wales, the Chinese Christian Church, the Church of God of Prophecy, Gospel Outreach, the Nazarenes, New Frontiers, Pioneer Churches, the Vineyard Fellowship and others, while groups such as the Assemblies of God, the Elim churches, the Fellowship of Independent Evangelical Churches, the Orthodox Church and others that would formerly have been on the periphery, are listed as having moved much nearer towards the mainstream. Diversity has triumphed over uniformity with Welsh Christianity being more of a patchwork quilt than a monochrome (or duochrome) blanket comprising of 'chapel' and 'church'. Although a far broader range of churches now serve the Welsh people, this does not mean that they attract vast congregations: according to different surveys, in 2006–8 only between 7 and 9 per cent of the Welsh population attended any place of worship. Curiously, however, according to the 2001 census, as many as 71.9 of the Welsh population described themselves as 'Christian' and only 18.5 stated that they had no religious affiliation at all. Whereas the facts enumerated above could give for gloomy reading, there are two trends that may be significant for the future.

The phenomenon of the liquid church or the emerging church has been the focus of some interest as witnessed by Zak's Place in Swansea's city centre, Solace, which meets in a Cardiff nightclub, and similar endeavours. In tune with the fluid, questing and provisional nature of post-modernity and responding to the fact that the institutional churches are not meeting people's felt needs, these ventures have been developed specifically by younger Christians for whom globalization, pluralism and a visual-based multi-media culture are the unquestioned norms. Whereas the inherited churches took the Enlightenment standards for granted, privileging rationality and the cerebral in which objective truth was measured in terms of sound doctrine, propositional revelation and the like, these new associations prize immediacy and spontaneity, they are highly participatory, with music and the visual being the medium through which spirituality is expressed. Their websites are arresting with most communication occurring in electronic form. The setting for 'doing church' is no longer church or chapel; there are no pulpits or pews. Sacred space is wherever people meet for sharing, discussion and the application of the gospel to their everyday concerns. For a generation suspicious of authority and alienated from religion in all its guises, the emerging church is at least trying to connect. 'The aim,' it has been said, 'is not necessarily to convert the unchurched but to give space for those who are seeking spiritual fulfilment.' Whether anything will come of this, it is too early to tell. The Spirit *needs* structures, and an element of institutionalism is essential for one generation's vision to be passed on to the next. The rather naive Jesus-centred spirituality, as much in reaction to an oppressive evangelicalism as to a stifling traditionalism one suspects, will need an underpinning in classical orthodoxy if it is to survive. Yet this movement does show that alternative pieties, still recognizably Christian, are being nurtured in the context of a post-modern Wales.

The second phenomenon is more interesting and, I suspect, more significant by far. One legacy from the twentieth century was that the evangelical movement was, on the whole, distrustful of anything that smacked of 'the social gospel'. A zeal for social commitment on the part of Christians was seen to compromise the biblical gospel, to undermine the spiritual nature of the church and, worst of all, to betoken theological liberalism. To suggest that sin could be analysed in anything less than individualistic terms was to invite suspicion and censure. The divide between 'liberal' and 'evangelical' often ran along these lines including a positive or negative (or noncommittal at best) attitude to social involvement. Within the last decade especially this bifurcation has broken down. The bulk of the churches listed in the *Church Diversity Index* are explicitly evangelical holding to the deity of Christ, the unique authority of the Word of God and salvation in terms of personal conversion and faith. Even within the mainline denominations including the Church in Wales, evangelical convictions are no longer marginalized but are accepted as being staple fare. While not diverging from these convictions, these churches are now engaging with the unchurched communities, many of whom are severely economically deprived, in a holistic way and making common cause with secular agencies and other faith groups, both ecumenical and non-Christian even. The churches have always been involved in charitable work. What is new is that in order to respond to post-industrial realities in the light of the gospel, the sect-type groups are aligning themselves with more liberal churches with whom they would formerly have had no dealings at all.

The focus for much of this has been Gweini, the Council of the Christian Voluntary Sector in Wales, established in 1999 under the aegis of the Evangelical Alliance, which has mobilized the considerable social capital that Welsh Christianity still possesses. Sick visiting, breakfast clubs for children, luncheon clubs for the elderly, youth activity and bereavement support are extended not to the faithful alone but to all, as are newer ventures such as care for asylum seekers and migrant workers, advice centres for debt management and personal finance along with help for those afflicted by drug problems and alcohol abuse. The Evangelical Alliance report *Faith in Wales: Counting for Communities* (2008) provided a sound rationale for this, linking orthodox biblical doctrine with a radical theology of discipleship. With 3,000 churches or chapels giving myriad local groups access to their property either free or for a minimal charge, 600 faith communities operating purpose-built community centres and 500 others actively participating in regeneration projects in partnership with local authorities and the Welsh Assembly Government, even in their minority status the churches plainly have a huge amount to give. According to Rhodri Morgan, former First Minister, in his introduction to *Faith in Wales*: 'Faith communities . . . even today offer a range of vital services which complement and enhance the work of government.'

Following its publication a decade ago, *The Span of the Cross* received favourable reviews and has served as a standard resource for those wishing to know more about the history of Welsh Christianity during the twentieth century. As well as contributing to the discussion within Wales, it has informed the wider analysis in the United Kingdom (see Callum G. Brown, *Religion and Society in Twentieth-Century Britain* (2006), Hugh McLeod, *The Religious Crisis of the 1960s* (2007), Keith Robbins, *England, Ireland, Scotland, Wales: The Christian Church, 1900–2000* (2008) and others). Some of the names mentioned in the final chapter, happily still with us in 1999, have now passed on: the poet R. S. Thomas, the historian Glanmor Williams and the philosopher D. Z. Phillips. But there is nothing contained in the text that I would wish to retract. To list my acknowledgements since then would be onerous. Suffice it to say that my debt to those mentioned in the preface to the first edition still stands (along now with Ennis Akpinar at the University of Wales Press) while the fact that I am now writing not from the School of Theology at Bangor but from the School of Theology, Religious Studies and Islamic Studies at the University of Wales Trinity St David is itself a comment on the changes in religion and society that have occurred during the last decade.

D. Densil Morgan
University of Wales Trinity St David
Lampeter
1 March 2011

Introduction:
a faith for the third millennium

Whatever continuities persist between the Wales of 1914 and that
of the beginning of the third millennium, a national profession of
explicit Christian faith is not among them. Putting to one side the
complexities of definition, it is safe to say that the Wales of 2000 is
secular and post-Christian rather than religious or devout. The
drift away from faith, common to all advanced European cultures
since the eighteenth-century Enlightenment, has appeared more
marked among the Welsh due, first of all, to the exceedingly tight
historical interpenetration between the development of the nation
and the story of the faith, and, secondly, to the very high profile of
institutional religion, whether Chapel or Church, which prevailed
at the beginning of the First World War. Although the precise
nature of the impact which Christianity made upon the British
during the Roman occupation remains unclear, it is obvious that
by the fifth century, when the Welsh nation and its language
emerged, the Cymry, or inhabitants of the Isle of Britain,
considered themselves to be Christian. Just as the dawn of
nationhood coincided with the intense religious revival connected
with Celtic saints such as Dyfrig, Illtud, Beuno and Dewi,
Christianity and Welshness evolved not so much side by side but
very often each as an aspect of the other. And what was true of
'the Age of the Saints' characterized the Middle Ages, the
Reformation period and much of the modern age as well. For a
millennium-and-a-half the Welsh could do no other than identify
themselves as a Christian people.

By 1914 that identification was beginning to break down.
Although, at the time, institutional Christianity was flourishing
and as many as half the population were still affiliated with one or
other of the Christian communions, many realized that the social,
cultural and economic transition which Wales was currently
undergoing had grave religious and spiritual implications which
boded ill for the future of the churches. However outwardly

prosperous Christianity appeared, there was considerable and often barely concealed concern as to its inner vitality, its doctrinal integrity and its ability to cope with change. If Welshness and Christianity had been virtually synonymous with one another even up to a generation earlier, by the time of the First World War the nation was undergoing a profound crisis of faith.[1] The crisis had no single cause, and therefore it had no simple or superficial explanation; those who put the blame wholly on such disparate malignancies as biblical criticism, the theory of evolution, liberal theology, the slackness of church discipline, 'football mania', encroaching Anglicization, or else 'dead orthodoxy', an otherworldly pietism, religious hypocrisy, bourgeois respectability, the churches' coolness towards the labour movement, a failure to engage in the class struggle, or whatever, oversimplify a situation which was bewildering in its complexity and all-embracing in its influence. It was, in fact, the heterogeneous nature of the situation which defined the then current malaise.

The purpose of this study is to describe the history of Christianity in Wales since 1914 and to analyse how it has tried to cope with the challenges of change. If, in the interim, the churches' crisis has expanded vastly and deepened considerably, secularization has failed wholly to eradicate religious institutions or totally to undermine the convictions by which they are still upheld. Even in a secular Wales, the faith persists and has done throughout the remarkable century which has by now all but drawn to a close. This book has been written in the belief that Christianity does have a future in the context of the Wales of the twenty-first century, and that in order best to prepare for that future we need to appreciate its history in the (albeit recent) past.[2]

The originality of this work, such as it possesses, stems principally from its attempt to draw together the various strands of the story of the faith in Wales within the bounds of a single narrative. Although I have relied heavily on the work of those scholars who have already published in the field, the fact that so many aspects of our more recent religious life remain unexplored has meant that much of the research contained herein is my own. Although by far the most fruitful way of doing history is according to theme rather than according to denomination, the current dearth of denominational history precluded, at this stage, my writing a more thematically based study. I hope, however, that the rather old-fashioned approach which I have followed will provide readers, and, hopefully, researchers as well, with a basis for further reflection on the various ways in which all Christians, irrespective of sect or ecclesiastical tradition, have responded to the challenge of their times and contributed to the wider history of their period. In order to produce a work of manageable size, there are many subjects which have been treated in a very cursory manner or else not at all. Readers who are fascinated by economic matters will, no doubt, be disappointed to find nothing on church finance in the following chapters despite the fact that financial considerations have been hugely important for all the churches throughout the century. The same is true of another aspect of Christian life which exists in a different, though (surprisingly, perhaps) not wholly contrary, milieu to that of economics: worship, spirituality and prayer. It is through hymnology and liturgy in the main that the faith has made its most telling impact on worshippers, but these are subjects which demand a much more detailed treatment than they are afforded herein. In fact the whole matter of twentieth-century Welsh spirituality requires a lengthy study of its own: I hope someone will be sufficiently enthused by the subject to rise to the challenge.

Throughout the study I have treated Wales as a unity despite the fact that clearly it is not. Although conscious of geographical and cultural divides between north Wales and south, rural Wales and the industrialized areas, English- and Welsh-speaking and many others beside, I have tried to write the story of Christian faith as a single though infinitely varied phenomenon. If, by doing so, I have emphasized cohesion and continuity at the expense of dissimilarity and discord, I hope further studies, probably drawing on local materials, will complement, challenge or even supplant my own analysis. I realize all too well that, far from being the last word on this complex subject, this is much more akin to a faltering and speculative introductory study. It has also been written, as it were, from the top down rather than from the bottom up. I have drawn heavily on materials contained in reports, journals and books which, because of their very nature, reflect the official views of ministers, clergy and church leaders rather than the everyday experience of the man, or more often the woman, in the pew. This is a grave weakness, though I suspect, at this juncture, fairly unavoidable. Until we have an overall history of twentieth-century

Welsh Christianity written from the public perspective, it will be very difficult to produce anything of a more personal, intimate and possibly more realistic nature.

The fact that I give what some would find an inordinate amount of space to doctrinal matters reflects not only a fixation of my own but a sincere conviction that what worshippers have actually believed about God, Christ and the gospel is a vitally important aspect of religious history. My own preferences (some would say prejudices) in this sphere will be patent from the beginning. All my sympathies lie with an open Christian orthodoxy, which, whether it be Nonconformist, Anglican, or Catholic, eschews a narrow sectarianism on the one hand and a sceptical theological liberalism on the other. Where Christianity has been faithful to these norms, it has, in my view, been most true to itself and most beneficial to society and the world at large. That I believe this to be the case has, no doubt, affected my analysis of the evidence, though the thesis can, I think, be sustained on the basis of a sound academic appraisal of the facts.

Although this assessment is written by a professional theologian from a specific faith perspective, I hope that it will be of sufficiently general interest to engage all readers who wish to know more of the part religion has played in the unfolding history of twentieth-century Wales.

~ 1 ~

The state of religion in 1914

Roman Catholicism

In 1914 the oldest of the Nonconformist traditions was the one which the majority of Welsh Dissenters suspected the most: it was 'the Old Faith' or the Catholicism of the Church of Rome. The thought that popery had anything in common with the other Christian communions which had dissented from the Church of England would have been incomprehensible to most chapel people, and the suggestion that the very word 'chapel' had anything but purely Protestant connotations would have been perplexing in the extreme. But the fact remained that, despite its claim to historic continuity with the most primitive Welsh Christianity, Catholicism's minority status and its perception as being something strange, foreign and markedly non-Anglican placed it squarely within the Nonconformist fold. Not all Welsh Nonconformists in 1914 were Protestant Nonconformists.

The proclamation of a Catholic vicariate in Wales had been made by Pope Leo XIII in 1895. Formerly annexed to the diocese of Shrewsbury, the six counties of north Wales and five in the south (excluding populous and industrialized Monmouthshire and Glamorgan), became a separate ecclesiastical area under the jurisdiction of the Westminster diocese with its own vicar apostolic. The choice for that office could hardly have been more propitious. Francis Edward Mostyn (1860–1939), the fourth son of Sir Pyers Mostyn, the eighth baron of Talacre, Flint, represented not only indigenous Welsh Catholicism in its landed guise but also a long family commitment to Wales and its culture. On his father's side the family had been Catholic since the eighteenth century, whereas through his mother, the Hon. Frances Georgina Fraser, daughter of Lord Lovat, the vicar apostolic could claim descent from at least three recusant martyrs. Within three years the vicariate had become an independent diocese designated by the ancient title of Menevia, while Glamorgan, Monmouthshire and over-the-border Hereford were established as the new see of Newport. Mostyn's appointment in 1898 as first bishop of Menevia was welcomed by the faithful, and for the next twenty-three years he would prove himself an exemplary leader of his flock.

Though shrewd and intelligent, the youthful Mostyn was little concerned with intellectual matters. His colleague at Newport, however, was his antithesis. John Cuthbert Hedley OSB (1837–1915), bishop of the see of Newport and Menevia since 1881 and of Newport alone following the reorganization of the dioceses in 1898, was the outstanding British Catholic bishop of his generation. A Northumbrian from Morpeth, John Hedley was educated by the Benedictines at Ampleforth and joined their order in 1855, taking 'Cuthbert' as his monastic name. Ordained priest in 1862, he was soon appointed instructor at the Benedictine study house at Belmont Priory, Hereford. His ascent within the diocese, and the order, was steady; from canon theologian he became auxiliary bishop in 1873 and bishop eight years later. He had a consuming interest in public affairs and in the years following the Vatican Council of 1870 he was cast in the role of apologist for the Church as well as being one of its most erudite pastoral teachers. An accomplished author, patristic scholar and theologian, this one-time editor of *The Dublin Review* brought rare intellectual distinction to the Welsh Catholic community. The balance between Francis Mostyn's effortless leadership qualities, his rootedness in Wales and its recusant past and a commitment to the success of his diocese, and John Cuthbert Hedley's experience, his Benedictine spirituality and intellectual acumen, served the Catholic Church in Wales well during the first decade or so of the twentieth century.

The outbreak of war and its aftermath weighed heavily on Bishop Hedley. He died, aged seventy-nine, in November 1915. His death opened the way for a closer union between the two dioceses, a move which had been contemplated for some time crystallizing in discussions at the National Catholic Congress which had been held in Cardiff during the previous July. Pope Benedict XV's response to the overtures from the diocesan authorities was contained in his apostolic letter *Cambria Celtica* of 7 February 1916. Affirming the historic particularity of the Welsh nation, Benedict announced that henceforth Menevia and Newport would be freed from the province of Birmingham (under whose jurisdiction they had been transferred in 1909) and established as a separate archiepiscopal province. The Newport diocese, now called Cardiff, would become the metropolitan while the name Menevia would be retained as Cardiff's suffragan. Herefordshire would also remain part of the new archdiocese, its Benedictine priory church at Belmont being promoted to full cathedral status. This rather curious arrangement of having two cathedrals in the one archdiocese, St David's in Cardiff which was staffed by secular clergy and Belmont by Benedictine regulars, lasted until 1919 when the status of the Hereford establishment lapsed. The cathedral of the north and west Wales diocese would remain at Wrexham.

There was much surprise that the archiepiscopate did not go immediately to Bishop Mostyn, ostensibly the strongest contender for the office. Instead James Romanus Bilsborrow OSB (1862–1931), a little-known prelate whose links with Wales had been confined to the few months he had spent as assistant at the mission at Maesteg two decades earlier, was appointed to the see. A Lancastrian from Preston, Bilsborrow's principal field of service had been in Mauritius where he had been both vicar general and bishop. Educated at Douai, he had become a Benedictine novice at Belmont. It was this connection with the province that had been influential in his being appointed first archbishop. The stresses of presiding over a province in wartime, however, along with bouts of severe ill health did not augur well for Archbishop Bilsborrow's success, and in 1920 he relinquished his office. It was in the post-war years that the Catholic Church began to make a real impact in Wales, though the institutional foundations for that success were laid in 1916.

For the majority of the Welsh population Catholics were at best an oddity, usually feared or distrusted and often despised. There was nothing in Wales corresponding to the strong indigenous working-class tradition of Lancashire, the North Riding of Yorkshire and Durham. By the nineteenth century the few pockets of residual Welsh Catholicism which had once flourished around Abergavenny and in the Holywell area of Flintshire had all but disappeared, while there were only a handful of landed families left to perpetuate the recusant tradition of Tory aristocracy: the Mostyns, the Vaughans of Courtfield and the Herberts of

Llanarth, Gwent. Despite Bishop Francis Mostyn's (admittedly limited) knowledge of Welsh, the tiny band of hereditary and landed Welsh Catholics was virtually indistinguishable from its Anglican counterparts. To the extent that Protestant Nonconformity was conscious of their existence at all, the indigenous Welsh Catholics were seen as remote, Anglicized and alien.

And then there were the Irish. Forced to emigrate initially by the appalling potato blight of the 1840s, by the last decades of the nineteenth century these poverty-stricken Irishmen and their families had arrived in their thousands finding employment in the lowliest of jobs: as labourers, navvies and dockhands. Although present in the valleys, in Merthyr especially, they were mostly attracted to the dock areas of Newport, Cardiff, Barry and later Swansea where their presence became considerable. For the most part they were poor, rural, uneducated and incontrovertibly Catholic. For Welsh chapelgoers they represented everything which Protestant evangelicalism existed to counter: clericalism, a sacramentalism so primitive as to be superstitious and a morality impervious to the blandishments of teetotalism and the keeping of the sabbath. Theirs was a religion of ritual and form: Friday abstinence, the confessional, non-participatory attendance at Mass or Benediction and a mystifying devotion to the Mother of Jesus. For churchmen and chapelgoers brought up on the Word, this was unreformed religion at its most reprehensible. If the Welsh Catholic community as a whole was perceived as being suspect, the considerable Irish element within it put it virtually beyond the pale. Such was the strength of prejudice in 1914 that the ancient Christianity of the Church of Rome was seen by many of the Welsh to be worldly and unregenerate if not, indeed, wholly reprobate.

Notwithstanding its reputation as being foreign, the Catholic Church saw itself increasingly as being attuned to the national aspirations of Wales. Its presence in the Welsh-speaking areas was sparse: within the diocese of Menevia there were twenty-seven churches and eighteen mission centres, seven in Caernarfonshire, six in Denbighshire, three each in Cardiganshire and Carmarthenshire, two on Anglesey and only one in Merioneth. In more Anglicized Brecon and Radnor there was one apiece, there were two in Montgomeryshire, six in Pembrokeshire and as many as thirteen in the old northern heartland of Flintshire. Eighty-seven priests, sixty of whom belonged to monastic orders, served 9,987 communicants out of a total population of some 900,000. In the Cardiff archdiocese ninety-two priests, forty-three secular and forty-nine regular, manned sixty-seven churches. There were 59,890 communicants from among a population of 1,631,109.[1] The main aim of the Church was the effective pastoral care of the faithful rather than proselytizing or evangelism, and with its staff of priests, secular and religious, most of whom were Benedictines (though there were Jesuits at Holywell, Passionists at Carmarthen and Capuchin Franciscans at Pantasaph to say nothing of the representatives of ten separate female orders), that aim was certainly achieved. From small beginnings the presence of the Catholic Church would become both substantial and significant during the decades which were to follow.

The smaller Protestant bodies

The Catholic Church had stood aloof from what had been the most wide-ranging survey of religious practice ever undertaken within Wales. The Royal Commission on the Church of England and other Religious Bodies in Wales and Monmouthshire had been convened in 1906 and published its report in eight exhaustive foolscap tomes four years later. In many respects the report was deeply flawed. Rather than contributing to the resolution of tensions between Anglican and Dissenter it merely added to them: the waspish condescension of its chairman, the Rt Hon. Sir Roland Vaughan-Williams, towards those who had volunteered as witnesses was often little short of scandalous. Whatever its weaknesses, however, it does contain invaluable statistical evidence to the state of religion during the years immediately prior to 1914. The report divided Protestant Dissent into two groups: 'the four great Nonconformist denominations', namely the Calvinistic Methodists, the Congregationalists, the Baptists and the Wesleyans, and 'the smaller denominations'. For the commissioners greatness was defined numerically. The lesser bodies, however, like the Catholic Church, had their own unique contribution to make to the rich religious mix which was Edwardian Christianity in Wales.

The oldest of the lesser denominations, and by this time among the smallest, was the Society of Friends. Pristine Quaker radicalism had long descended into a domesticated humanitarianism, and few Welsh people in 1914 would have related the pacifist gentility of contemporary Friends to the abrasive militancy of a John ap John, a Francis Gawler or a Dorcas Erbury 250 years earlier. The Quakers were the absolute antithesis of the Roman Catholics: their faith was egalitarian, anti-clerical and unsacramental, their only authority being that of 'the inner light' or divine conviction of the individual soul. They allowed full equality to women in the worship and government of the congregations and took pride in upholding 'the ancient testimony of the Society against all war'. Before the First World War there existed just eight Welsh Quaker congregations comprising of some 250 attendant members with another two score scattered abroad. Four of the meetings were in mid-Wales, at Aberystwyth and inland at Llandrindod, Pen-y-bont and Llanbadarn (Radnorshire); there were three in south Wales, at Swansea, Neath and Cardiff, and just one in north Wales at Colwyn Bay. Although each congregation was self-governing, there was a connexional link through the Western Quarterly Meeting and all Friends were invited to the Yearly Meeting which provided a platform for each congregation throughout England and Wales.[2] Despite the small size of their movement, Friends still maintained a distinctive witness through humanitarian and educational work and their well-known stand against war.

If the Quakers had emerged from among the left-wing sectaries of the Commonwealth period, the Unitarians' roots were in the much more sober soil of Puritan Presbyterianism. The Presbyterians had been the least radical of the seventeenth-century Puritans who had left the Church of England at the Restoration not through choice but compulsion. Their emphasis on sobriety, morality and a learned ministry had made them much more doctrinally minded than the Quakers. It was in the early eighteenth century that a section of the Welsh Presbyterian movement, then merged with the Congregationalists, voiced doubts concerning the prevailing Dissenting orthodoxy, and a century later a full-orbed though small Unitarian movement had developed with its centre in Cardiganshire. 'The changes in the form of doctrine', related the Revd Rees Jenkin Jones, 'have been from

Calvinism . . . to Arminianism, from Arminianism to Arianism, from Arianism to a kind of Unitarianism.'[3] Fifteen of the movement's thirty-four churches were situated along the Aeron and the Teifi between Lampeter and Llandysul, the remainder being in Glamorgan with one, Cefncoedycymer, just north of Merthyr in Brecknock. The churches, all of which were congregationally governed, met together either in the South Wales Unitarian Association which conducted its business in Welsh, or the English-speaking South-East Wales Association. The movement's 3,000 members were served by eighteen ministers nearly all of whom had been educated at the Presbyterian College in Carmarthen. The most liberal of the Nonconformist denominations (including the Quakers), the Unitarians partook of all the mores of Welsh Dissent, its puritanism and Bible-centred worship, though its rejection of evangelical belief was total.

Like the Quakers and Unitarians, the Scotch Baptists could trace their indirect lineage to the religious upheavals of the seventeenth century. The Baptists established a presence in Wales in 1649 but it was only in 1779, under the influence of the Evangelical Revival, that they began to make inroads into the north. If the revival attracted many it repelled a few, and among those who reacted against its emphases was the Merionethshire Baptist leader, J. R. Jones. Following the lead of the Scots Dissenters, Robert Sandeman and John Glas, Jones severed his links with the mainline denomination in 1795 and formed a new connexion of 'Scotch' Baptists with branches in many parts of north Wales. Doctrinally Calvinist and congregationalist in structure, Jones's churches strove to restore New Testament Christianity in its purity. Communion was held each Sunday and the idea of a salaried ministry was rejected. This restorationist ideal was renewed in the mid-nineteenth century when some half of the churches joined fellowship with the Scots-American Alexander Campbell's 'Churches [or 'Disciples'] of Christ' in 'discarding all formal creeds and all practices and methods of church order for which no justifying precept or example could be found in the New Testament'. The best known of the Campbellite churches was Berea, Criccieth, where Lloyd George's brother, William, was an elder and where the Chancellor of the Exchequer himself had been raised and baptized. By then there were twenty-four Scotch Baptist or Campbellite congregations all of which

were confined to north Wales, chiefly in the Ardudwy area of
Merioneth, parts of Caernarfonshire and around Rhosllannerchrugog in Denbighshire. Their total membership was 1,075. Despite
their sectarian beginnings, both the Scotch Baptists and the
'Disciples' were on increasingly good terms with their fellow
Nonconformists, particularly the regular Baptists; indeed, the
Criccieth church would merge with the latter in the 1920s. Their
original ideal, though, remained valid. As William George had
stated to the Royal Commission, 'I regard the position taken up by
the Churches of Christ as a standing protest against creeds and
priestism in all its forms'.[4]

'If they could be a little more democratic, there would be one
Methodist body soon.'[5] It would be some time before this
complaint against the Wesleyans, voiced in April 1907 by the Revd
E. C. Bartlett, Bible Christian minister in Swansea, would be
rectified, but even then plans were underway to create a more
unified Methodist witness in the land. By 1914 the Bible
Christians along with two other smaller denominations, the New
Connexion and the United Methodist Free Churches, had become
the United Methodist Church, a Methodist body whose only
disagreement with both the parent body, the Wesleyans, and the
influential though less numerous Primitive Methodists, was not
about doctrine but about polity. All of the Methodist groups
combined Arminian theology with a strong evangelistic thrust,
but whereas the Wesleyan Conference vested authority in the
hands of the preachers, and the United Methodists granted equal
authority to ministers and laypeople, the Primitives, as the most
consistently working class of all the Methodist bodies, retained a
proletarian scepticism towards the professional ministry as a
whole. 'Our ministry', according to the secretary of their South
Wales District, 'is very largely a lay ministry.'[6]

All of the smaller Methodist groups in Wales were English in
tone and derivation. The strength of the Bible Christians had been
in the valleys of south-east Wales and as far to the west as Neath
and Swansea where they had ministered almost exclusively to West
Country folk who had flocked there in the late nineteenth century
seeking work in the mines and tinplate mills.[7] The New
Connexion's presence had been confined to east Flintshire and the
Cheshire border while the original United Methodists, though
retaining a few Welsh-speaking congregations on Anglesey, mostly

served the population of the north-east.[8] If, at the time of their amalgamation, the United Methodist Church's combined Welsh membership figure was 4,146 communicants in sixty-five congregations, the Primitive Methodists possessed 147 churches with a membership of 8,308.[9] They too catered for the immigrant workforce of north-east Wales, the valleys and the large industrial conurbations of the south, as well as the indigenous Anglo-Welsh population of south Pembrokeshire and the border lands of mid-Wales.

When at its most uncompromising, evangelical religion had always posited a gulf between converted and unconverted or the saved and the lost, and it was among the smaller nonconforming sects that this juxtaposition was most readily manifested. 'We stand in a great measure separate from the ordinary Christian work of the district' confessed Mr Henry George Lloyd of Newport, Monmouthshire, on behalf of those Christians, 'sometimes known as Brethren', who shunned not only the world but a worldly church in order to maintain the purity of the gospel in the close fellowship of their evangelistic halls.[10] The impulse to gather 'pure' churches of regenerate believers had predated the 1904–5 Revival, and the thirty-eight Brethren assemblies which Henry Lloyd listed, thirty-six of which were in south Wales, witnessed to the spread of 'Plymouth' Brethrenism, in the urban centres at least, from the late nineteenth century onwards. Yet one of the fruits of the Revival was the increase of support for independent missions, free of the larger denominations, whose members were intent on preserving the joy of salvation which had been so widely felt in 1904. By 1914 the 1,000 adherents of those thirty-eight assemblies had increased, and one suspects that the variety of halls, tents and independent missions which were included in the Commission's statistics[11] was evidence of the vitality of an intense revivalism. Due to the paucity of direct evidence a correct calculation would be impossible, though it can be surmised that some 2–3,000 worshippers, from Llanelli in the west to Newport in the east, would have met in those unprepossessing halls to break bread every Lord's Day morning and to preach a stern gospel to the unconverted every Sunday night.

If the proliferation of independent evangelistic halls in industrial south Wales was one result of the 1904–5 Revival, another was the spread of Pentecostalism. It was through the vision granted to Daniel P. Williams (1883–1927), a young Carmarthenshire coal-miner, that the first explicitly Pentecostal denomination in Wales was born. Williams, a Congregationalist from Pen-y-groes, Llanelli, received the baptism of the Holy Spirit accompanied by speaking in tongues while at Aberaeron in the summer of 1908. Bidden by a word of prophecy, he withdrew from his local church and, joining with a few like-minded believers, formed a separate Pentecostal congregation. Believing that the full range of pentecostal gifts was being restored to the church, 'Pastor Dan' was soon appointed the congregation's apostle while his brother, W. Jones Williams, became its prophet. Links were forged with other Pentecostal groups, and in 1916 this loose charismatic confederation became The Apostolic Church (*Yr Eglwys Apostolaidd*). Although rooted, mostly, in the anthracite valleys of west Wales and in the villages surrounding the tinplate capital of Llanelli, the movement soon fostered an international vision and through its annual August convention, Pen-y-groes would become a mecca for Pentecostal believers from many lands. By 1920 what had begun as a distinctly Welsh movement in language and sentiment, had become part of a wider British Pentecostal network linking groups at Bournemouth, Glasgow, Hereford and Bradford. Although the Welsh element was never thereafter to predominate, this (by then) highly centralized working-class religious body would retain its links with the principality through its small knot of churches mainly in the valleys. Though Pentecostalism would always remain a minority faith in Wales, its appeal among a section of the working-class population can hardly be denied. Although unsophisticated, it afforded ordinary people a taste of the vitality and excitement of New Testament faith at its most elemental. It, too, had its contribution to make to the wider religious scene.

Of the other smaller churches and denominations, the Salvation Army was the most numerous with 1,266 'soldiers' based at thirty-three stations throughout Wales, the majority of whom were in Glamorgan and Monmouthshire. The Presbyterian Church of England possessed four churches in Wales with 1,206 communicants, while such bodies as the Catholic Apostolics, the Christadelphians, the Moravian Church, the Reformed Church of England, the Seventh Day Adventists, the Swedenborgians and a handful of Lutheran missions in the dock areas serving German immigrants and seafaring Scandinavians, all maintained their (albeit tiny) witness. Only the Christadelphians had more than a hundred adherents; the rest less than a score, nevertheless Welsh Nonconformity was enriched by the presence of each of these lesser groups.[12]

The principal denominations

If the smaller sects and groupings filled their allotted spaces in the Welsh religious mosaic of 1914, the influence of 'the four great Nonconformist denominations' remained massive. Ever since the combined force of the Calvinistic Methodists, the Independents or Congregationalists, the Baptists and the Wesleyans was seen to have outstripped that of the Established Church in 1851, Welsh nationality had come to be defined for many in terms of Protestant Nonconformity. 'The Welsh', said Henry Richard MP, the most influential of Wales's political Dissenters of the early Victorian era, 'are now a nation of Nonconformists'.[13] The development and rapid triumph of a highly populist Dissenting culture had been remarkable. From a marginal and generally middle-class movement whose strength, such as it was, had been in the border areas of Wrexham and Gwent, the Older Dissent established itself in south-west Wales in the early eighteenth century moving north by the 1780s. Its transformation had been due to the Evangelical Revival, a spiritual movement initially within the Anglican Church which revitalized Welsh Protestantism as a whole.

The culture which issued from this ascendancy was a culture of the Word. Its growth had been rooted in widespread exegetical preaching, its piety had been nourished by the application of scripture both from the pulpit and within *seiadau* or fellowship groups, and its doctrines mutually inculcated in thousands of all-age Sunday schools. The puritan virtues of honesty, thrift, sabbatarianism and hard work, sobriety and chastity (sometimes observed more in the breach than in fulfilment), were highly prized, while a spirit of moderation and gradual social improvement through education were also fostered. Religious revivals had animated each aspect of this culture and replenished its adherents during virtually each successive decade since 1735. The doctrinal homogeneity between the four main denominations (and beyond) was profound: it comprised, in the main, of a moderate Calvinism whose catholicity was such as to embrace even the evangelical 'Arminianism' of the Wesleyan body.

By encouraging an individual response to the biblical message and a personal application of its precepts to everyday life, a process of self-improvement and democratization had been made inevitable. With the widening of the franchise after 1868, Dissent became politically viable. In Wales it produced a victory for Liberal radicalism and a near demise of the Tories. Literacy had fostered an equally inevitable intellectual curiosity and as early as 1815, when *Seren Gomer*, the first Welsh topical magazine, was established, the market for books and periodicals had flourished. With the implementation of a compulsory system of elementary education in the 1870s, a foundation for widespread social change had been laid. However, the expansion of horizons and the rapid economic growth which characterized the later-Victorian era provided Nonconformist Wales with its first serious challenge, that of modernity. Phenomena such as Anglicization, increasing social mobility, the influence of sports, entertainments and pastimes hitherto deemed inimical to the puritan ethos and, by the 1880s, the spread of secondary, college and university education, would soon undermine Nonconformist foundations. Just as the theology of Dissent was having to meet the challenge of Darwinianism and Biblical Criticism – a particularly hazardous endeavour given the explicitly biblical basis of Nonconformist culture – so the axioms of Dissent were being increasingly questioned, by the younger generation especially. 'I trust that you received due amusement and entertainment in the preaching meetings', wrote David Lloyd George to his fiancée in August 1886. 'Who won the buckle? Who raved most deliriously about the agonies of the wicked's doom and about the bliss of every true Calvinist's predestination? I hope you have sunk no deeper in the mire of the *Cyffes Ffydd* & other prim orthodoxies.'[14] Scepticism such as this was rarely divulged openly, but there was a growing number, both among the new professional middle class and beyond, who were rejecting not only Dissent but the Christian orthodoxy upon which it stood. Although Welsh Nonconformity would continue to flourish outwardly, by the turn of the century the corrosive effect of agnosticism, an incipient atheism and general secularization was beginning to be felt.

Whatever the effect of secular modernity, the extent of Nonconformist influence upon Wales by 1914 remained enormous. The largest of the four principal denominations was Calvinistic Methodism. With 185,000 communicant members, 335,000 adherents and 178,000 on its Sunday school roll, the *Hen Gorff* or 'the Connexion', was dignified, self-assured, disciplined and sober. Its polity was presbyterian, authority being vested in its eldership who would meet monthly in twenty-one area meetings, nine of which were in south Wales and twelve in the north. For two generations the Welsh Calvinistic Methodists had existed, uneasily but doggedly, within the bounds of the Established Church, but such were the tensions of this dual allegiance that secession would become inevitable. The breach had occurred at Bala in June 1811 when Thomas Charles, an ordained clergyman of the Church of England and undisputed leader of the Welsh Methodists, had ordained nine preachers to administer the sacraments among the north Wales societies. Two months later a similar meeting took place at Llandeilo, Carmarthenshire, when the south Wales Association, also under Charles's presidency, ordained thirteen more to minister to the Connexion's societies in the south. The foundation for Welsh Calvinistic Methodism's governing structure had thus been laid, and thereafter the two annually held Associations, one in north Wales and the other in the south, would provide the focus for the movement's connexional existence. In 1864 the General Assembly was first convened in order to supplement the work of the two Associations. Though matters of common concern such as literature, Sunday school organization, insurance and the organization of the English-language churches would be put within its ambit, the Assembly would never usurp the Associations' function as the principal manifestation of denominational authority.

Despite a loosening of its Calvinist bonds, the *Corff* still adhered to its 1823 Confession of Faith. The scholastic element inherent in its creed had never stifled experiential faith or a lively evangelicalism. The missionary task both at home and abroad rated highly among the Connexion's priorities, and by 1914 the fifty Forward Movement home mission halls as well as the flourishing foreign mission field on the Khasian Hills in Assam on India's north-east frontier, witnessed to the denomination's commitment to the expansion of the faith. By 1914 the Indian mission could record the existence of 370 churches, 240 mission centres, 30,000 converts and a further 6,000 baptismal candidates since its establishment sixty years previously. There was even a small mission centred at Quimper, where the Revd W. Jenkin Jones had persevered heroically but ultimately fruitlessly to spread the Methodist gospel amongst the Bretons.

If the Connexion's confessionalism had encouraged rather than impeded missionary growth, neither can it be said to have militated against the cultivation of a learned ministry. Ever since 1833 when Lewis Edwards had braved the elders' wrath and insisted on reading for a degree in Classics and Theology at the feet of the great divine Thomas Chalmers at the University of Edinburgh, the Welsh Calvinistic Methodist Connexion had prided itself on the academic credibility of its ministers. The standard of entry to its two theological seminaries, at Bala and Aberystwyth, was high, and a good proportion of their students were graduates, either of the colleges of the University of Wales, or of Oxbridge or the ancient Scottish universities. Owen Prys (1857–1934), principal of the Aberystwyth seminary, was a graduate of Trinity College, Cambridge, while John Morgan Jones, Merthyr Tydfil (1861–1935), had graduated at St John's in the same university; John Hughes, Liverpool (1850–1932), and William Evans, Pembroke Dock (1838–1935), had studied at Glasgow, while John Puleston Jones (1862–1925), the pastor of Penmount Chapel, Pwllheli, had gained an astonishing first-class honours degree in modern history at Benjamin Jowett's Balliol – since early childhood Puleston had been totally blind. Despite the intellectual brilliance of the Calvinistic Methodist pulpit when at its best, its occupants drew their authority from their solidarity with their congregations. Cultured and theologically literate, these pastors yet shared the same class background as their flocks and were wholly identified with their aspirations. Though represented throughout Wales and serving the Welsh diaspora in England, Patagonia and beyond, the *Corff*'s geographical strength in 1914 was in the rural areas of north and west Wales while its ministerial complement stood at 971.[15]

The second largest Nonconformist denomination was the Congregationalist. Its 1,124 churches, 160,000 members and 145,000 Sunday school adherents were served by 655 full-time pastors. The Welsh Congregationalists, Independents or *Annibynwyr*, were comprised of self-governing congregations whose members had long been loath to describe themselves as a denomination at all. Classic independency had been born of radical seventeenth-century separatism and its ideal that 'the kingdom of God was not begun by whole parishes but rather of the worthiest, were they never so few' had preserved a sometimes abrasive assertiveness in the face of prevailing social pressures. For a century and a half the movement's most distinguishing factor had been the sovereignty of the individual fellowship, yet by the mid-Victorian era its aversion to connexionalism was being eroded both by the rapidity of its own expansion and by the forces of social uniformity. Since the founding in 1872 of the Union of Welsh Independents, the movement's disparate congregationalism had gradually succumbed to the appeal of centralization. The support given to the Union's Weaker Churches Fund established in 1895, to its central Bookroom opened in Swansea in 1907 and its Ministerial Assistance Fund begun in 1911, had cemented inter-congregational unity and by 1914 Welsh Independents were not nearly as independent as their reputation had once suggested.

'The Independents', reported the Royal Commission, 'are . . . thoroughly evangelical and Protestant in doctrine and character.'[16] They were also thoroughly working class. The élite ethos of the Older Dissent had been dissipated by the Evangelical Revival's populism, and by the nineteenth century Welsh Congregationalism had taken on a proletarian guise. The eagerness of Victorian Wales to nurture Nonconformist culture had been a reaction partially to the lack of social opportunity under which the ordinary people had been forced to exist. Despite the improved situation of later Victorian Dissent, the rustic character of much chapel life persisted, and as always education remained the most effective route to self-cultivation and personal advancement. Although Oxbridge had been open to Nonconformists since the 1870s, the majority of ordinands at the Independents' two Welsh colleges at Bangor and Brecon (along with the non-aligned Presbyterian seminary at Carmarthen) sought an academic grounding in an environment less exalted than the older universities and much closer to home. 'The students [in the two seminaries] are drawn for the most part from the working classes', continued the Commission's Report. 'Of 44 men now in college 25 had been engaged in manual labour before commencing to preach.'[17] Such a cross-section of the Independents' ministerial candidates was a true reflection of the constitution of the movement's churches as a whole.

Ever since the early nineteenth century the Welsh Independents had built up a reputation for progressive action and thought. Independents such as Dr George Lewis (Llanuwchllyn), Samuel Roberts (Llanbryn-mair), Ieuan Gwynedd, David Rees (Llanelli), Gwilym Hiraethog, Michael D. Jones and others had been in the vanguard of Nonconformist radicalism. By the Edwardian era this radicalism had blended with the wider, more bourgeois, 'Nonconformist Conscience' to express itself in a series of moral and political issues from temperance to the disestablishment of the Anglican Church. The movement's progressive character, which had by then found a political outlet in the Liberal Party, was a natural extension of its earlier social concern. It is no coincidence that some of the labour movement's earliest Nonconformist supporters were Independents, the lawyer Daniel Lleufer Thomas (1863–1940) and the Revd T. E. Nicholas (1879–1970), the controversial minister at Glais in the Swansea Valley, being cases in point.

If, by the turn of the century, Independents were being attracted to the socialist cause in politics, they were also succumbing to the appeal of liberal ideas in theology. Although the Revd R. E. Peregrine, minister of Zion Chapel, Rhymney, had told the Royal Commissioners that the Welsh Congregationalists 'believe everything which is commonly called the orthodox Christian religion',[18] by 1914 that orthodoxy was being interpreted in an increasingly liberal way. By the outbreak of the First World War the movement's traditional Calvinism was beginning to be superseded by an optimistic Hegelian modernism, while David Adams ('Hawen') (1845–1923), the denomination's most outspoken theological liberal, had by then been transformed from an object of suspicion into a veritable prophet and sage.[19] Influential academics of the calibre of Dr Thomas Rees (1869–1926), principal of the Bala-Bangor College, his successor the Revd John Morgan Jones (1873–1946) and Dr D. Miall Edwards (1873–1941), professor at the Memorial College, Brecon, would become liberal theology's ablest interpreters among wartime and post-war Independents, while the liberal themes of humankind's inherent goodness, human perfectability and the Kingdom of God as an ethical concept would be constantly reiterated by the movement's most popular preachers. It would not be until the 1930s under the influence of Karl Barth and the revival of Calvinistic confessionalism, that Welsh Congregationalists would be recalled once more to the fullness of their doctrinal inheritance.

Like the Independents, the Baptists' roots were in radical seventeenth-century Puritanism. Their congregational polity had always been qualified by each individual church's loyalty to its local association, and since 1866 the country's dozen associations had been strengthened by the establishment of the Baptist Union of Wales. For Baptists church membership was confined to responsible Christian believers whose seal of individual commitment was baptism by total immersion. Although present throughout Wales, their strength was in Pembrokeshire and Gwent, and because of their long experience of holding forth in traditionally bilingual areas, they coped more successfully than the Independents and Calvinistic Methodists with the potentially traumatic challenge of Anglicization. There were 940 Baptist churches in Wales at the outset of the First World War, most of which practised closed communion (i.e. they restricted communion to those who had been baptized by immersion). Baptist believers totalled 125,000 with 140,000 attending their Sunday schools along with 592 salaried pastors.[20]

Among a generally proletarian and populist Nonconformity, Baptists were the most proletarian of all. Unlike the Calvinistic Methodists, the ideal of a trained, professional and learned ministry was not regarded as essential: 'All the better if a young man is well trained but good preaching is regarded as more essential for the pulpit than scholarly attainments.'[21] This did not, however, preclude the encouragement of academic prowess when the opportunity arose. The two Baptist seminaries, the one founded at Llangollen in 1862 and located at the university city of Bangor since 1892 and the other, founded at Abergavenny in 1807 and removed to Cardiff, via Pontypool, in 1893, had respectable academic pedigrees. Dr Thomas Witton Davies (1851–1923), first professor of Semitics at the university at Bangor, had been a Hebrew tutor at the city's Baptist seminary, while Dr William Edwards (1849–1929), the Cardiff principal, had combined scholarly rectitude with an unshakeably conservative evangelicalism. For these men scholarship was the handmaiden of faith, and saving faith could only be inculcated through preaching. 'There are also in the Baptist ministry', concluded the Commissioners' Report, 'many pastors and preachers who are practically self-taught'.[22] It was not the academics but preachers such as E. T. Jones (1857–1935), minister at Llanelli's Zion Church, and Charles Davies (1849–1927), the silver-haired patriarch of Tabernacle in Cardiff's Hayes, who wielded the real influence among the Welsh Baptists before, during and well after the First World War.

If the Calvinistic Methodist Connexion was the one indigenous Welsh denomination, the Wesleyan Methodists had come into Wales from the outside. During his lifetime John Wesley had been happy to leave the evangelization of Wales to Howell Harris and his Calvinistic Methodist colleagues; his disciples, though, were not nearly so reticent. The Wesleyan movement made its first inroads into Wales in 1800 and made steady gains thereafter as far west as the Vale of Clwyd and as far south as Plynlymon. Despite its use of Welsh-speaking missioners and its relative success in Welsh-speaking areas, authority was wielded by the English Conference and it was not until 1897 that permission for the formation of a separate Welsh Conference was granted. Such organizational tardiness prevented the movement from rooting itself extensively in Welsh Wales, while the centralized nature of its governance militated against its long-term effectiveness as a whole. The Conference first met at Machynlleth in 1899, and organized the movement's churches into three separate circuits, one covering south Wales and two others covering the north. Ministers were ordained to work the circuit and would never be allowed to settle in any one place for more than four years before being moved on. The fact that they were trained in the denominational colleges at Richmond in Yorkshire, Didsbury in Manchester, Headingley in Leeds or Handsworth in Birmingham, further emphasized the difference between Wesleyanism and the rest of mainstream Nonconformity. Ironically though, the English bias of its training did little to diminish the commitment which such ministers as Evan Isaac (1865–1938), D. Tecwyn Evans (1876–1957) and E. Tegla Davies (1880–1967) had to Welsh language and culture. By 1914 there were 41,422 Welsh Wesleyan Methodists of whom 112 were ordained and serving ministers. The movement possessed some 650 chapels, more being situated in north Wales, the north-east especially, than in the south.[23]

In terms of membership the combined numerical strength of Welsh Protestant Nonconformity in 1914 was approximately 535,000 out of a total population of some 2,450,000. In other words nearly one Welshman or Welshwoman in five was a baptized and communicant Nonconformist. With some 500,000 attending Nonconformist Sunday schools including tens of thousands of non-communicant children, as well as considerable numbers of adherents or 'listeners', that is, those who would regularly attend services though not church members themselves,[24] on the eve of the First World War Nonconformity was the most single significant institution which Wales possessed. Its apparent strength, however, masked grave internal weaknesses: an inability to keep pace with the growth of population, a progressive undermining of its doctrinal standards, its inability both to stem the flow of religious indifference and to challenge effectively the intellectual forces of agnosticism, the over-politicization of its message during the campaign to disestablish the Church of England, and its failure to provide a credible alternative to the appeal of a revived Anglicanism. The reply given by the Congregationalist Dr Thomas Johns, pastor of Llanelli's Capel Als, to a question put by the Royal Commissioners in 1907, was grossly over-sanguine: 'I believe Nonconformity is permanent.'[25] Nevertheless there is no doubt that a huge number of Welsh people defined not only their religious lives but their class affiliation and national identity according to the standards of Protestant Dissent. For them, and for many who observed Wales from the outside, Wales and Nonconformity – for good or for ill – were virtually synonymous.

The extent of Welsh Anglicanism by 1914

'Sir, you have the satisfaction of knowing that you are helping not a dying Church, not a decaying Church, but a living, a reviving, a rising church.'[26] The words of Canon William Evans, the evangelical vicar of Rhymney, to the secretary of the Church Pastoral Aid Society in 1887, encapsulated perfectly the spirit of rejuvenation which pervaded the Anglican Church in Wales during the last three decades of the nineteenth century. By the mid-Victorian era Robert Peel's restructuring of the establishment had had a half century to take effect: pluralities had been abolished, absenteeism had ceased, church buildings had been extensively refurbished and finances had been released to facilitate church extension. The effectiveness of episcopal oversight had been increased and, since the election of Joshua Hughes to the see of St Asaph in 1870, its nature was felt to be more in tune with national aspirations of the Welsh people. By the turn of the century Welsh Anglicanism had become a force to be reckoned with. 'There is a vitality, a growth, that shows itself in every direction', stated Thomas Lloyd, vicar of Rhyl and rural dean of St Asaph during the proceedings of the Swansea Church Congress in 1909. The preceding decades had witnessed the development of a higher concept of office among the clergy, a deepening of devotion among the laity, a renewed sense of mission, a fresh appreciation of the value of sacrament and creed and a definite reversal in the Church's fortunes. 'Nothing is more remarkable than the immense advance made by the Church in the public esteem', Lloyd claimed.[27] Robert Williams, vicar of Llandeilo Fawr reiterated the same sentiment: 'During the last thirty years the growth [of the Church] has been wonderfully rapid in all parts of Wales, and this growth has synchronised with a change of attitude on the part of the people . . . Once more the Church is the "Old Mother" of Welsh religious life.'[28] By 1914 Henry Richard's 'nation of Nonconformists' had been undermined not only by the increasing prevalence of irreligion but by substantial renewal within the Church in Wales.

On the eve of the First World War[29] the 990 parishes of the four ancient Welsh dioceses of Bangor, St David's, St Asaph and Llandaff were manned by 1,597 incumbents, assistant clergymen and others. The largest diocese was St David's which covered Pembrokeshire, Carmarthen and Cardiganshire, parts of west Glamorgan, Breconshire and most of Radnor. This vast predominantly rural see included 4 archdeaconries, 29 rural deaneries, 415 benefices and 595 actual churches. In 1914 its 544 clergy baptized 5,728 children and adults, its bishop confirmed 3,500 candidates, its Sunday schools contained 55,045 scholars while 51,330 communicants attended Easter services. Since 1827 the diocese had had the distinction of being home to St David's College, Lampeter, the Welsh Church's alternative to the two ancient universities. Although technically a university in its own right, it was in effect a seminary for the Welsh Church. In 1914 virtually all of its 150 students were native Welshmen, most of them from within the diocese itself, and bound for orders in the Anglican Church. Those following arts courses would sometimes proceed, via the college's much valued affiliation scheme, to either Oxford or Cambridge in order to read for a degree in theology before returning to serve the home Church. Though geographically isolated and somewhat introverted in character, Lampeter had made a significant contribution to the life of the Church in Wales for generations, a contribution which would persist well after disestablishment had come to pass.[30]

The second south Wales diocese, Llandaff, though not geographically extensive, was bustling, populous and in places highly industrialized. It included most of Glamorgan and all of Monmouthshire as well as parts of Brecknock and Hereford. Its 256 parishes containing 451 churches and mission centres were serviced by 246 vicars and rectors, as many as 256 curates and 19 other clergymen who served in different capacities. In 1914 13,952 were baptized, 5,500 were confirmed, 57,954 attended Easter Communion while 96,048 were regularly present in parish Sunday schools. Since 1892 it had hosted St Michael's College, situated originally at Aberdare but since 1907 relocated to Llandaff itself, a theological college in the Tractarian mould established specifically to provide devotional training for graduate ordinands immediately prior to ordination. By 1914 its two dozen or so students, most of whom were Lampeter men, along with a staff of three were contributing to the progressive catholicization of the Welsh Church, a process which had begun in earnest some thirty years previously. According to an inspection undertaken for St Michael's and published in September 1914, the practice of the college was 'distinctive of one school of thought in the Church'.[31] By then significant parts of the Llandaff diocese and other parishes throughout the country were succumbing to the Tractarian influence.

In north Wales St Asaph diocese covered Flintshire and Denbighshire as well as parts of Montgomeryshire, Merioneth and Caernarfonshire. Fourteen of its parishes were situated beyond the English border in Shropshire. Mostly agricultural in nature, though including the conurbation of Wrexham and the populous communities of the north Wales coalfield, it included 191 parishes, 227 churches, three archdeaconries and seventeen rural deaneries. Its clergy consisted of 298 vicars and curates who in 1914 baptized 3,595 children and adults, held Easter services for 30,542 communicants and taught 32,044 Sunday scholars. Confirmation candidates for that year were around 5,000. Still in the north, the smallest of the Welsh dioceses was that of Bangor which included the counties of the ancient kingdom of Gwynedd: Anglesey and most of Caernarfonshire and Merioneth as well as parts of Montgomeryshire towards mid-Wales. Its two arch-deaconries and fourteen rural deaneries contained 142 often mountainous and sparsely populated parishes of 254 churches which were served by 144 incumbents and 68 curates. In 1914 they officiated at 1,313 baptisms, attended to 15,706 Easter com-municants and provided Sunday school instruction for 12,515 people. During that year approximately 3,000 candidates were confirmed.

Whereas the total Welsh population before the War was estimated to be 2,450,000, in 1914 the Anglican Church baptized 24,500 children and adults, confirmed 17,000 candidates, welcomed some 155,500 to its altars at Eastertide and taught the essentials of the Christian faith to 196,000 in its Sunday schools. If one in five of the Welsh population was Nonconformist, 13 per cent belonged to the Established Church. If this was less than the total number of Nonconformists, it represented significantly more than any single Christian denomination at the time. Much more significant was the fact that Welsh Anglicanism was a growing phenomenon whereas mainstream Dissent was a contracting force.

The renewal of Anglican fortunes can be traced to a number of sources. Along with the structural transformation already men-tioned, a new breed of reforming bishop had not only created change but had provided an example of energetic and committed pastoral leadership which was emulated by their successors. Between 1849 and 1882 Alfred Ollivant had presided over the rejuvenation of the Church throughout Llandaff and especially in the valleys. Additional parishes had been created, over a hundred new churches were built where the population was at its thickest while the diocesan provided leadership, support and considerable inspiration for his clergy. He was indubitably the most effective of all the Welsh bishops of the mid-nineteenth century. Although his successors, Richard Lewis (1883–1905) and Joshua Pritchard

Hughes, who remained in office until 1928, were not of the same character as Ollivant, they and their people benefited greatly from the example of firm and conscientious leadership which had now become the norm. Neither Connop Thirlwall who presided over St David's between 1840 and 1874 nor Vowler Short who served at St Asaph from 1846 to 1870, had the gift to fire the popular imagination, while the efficient and devout James Campbell at Bangor (1849–90) was unassuming as a diocesan leader. Nevertheless, unlike their absentee and pluralist predecessors, these were men of integrity who laboured within Wales and among their clergy. By the first decade of the twentieth century, each of the Welsh bishops – John Owen who had succeeded Basil Jones at St David's in 1897, A. G. Edwards who was Joshua Hughes's successor at St Asaph from 1889 and Watkin Herbert Williams at Bangor (though far from being above criticism, as will become apparent) – was hardworking, resident and indigenously Welsh. If their ambiguous attitude to Welshness, their social superiority and their hierarchical understanding of the dignity of their office put them well above most of their own clergy to say nothing of the huge majority of their fellow countrymen, they did at least represent the change in outlook which by 1914 had transformed Welsh Anglicanism.

It was not the bishops but the parish clergy who represented the Church among the people at large. Just as the nature of the bench of bishops had improved, a new and zealous type of parish priest was becoming more the norm than the exception. Even such an inveterate Dissenter as Henry Richard had complimented the Welsh Church on the change which had occurred within the ranks of its ministry: 'There are among them men of piety, learning and eloquence who would do honour to any church', he had claimed.[32] It was the missionary fervour, practical holiness and preaching abilities of the evangelical clergy which spearheaded the parochial transformation of the Church between *c.*1850 and 1875. Almost invariably natives of 'the evangelical heartland' of west Wales,[33] they shared the same social background and culture as the people at large. If Ollivant's strategy had made Llandaff Wales's most vibrant see, it was due to their efforts that the strategy was translated into fact. Being Welsh in both speech and sentiment, their claim that the Established Church represented *'Yr Hen Fam'*, 'the Old Mother' or ancient Church of the Welsh nation, carried considerable conviction.[34]

However effective evangelicalism had been in renewing the witness of the Church, it was not the sole engine of reform. By the 1880s the evangelicals were being eclipsed by the influence of J. H. Newman's Tractarians and their ritualist successors. Not only was 'Puseyism' gaining ground in the parishes, but its practitioners were reaching higher levels within the Church hierarchy as well. If evangelical Christianity emphasized belief in 'Christ crucified' through the preaching of the Word, the Anglicanism of the Oxford Movement was sacramentalist, catholic and unashamedly 'High Church'. Its focus was not the pulpit but the altar; despising the Reformation it looked back wistfully to the medieval past. Whereas the first generation of Tractarians – which included the Welshman Isaac Williams as well as J. H. Newman, E. B. Pusey and John Keble – were interested in doctrine alone, the implications of that doctrine would thoroughly revolutionize liturgy and practice. The establishment of a new church at Isaac Williams's family seat at Llangorwen near Aberystwyth in 1841 illustrates the impact which the Oxford Movement would have on the Church in Wales. Modelled on Newman's own church at Littlemore outside Oxford, it had an altar rather than a communion table, its first incumbent (Lewis Gilbertson) wore a surplice and stole rather than a black gown, while worship included Gregorian chants led by a parish choir. Archbishop A. G. Edwards's recollection of hearing the evangelical David Parry of Llywel, 'Y Gloch Arian' ('The Silver Bell'), preaching to the boys of Llandovery School in 1860 – 'a short little man draped in a heavy black gown, he stood like a statue in the pulpit' – would become characteristic of a past age.[35] The wearing of the black Protestant preaching gown was falling out of favour while eucharistic vestments would eventually become the norm. It was in the Bangor diocese that Tractarian thought would first take root,[36] while by the late nineteenth century the policy of the marquis of Bute's trustees to undermine the evangelical character of Llandaff through appointing ritualist clergy to incumbencies in their gift had largely paid off. By 1914 formerly evangelical parishes such as Aberdare, Merthyr, St Mary's Cardiff and Dowlais had been thoroughly catholicized – not infrequently through the labour of Bangor men – while St German's in Roath had become the ritualists' showpiece. In his evidence to the Royal Commissioners, Canon Frederick J. Best, vicar of St Margaret's, the mother church of the parish, reported as to the ceremonial which was used in worship. It included the wearing of such vestments as the amice, alb, girdle, maniple, stole and chasuble: 'The colour of the chasuble varies with the seasons.' The eucharist was referred to as the 'mass', the offering priest would invariably be assisted by an acolyte among whose tasks would be to administer the lavabo or pouring out of water to wash the tips of the server's fingers. The sanctus bell would mark the moment of consecration followed by the elevation of the host. Frequently the only one to communicate would be the priest himself.[37] This revolution in ceremonial illustrated the ascendancy of the Catholic ideal over the Welsh Church's traditionally Protestant and Reformed concept of divine grace. Its significance was not trivial but deeply doctrinal. Even if Anglo-Catholicism made less headway in St David's and St Asaph,[38] such was its influence by 1914 that the Church in Wales was beginning to see itself as more Catholic than Protestant and was pointedly critical of Protestant Nonconformity as a whole. Whereas some of the disapproval was politically motivated, much stemmed from a mutually exclusive understanding of the Church. When asked by the Royal Commissioners whether there was any common doctrinal ground between Nonconformity and the Welsh Church, many clerics answered in the negative. For D. Watcyn Morgan, vicar of Llanelli, there was no question of co-operation with those who had made a schism in the Body of Christ: 'they themselves deserted the usages and the practices of the Church of England of their own accord', he claimed.[39] J. E. Jones, the vicar of Brymbo, stated that

> the differences [between the Church and Dissent] are too great to admit of anything in the way of religious co-operation . . . We do not agree as to what constitutes the church and the mode of admission into the church, and what is necessary for orders, and the importance of sacraments; we do not agree about those things.[40]

The vicar of Brecon, Edward Latham Bevan, reiterated this conviction forcefully. Co-operation on religious matters was impossible, he claimed, 'because the Church of England regards the orders and sacraments of the Nonconformists as invalid'. This was not a matter on which one could be equivocal: 'It is manifestly impossible that we can both be right.'[41]

Despite being distasteful to evangelical churchmen and causing many Nonconformists virtual apoplexy, the appeal of 'High

Churchmanship', whether Anglo-Catholic or not, was obvious. It was a coherent religious system integrating doctrine, liturgy and rigorous discipleship. Unashamedly supernaturalist, it preserved continuity with the primitive church and the intervening Christian centuries. Whereas Nonconformity was seen as being fractious and divided, and evangelicalism as pietistic and narrow, Catholicism with its rounded doctrines of creation and redemption and sacramental appeal to the senses, presented a very satisfying version of the faith. When Timothy Rees of Cross Inn, Cardiganshire, forsook Nonconformity for a Catholic Anglicanism, he was attracted above all by the wholeness of its faith: 'The divisions in Nonconformity and its lack of historic continuity made him decide to seek for Orders in the ancient Church of the land.'[42] If Protestantism was austere, negative and moralistic, Anglo-Catholicism seemed to be setting the pace for the future.

By 1914 the perceived virtues of Welsh Anglicanism were finding favour with an increasing number of Welshmen and women. 'Is it not obvious', stated Frank Morgan, tutor in modern history at Keble College, Oxford, and one of the Welsh Church's most able laymen,

> that the Church, by its maintenance of a definite standard of religious belief enshrined in its Creeds and its Prayer-Book, by the importance it attaches to pastoral ministrations, and by its inculcation of a true spirit of reverence, is contributing to the religious life of Wales what no Nonconformist body has been able to contribute?[43]

Whereas it was the evangelicals who had secured the Church's popular missionary success, it had been the High Churchmen who had animated Welsh Anglicanism with that spirit of reverence and provided a fresh appreciation of the value of sacrament and creed. Between them the fortunes of the Church in Wales had been significantly improved.

The implications of the disestablishment campaign

The final stages in the long campaign to disestablish the Welsh Anglican Church began with the Liberal landslide in the general election of 1906.[44] Now each of the Welsh parliamentary seats apart from Merthyr's second seat which Keir Hardie held for Labour, was occupied by a Liberal. Every single Welsh member was in favour of disestablishment and disendowment while the election of a Liberal government meant that the party's long-standing policy could be translated into action. With Lloyd George now holding Cabinet office, action seemed imminent. But to the dismay of many, rather than proposing a bill to sever the link between church and state, the government proposed a Royal Commission to investigate the state of religion in Wales. This prevarication was indicative of a fundamental change of mood occurring at the time. What had been a burning issue of contemporary relevance three decades earlier, had by 1906 become of secondary importance at best. The disadvantages under which Nonconformists had laboured had long been redressed. The tithe had been commuted, church rates had been abolished, burial and marriage laws had been passed granting Dissenters full and binding rights, the two ancient universities had opened their doors to (male) Nonconformist students while the restructuring of the franchise system had spelt the near absolute demise of the Tory squirearchy's influence on the new Welsh county councils. The remedying of religious grievances had undermined the passion and even the demand for radical legislation. But even more significant was the fact that purely religious concerns were being eclipsed by secular and temporal matters. By the twentieth century Welsh public opinion was focusing much more explicitly on such vital issues as unemployment and industrial oppression, fairer working conditions and pay schemes, the problems of malnutrition and proper housing. With a rising class consciousness, the question of disestablishing the Welsh Anglican Church seemed increasingly peripheral.

No one realized this more than David Lloyd George, since 1908 Chancellor in Asquith's government. Exercised by much more absorbing topics of which the running of the Exchequer would become paramount, his interest in the church–state question and in matters particular to Wales had long abated. Having held private consultations with both the bishop of St Asaph and Randall Davidson, the archbishop of Canterbury, it was he who had proposed the setting up of the Royal Commission in order ostensibly to prepare the way for disestablishment. He had in fact agreed to bide for time during which a compromise measure protecting the Church's endowments could be drafted. This, of course, was guarded assiduously from his most loyal supporters, the still strong body of Protestant Dissent. The ensuing years were taken up by a host of parliamentary battles: the radical Pensions Act of 1908, the sterling attempt to pass the 'People's Budget' of 1909, the equally radical National Insurance Act of May 1911 and the Parliamentary Act of the following August curtailing drastic- ally the powers of the House of Lords. By then the Commission had fulfilled its remit and produced its report, the most detailed assessment ever of religious life in Wales. Further procrastination was now made impossible, and on 23 April 1912, the third Welsh Disestablishment Bill was introduced to the House of Commons by the home secretary Reginald McKenna, the member for North Monmouthshire.

Based on a previous Bill of 1909, the third measure stipulated that all pre-1662 properties would be secularized and that a number of Welsh Church Commissioners would be appointed to oversee the transferral of Church assets, namely cathedrals, dean- eries and bishops' residences, churches, vicarages and rectories and all glebe lands, to a Representative Body of the new Welsh Church. The educational establishments of St David's Lampeter and St Michael's Llandaff would be exempt from this process. Income from the Queen Anne's Bounty and parliamentary grants since 1800 was to be discontinued while all parochial endowments were to be transferred to the county councils. Although represent- ing a still substantial financial loss, this measure was much more moderate than previous planned legislation. Despite their con- tinued vigorous opposition, Welsh Churchmen were in fact much less disheartened than they had initially feared. The Bill itself did not finally pass through the Commons until January 1913 only to be rejected by the Lords; it was moved again in the following July and summarily rejected by the Upper Chamber once more; its third passage was rushed through during the summer of 1914 by which time the vastly more pressing matter of war finally ensured its acceptance. To the jubilation of some but to the relief of many, the Welsh Church Act reached the statute books on 18 September 1914 with the proviso that it would not be enacted for a full year after the cessation of hostilities. The war years would see further developments basically advantageous to the newly disestablished Welsh Anglican Church. Most important of all, the conflict afforded Churchmen time to adapt to their new status and prepare for self-government, a task which they undertook with professionalism and considerable resolve. Yet it was impossible not to conclude that the strains of *Hen Wlad fy Nhadau* sung by the Liberal Dissenting members which echoed through the Westminster corridors in September 1914 sounded an empty victory.

The hugely protracted disestablishment campaign did little credit to either Nonconformist or Churchman, though it would be the chapel rather than the Church which would suffer ultimately most grievously. What had been in the 1860s a crusade for righteousness had degenerated into a mean-spirited and unedifying political *imbroglio*. A. G. Edwards, who was no mean political operator himself, laid the blame squarely at the door of Henry Richard MP, former leader of the Liberation Society and the evil genius of political Dissent: 'He belonged to an eminent group of Nonconformists whose early enthusiasm for religion had been wholly translated into politics', he claimed.[45] This did less than justice to an honourable man. What was incontrovertible was that, although nominally religious, the second generation of parliamentary Nonconformists had become in fact deeply sceptical. From 1893 matters of principle had to a large extent yielded to questions of finance. The moral implications of establishment had been replaced by the economic considerations of endowment. Lloyd George and his radical colleagues announced that they would be content with no less than the full despoilment of 'an alien Church'. This had been countered by an equally unyielding policy of Anglican 'Church Defence'. Its master-strategist had been A. G. Edwards who had replaced Joshua Hughes at St Asaph in 1889, ably assisted by John Owen, his dean, a man who was soon to become bishop of St David's. Edwards's parochial experience was negligible, Owen's non-existent, the one having risen through the Church's hierarchy via the headmastership of Llandovery College and the other by way of a Lampeter professorial chair. Both were to make their reputation not so much as pastors, administrators and certainly not as preachers, but as ecclesiastical politicians. Under their highly effective leadership, 'Church Defence' became an out-and-out war against popular Nonconformity and, alas, against the voluntary and democratic Welsh-speaking culture from which it had sprung. From 1890 the extremist mentality triumphed, compromise became impossible, and vengefulness, meanness of spirit and crass materialism seriously undermined spiritual integrity on both sides. In fact the campaign became the focus for a host of resentments which had more to do with social and cultural differences within the Welsh nation than with the essence of the Christian faith itself.

The fact that the most vocal representatives of the hierarchy chose to fight Nonconformity on what became a class-bound and virtually anti-Welsh platform highlights the severe ambiguities under which contemporary Welsh Anglicanism laboured. On the one hand the Established Church had prided itself on being 'the ancient Church of this nation'; on the other it gloried in its social status as the church of the Anglicized aristocracy. Having a genuine concern for the *gwerin* or native working people, its prelates were often felt to be aloof and self-important. 'There is a distinct cleavage between the Nonconformists and Anglicans', reported a Llanelli Presbyterian pastor in 1907, 'partly accounted for by differences of doctrine . . . but more, I think, because of the different status or prestige of establishments.' Inter-ministerial cordiality, though highly desirable, was virtually impossible, for 'we are Dissenting ministers, and the Jews have no dealings with the Samaritans'![46] 'I would like for them to work with us', claimed the Congregationalist patriarch, Dr Thomas Johns, 'but they are always keeping aloof.'[47] Whereas there was nothing indigenously Welsh about Nonconformity, Calvinistic Methodism excepted, Churchmen could take pride that their communion represented a Christianity which was as old as Wales itself. Sometimes with scholarly acumen, often with partisan zeal, the defenders of the establishment would invariably emphasize the national character of their Church. 'If I am asked whether the Church is national in Wales', stated A. G. Edwards, 'I should say that it is the only institution in Wales which can be called national.'[48] For him the ancient Welsh Church had existed prior to the birth of the British state and before the coming of the Saxons and the Normans. In the early medieval period a fusion had occurred between the English Church of Augustine and the native Welsh sees which, by the time of Geraldus Cambrensis, had been complete. Thereafter England and Wales shared the same ecclesiastical communion which fully accepted the jurisdiction of Canterbury. Older than the Act of Union, it embodied the spiritual, ecclesiastical and thereafter the political union of the two nations: 'The Catholic

Church was there before the union, and after the union, and it was the same church from an ecclesiastical point of view.'[49] Given the bishop's presuppositions there was nothing particularly erroneous about his theory. Its weakness, however, was that it too readily sanctioned the powers of the status quo. Rather than working to Wales's advantage, this popular unionism tended to undercut the claims of Welsh particularity in favour of the well-being of the stronger partner. It served as a ready excuse to Anglicize the Welsh Church.

This bias towards England was most readily expressed in Edwards's long antipathy towards the use and extension of the Welsh language. Although Welsh-speaking himself, by the early twentieth century his anti-Welsh reputation had reached the point of notoriety. During his period as warden of Llandovery College in the 1870s he had banished Welsh from the curriculum, turning the establishment into a minor public school in the English mould. His highly public clash with David Howell, 'Llawdden', arch-deacon of Wrexham and future dean of St David's, at the beginning of his episcopal tenure disclosed the strength of feeling which existed between the patrician, hierarchical and Anglicizing element within the Church and the indigenous, patriotic and proletarian tradition which Howell espoused.[50] For Edwards the Welsh language was a source of derision and contempt, 'the last refuge of the uneducated'[51] and something to be apologized for; it was certainly never to be afforded any official status. Yet the Church's principal missionary gains had been made by Welsh-speaking clergy among Welsh-speaking people during a time when national sentiment was increasing in strength.

More remarkable than Bishop Edwards's anti-Welsh bias was that of his principal colleague and coadjutor, Bishop John Owen, a former Methodist 'Son of Lleyn'. Even after being appointed professor of Welsh at St David's College, Lampeter, he resolutely (and bizarrely) refused to speak the language with his students. Welsh could be studied (through the medium of English) but on no account was it to be used. Although he never divested himself of a thick Caernarfonshire accent, he was never once known to have spoken Welsh with any of his fellow clergy. Recounting an interview with Owen during the 1920s, D. Parry-Jones, then a junior curate in Pontarddulais, remarked on the linguistic incongruity of the situation, adding: 'I never spoke in my own native tongue to any

Welsh bishop until I was over eighty years of age! I would not dare do so.'[52] Such would be the long-term influence of 'the St Asaph Policy'. 'Neither by temperament nor by training nor by conviction is the new Bishop a strenuous reformer', the radical journal *Young Wales* had reported on Owen's appointment to St David's in 1898. His refusal to reinstate Welsh at Llandovery (where he had followed Edwards as headmaster), his continuing support for his diocesan in his clash with 'Llawdden' by which time he (Owen) had become St Asaph's dean, and his having voted against the appointment of a Welsh-speaking principal at Lampeter were all noted: 'Since his elevation he has gone out of his way to allude to the Bishop of St Asaph as his "great and loyal leader".' The radicals' prophecy that 'The national party in the Church has nothing to expect from Bishop Owen'[53] was more than amply fulfilled.[54]

This apparent 'pandering to England [and] ridiculing the Welsh language'[55] must be understood in its cultural and historical context. Ever since the sixteenth century when Wales was incorporated into the English state and the status of its language downgraded, a deep strain of inferiority had infected the Welsh national consciousness. The legal and objective inferiority conferred on Welsh nationhood, especially on its most obvious point of differentiation, namely its language, produced in successive generations of Welsh people a subjective sense of ambivalence and often shame concerning the essence of their own national identity.[56] Those who lived in the closest proximity to the centres of power frequently felt this ambivalence most keenly. The Anglican Church had always been linked with status, power and privilege; its bishops would sit in the House of Lords. It is hardly surprising that its senior clerics would fight tenaciously to retain a status which had been conferred upon them by what they regarded as culturally and politically the superior partner. Consequently any popular movement which was more confident in its own national identity, especially if it were linked with Liberalism and Nonconformity, would be far more likely to be seen as a threat than a challenge. 'I am half an Englishman and half a Welshman', mused A. G. Edwards, 'and I have been labouring between the two all my life.'[57] Edwards's identity crisis coloured not only his diocesan policy but much of the life and witness of the Church in Wales well into the mid-twentieth century. It was compounded rather than resolved by the disestablishment campaign.

The intransigence and bigotry which both sides displayed during the campaign created wide disillusionment with Christianity among many who were already drifting towards the boundaries of their respective churches. A surfeit of zeal was being expended on secondary matters and everywhere spirituality was being sapped. In many the religious impulse had become virtually extinct. According to one loyal and fair-minded Welsh Churchman,

> Too much time was wasted . . . in slandering, backbiting and reviling one another, and in arousing a spirit of antagonism and hatred . . . [all of] which was corroding the life of the Church, overshadowing her brightness, diminishing her influence and bringing the whole gamut of religion into discredit.[58]

In his address before the 1909 Church Congress, Frank Morgan's incisive assessment of the over-politicization of Dissent could equally well have been applied to his own communion. The result of a half century of agitation for disestablishment, he claimed, had been to intertwine politics and religion much more tightly than had hitherto been the case:

> This process, it should be noted, is quite distinct from that which is often confused with it, but is really its converse – the bringing of religion to bear upon politics. While there is much to be said for the latter process, there is nothing to be said in favour of the former; yet, unfortunately, it is the former that has been predominant in Welsh Nonconformity for the last generation. The quiet, earnest, religious Nonconformist has been pushed more and more into the background to give place to noisy politicians – many of them politicians first and ministers of the Gospel second.[59]

Yet for all that there remained a vast concourse of faithful Christian believers, both Churchpeople and Nonconformist, who stayed well above the fray and whose task it would be to deliver the gospel message to an increasingly secularized and alienated generation.

The social and religious challenge

When Dr John Williams, Brynsiencyn, the most popular Noncon-formist preacher in north Wales died in 1921, it was said of him, not without sympathy:

> The farthest that his vision extended was to improve things as they
> stood, to get the master to be more considerate and the servant more
> conscientious but not to build a new world on new foundations. His
> concern was to make religion permeate all things but to revolutionize
> nothing.[60]

The most pressing problem which Nonconformity, still Wales's
principal religious tradition, had to face was that of responding to
the secularizing process which accompanied modernity. The
gradual improvement of the individual may have chimed in
perfectly with Victorian progressivism, but it was less relevant to a
generation which was beginning to interpret history in terms of
competing economic forces manifested in the differing values of
each social class. For more and more of the Welsh, not only in
industrialized south Wales but in other parts of the country as
well, a status quo which sanctioned unbridled capitalism and perpetuated the social divide was no longer an option: fundamental
change was essential. But Nonconformity, still enamoured of the
ideology of the individual and enmeshed in the politics of the
Liberal Party, found this disconcerting. Far from being a healthy
challenge, the doctrines of socialism were perceived as a severe
intimidation.

Following its foundation in 1893, the Independent Labour Party
(ILP) made rapid progress in parts of Wales. Its main centres of
support were Merthyr Tydfil and the Rhondda Valleys where
branches proliferated well before the turn of the century, and
within a few years Rhosllannerchrugog on the north-eastern
coalfield and Blaenau Ffestiniog in the heart of the Merioneth
slate districts. In 1900 the ILP had merged with the trade unions
and the more theoretical Fabian Society, established a decade and a
half previously to popularize the socialist creed, in order to create
a new body to represent the working people: the Labour Party. Its
success was marked by the immediate election to Westminster of
the Scotsman Keir Hardie, the ILP's founder, as junior member for
Merthyr and Aberdare. By 1906 Liberal Wales had returned six
Labour members, a rate of success which was a portent of what
was to come. If the Labour Party existed in order to represent in
Parliament (initially) the rights and welfare of manual workers,
full-blown socialism advocated not the utilization of capitalism in
favour of the less well-off but its wholesale rejection and

destruction. As the representative of the people, central government would take possession of all private property. Everyone would be expected to contribute towards the common good and receive, in turn, a portion of the common benefit; only thus would a fair, just and equitable society be created. By 1914 what had begun as a minor interest of a few enthusiasts had become a surging popular movement and as such faced the chapels with a momentous problem. How would they respond to its claims and how would it view their religion? In a conference of Cardiff ministers convened on 5 January 1912 to discuss the social question, the Revd John Morgan Jones, Calvinistic Methodist pastor of the Pembroke Terrace Church in the heart of the town, plied the conventional wisdom; 'the Gospels support no single social theory or propaganda', he claimed, and 'the evidence of the gospel is either negative or neutral on the subject'.[61] Had the powerful Nonconformist establishment displayed in the past the same neutrality and disengagement towards the Liberal cause, such an answer may have rung true. The truth, of course, was that such studied impartiality appeared wholly disingenuous; the chapels were being seen as a buttress to the status quo. It hardly augured well for their developing relationship with the Labour movement.

Yet Nonconformity's leaders were right to be wary. They were sufficiently astute to realize the dangers of lending support to a doctrinal system which could well become incompatible with the gospel. For socialism, when at its most consistent, offered people an alternative world-view replete with its own programme, philosophy and absolutes. If taken to its logical conclusion it could prevent men and women from confessing Jesus as Lord. Whereas there was so much in socialist propaganda which the Christian mind could affirm – its burning social concern and zeal for justice and fairplay – it was equally true that it possessed contradictory elements – a materialistic philosophy and humanist preconceptions – which Christian faith would have no choice but to challenge and reject. But the fact was that by 1914 Nonconformity was ill equipped to do so. The retreat from biblical authority, the lure of a liberal creed which downplayed the supernatural and tended (like socialism) to deify humankind, and an inability to formulate an adequate, orthodox and biblically realistic doctrine of society rendered the chapels ineffectual in the face of Labour verve, analysis, commitment and idealism. And when hugely skilled Labour propagandists used the language of religion – the Sermon on the Mount and the coming of God's Kingdom on earth – as did Keir Hardie and the Revd T. E. Nicholas, and were assisted by a bevy of intellectually distinguished young ministers whose grasp of the biblical revelation was not nearly as sound as their commitment to the Labour cause (the Revds Herbert Morgan and R. Silyn Roberts exemplifying this trend), the consequences for the future of Welsh Nonconformity were dire. For many within the rising generation it was the Labour movement and not the Christian churches which would provide the people with an albeit temporal salvation and usher in a utopian kingdom of righteousness. The churches, having either retreated to an other-worldly pietism or to a theologically defective individualist Idealism, were already forfeiting the allegiance of working people. 'Nonconformity', according to one recent authority, 'would never really recover its previous status in society because it had eschewed the only path that might have ensured success: namely, a spiritually informed commitment to politics.'[62] Alas, after August 1914 both politics and religion were to be severely put to the test with the cataclysm that was about to descend.

2

Christianity and the First World War, 1914–1918

Initial response to the conflict

In his New Year's message to his flock, Bishop Joshua Pritchard Hughes of Llandaff listed some of 'the grave uncertainties, the possible difficulties [and] the certain anxieties' which he foresaw during 1914. Apart from the inevitable matter of the disestablishment of the Church, he mentioned the threat of insurrection in Ireland and 'the many difficult social and industrial problems' which had become so prevalent within his diocese.[1] The one thing he did not mention was the possibility that by mid-summer Britain would be plunged into full-scale war. Yet even then Germany, which since the days of Chancellor Bismarck had developed from being a fairly loose confederation of separate states into the strongest unified power in Europe, had become deeply threatening to some of her neighbours. The triple alliance between Germany, Austria and Italy was felt to be sufficiently intimidating that a triple *entente* was established between Britain, France and Russia to counter-balance the Kaiser's increasing influence. A massive build-up of arms served to intensify an already volatile international situation. Whereas Austria had designs upon Serbia, Russia was pledged to its defence in the eventual hope of winning Serbia for itself. So when Archduke Franz Ferdinand was assassinated by a Serb at Sarajevo on 28 June 1914, the spark which would cause the conflagration had been ignited. Austria, declaring war on Serbia, pitched itself against Russia, thus implicating Germany which had promised to support its ally come what may. To defend Austria Germany needed to immobilize France which could only be done by occupying neutral Belgium which stood in its path. But Britain, alarmed at the prospect of German domination of Europe, had pledged itself to Belgium's defence. So when, on 4 August 1914, Germany did invade Belgium a major war became inevitable. Few realized how protracted that

war would become or imagined the nature of its effect upon
society or religion both in Wales and elsewhere.

Whereas Bishop Hughes's attitude to the war would reflect the
values of the Anglican establishment, it was chiefly due to the
influence of David Lloyd George, chancellor of the Exchequer and
the Liberal Party's most dazzling operator, that Nonconformist
Wales put aside its scruples and supported the war wholeheartedly. The mood initially was serious rather than jingoistic; no
one relished the idea of conflict and Wales's leaders spoke in terms
of moderation and even respect. Though currently corrupted by
Prussianism, Germany was, nevertheless, the home of culture and
civilization and remained the cradle of the Protestant
Reformation. It was only afterwards, in response to propaganda
concerning German atrocities, including the falsely reported
burning of the university library at Louvain, the Zeppelin raids
over the east coast in January 1915, the sinking of the civilian liner
Lusitania, the publication of Lord Bryce's report on enemy
outrages (the contents of which were discovered later to be
factually inaccurate) and the execution of nurse Edith Cavill in
October, that moderation gave way to widespread anger and
revulsion.[2] Meredydd Ffoulkes had been in training as a junior
physician in Lowestoft, Suffolk, when war had been declared, and
had treated many of the Belgian refugees who had arrived there at
the time. 'I have never seen people in such a pitiable plight in all
my life', he wrote to his parents in Llanberis, near Caernarfon, in
October 1914:

> So many of them had a look of terror on their faces. The old people
> did not seem to realise where they were, and kept asking if they were
> safe from the Germans . . . Apart from the sacking of towns, the stories
> of cruelty related by these poor refugees are sufficient to debar the
> Germans from any claim to culture and civilisation.[3]

Reports such as these strengthened the already massive consensus
that Britain had behaved honourably in taking up arms. Germany
had flagrantly violated international law, had flouted public
opinion and left Britain no choice but to honour long-standing
treaty links which went back as far as 1839. 'We cannot as a nation
break our plighted word,' stated Bishop Hughes; 'we cannot stand
by in our seagirt isle and see the weak trampled upon, robbed and

outraged by a cruel and relentless horde as long as we have power to hold out our helping hand to support and protect those who call to us for help.'[4] The bishop's sentiments were echoed by virtually all Welsh Nonconformists, even those who had built a reputation on political radicalism. 'As the Lord liveth we had entered into no conspiracy against Germany', said Lloyd George to a vast congregation of Free Church people and London Welshmen in the City Temple, Westminster, in November 1914. 'We are in the war from motives of purest chivalry to defend the weak.' Belgium was, like Wales, a small nation, 'a poor little neighbour whose home was broken into by a hulking bully', and were it not for the Christian resolve of its allies, it would surely perish. However regrettable, therefore, the war was both inevitable and just. 'We are all looking forward to the time when swords shall be beaten into ploughshares', he said, but in the meantime there was no alternative but to fight.[5]

Rhetoric like this was replicated a thousand times from platforms and, alas, pulpits throughout the land. Biblical allusions to the Good Samaritan, Naboth's Vineyard, the divine righteousness and God's protection of the weak, were used to dispel quasi-pacifist qualms and justify the decision to go to war. 'It has become our sacred calling to take up arms,' said the Revd Thomas Charles Williams in September 1914, ' "he that hath no sword, let him sell his garment and buy one".'[6] Scriptural language was commandeered for militaristic use and Nonconformist ministers and Anglican prelates became recruiting officers. This occurred nowhere more than in the Welsh heartland of Gwynedd where Calvinistic Methodism's two most popular preachers, Thomas Charles Williams of Menai Bridge and John Williams, Brynsiencyn, became the war effort's most vocal apologists. Both were men of consummate ability; T. C. Williams was debonair and intellectual, whose fashionable pulpit delivery was as revered in the bourgeois world of London Nonconformity as it was among the chapelgoers of north Wales, and John Williams, the idol of the preaching meetings, whose direct style had ensured lasting affection far beyond the bounds of his own denomination. Both were close friends of Lloyd George, and the chancellor, wily as ever, knew how to manipulate his relationship with these key Welsh Nonconformists to the full. The creation of the 38th (Welsh) Division, where volunteers would be able to use their own language and where their religious needs would be met to the full, was one of the chancellor's ploys for enticing Nonconformist Wales into the war. His appointment of General Owen Thomas, an Anglesey Congregationalist and the only senior Welsh-speaking officer in the regular army, as its commander-in-chief reinforced its appeal. The (by now) notorious photograph of the Revd John Williams, resplendent in clerical collar and the uniform of the 38th Welsh, standing in the garden of 11 Downing Street in the company of Lloyd George and the philosopher Sir Henry Jones, illustrates the extent of Welsh Nonconformity's compromise with the political establishment of the time.

Those who were not deceived by the pious rhetoric of the war's supporters were scarce indeed. Few conceived of the hostilities in terms of a clash of conflicting imperial interests or doubted that Britain's intentions were anything but altruistic. In the popular mind the conflict was seen in apocalyptic terms of good against evil and God versus the devil. 'This war is being fought not only between temporal powers but more especially between spiritual mights', it was claimed, 'between the kingdom of darkness and the kingdom of light.'[7] Those brought up on evangelical religion, with its absolute antitheses of salvation and damnation, darkness and light, were likely to interpret the war in an unsophisticated way. This was true of those who delivered sermons as well as those who listened to them.

> Is our cause a just one? [asked the Congregationalist T. Esger James in March 1915] Yes, if it is just for the strong to support the weak; yes, if the Lamb and not the beast is to rule . . . Yes, for this is a battle between truth and error, between light and darkness, between righteousness and unrighteousness, between Christ and Anti-Christ, between the beast and the Son of Man.[8]

However much truth was contained in allied accusations of German arrogance and militarism, such an absolute duality served as a convenient cloak to cover the self-interest of the two rival factions. Those who attempted to inject some realism into the situation were treated harshly. The Revd J. Puleston Jones, the blind minister of Pwllheli's Penmount Chapel, was vilified and ostracized by some from within his own community, while the windows of the Congregationalist College at Bala-Bangor were vandalized because of Principal Thomas Rees's refusal to bow totally to anti-German sentiment. These men's crime was to have suggested, in the columns of their respective denominational journals, that Britain's declaration of war may not have been made for totally disinterested reasons and that Britain would do well to exert a measure of self-restraint.[9] 'I note . . . that you have in *Y Tyst* (among other papers) been expressing *Christian* views on this terrible European conflict', wrote D. R. Daniel, an erstwhile colleague of Lloyd George, in a letter to Thomas Rees in October 1914. 'To find anyone with sufficient courage at the present time to stand boldly for such obsolete opinions is to me at any rate wholesome and invigorating and I heartily wish strength to your hand.' What Rees had done was to urge against a simplistic appraisal of the international situation and to apply a measure of national self-criticism. Already deeply disenchanted with Lloyd George's opportunism, Daniel's views were uncommonly critical:

Christianity, which for some years I had been forced to believe was only a thin veneer over the civilization of this and other so-called Christian nations has for the last two months been totally erased leaving no trace behind. Our preachers of all denominations have been swept into the vortex of militarism . . . Liberalism, Labour yea the Positivists are all infected by the virus . . .

Daniel was resident in London at the time and his observations reflected the more blatant jingoism of English Christianity's initial response to the war, especially that of W. Robertson Nicoll and *The British Weekly*. None the less he was not blind to the unhealthy tendencies which were growing daily more common among his compatriots at home:

The 'neutrality of Belgium argument', as it has been so assiduously presented on its altruistic side, is of course irresistible. At the same time it takes a rather 'strong man' possessing any knowledge of modern history and the tortuous ways of diplomats, to believe that anything so disinterested is possible on the part of any European Chancellery . . .

Christian ministers, he suggested, should decline from making simplistic assertions which merely served to reveal their political naïvety. To inculcate hatred for the enemy even in the cause of national victory, was a negation of the gospel, 'and to read such twaddle and rickety sophistry as is written by your fellow minister the Rev Robert Williams MA Glanconway in the *Cymro* would be amusing were it not so sad'. So much of the more recent out-pourings of the English denominational press, he claimed, were 'too nauseating to be read'.[10]

Such critical realism as this, at such an early juncture of the war, was rare. The general view was that war was inevitable, that the British cause was just and that Wales was proud to play its full part in defence of King and Empire. It was when people realized that the war would not be 'over by Christmas', when battle-scarred men returned for leave with horrendous stories of life in the trenches and when the body count reached thousands and tens of thousands, that popular idealism cooled and doubts as to the wisdom, if not the justice, of the war surfaced. The recruiting zeal of the ecclesiastical leaders would seriously rebound upon them as the incongruity of Christ's followers urging young men to take arms registered increasingly upon the populace. The reputation of John Williams especially was damaged beyond repair: for the mothers of Anglesey he became 'the one who sent our boys to be killed'. All the major denominations, including the Anglican Church, were perceived to have endorsed the war effort whole-heartedly and to have discarded all that was distinctive in the Christian faith and ethic according to the demands of the moment. Rather than providing a moral code, a set of values and a knowledge of God which could transcend temporal and merely national considerations, institutional Christianity appeared to have become a function of the imperial cause. This was to bode ill for its fate in post-war Wales. As Lloyd George's reputation plummeted after 1919, so too did the matrix of causes with which he had been connected: Liberalism, the implicit purity of the national interest and a populist and increasingly ineffectual Welsh Nonconformity. Secularization would have occurred anyway. What the First World War did was to hasten its process and provide succeeding generations with a brutal if convenient historical divide between a religious and post-religious phase in the develop-ment of modern Wales.

Christian witness at the front

By the end of the war nearly 11 per cent of the Welsh population, an estimated 227,000 men, had served in the armed forces, some 10 per cent of whom had perished. There was not a village, town or parish without its list of war dead: even today those brass plaques or chiselled marble monuments in innumerable communities bear silent witness to the grief felt for a lost generation. The effect of war, whether from aboard ship (the maritime tradition of coastal districts from Pembrokeshire to Anglesey and the tip of Llŷn ensured that a substantial minority of Welsh youth served with the Royal Navy or Merchant Marine) or on land, whether in the heat of Salonica, Mesopotamia and Palestine or from the trenches of Belgium and France, was often traumatic: 'Hell! Hell! Hell! O merciful God, what is man?' cried Lewis Valentine during the height of the third Ypres campaign in August 1917: 'Woe – blood – madness! . . . Torn flesh, shattered bones. Halt, O God, this mad fever . . .'[11] Letters written, diaries kept and reminiscences subsequently published by serving Welsh soldiers witness to a sometimes bewildering range of emotions engendered by the conflict: even when sorely tested, though, faith, for thousands, was never wholly extinguished.

Awaiting transportation to France in October 1915, Herbert Williams, a young man from Rhosllannerchrugog, Denbighshire, assured his minister of his intention to keep the faith: 'Well Mr Jones they (*sic*) are a lot of temptations in this camp but thank God I have had strength to overcome them all. I shall never forget my vow and the religion in Jesus Christ (*sic*).'[12] Six months earlier Herbert Richards, his friend and fellow Rhos chapel member, had described the dire awfulness of trench life:

> I was staying last week about half a mile from the fireline. It was allfull (*sic*) on times there with the rolling of the guns. You would think that the end of the world had come. The German coalboxes were droping (*sic*) quite near to us rocking the houses down and shaking the place but I am still alive. It's the One Above that I'm to thank for all this. I believe that you all are praying for me.[13]

Thomas Jones from Pennal, Merioneth, a private in the 16th Battalion Royal Welch Fusiliers, wrote regularly to his brothers from the front describing the desolation which he encountered but always mentioning the help he gleaned from prayer and when possible worship, and assuring them of his faith in God's protection. He was struck forcefully early in 1916 by the sight of a crucifix standing unscathed and alone outside a totally wrecked church building, which he perceived as a sign of God's providential ruling despite the madness all around.[14] Thomas Owen, a native of Anglesey, kept a diary in which his descriptions of the horrors and hardships of the Somme were interspersed with petition and prayer:

> Mi oedd mor galed arnaf os (*sic*) eiddwn yn gyrnu fel deilen, ac yn yr un modd mi eiddwn yn drio gweddio ac mi gefais fy gwrandaw, ac fy amddiffyn trwy ddiolch am nerth a chysgod pan oedd hi yn ofnadwy arnom. [It was so awful that I shook like a leaf, yet still I tried to pray and thankfully I was heard and protected when all things were so terrible.]

Scriptural verses learned at Sunday school brought comfort and served to make some sense of the horror in which he found himself:

> Yn y nos byddaf fel llygoden yn gwachiad (*sic*) a rhyw 200 yards sydd rhyngddo (*sic*) a gelyn, ac mae nw yn bifario (?*sic*) yn oleu, welais waeth lawer gwaith, ond ella heno bydd hi'n bwys arnom, ond toes ond disgwyl y goreu, os bydd Duw gyda ni, bwy (*sic*) all fod i'n herbyn. [During the night I watch like a mouse there's 200 yards between me and the enemy, and their barrage (?) is bright though I've seen worse many times, but perhaps tonight it will come upon us heavily, but we can only hope for the best, if God is for us, who can be against us.][15]

Both men were killed soon afterwards. In one of the more unlikely scenarios of the war, the Revd D. Cynddelw Williams, chaplain in the 38th Welsh, came across a bible-study group being conducted in a shell-hole during a pause in the Battle of the Somme: 'Another scene which impressed itself upon me', he recorded in his diary in November 1916, 'was coming across 5 or 6 of the boys in a shellhole, 2 of whom had testaments in their hands. They were discussing some scriptural truth in a most dangerous spot: just to have raised their heads would have invited enemy fire.'[16] W. G.

Jones, a medical orderly serving with the 15th Division Royal Welch Fusiliers, had the opportunity to reflect upon his battle experiences while recovering from his wounds in Blackpool in April 1917. 'Though we had no religious services, never did I experience the presence of God so strongly as I did in France,' he wrote. 'By nature I am not one of the brave, but out in France I moved amongst death without any fear whatever. I can account for it only by reference to this power and consolation of my religion.'[17] While marching to La Boiselle in October 1917, Lewis Valentine, a student at the University of Wales, Bangor, serving as an orderly in the Royal Army Medical Corps, discovered the bodies of some of his officers in a dug-out. First they were buried, then 'We had a prayer meeting in the evening; though in semi-darkness the divine presence illuminated the place.' He had written in his diary the day before: 'To Thee o God, I commend my life; [though life?] is most sweet but "Thy will be done".'[18]

Examples of faith under fire are not hard to find; they bear poignant witness to the effectiveness of the churches in inculcating true experiential Christianity in their young men before the war. Whereas nominal Christianity was shown to be worthless in the trenches, true faith, often when reinforced by the objective potency of sacramental symbolism, was revered by many. Writing to his former parish priest, the Revd D. L. Prosser, vicar of Pembroke Dock, Corporal Frank Reed of the 6th Welsh Regiment stated in April 1916: 'Every Sunday morning at 7.30 we have Holy Communion which is a great help to men leaving for the trenches in the night.'[19] Years later the poet and artist David Jones, whose *In Parenthesis* remains a uniquely evocative verse portrayal of trench life, described the effect that coming across a celebration of the mass near the front line had upon him. A London Welshman and nominally an Anglican, he had joined the 15th Battalion Royal Welch Fusiliers early in 1915, was wounded at Mametz in June 1916 and was later involved in the Passchendaele offensive. While looking for firewood during a lull in the battle of the Somme he chanced upon an outhouse:

what I saw through the small gap in the wall was not the dim emptiness I had expected but the back of a *sacerdos* in a gilt-hued *planeta*, two points of flickering candlelight no doubt lent an extra sense of goldness to the vestment and a golden warmth seemed, by the same agency, to lend the white altar cloths and the white linen of the celebrant's alb and amice and maniple . . . You can imagine what a great marvel it was for me to see through that chink in the wall, and kneeling in the hay beneath the improvised *mensa* were a few huddled figures in khaki.[20]

It was through this powerful image and the subsequent pastoral ministrations of the celebrant, Fr Daniel Hughes SJ, Catholic chaplain to the 38th Welsh Brigade, that Jones forsook his conventional Anglicanism for the Church of Rome. The blend of Christian symbolism, mythology and allusion to medieval Welsh literature contained in his later creative work would establish David Jones's reputation as a major twentieth-century Christian poet and artist.

Yet it was not only Anglicans and Catholics who set great store upon the eucharist; Free Churchmen too came to appreciate the objective character of the sacrament in a fresh way. Partaking of the Lord's Supper in a trench, or within the sound of battle, was frequently a very moving experience. 'We have a religious service every Sunday in a farmyard adjacent to where we are billeted', Thomas Jones informed his brothers in January 1916. 'After writing these words I will go to the Welsh service where we shall partake once more of the Lord's Supper.'[21] W. T. Davies, a Calvinistic Methodist ordinand and stretcher-bearer with the 45th Field Ambulance RAMC, wrote from France on 29 October 1916:

I did manage this morning to attend a communion service in a hut some distance away. The officiating minister was a C of E clergyman. Needless to say the 'great things' seemed more precious than ever. I've been impressed many times by the nearness of the spiritual world. Perhaps things being what they are, one would look for it to be otherwise but it is not so. It's an all round testing time. We are put to the test, but so also is God and his Christ (I write with all reverence). There cannot be any doubts lurking in one's mind with regards to the essential things of the Xtian religion after an experience 'out here'.[22]

The sacrament retained its potency as much in the heat of Salonica as in the mud of France.

I have had the privilege of having one communion out here [wrote Private B. J. Evans on 13 December 1916]. This was the first communion of this kind I have ever received. It had a peculiar effect on me. I could think that never before had I been present in such a beautiful communion. My spirit was well blessed in that service. It is a glorious fact for me that although I am far from home, far from friends and relations, yet heaven is as near to me here as it was in Wales, and God is as eager to hear and answer our prayers out in this wild country as he was in the quiet, comfortable home amongst the hills of Wales . . . '*Mae Duw yn llond pob lle, presennol ym mhob man.*[23]

Iorwerth Davies, an apprentice pharmacist from Machynlleth and latterly a Congregationalist deacon in churches in Lampeter and Aberystwyth, had been turned down by the South Wales Borderers on grounds of poor health, but was eventually accepted by the RAMC as an orderly. Sixty years later he recollected vividly a communion service held in a derelict carpenter's shop on the Struma front in Salonica in 1917. A white cloth covered the carpenter's bench as he knelt, with half-a-dozen others, in the shavings; it was Christmas day, and the significance of both occasion and location was immense: 'I'll never forget that, because it was a very, very sacred, and very impressive little service that we had . . . in the carpenter's shop.'[24] Sometime before the experience which was the basis for that recollection, the Revd Cynddelw Williams quoted from a letter in which a young man described a communion service which he, too, had recently attended:

It was held in an old French barn, but nevertheless had it been a cathedral, it would never have been more beautiful, for the Spirit of God was present without doubt. You were as if carried away from the world and its sound of guns and war and lifted up to some unseen elevated plane . . . The hour spent in that French barn I shall never forget, and I thank my heavenly Father for his great blessings of a Christian home and upbringing.[25]

A week later that young man was dead.

The mention of military chaplains raises serious questions concerning the integrity of the Christian witness during a time of war. For some Christians, bearing arms was (and is) seen as incompatible with a profession of faith in the Christ who charged his followers to turn the other cheek and told Peter, the chief among the disciples, to put away his sword. Although Welsh Anglicanism, which represented the values of the religious establishment, could more easily reconcile Christianity with military service, Nonconformity tended to be much more pacifist in tone. 'We had been brought up in a tradition that was wholly unmilitaristic, peaceful if not pacifist',[26] wrote Morgan Watcyn-Williams, the son and grandson of Calvinistic Methodist ministers and during the war a captain in the Royal Welch Fusiliers. Radical Dissent had drunk deeply at the well of non-violence and the reputation of Henry Richard, Wales's foremost Nonconformist radical of a generation earlier, was as much as 'the Apostle of Peace' as of a doughty fighter for Dissenting rights. Yet Welsh Nonconformity's virtually unqualified support for the war required a radical reappraisal of its attitude to conflict as such. Although Nonconformist chaplains did not bear arms, their very presence at the front imposed dilemmas as to the relationship between Christianity and the war. When initial popular idealism waned and the scale of carnage began truly to register, it was not surprising that Welsh Dissent would be accused of gross hypocrisy. The chapels would be called to return to the anti-militarism which had characterized their earlier stance.

Yet the presence of Nonconformist chaplains on the field of battle did not invariably point to insincerity. The conventional picture of the jingoistic padre whose ministry consisted in sanctioning the allied cause (a picture which was created principally by such influential post-war authors as Robert Graves, Siegfried Sassoon and Frank Richards, all of whom had served with the most conspicuously Welsh of all the regiments, the Royal Welch Fusiliers), was at best incomplete. The bravery, integrity and spiritual seriousness of many regimental chaplains clearly impressed the fighting men. Perhaps the most revered among them was D. Cynddelw Williams, a Calvinistic Methodist minister in Pen-y-groes, Arfon, who volunteered for service with the 38th Welsh in October 1914. He served at Ypres and on the Somme (where he earned the Military Cross) and was clearly highly effective as a Christian pastor:

Sunday July 16th [1916] [wrote David Evans, a Caernarfonshire quarryman, in his diary] . . . 6 p.m. N[on] C[onformist] Service in the trench = Chaplain D. Cynddelw Williams BA. He followed us all the way through rough roads, scattered and muddy trenches, and at many times under heavy fire, and always doing all he could for us. Casualities (*sic*) which occur almost every day. He would be the first in the danger to attend the wounded. He won his DSO many times over through his silent duty and life sacrifice.[27]

Captain Morgan Watcyn-Williams wrote:

I heard the padre constantly for twelve months, now in a ruined house, now in an orchard behind Arras with the apple tree in bloom, and again inside the walls of a little French school; he had ever the same straightforward message – a Power greater than war, love stronger than death, and sacrifice the very gate of heaven. He was frank too, with a directness that could be disconcerting, even when it helped . . .

Down on the Somme he won his MC. All round Delville and Longueval and Guillemont the wounded came pouring in, but the padre never hesitated, and out among the falling shells and flying splinters carried on with the work of rescue.[28]

His reputation among the Welsh troops bore comparison with G. E. Studdert-Kennedy, 'Woodbine Willie', the best-known and most widely respected of the English chaplains,[29] though what is particularly significant is the fact that he was not unique. There were others: fellow Presbyterians like D. Morris Jones MC and, in Salonica, David Williams (both of whom were to have a lasting influence on a generation of post-war Calvinistic Methodist ministers as professors in the denominational seminary in Aberystwyth), Baptists such as A. Rhys Morgan MC, Congregationalists like Evan Mathias and Peris Williams (who were mentioned in dispatches) and Churchmen such as W. T. Havard MC and Timothy Rees MC (subsequently bishops of St Asaph and Llandaff respectively). There was also 'old Evans the padre' whose resolve and gallantry was recorded by Ll.Wyn Griffith in his *Up To Mametz* in 1931: 'There's a man for you Griff. If I come through this bloody business, I'd like to go to that man's church.'[30] The character upon whom Evans was based was Peter Jones Roberts, a Bangor Wesleyan minister, who had served in France along with his three sons, Glyn, Iori and Aubrey:

Yes, Peter Jones Roberts was the padre [Ll. W. Griffith acknowledged afterwards], and a better man never lived . . . Looking back upon it all now, I am more convinced than ever that his sincerity, in small things as well as great, was the secret of his tremendous influence over everybody. By this I mean – and I hope you will not misunderstand me – that he made no attempt whatever to imitate the conventional (and useless) padres in their heartiness and 'I am one of you, damn it, pass the whisky' sort of pose. He was what he was, a 'gweinidog' in khaki, convinced that his mission in all that madness was to stand for better things, unashamedly, reminding us by his very presence that the things and thoughts that had influenced us for good in our childhood were still valid and authentic and ever-lastingly 'there'.[31]

The sincerity and effectiveness of the best of the padres did not, however, minimize the ambiguities inherent in the general situation. The fact that Cynddelw Williams and Peter Roberts were commended for their outstanding bravery and the quality of their Christian witness suggested that there were others in whom these virtues were lacking. 'We have a new addition in the shape of a C of E chaplain who is attached to us for messing' wrote Captain Meredydd Ffoulkes from the Depot of the 38th Welsh in Winchester shortly before departing for France in September 1915. 'He is . . . from St Asaph and a native of Newcastle Emlyn. He seems a very nice man but, so far as I can see, is not likely to hurt himself through overwork.'[32] Lewis Valentine had occasion to criticize the chaplains for their lack of sympathy with the men and for standing on their dignity, 'It appears to me that many of them think more of their status than of the Kingdom of God.'[33] He was scandalized a month later by a sermon he heard near the front in Belgium. 'The service was so cold, the message so poor, [the chaplain's] words so anti-Christian', he wrote. 'He attempted to justify war. We listened not to a servant of Christ expressing "the convictions which burned in his heart" but a military officer addressing soldiers according to the convention.'[34] Rather than bringing a truly Christian perspective to bear on the admittedly perplexing circumstances in which the troops found themselves, the danger of worldly clerics was to oblige the military authorities by becoming mere appendages to the war effort and to reflect not Christ but the status quo. Whereas what was needed was a wider vision which would transcend nationalism and offer some insight into the ultimate mysteries of life and death and sin and suffering, cheap consolation and worldly wisdom, especially if dispensed from the safety of a base camp, would only serve to tarnish the churches' subsequent reputation. The evidence available, though, suggests that Wales was well served by its military chaplains (probably because they were almost invariably volunteers rather than professional men), and that the Christian cause did not suffer inordinately through their example. Often the opposite was the case. Writing from Mesopotamia in January 1918, Private J. S. Bowen informed Principal Owen Prys 'that Professor [David] Williams is idolised by his men and makes an ideal chaplain'.[35] Like Cynddelw Williams in France, the reputation which David Williams gained among the Welsh troops in the east was enormous: 'All over Wales', wrote Morgan Watcyn-Williams years after the war, 'I keep running into men who speak of him as I have heard no other padre described except "Tubby" Clayton and "Woodbine Willie".'[36] Although they were comparatively few in number,[37] the faith, fortitude and bravery of these men did much to secure a healthy respect for the churches' witness during this dire time and afterwards.

The pacifist option

Despite being deeply pacifistic, Welsh Nonconformity found itself almost wholly in favour of British intervention in the war. Radical Nonconformity's abhorrence of war was neither superficial nor hypocritical but totally genuine (a point which has been lost on many subsequent commentators), yet such were the circumstances of the time that both leaders and laymen found themselves in support of the current war policy. When such level-headed and principled Nonconformists as Sir Owen M. Edwards and Llewelyn Williams MP came out in favour of Britain's stand, they were not acting in bad faith but reflecting the conscientious opinion of a considerable section of enlightened Dissent. This was especially true during the earliest stages of the conflict, though it continued to the end. 'In many things', mused Morgan Watcyn-Williams, 'I was a conscientious objector in khaki', yet despite his mounting horror at the futility of the fighting and 'its slow murder of the soul of man', he persisted in his belief that the war had had to be fought: 'It was clear to me that Britain, bound by her treaty obligations . . ., had no option but to enter the war on the violation of Belgium.'[38] Although the unease he felt at the scale of the carnage was patent, for him this reference point remained a constant. Professor David Williams was Watcyn-Williams's equal in moral sensitivity, yet his opinion was also unequivocal. 'Our country in the state of things in which we stood last August', he confided in his diary in 1915, 'had no option but to fight . . . To fight is the only honourable thing for a citizen of that country, for its very existence is at stake.'[39] Cynddelw Williams had fewer qualms than most in supporting Britain's part in the war effort, yet even he admitted readily that militarism and Christianity were incompatible, 'but since our country was obliged to partake in the present great Armageddon', he knew that the Welsh soldiers among whom he was currently serving would bear their burden as bravely as any.[40] Jingoism and warmongering found scant favour with the most responsible among Welsh Nonconformists, and those who were perhaps surprised to find themselves toeing the official line did so with wariness rather than with excessive zeal.

Yet there was still an uneasiness about the wholesale nature of Nonconformity's response to the crisis, and jingoism, when it did occur, merely served to compound the disquiet. D. R. Daniel, as we have seen, was among the first to voice his doubts, and he did so unflinchingly. 'Nothing has pained me more than to see our ministers rushing to the platforms to persuade their listeners to enlist', he wrote to a friend during the autumn of 1914, 'while they stay at home to pray for them for a better wage than the poor fellows will ever get for giving up their bodies to be damned!'[41] Like Daniel, the journalist T. Gwynn Jones, recently appointed to an academic post in the University College of Wales, Aberystwyth, had been afflicted by serious doubts as to the validity of Christianity as practised by contemporary Nonconformists. He was greatly disturbed in October 1914 by the chapels' acquiescence, if not their active compliance, in the persecution of Professor Herman Ethé, a German national and the most learned academic on the college staff. He expressed his general disquiet in a brave and striking address 'Croes ai cors?' ('The cross or the swamp?') given at the Calvinistic Methodists' Tabernacle Chapel in the town on 10 February 1915. All wars he claimed, the present war included, were the result of a clash of imperialisms. Germany was merely doing what other imperial powers had always done, namely expanding its influence by force. The present means may have been sophisticated but the compulsion was as primitive as ever: 'the strong inflicting its will on the weak through the force of arms, through deception and hypocrisy, through theft, violence and coercion'. Although he cited Germany, he did so in order to exemplify the ways of all imperial powers, Britain included. Under other circumstances this would have been unremarkable; in this context it was highly dangerous. Ethé's persecutors were men of influence in both university and town, and local Calvinistic Methodism had become deeply embedded in the status quo. Yet despite having to wrestle with serious spiritual doubts, Gwynn Jones was clear that following Christ meant a rejection of the ways of the world: it was either the cross or the swamp.[42] Writing a few months later he stated: 'I am surer than ever in my opinion that there should only be one Christian Church, and that it should condemn every war without favour. Today the god of Europe is nothing more than a row of tribal deities.'[43] Although he was not officially a church member, he would attend Sunday worship regularly; in fact he and the Tabernacle pastor, the Revd R. J. Rees were personal friends. That friendship was finally fractured during a Sunday evening service in September 1915. Rees offended Gwynn Jones mightily by calling upon God to grant Britain victory; his prayer, claimed Jones, was 'no better than a barbarian's appeal to the god of his tribe'.[44] Unable to bear any more, Gwynn Jones rose and left: he would never return to the chapel again. His long-standing agnosticism hardened into a rejection of official Christianity; all he had left was a stubborn admiration for the Galilean rabbi whom he still believed to be the Prince of Peace.

If D. R. Daniel and Gwynn Jones had found themselves on the periphery of the Christian community, Puleston Jones and Principal Thomas Rees were somewhere near its centre. Neither came out initially against government policy *per se*; their complaint rather was against the pitch of anti-German rhetoric, which they believed to be both uncharitable and sub-Christian, and the need for a balanced appraisal of the crisis. Yet the invective to which they were subjected shook even their equilibrium. As well as having to face considerable criticism locally, Puleston was taken to task vigorously by a correspondent styling himself (pretentiously) 'Oxonian' for having suggested that ministers of the gospel should refrain from acting as recruiting sergeants: 'How is urging the young men of

Wales to respond to the call and to give themselves unstintingly to the service of their country and laying down their lives for her in the present crisis inconsistent with a minister's calling?' he asked. In 'Oxonian's' view all ministers should bring as much pressure to bear as possible on those in their charge 'and make sure that every man who refuses to respond to this call is in danger of forfeiting his very soul'.[45] The desire to make the nation's cause synonymous with that of the truth and identifying patriotism with salvation was one which, in less heady times, would have dismissed swiftly as heretical and idolatrous. Yet theological orthodoxy had become an early victim of the war fever. According to a columnist in the Anglican weekly *Y Llan*: 'The soldier who sheds his blood on the field of battle in a just cause is only doing what Christ did, and he can be sure that he has Christ's approval and his blessing.'[46] 'Oxonian', for his part, had no compunction about praying for a British victory, asking God's blessing on British guns and bombs and heartily desiring Germany's downfall. This was a clash between Christ and Anti-Christ, between the people of God and the hordes of the devil. Those who found the crusade distasteful should examine their consciences and support the war effort wholeheartedly.[47] The suggestion, of course, was that Puleston was little more than a traitor.

If the tone taken by 'Oxonian' was crass and belligerent, the treatment meted out to Thomas Rees was vicious. According to the editor of *Y Llan*, Rees was guilty of treason[48] while the *Western Mail*, the principal south Wales daily, accused him of performing 'a gross and unpardonable act of disloyalty' in suggesting that Britain may not have been guiltless in the present conflict. The statement that, by going to war, Britain was only defending its own economic and political interests was 'baseless and inexcusable': 'These ridiculous perversities would not claim a moment's attention' it continued 'but for the fact that they appear over the signature of a leader of Welsh Nonconformity' and 'a burning and shining light among Welsh Congregationalists':

> If his statements are not publicly repudiated by those who can speak in the name of Welsh Nonconformity serious harm may be done to the national and patriotic movement in Wales initiated by Mr Lloyd George and Mr Asquith . . . The need for official action to counteract the pernicious effects of the Rev. T. Rees's letter is the greater seeing that in Wales . . . the popular leaders are the religious leaders.[49]

The effect of this and other attacks[50] was wholly counter-productive; it merely stiffened the resolve of both Puleston Jones and Thomas Rees to challenge popular prejudices and opinions. 'I confess I have had a somewhat worrying time' stated Rees later, but it had been little to his opponents' avail: 'I have been considerably battered from various directions. But I have won into a position where I feel peace within and the storm without is realising that it is beating in vain.'[51]

By that time the Fellowship of Reconciliation, an explicitly pacifist Christian group which had been formed in late December 1914, had become a rallying point for all those who were disenchanted with the churches' attitude to the war. Its first national secretary was the Revd Richard Roberts, a native of Blaenau Ffestiniog currently serving as Presbyterian minister in Crouch Hill, north London, while another Welsh Presbyterian, George M. Ll. Davies was appointed his associate. The Fellowship's first Welsh branch was established in Bangor, the home of Thomas Rees, in June 1915 following a public meeting at Prince's Road, the Presbyterian church where Puleston Jones had previously ministered. A second branch was formed at Wrexham a day later. Each provided a local platform from which the pacifist standpoint could be argued and developed. The feeling among those Nonconformists least enamoured of the current trends was that the chapels' formerly mild 'pacificism' had been shown up for what it was and that the need now was for a far more thoroughgoing 'pacifism', an absolute stand against warfare in all its guises.[52] Rees and Puleston Jones, George M. Ll. Davies and, to an extent, T. Gwynn Jones, would soon find themselves in the vanguard of the new movement. This was something for which Rees had yearned. 'You see I am in open revolt', he had informed his friend, the Revd J. T. Rhys, on 3 April 1915, and '. . . I will join any rebellion that comes along . . . I mean . . . to make the anti-war position recognised and of some authority in North Wales politics and religion, but it will take some time'.[53] Some months later he reiterated both his faith and his resolve: 'I feel strongly that we have a great work ahead to arrive at a Christian statement of international politics and to win a calculable body of public opinion in its support. But that time is scarcely yet.'[54]

In fact a major opportunity for producing such a statement and making an issue of the anti-war position came during that very

month with the passing, on 19 January 1916, of the Military
Service Act which introduced conscription for single males between
the ages of eighteen and forty-one. A national register of all men
eligible for military service had been instituted in May 1915, and
with the appointment of Lord Derby as director-general of
recruiting in the following October, it was obvious in which
direction the government was moving. For the first time during the
course of the conflict, pacifists could find themselves being
imprisoned for their opposition to official policy. The fact that the
state sought to impose its will on individual citizens did much to
restore the older divide between Churchmen and Dissenters. Welsh
Anglicans were in full agreement with the idea of compulsory
service but it gave even Lloyd George's most faithful Nonconformist supporters pause for thought. 'The acknowledgement of
the state's right to force its young citizens, against their own reason,
conscience and inclination, to maim and kill their fellow man,
indicates the extent to which the Kingdom's morals have
deteriorated', wrote the Baptist Ungoed Thomas in March 1916.[55]

The radical journalist E. Morgan Humphreys, an erstwhile
friend and admirer of Lloyd George and (admittedly critical)
supporter of the war, found that the conscription measure
strained his loyalty one pull too far. 'Nonconformity was built on
the rights of conscience', he wrote, 'and once authority is granted
to a state or an army or an official to trample those rights
underfoot the foundations of Nonconformity will crumble.'[56]
Humphreys, who did not in fact conscientiously object to the war,
had found himself in difficulties at the beginning of the conflict by
allowing J. Puleston Jones, D. Francis Roberts and others freedom
to express their opinions in the Calvinistic Methodists' newspaper
Y Goleuad of which he was the editor. The paper's committee,
headed by the Revd John Williams, Brynsiencyn, had even then
sought to kerb his editorial openness. A further clash between the
editor and his board occurred in October 1917 after the publication of a ringing endorsement of Asquith, the leader of the anti-
conscription group within the cabinet, which was construed by
John Williams and others as an open indictment of Lloyd George
and his policies. 'I well know that there are a great many in Wales
who today revile the Prime Minister', wrote the Methodist leader,
'and are doing their best for the cause of Mr Asquith.'[57] The
upshot of this perceived act of disloyalty was that Humphreys,

whose journalistic and editorial ability was unsurpassed, lost his job.[58]

By this time the premier's reputation had been tarnished badly in Free Church circles, especially since his refusal to contemplate a negotiated settlement with Germany had become known. Asquith, for his part, was said to be in favour of accepting Germany's tentative offer of exploratory peace talks. John Williams, Sir Henry Lewis and others who comprised the coterie of Lloyd George's die-hard Nonconformist supporters were finding themselves in an ever more isolated and uncomfortable position. Christian pacifism had by then established itself in Wales, partly on the basis of a reasoned religious critique of war on the pages of *Y Deyrnas* ('The Kingdom'), an increasingly influential monthly journal which first appeared in October 1916 under the editorship of Thomas Rees and others,[59] and also due to publicity generated by the repeated appearances before the authorities of young men who had refused to serve in the forces. The Act had stipulated that exemption should be granted to those who could convince locally convened tribunals either of their indispensability at home or else that their religious convictions precluded them from taking up arms. Those who refused service on religious grounds were to be employed in alternative occupations.

Ben Meyrick, a native of Gelli-gaer near Caerphilly and a student at the Bangor Baptist College, was one of the first to refuse either military or alternative service. He did so 'because I conscientiously object to taking up arms [and] as a preacher of the gospel of Jesus Christ [I] believe that it is entirely wrong to kill or to have anything to do with war'.[60] He was refused exemption, and despite a series of appeals culminating in appearances before the magistrates and even the King's Bench Division of the High Court, he was sentenced in October 1917 to two years' imprisonment with hard labour.[61] Whereas the majority of north Wales objectors made their stand on specifically religious grounds, in south Wales opposition tended to be more politically motivated and was linked almost invariably with the Independent Labour Party. Merthyr Tydfil and Aberdare became centres of socialist opposition to the war, though even there political and religious convictions often coalesced. During the war Hope Chapel in Merthyr, where the Calvinistic Methodist stalwart the Revd J. M. Jones had ministered for many years, became a centre for both social radicalism and Christian pacifism, while the Revd T. E. Nicholas had already become renowned for his unorthodox though specifically Christian brand of socialist internationalism. David Thomas, the north Wales organizer of Fenner Brockway's mainly secular No-Conscription Fellowship also served as the north Wales secretary of the ILP. Though the defence he made before his local tribunal on 2 May 1916 was on political grounds, 'I believe the present war . . . to be the natural result of the constant struggle between the Powers for domination and gain', the efforts for international harmony in which he was involved were wholly compatible with religious faith. 'I believe that course to be the only one that is consistent with the spirit of Christianity', he claimed.[62] Unlike Meyrick, his dispensation allowed him to spend the next two years as a non-combatant doing agricultural work near Wrexham.

Although Thomas Rees and others contended for pacifism as a valid political option, the cause was seen by most of its Christian adherents as a specifically moral issue. Its ideal stood independently of political considerations. For Welsh pacifists the pragmatic grounds for adhering to a policy of non-violence were advanced in order to validate a moral opinion which had been derived elsewhere, usually from the ethical portions of the New Testament interpreted in highly idealist and individualist terms. This was true of virtually all of those who contributed to *Y Deyrnas*. Rees and his fellow editor, his Bala-Bangor colleague Professor John Morgan Jones, were liberal modernists of pronounced opinions and even those whose thought ran along more orthodox lines – Puleston Jones and the Baptists H. Cernyw Williams and E. K. Jones for instance – belonged to a generation which interpreted Christianity almost exclusively in an individualistic way. The concept of the corporate seemed somehow beyond them. Puleston Jones's review of P. T. Forsyth's remarkable but flawed *The Christian Ethic of War* illustrates this vividly. Unlike many of his fellow pacifists, Jones refused to downgrade Christian theology in favour of a more humanitarian version of the faith. He appreciated the Scottish Congregationalist's emphasis on an objective atonement wrought by God through Christ's unique sacrifice for mankind. It was the whole ministry of Christ in his life, death and resurrection rather than the ethical teaching of the Sermon on the Mount which should provide the basis for Christian faith and discipleship. Yet the Welshman shows no appreciation of two of Forsyth's most incontrovertible points – which would later be argued vigorously by Reinhold Niebuhr in *Moral Man and Immoral Society* (1932) – that collectives are less moral than individuals and that love manifests itself within social structures as justice. 'The obvious criticism of these views', wrote Jones, 'is that a Christianity which means one thing to men as individuals and another to nations would have nothing worth offering to the world.' If gentleness, forgiveness, flexibility, peace and tolerance are relevant to persons but irrelevant to national entities, 'then we can bid farewell to a gospel which is able to save the world's institutions as well as its character'. 'Love', he insisted, 'is the same between two nations as it is between two individuals.'[63]

An inability to face the implications of corporate morality and explicitly social ethics and an idealism which had scant appreciation for the depths of human malignancy and evil were the principal intellectual weaknesses of Welsh pacifism during these years. It was a weakness that mirrored the crisis of late-Victorian and Edwardian Nonconformity. Lacking an adequate doctrine of structural sin and corporate redemption, no matter how vigorously pacifist Dissenters protested at the undoubted horrors of war, they failed to provide a sufficiently realistic philosophy whereby conflict could be overcome and abolished. Whereas pacifism became a potent individual witness, it remained unconvincing as a political strategy: 'It is a useful protest but useless policy.'[64] Unskilled in the compromises of power, a fact illustrated by their increasingly muddled attitude to Lloyd George, most Welsh Nonconformists found the multiplicity of ambiguities which the war had revealed to be ever more perplexing. This was equally true of those who yearned and campaigned for peace.

There is little doubt, however, that the general sense of revulsion which the conflict had engendered created a climate of opinion which was progressively conducive to peace-making if not to unambiguous pacifism. Some pacifists continued to be reviled. 'Say what you will our churches are full of wild militarists', wrote a north Wales Baptist minister in 1917. 'There are those on Anglesey who curse [Ben] Meyrick and others who bless him. There's little logic in their reasoning as you know. "What makes him any better than my son?" is the usual retort.'[65] Many though were afforded both a grudging and often an explicit respect. One correspondent 'Formerly from the Rhondda', who was still a serving soldier in France, wrote to the secretary of the Bala-Bangor College expressing his disquiet that an Aberdare Congregationalist church had withdrawn its usual financial support in protest at the staff's pacifist activities. 'It grieves me that chapels in connection with the Independent denomination have taken up such a narrow view and are so unfair to those who have stood so unflinchingly for the rights of conscience', he wrote. 'I along with others am eager for Prof. Tom Rees to know that he is not without support (even among those who do not always agree with him) in the battle for freedom of opinion.'[66]

The number of Welsh conscientious objectors was small: some thousand in comparison to the 280,000 men who served in the armed forces.[67] The percentage of those who refused, for specifically religious reasons, to bear arms was smaller still. Yet there is little doubt that the stand they made did much to create a situation which favoured pacificism and freedom of expression. Their witness was augmented by that of the 150 non-combatants, most of whom were theological students or undergraduates in the University's constituent colleges, who took advantage of General Owen Thomas's plan to form a specific unit of the Royal Army Medical Corps in connection with the 38th Welsh Division. From January 1916 onwards 36 Calvinistic Methodist ordinands, 15 Anglican students from St David's College, Lampeter, 12 students from the Cardiff Baptist College and 12 Congregationalists from the seminaries at both Carmarthen and Bala-Bangor, a further two dozen pre-ordinands presently enrolled in the University colleges of Aberystwyth, Cardiff and Bangor as well as 15 medical students and 30 or so preparing for careers in schoolteaching in the different normal and training colleges, joined 'God's own', or the Welsh Students' Unit of the RAMC. They were joined by thirty-five mainly English Methodist ordinands from the Headingley, Didsbury and Handsworth colleges as well as a Salvation Army officer, five Roman Catholics and a Jew.[68] Although the Noncon-formists among them were for the most part pacifist in conviction, the fact that they sought to fulfil their religious witness by enlist-ing, albeit as non-combatants, illustrates the tensions inherent in the movement at the time. Anti-militarism in its absolute form was chosen by very few indeed.

The most substantial contribution made by the Welsh pacifist movement was in helping to create a post-war consensus which put peace near the top of the agenda. The churches' increasing embarrassment at the level of compromise and naïvety which they had displayed in 1914 produced a heightened sensitivity to internationalism and the need to preserve the peace almost at any cost. The idealism which became prevalent during the 1920s and which found its expression in the Christian youth movement Urdd y Deyrnas ('the League of the Kingdom'), the Student Christian Movement and in such progressive publications as *The Welsh Outlook* and *Yr Efrydydd* ('The Student') reflected the feeling that a new world order could be achieved and that the Christian church was being given a unique opportunity both to redeem itself and provide a vital social leadership for the community at large. Liberal optimism was revived and support for the League of Nations Movement and COPEC, the Conference on Christian Politics, Economics and Citizenship, became practically universal. The measure of acceptance accorded to the pacifist movement was made explicit in 1923 by the election of George M. Ll. Davies, the most charismatic (and perhaps most enigmatic) of the Welsh pacifists, to represent the University of Wales seat in Parliament. This was seen by many as the ultimate validation of their creed. It would not be long, however, before grave social and economic crises at home and the threat of totalitarianism abroad would dissipate current idealism and challenge many to reassess their most cherished assumptions. In 1920, however, the pacifist option was felt to be valid for more than a few.

The religious legacy of the war

The early expectancy that the war would lead to national repentance and religious revival soon evaporated. One of the first meetings which Cynddelw Williams had with a front-line soldier, 'a Private Lewis from the South', whom he had met at the brigade headquarters at Bournemouth in November 1914, had suggested that the crisis might in fact be leading men to faith. 'When I asked him was it true that everyone in the trenches was praying he replied, "You can be sure that they are, what else would you do with men dying all around you".'[69] Alas, this was not to last, as Cynddelw would find out for himself after he arrived in France a few months later. Although occasional reports of a renewal of faith and spirituality, both in the front line and at home, persisted, after mid-1915 expectancy had given way to a harsh realism. 'Danger and the daily possibility of death are not abnormal things now', wrote John David Jones in 1917. 'They are rather in the normal course of events; they have become part of the every day routine of life, and as such fail to bring about that revival of thought and religion which some people have so flamboyantly asserted.'[70] A letter signed by Sgt Tom Pyke of the 17th Royal Welch Fusiliers and dated 22 August 1916 was more typical of an earlier confidence:

> I would like you to see the great changes that have occurred in the lives of many of our boys in France. Despite the awfulness of the war, flashes of goodness still break through the thick clouds and there are hundreds and hundreds of those who have perhaps never acknowledged God in prayer that have at last come truly to realise their state before God and need for him.[71]

It was this need to address the spiritual crisis which had been revealed during the initial phase of war that had prompted the archbishop of Canterbury and others to inaugurate, belatedly, 'the National Mission of Repentance and Hope', a country-wide Anglican venture scheduled for the autumn of 1916.[72] 'This mission is a great war against sin', stated the editorial of the Churchmens' periodical *Y Cyfaill Eglwysig,* 'a war against uncleanness, deceit, miserliness, drunkenness and unlovingness. It is a crusade against the nation's neglect of the Lord's Day and the Lord's house, yes of God's Son as well.'[73] For Canon William Williams, diocesan missioner of St David's, it was a golden opportunity to respond to God's call through the war: 'It is intended through the Mission to open the nation's eyes to perceive God's providential hand chastising her for her sins in order to purify her in the cauldron of suffering', and by so doing 'to make Britain more deserving of victory'.[74] Despite the zeal of a few Churchmen, it was obvious that this crusade for a renewal of individual piety would have little effect upon the churches and virtually none upon those beyond their walls: religious renewals wrought by committees seldom do. The huge insensitivity of using peoples' suffering as a moral and spiritual means to military victory seemed hardly to have dawned on the Mission's protagonists. Yet it was the simplistic nature of its message, that a renewal of conventional religion would solve the nation's problems, which militated against its ultimate effectiveness. Nothing was mentioned about the metaphysical difficulties which the war had disclosed or that the scale of suffering demanded a more sophisticated approach to the church's apologetic task. Neither did repentance include social and political sins, nor the recognition that the government's own policies may have contributed to the declaration and perpetuation of the present war. 'It is doubtful whether the Church has ever before been called upon to partake of such a vast task', wrote the editor of *Yr Haul*,[75] and it is hardly surprising that, by the end of the year, the general response to the missionary meetings throughout the parishes and dioceses was that 'nothing very spectacular happened'.[76] By then Welsh Churchmen, having tired of the spiritual challenge of the war, were preparing for disestablishment. Having reconciled themselves to its inevitability, interest in the steadily unfolding plans for creating a new, independent Welsh province within the Anglican communion increased throughout 1917. If the National Mission's effect was minimal with the war revealing momentous weaknesses in each of the churches' evangelistic and pastoral strategies, Welsh Anglicans could at least contemplate the potentialities for creative change which would soon be afforded by the formation of the Church in Wales.

Yet for the more perceptive it had become apparent that the values and certainties of the old world had vanished permanently. 'In some sense I suppose we have all left the old order of things behind us forever', wrote Alfred Jenkins, an RAMC orderly, from the Colchester camp sometime in 1916. 'The war has slain the past as well as the living and those who would go back to it would be history's greatest cynics.'[77] Pessimism had replaced optimism, hope had given way to despair; the idealism of the late summer of 1914 had, within a year and a half, transformed itself into a worldly cynicism. 'When the war started I never as much as dreamt it would last as long as this' wrote Corporal Leslie Griffith to his local vicar from France in April 1916. The cost, he claimed, had been too much already; 'Really speaking I don't quite see what we are fighting for. I quite see that we are helping Belgium, but don't you think we have suffered enough?' His opinion, that 'the world has become uncivilized since this awfully damning war

commenced', had by then become commonplace.[78] 'I dont care
how soon the war his (*sic*) over I am geting (*sic*) tired of it', wrote
Herbert Richards to his minister, the Revd E. K. Jones of Rhos, as
early as 19 March 1915. 'I would give anything to get home . . .
There is (*sic*) hundreds of lives lost out here, its allfull (*sic*).'[79] This
was the authentic and anguished voice of a whole generation of
young men often not yet out of their teens. Many would not live to
reach twenty.

If many of the more reflective among Welsh Churchmen had
been chastened by the extent of the carnage, Nonconformists had
been increasingly appalled by the pragmatism of Lloyd George.
His advancement through the highest echelons of government –
from the chancellorship to minister of munitions in May 1915 to
minister of war in July 1916 to be followed by the ultimate
achievement of the prime ministership itself by the December –
had been followed, even among Welsh Liberals, with a growing
sense of unease. The wizard's spell seemed to be weakening, a fact
confirmed by the outcry against compulsory military service
which occurred from January 1916 onwards. The Criccieth
Baptist's refusal to contemplate anything short of Germany's total
capitulation whatever the cost in British lives, and his determination to enforce conscription in order to achieve this aim, was more
than many could endure. 'I can hardly understand Mr Lloyd
George,' wrote the Bangor solicitor J. Pentir Williams, 'a man
whose whole position is attributable to the fact that his
predecessors and he himself earlier in his career fought so hard for
freedom of speech and of conscience.'[80] Liberals and Nonconformists widely believed that he had betrayed their one single core
conviction: liberty of conscience. The change of mood was nowhere better recorded than in the General Assembly of the
Calvinistic Methodists held at Colwyn Bay in May 1916.
'Although we as an Assembly promise to do what we can to
support the government in its intention to bring this war to a swift
and satisfactory conclusion,' read the deliberation, 'nevertheless
we stand by our convictions in the matter of peace and individual
conscience.' The motion was proposed by none other than John
Williams, Brynsiencyn, and seconded by T. C. Williams, Menai
Bridge.[81] Although both men continued to afford the premier their
fullest personal support, their willingness to move this motion
illustrated how critical the situation had become. The message

this sent to Lloyd George could hardly have been clearer. For him and for the older Liberal-Nonconformist hegemony, the writing was on the wall. The utter disenchantment felt by Lewis Valentine following the announcement of the 'khaki election' in November 1918 was indicative of earlier doubts:

> The Church has hardly stirred [he wrote on 1 December 1918]. She has sold her soul and was unfaithful to her ideals even at the beginning of the war so that now she is merely contemptible. Is little David from Criccieth among the 'Spoilers'? His colleagues are a hellish bunch – the enemies of democracy. He will have to pay dearly for forcing an election upon the country before the soldiers have had a chance to return home.[82]

The next entry in his diary, 19 December 1918, illustrated vividly the sea-change which was already taking place. 'Yesterday I voted for the first time, for E. T. John, the Labour member for Denbigh.'[83] The wizard's spell had been broken forever.

Preparations for the post-war settlement were being made long before the conflict ceased. Despite the comfort which many Christian believers gleaned from their faith, the war had also served to reveal the extent of immorality and irreligion among the men. Alfred Jenkins, an obviously sensitive Calvinistic Methodist ordinand (who would later be killed), was shaken by 'the indescribable filthiness of the daily talk' and appalled by the moral laxity at the front: 'It is only too certain that a tragically large number have made acquaintance with sexual sin since their enlistment', he said.[84] The squalor and carnage of the war inevitably created hard-heartedness of an extreme kind. 'The men out here are sinful', wrote Lewis Valentine in November 1917. 'They play the fool with themselves, but they will not be convinced that there is such a thing as sin.'[85] Among those of Jenkins's acquaintance there were many who were 'aggressively hostile to religion and boastfully immoral'.[86] Even when not openly immoral, most men made no pretence of possessing a vital religious faith. 'Estimated by almost every criterion', Jenkins continued, 'prayer would seem to be a negligible factor in the lives of the vast majority of soldiers.' Both he and Valentine described the religious indifference of the men in similar terms:

> The majority of men cling vaguely to some sort of faith in the existence and sovereignty of God [Jenkins stated]; a comparatively small number

have a personal faith in Jesus Christ . . . and fewer still believe in the church as a divinely appointed agency for the world's upliftment. [87]

It is difficult truly to analyse their attitude to religion [wrote Valentine, 26 October 1917]. The war has made some doubt God's love, but the conflict and carnage has deepened others' faith in God. Many believe in God's sovereignty but I am afraid there are but few who actively trust in Christ.[88]

'At this point I should like to touch briefly upon some strange contrasts in the personality of the men', wrote John David Jones. Foulness of language would often go hand in hand with perfect courtesy; tolerant treatment of German prisoners would coexist with frequent vindictiveness towards their own; selfishness and scheming one minute were complemented by tenderness, devotion, heroism and exquisite self-sacrifice the next. For those brought up with a belief in the goodness of God and man, it was perplexing in the extreme. Traditional perceptions were being challenged daily and that 'small minority who, in spite of great disadvantages, are endeavouring to weigh up the things that matter', were finding themselves having radically to reassess their creeds. 'What is the inner mind of these men about religion?', he continued. 'Perhaps the most obvious thing that strikes one is the hazy idea which most men have of what the Christian religion is.' For many it had been portrayed as a joyless legalism rather than a living faith, and although there was a general admiration of the Christian virtues, 'the tragedy is that they never connect these things with Christianity and Christ'.[89]

The scale of institutional Christianity's involvement in the war was felt by some to have compromised the churches' integrity. Lewis Valentine especially felt this keenly. 'I am seeking to make myself resourceful to meet the many difficulties of the post-war days', he wrote on 13 November 1917. 'The peril which the church is in is really great and something must be done to safeguard the future of Christianity in our islands.'[90] Writing from Macedonia in September 1918, Private J. S. Bowen also wondered how the churches would cope with the vast changes of the post-war world: 'I often wonder what the result of it all will be, what effect will it have when we all come home? . . . I pray God [the church] will have a message, a divine all-conquering message, that will sweep away all things that make war possible and so create an atmosphere that will make a repetition of this horror impossible.'[91]

The fundamental theological problems that the First World War had revealed were those of the personhood of God, whether and how He responded to man's plight and his prayers, and of providence and theodicy; in the face of such suffering and slaughter as this, how could the goodness of God be reconciled with his omnipotence? It was Alfred Jenkins once more whose comments were most perceptive. 'The problems of war have always challenged faith,' he told his college principal, Owen Prys, 'but a world organized for slaughter is something new and has bred a sense of dominant materialism which has darkened the spiritual outlook of many.' Despite the unique horrors which the concept of total war had introduced, he believed that the religious questions which men currently faced were new in scale rather than in kind: 'It would be truer as a general statement to say that the old difficulties have been intensified rather than new ones have arisen.'[92]

The way in which military chaplains, private Christians and professional theologians applied the gospel reflected the ways in which they interpreted their faith. For staunch Calvinists like Cynddelw Williams, the war merely reinforced a prior belief in people's innate pride and corruption and God's graciousness in the outworking of his sovereign design. When a colleague pulled him from a burst of shellfire into a nearby trench, he (the colleague) was taken to task for his lack of faith. '[Williams's] life was portioned out for him and he could face all its situations with equanimity. When I asked him to distinguish his views from the fatalism of the men many of whom believed their number was on a certain shell or bullet, he poured theology into me!'[93] Cynddelw's young colleague, though, whose experiences in the trenches would confirm his calling into the Christian ministry after the war, held to a more liberal creed. Rather than emphasizing God's transcendence, Watcyn-Williams's battle theology was one of the divine immanence, of God's immersion in the pain of a suffering world. Liberal theology had been fashionable among the younger generation of Welsh Nonconformist ministers since the turn of the century.[94] Ironically perhaps, the tragedy of war did not deal liberalism a death blow but gave it a new lease of life. 'The effect of the war on our theology is already immense', wrote

R. S. Rogers, a liberal Baptist theologian, in 1917. In his opinion
the fighting had utterly destroyed what remained of the chapels'
residual Calvinism; he would have regarded Cynddelw and those
like him as relics from the past. From now on the only righteousness which mattered would be social righteousness, not the
justification of the individual soul, while traditional teaching on
eternal punishment was everywhere yielding to faith in 'the wider
hope' of universal salvation.[95] As the war began J. Puleston Jones
had commented on the current trend towards a conditional
immortality: 'We have lost the old idea of hell but have hardly
found anything definite to put in its place.'[96] The trauma of
having to witness the destruction of a generation of young men in
what many still believed to be a just cause underlined the waning
appeal of the older belief. 'One of the immediate effects of the
war', wrote the Congregationalist layman Beriah Gwynfe Evans,
'will be to revolutionize our opinion of God's judgement.'[97] The
same would be true of the divine omnipotence and impassability.
For the liberal theologians such as Thomas Rees and Miall
Edwards the divine sovereignty would have to yield to a partnership in which God and man worked together towards the outworking of his will.[98]

If there was something inappropriately theoretical about the
way in which traditional dogmas were reworked by the professional theologians at home, the sermons of the chaplain David
Morris Jones of the 14th Battalion Royal Welch Fusiliers (who,
like Cynddelw and Morgan Watcyn-Williams, was a Calvinistic
Methodist whose bravery earned him the MC) at least illustrate
the way in which liberal theology tried to provide an immediate
answer for the needs of the front.

> Religion is really helpful [he said in a sermon on Isaiah 46: 1–4]. Its
> essence is in its helpfulness. If it doesn't help then there's something
> wrong with you or with God or with worship. Some of you regard
> religion as a hindrance, a nuisance and an encumbrance. It is because
> you have a wrong conception of religion. You identify it with
> ceremonies, dogmas, practices. Those are idols – the imperfect
> expression of your religious ideas and feelings.

Liberalism was a theology of experience and feeling. It
downplayed dogma in favour of 'life' and had little to say about

sinfulness and judgement. The tendency was to see Christ's sacrifice in terms of his sympathy with man rather than as an atonement for sin. One experienced God's presence through the suffering of a bleeding humanity. 'If you find you have to carry these [idols]', Morris Jones continued, '. . . take it that you have not found true religion. God delivers, God saves, God helps, God gives courage, God suffers for and with you – God carries you.'[99]

For the liberal theologians the dividing line between God and humanity was imprecise and the boundary between the church and world was blurred. When seemingly irreligious men could display outstanding bravery and stupendous self-sacrifice, conventional orthodoxies were put at risk. 'If you find that the orthodox expressions of religion are a worry to you', Morris Jones said, '. . . look around to see if the life-giving . . . power of God is still working within you, entering . . . perhaps through the love of your friend, or [his] sympathy.' Liberal idealism held that God and man were basically one, and even when men could not acknowledge the fact, God was 'the source of courage, goodness, sacrifice [and] cheerfulness which strews our land today like the common grass'.[100] More than anything the gospel taught the divine Fatherhood: 'The fundamental fact in Christ's teaching is the doctrine of God's Fatherhood.'[101] Christ revealed that Fatherhood through uniting himself with mankind in all its woes. 'God is like Jesus, He is Jesus and Jesus is God', he said while expounding John 14:8. 'Jesus is God living under human conditions and limitations. Jesus' life is God's life. All the virtues of God – holiness, purity, self-sacrifice, his power over life and death – are God-like. Jesus is a human summary of God.' Morris Jones did not deprecate the fatalism of the ordinary soldier or his faith in chance or in luck. This was not mere superstition or unbelief, he claimed, rather 'a stammering way of entrusting ourselves to God'. Even ostensibly irreligious men were incurably spiritual. It was the chaplain's task to direct their stammering faith to the right goal.

> It is not mere chance [he concluded in a sermon on Psalm 55: 27]. It is a kinder, closer, better power than that. Whatever it is my message this morning is that God represents all the good elements in Luck and that all our needs are satisfied in him. Instead of casting your burden on Luck, cast it on God whose sympathy and mercy are higher than

anything we know in this world, whose power also is infinitely wise shaping and arranging everything for the highest welfare of mankind.[102]

Not even the horrors of Passchendaele and the Somme could destroy the liberal theologians' faith in God's benevolence through the upward path of evolutionary progress.

The religious legacy of the First World War in Wales was ambiguous. The psychological scars which many suffered were revealed by a common reticence among ex-soldiers to mention their wartime experiences; there were others, however, who looked back at the war with something akin to nostalgia. Only a month after the slaughter inflicted on the Royal Welch Fusiliers at Mametz on the Somme, Meredydd Ffoulkes remained totally enthusiastic about all that he been through. 'I would not have missed it for the world', he told his parents, ' – it has been a wonderful experience.'[103] Similarly, whereas the carnage had turned many against God, it was through the war that many had found their faith. Morgan Watcyn-Williams is a case in point: his burning Christian conviction, which fuelled his subsequent ministry in the Merthyr Tydfil of the depression, had been confirmed on the Somme. It became common during the inter-war years for Methodist elders, when being commissioned by their presbyteries, to attribute their conversion to their wartime experiences.[104] Many returned with a renewed resolve to serve God and their fellow man and to do their utmost to prevent the tragedy of war from happening again. 'I dream, no I know that God has great things for you to do', confided Lewis Valentine on St David's Day 1917. 'Following this war you will return to raise the white standard of peace.'[105] Valentine, whose post-war pacifism was deeply Christian in tone, typified the most idealistic of his generation. Returning to complete his degree, with first-class honours in Semitics in 1919, he proceeded to the Baptist ministry and would be much influenced by the renewal of Barthian ortho-doxy in the 1930s. Like many Welsh-speakers at the time, he aligned himself with Plaid Genedlaethol Cymru, the Welsh Nationalist Party, and became their first parliamentary candidate in 1929.

Despite the opinions of some of Nonconformity's more liberal theoreticians there is little evidence that the First World War created any completely new theological difficulties, though certainly the old problems – theodicy, suffering, the fate of those who died without an explicit faith in Christ – were given a new potency. What would become apparent was that the assumptions of the past would be challenged radically. 'Great things are happening in this awful cataclysm of war', wrote William Morgan, vicar of Glanogwen, Bethesda, to his rural dean in August 1917. 'Social systems are changing before our very eyes. A new world is being born. It is the time of our visitation.'[106] By late 1917 a war-weary people was yearning for peace, 'And what then?', asked the editor of *Y Cyfaill Eglwysig*, the least bellicose of the Welsh Anglican publications. A greater fear of God, certainly, a deeper spirituality and unity among Christian believers, Churchmen and chapel people alike. But what was more significant was the general insistence on social righteousness.

> Men must be respected *because* they are men – apart from riches, status or colour. The workers must be given better housing, reasonable working hours and a living wage. If we persist on the old lines . . . after the war . . . even if the enemy will be defeated, Britain will certainly not have won.[107]

Welsh Anglicans returning from the front were as insistent as Nonconformists on the need for social justice. After having experienced the camaraderie of military life, there would be a great need 'to create such an environment . . . [where] there will be no falling back into the old life with its false standards, class interests, strifes, bitterness and jealousies'. Frank Beddows of Pembroke Dock warned his vicar, the Revd D. L. Prosser, that this would be 'the hardest task the clergy will have to perform'. The old culture of deference would eventually be overthrown. 'This wholesale acceptance of other folk's opinions on trust, [which] men were pleased to call faith', he said, would cease. A generation, having experienced reality in the raw, would make up its own mind as to what constituted both falsity and truth. It would no longer be sufficient 'to receive teaching as sops from the ecclesiastical spoon'.[108]

This, perhaps, was the most significant aspect of the change to have affected Welsh religion by 1918: Christianity would be forced to respond to the social challenge. 'I believe that the churches should put a much greater emphasis in their Confessions of Faith on social and political questions', wrote Robert Pritchard, a correspondent in the Methodist *Goleuad*, '. . . rather than being suspicious and contemptuous of those who are working in that direction.' He foresaw huge problems were Nonconformists to yield social reforms to political movements outside the churches rather than tackle these issues themselves,[109] a point which was confirmed by the ever-trenchant Alfred Jenkins:

> The questions that men will ask of the Church when they return will be: Are you prepared to lead in the social movement that has declared war on a system based on monopolism, which keeps the land locked up in the interests of a few [and] which condemns millions of our population to live in rack-rented, overcrowded dwellings? . . . The Church must not count on the devotion and loyalty that were merely part of a family tradition and heritage, for these have been shrivelled up in the experiences of war . . . [Moreover] if the basis of church membership will still invoke the pale ghosts of ancient creeds and musty dogmas rather than challenge the moral heroism of men, the Church will not attract those who . . . have learned to suffer and endure.[110]

Yet it was apparent even then that post-war Wales would be a new, strange Wales, where the old values would be put aside and Christianity be increasingly regarded as an anachronism. The religious indifference which had worried church leaders in 1914 had not been stemmed. The most poignant entries in Cynddelw Williams's diary were those written after the close of the war in 1919. Having returned from France in order to serve the troops on the home front, he was mystified by the religious apathy he discovered. 'The chaplains try their best to get men to attend religious services in the warm and comfortable rooms provided, but very few come.' Try as he might, the response to his pastoral work was minimal. His only comment on the services he arranged for the troops of the South Wales Borderers and the Welsh Regiment at Aldershot in October 1919 was the terse: 'Nobody came.'[111] For many the war had seemed to have killed the religious instinct stone dead. It would be the churches' thankless task to have to witness to the gospel in a time such as this. Following his return from France in 1919, Lewis Valentine felt himself to be like an old man in a children's service. 'The sacrifice of the last five years had done little to awaken the people,' he wrote, 'rather there seems to be a very selfish spirit abroad.' As for the future? 'Not even a magician can tell where this world is headed.'[112]

3

Anglicanism and Catholicism, 1920–1945

The first decade of the Church in Wales

During the summer of 1917 the Revd William Morgan, vicar of Bethesda in the Ogwen Valley in north Wales, had written to his rural dean expressing his hopes and fears for the future of the Anglican Church after disestablishment. The Disestablishment Act had finally been passed in September 1914 though the First World War had prevented it from being put into practice. By August 1917, however, Churchmen were beginning to prepare for the practicalities of change. After having been forced grudgingly to accept the inevitable, many clergymen had become cautiously optimistic as to the potentially beneficial effect of the Church's proposed new status. The crisis, it seemed, had become a challenge:

> I hope [Morgan wrote] . . . that . . . [many] will make an effort at this supreme juncture in its history to popularise, democratise, and nationalise the old Church of our Fathers so that it may become once more as of old the spiritual home of the Welsh people. A fervent (Nonconformist) Welsh Nationalist, who clearly knew all about it, told a friend of mine the other day, 'I hear you are forming a scheme of government for the Church after Disestablishment. For God's sake be wise. These – meaning Nonconformists – are tumbling to pieces. The people will come back to you if you proceed wisely'. This is the spirit that is abroad.[1]

Whereas the Church had been guilty of standing apart from the principal issues which had exercised the Welsh people in the past and 'it is said of her that she has no sympathy with the people, their health, their homes, and their material welfare so that the masses either go elsewhere or stand aside from religion altogether', now was the time to redress the situation. The perceived weakness of Nonconformity served to emphasize Anglicanism's potential strength. Were the Church in Wales to become once more the Church of the Welsh people, could not the slide into indifference and irreligion be halted? As disestablishment loomed, this became the hope of more and more members of the Anglican Church in Wales.

Although disestablishment had been postponed until the end of the war, the process of disendowment (which was even more emotive than the question of status) began immediately. The Welsh Church Commissioners were appointed who, under the Welsh Church Act, would have sole responsibility for the new Church's temporalities. The Act itself stipulated that henceforth patronage would be abolished, that the four Welsh bishops would forfeit their seats in the House of Lords, that the King would forgo his position as the Church's sovereign head, that ecclesiastical courts would be stripped of their former coercive powers and that ecclesiastical law would be restricted to the sphere of the Church alone and not regarded as an aspect of the civil law. Whereas these changes revolutionized the status and character of the Welsh Church, it was the financial implications of disestablishment that caused most bitterness. According to the Act, all ancient (pre-1662) endowments were to be diverted to secular use, their capital being divided between the Welsh county and borough councils and the University of Wales, while tithe monies would be transferred to the local authorities. An Amending Act passed in 1919 cushioned the financial blow, first by allowing the Commissioners to charge a levy on all endowment payments which were being transferred to the secular bodies and secondly by securing for the Church a Treasury grant of £1 million; nevertheless the financial strains were considerable. What the normally placid Bishop Hughes of Llandaff had described as 'the cruel and uncalled for and absolutely unjustifiable attempt . . . by the government of the day to cripple and paralyse the Church in the four dioceses of Wales',[2] had come to pass.

A national convention, including delegates from each of the diocesan conferences which had met in Cardiff in October 1917, had already established the new Church's machinery of government. This would consist of a Governing Body of the four bishops along with clerical and lay members, and a smaller Representative Body which would have jurisdiction over the Church's properties.

It was on 31 March 1920, on the Wednesday of Holy Week, that all preparations were concluded and the Welsh Church Act at last came into full operation. The new Welsh Church (only later, in 1921, to be called 'The Church in Wales') was an autonomous body, no longer under the jurisdiction of Canterbury, and in status merely one independent Christian denomination like the rest. What the Nonconformists had campaigned for for two generations, and what the Anglicans most dreaded, had at last occurred.

The most powerful personality on the bench of bishops was A. G. Edwards, bishop of St Asaph since 1889 and despite his seventy-one years quite as formidable as ever. His ambivalent attitude towards Welsh nationhood has already been mentioned. The 'St Asaph Policy' of all-out war against Nonconformity and everything which it signified, namely popular democracy, the value of individual rights, Liberal politics and proletarian Welsh-language culture, had prevailed throughout the disestablishment campaign. Professor W. J. Gruffydd's acidic description of Edwards, 'y dyn mwyaf trychinebus a welodd Cymru erioed' ('the most disastrous man that Wales has ever seen'),[3] reflected accurately how he was viewed by a not insubstantial section of Welsh opinion. His faithful lieutenant, Dr John Owen, a former Calvinistic Methodist and since 1897 bishop of St David's, had been the Church's chief strategist during the defence campaign. Owen's humble, Nonconformist background on the Llŷn Peninsula had not prevented him from supporting Edwards to the hilt in every controversy in which he had been involved. He had long evolved into what his senior had always been, an establishment-minded Tory of the bluest hue. Neither Watkin Herbert Williams, son of one of the oldest landed families in north Wales and since 1899 bishop of Bangor, nor the inoffensive Joshua Pritchard Hughes, bishop of Llandaff since 1905, was of the same calibre as Edwards or Owen. When, on 7 April 1920, the bishops in conclave chose the new province's first archbishop, the outcome was inevitable: Edwards was elected having been proposed by Owen. Prominent among those present at the new archbishop's enthronement in St Asaph Cathedral on 1 June 1920 was David Lloyd George, formerly the most fiery of all the disestablishmentarians. The prime minister's radicalism had long become a thing of the past.

For the first quarter-century of the new Church's life financial considerations were all-consuming. Maintenance of clerical stipends at a realistic level was seen as the initial imperative. Careful management and a wise investment policy made up for the most substantial losses which disendowment had caused, while Churchpeople, though previously unfamiliar with the voluntary principle, gave generously towards the parish quota and diocesan levy despite the dire economic hardship of the inter-war years. The landed class, though not particularly numerous in Wales, was well represented within the Church and many of its members made handsome contributions to both diocesan and provincial funds. By the late 1930s it had become apparent that the Church, though far from being opulent, was on as sound an economic footing as it had been prior to 1914.

The carefulness which characterized matters of finance was replicated in other areas of church life. Having embraced disestablishment reluctantly and against their will, Welsh Anglicans were neither by conviction nor temperament bold innovators, yet the swift creation of two new dioceses showed at least some desire to take a fuller advantage of their new-found independence. The archdeaconry of Monmouth had for centuries been part of Llandaff and had been nearly as deeply affected by the immense population increase which accompanied the Industrial Revolution as the more westerly parts of the diocese. As well as covering the lush and lightly populated rural areas around Abergavenny, Chepstow, Raglan and Usk, it contained the old iron- and coal-producing regions of Pontypool, Tredegar and the Sirhowy Valley and Newport to the south. The upgrading of the archdeaconry to full diocesan status would ease the burden on bustling Llandaff and its ageing bishop. The principal architect of the proposed new see was its resident archdeacon, Charles Green, the Welsh Church's most accomplished canon lawyer and a constitutional expert of undoubted stature. It was he who chaired the commission charged with creating the new diocese and he did much to secure its financial viability. The decree announcing the creation of the Diocese of Monmouth – not Caerleon or Usk or even Newport as had been suggested – was made by the Governing Body on 29 September 1921; secession from the parent diocese occurred on 18 October and Green was elected its first bishop on 18 November. His consecration took place at Llandaff on 21 November before he was enthroned at St Woolos' parish church, Newport, pro-cathedral of the new see, on 3 January 1922.

If Green's appointment smacked of inevitability, it was also wise and quite fitting. At fifty-eight he had served six years as archdeacon of Monmouth having previously spent twenty-six years as curate and vicar of the parish of Aberdare. Having been educated at Charterhouse and Keble, this son of a moderately well-connected Carmarthenshire squire-parson reinforced his social standing by marrying Kathleen, the daughter of Sir William Thomas Lewis, later Baron Merthyr of Senghenydd. By background, kinship and ability, he possessed all that was required to make an ideal prelate. Yet there was no doubt about his spiritual stature or the seriousness with which he viewed his priestly calling. He had left Oxford (where he had been president of the Union) thoroughly imbued with the ideals of Tractarianism in its later ritualist phase, and had consolidated the Anglo-Catholicism of the parish of Aberdare which he inherited from his predecessors, Evan Lewis and Richard Bowen Jenkins, with zeal and efficiency. The Catholic doctrine which had long been the mainstay of the parochial teaching was augmented by a more elaborate ceremonial, regular confession, the use of altar lights and eventually by a daily celebration of the eucharist. Although he remained diligent in his studies (he took the Oxford DD in 1911) Green proved himself to be a capable parish priest and skilled organizer, yet the privileged world he inhabited was aeons away from that of the working parishioners towards whom he showed a genuine if paternalistic care. When asked by the Royal Commissioners of his knowledge of the workings of local Dissent, 'I have not the remotest idea' was his candid reply.[4] He admitted that had never been inside a Nonconformist chapel despite there being thirty-four of them within the bounds of his parish. Neither would later resolve broaden his experience of Christian communions more Protestant than his own. He became bishop of Monmouth, from whence he was translated to Bangor in 1928 (becoming archbishop of Wales following A. G. Edwards's retirement in 1934), and in those positions his only ecumenical interest was in possible rapprochement with Rome.[5] Throughout his career Chapel and Church, though geographically coextensive and sharing a common commitment to the spiritual benefit of the people of Wales, would exist as though in parallel universes.

Green's work in Monmouth was assiduous and effective. He immediately created a clutch of new parishes in the most highly industrialized parts and amalgamated many of the smaller rural livings. His concept of episcopal authority was of a piece with his ultra-High Churchmanship. He was adamant that the bishop alone 'is the channel through whom our Blessed Lord, the Head of the Church, confers authority externally to act in his name in this part of the vineyard'.[6] This monarchical authoritarianism which was given its most scholarly apologia in his *The Constitution of the Church in Wales and its Setting* (1937) was always tempered with kindness and consideration, yet it perpetuated the trend towards a virtually medieval concept of hierarchical rule which did little for the Church's image as being for the common people. It was only after the election of Timothy Rees to Llandaff in 1931 that attitudes began to change and the Church in Wales would be perceived to shed at least some of its aristocratic pretensions.

If population growth had necessitated the division of Llandaff, geographical expanse required the creation of a second diocese in south-west Wales. St David's was the largest diocese in England and Wales covering 2,238,000 acres. It was huge and unwieldy and, apart from the area around Swansea and parts of east Carmarthenshire, sparsely populated. There had long been talk of dividing St David's into three: Brecknock and Radnorshire; the part of the diocese which was situated in Glamorgan; and the western seaboard counties of Carmarthen, Pembroke and Cardiganshire. Economics, however, dictated that there could only be a single division, and in April 1923 the archdeaconry of Brecon was joined to the deaneries of east and west Gower to create the disestablished Church's second new diocese, Swansea and Brecon. As the bulk of the population was situated towards the south, from Ystalyfera to as far down as Swansea, the ancient and lovely priory church of St John's, Brecon, became the cathedral. Much of the credit for the diocese's formation was due to Dr John Owen who was even tempted, like Charles Gore who had left Worcester for newly created Birmingham, to leave St David's in order to become Swansea and Brecon's first bishop. The temptation was resisted and the honour and responsibility went instead to Edward Latham Bevan, former archdeacon of Brecon and since 1915 suffragan bishop of Swansea. Like Charles Green in Monmouth, Bevan was the strongest and in truth perhaps the only serious candidate for the post, but unlike Green his appointment did not go smoothly. Ostensibly he was perfectly positioned for the work.

Well-connected and patrician, the son of an exceedingly wealthy
squire-parson of huge standing within the diocese, Bevan had
been vicar of Brecon before following his father as the local
archdeacon. But like practically all within the principality's upper
class, he spoke no Welsh. With staggering perversity it was Archbishop Edwards who insisted that the consensus which had prevailed since 1870 requiring all bishops to speak Welsh should be
upheld, this despite Bevan's rootedness in the area and his
undoubted qualifications for the job. However, Edwards did not
get his way and on a very close vote indeed, Edward Latham Bevan
exchanged his suffraganship for the full title of first bishop of
Swansea and Brecon. He was genuinely delighted to have been
elected and thereafter spent much of his considerable personal
fortune in improving the fabric of the cathedral, its deanery in
Priory House within the close, and the adjoining canonry in
Tower House. He died in harness, aged seventy-three, in 1934.

The forging of a new identity

By the late 1920s the new province had begun to find its feet and
develop its own specific identity. St David's remained geographically the largest of the Welsh dioceses, and following the death of
John Owen in 1926 its oversight was undertaken by David Lewis
Prosser, the fifty-eight-year-old former vicar of Pembroke Dock
and archdeacon of St David's. The social convention which had
deprived Bishop Bevan of a knowledge of Welsh was also true of
Prosser, despite his having been born in a Carmarthenshire rectory
and educated at Llandovery College. This was a much more
significant drawback at St David's than at Swansea and Brecon
and compounded the Church's old ambiguity on the question of
language and nationhood. Yet a more hopeful sign of the Church's
integration into the life and aspirations of its ordinary folk came
with the wholly unexpected appointment of the diminutive (5ft
½in.), warm-hearted and unpretentious Dr Maurice Jones –
'Meurig Prysor' – as principal of St David's College, Lampeter, in
1923. The son of a monoglot Welsh-speaking village shoemaker
from Trawsfynydd in Merioneth, Maurice Jones was wholly
impervious to the social snobbery, the anti-Welsh bias and the
anti-Dissenting antipathy of the hierarchy. His scholarly

credentials were impeccable: from the Friars' School in Bangor to Christ's College, Brecon, and thence to Jesus College, Oxford, where he read theology. (He was an exact contemporary of Sir John Morris-Jones in all three places earning an Oxford first for Morris-Jones's third!) Apart from short curacies in Caernarfon and Welshpool, his ministerial career had taken him to such exotic locations as Malta, South Africa and Jamaica as a military chaplain before he returned to a comfortable Jesus College living in Oxfordshire. His links with his *alma mater* were close; he served terms as University and College examiner and was awarded the DD in 1914 for his *The New Testament in the Twentieth Century*. Yet his abiding passion was for the mission of the Church in the land of his birth. His fourth attempt at securing an academic appointment at Lampeter was successful.

The influence of St David's College on the life of the Church in Wales during its first half-century was immense. It supplied over half its clergy and its mores were reproduced in parishes throughout the land. Jones inherited a dispirited institution, riven by factionalism and held in low esteem by senior members of the Church. SDC (as it was known) was taken for granted by Welsh Anglicans and was peripheral to the life of Wales as a whole. During Jones's fifteen years of tenure he managed to raise the college's profile and morale, to place it on a steady financial footing, to increase the student body from 98 to 200, to attract ordinands from the county schools rather than the public schools of Llandovery and Brecon, to enhance the status of the Welsh language in its life and to affirm that which Christians of all traditions held in common. Were it not for the continued and stubborn refusal of the University of Wales to accept the validity of Lampeter degrees, he would have brought the college even further into the mainstream of Welsh social and academic life. Apart from the election of Timothy Rees to Llandaff and despite the hierarchy's continued failure to appreciate his (Jones's) talents, it is difficult to imagine a more inspired appointment within the new Church during these years. For all his undoubted qualities, though, Maurice Jones failed to quash the petty rivalries which marred Lampeter life throughout this time; but it was only after his retirement in September 1938 that the simmering animosity between the cantankerous Anglo-Catholic Professor W. H. Harris and the unbending and humourless Edwin Morris, professor of theology, came to its unedifying and public climax.[7] Yet for all that, the Lampeter contribution to the witness of the Church in Wales was salutary and beneficial up to and well beyond the outbreak of war.

St David's College was not the only institution through which the disestablished Church maintained its witness. As well as being the centre of the diocese and home to one of the constituent colleges of the University of Wales, since the late nineteenth century Bangor had housed seminaries which served both the Congregationalist and the Baptist denominations. The specific Anglican presence within the university was represented by the Church Hostel which, like Pusey House in Oxford, had become the focus for Prayer Book spirituality of a Catholic hue and undergraduate pastoral care. Its warden was responsible for overseeing ordinands from both of the north Wales dioceses and, following the establishment of the University's faculty of theology in 1922, contributing to its academic life. What would transpire to be a significant move in the later history of the Church in Wales was made in 1931 with the appointment of the Revd Glyn Simon, a twenty-eight-year-old south-Walian clergyman, to the warden-ship with teaching responsibilities in Christian doctrine and the philosophy of religion. Despite his shy disposition and somewhat arrogant manner, Simon soon gained a following both within the university and among the younger, more Catholic-leaning clergy in the diocese. He was disciplined, even rigid, with a commitment to the full gamut of High Church practices including the sacrament of penance and clerical celibacy. There was never any question, though, about his wholehearted loyalty to the Anglican Church, and throughout the 1930s a stream of able Nonconformist undergraduates sought confirmation into the Church of Wales (and its ministry in many cases) having felt the pull of his influence: 'The rapidity with which Glyn acquired the reputation of being an *enfant terrible* is remarkable and he certainly lived up to this role in which he was cast.'[8] When Simon proceeded to the wardenship of St Michael's College, Llandaff, in 1939, his future as a leader within the Church was secure. He was young, determined and embodied the ideal to which the new Welsh Church aspired: a Catholic Anglicanism, more confident in its independence of Canterbury and in tune with both Wales (though Simon's explicit sympathy for Welsh culture and nationhood would only fully develop later) and the modern world. By 1945 (and despite the war) there was a boldness and sense of assurance within the Church that a quarter-century earlier no one would have dared to predict.

Simon and others represented a trend of mild optimism which ran counter to much which characterized Welsh, and to a lesser extent Church, life during much of the inter-war period. The progressive catholicization of the Church in Wales, which was illustrated by the institution in 1925 of a daily eucharist at St David's College, the use of eucharistic vestments in 1933 (even by Maurice Jones, its decidedly 'Protestant' principal) virtually without demur, the ever more central role played by St Michael's College in the province's affairs and, following A. G. Edwards's retirement in 1934, the appointment of the openly Anglo-Catholic bishop of Bangor, Charles Green, as his successor. Yet most of this was decidedly cautious, conservative and traditionalist in tone. Green's High Church theology blended with an erastianism which was practically gothic in style while 'Y Tad' (Father) H. R. Johnson, vicar of St Mary's in Cardiff and formerly the most influential of all of St Michael's College wardens, was equally uncomfortable with such regrettable innovations as the Higher Criticism of the Bible and the Christian Socialism of the later Anglo-Catholics. For all its rhetoric as the Church of the people, the disestablished Church in Wales remained hierarchical in nature, aristocratically inclined and still very ambivalent about its status. As late as 1935 its Governing Body comprised six barons, ten baronets, five knights, eleven titled ladies, three sons of peers, two generals, one vice-admiral, one brigadier-general, sixteen colonels and an assortment of majors, captains and members of the gentry many of whom would arrive in their chauffeur-driven Rolls Royces for the annual three-day meeting at Llandrindod.[9] There was something rather inappropriate about this gathering when in the industrial valleys not thirty-five miles to the south, men, women and children in their tens of thousands were afflicted by unemployment, deprivation and considerable hunger. While Wales suffered the Church seemed to be concerned only with its own internal affairs: the administration of the cathedrals, the stipends of curates, marriage legislation, the grouping of rural parishes, the running of Sunday schools and the like. There was virtually no mention by the Governing Body of the burning issues of the day, unemployment and social unrest at home, the rise of fascism abroad, nor of any specifically Christian response to their challenge.[10] Neither were Churchmen in any way conscious of such trends in contemporary theology as the rise of the Barthian movement on the continent and its implications for church and society at large. It was the Nonconformists who kept their academic and cultural links with Europe intact in a way which made the Lampeter–Oxbridge axis seem quite parochial in comparison. The former Baptist pastor Gwilym Davies was Wales's most vital link with the League of Nations, spending as much time in Geneva during the inter-war years as in Cardiff; during the mid-1930s Ivor Oswy-Davies, a Presbyterian ordinand and student of Karl Barth's in Bonn, kept his denomination closely informed of the latest developments in the German Confessing Church's struggle against Hitler, while one of the last to leave France before its occupation by Nazi forces in 1939 had been the deeply committed Calvinistic Methodist layman and noted Francophile Ambrose Bebb.[11] Whereas Welsh Churchpeople fought shy of any specific social application of Christianity, Nonconformists did much to devise a Social Gospel which, although ultimately ineffective (due in part to a lack of a doctrinal underpinning which a Catholic orthodoxy could have provided), at least attempted to engage with the problems of the everyday world. On the whole the Church in Wales still stood apart from the concerns of the people.

Against this backdrop the election of Fr Timothy Rees, a member of the Anglican monastic order the Community of the Resurrection and Mirfield's finest mission preacher, to the bishopric of Llandaff on 25 March 1931 displayed considerable flare and imagination. Rees was fifty-seven years old, a native of Cardiganshire, Nonconformist by upbringing and Lampeter educated, who had trained for the priesthood at St Michael's College when it had been situated in Aberdare. His parochial experience had been within the Llandaff diocese as curate of Mountain Ash from whence he had returned to St Michael's as chaplain and tutor. His experience of the 1904–5 Revival had been positive.

> It has taken us nearly half a century to discover that a man can be a Catholic and an Evangelical too . . . [he had said at the time] And not

only that, we are discovering . . . that the Catholic is very high and dry when he is devoid of all Evangelical fervour, and the Evangelical is very narrow and very shallow when divorced from the Catholic order. We are now beginning to discover that these two things co-exist side by side, not only in the same Church but in the same Churchman.[12]

This catholic evangelicalism had become the most distinctive characteristic of his witness and ministry while he was a member of the Community of the Resurrection at its house in Mirfield, Yorkshire, which he had entered early in 1906. Much attracted by both the religious life and Charles Gore's liberal catholicism which was much more world affirming, biblically open and socially engaged than the near fundamentalist High Churchmanship of the earlier Tractarians, his talents as a missionary and evangelist had been quickly appreciated. Having made his profession as a full member of the Community in July 1907, for the next quarter-century Rees became the order's principal preacher leading innumerable missions throughout Britain and its Empire, in New Zealand, Canada, India and Ceylon. Wartime service as a military chaplain had given him an even deeper sympathy with those who were on the periphery of the church and his concept of mission had always included social service as well as individual salvation. Between 1919 and 1922 he had ministered to undergraduates at Mirfield's hostel at the University of Leeds before being appointed warden of the Community's theological college in Mirfield itself. The return to Llandaff at such a critical juncture in its history of this most unassuming of men, a proficient hymnist (in both English and Welsh) and superb preacher whose theology of a suffering God was born of his feeling for the afflictions of ordinary people,[13] augured well for the diocese and for the province as a whole. According to a Nonconformist minister present at the enthronement service in Llandaff Cathedral on 24 May 1931, it signified 'a new epoch in the history of the Church in Wales'.[14]

Timothy Rees stated his episcopal aims with indisputable clarity: it was to bring the power of the gospel to bear on diocesan life as a whole. 'My heart goes out in sympathy to the broken lives and the broken hearts that are the result of this depression', he said in his enthronement address. 'Would God that I could do something to help. Would God that I could make some

contribution to the solution of this crushing problem.' Within a
year unemployment in Wales would reach its peak of 42.8 per cent
of the male population. Within the diocese of Llandaff tens of
thousands had been made idle, 13,000 in the borough of Merthyr
Tydfil alone. The Rhondda and Aberdare valleys were equally
devastated as was the Vale of Taff and the area around Pontypridd. The crisis was wholly calamitous. The population declined
sharply as families left in their droves, their menfolk seeking work
elsewhere. In the Rhondda 21,371 people left in the ten years
following 1931, while between 1921 and 1935 the Cynon Valley
lost 13 per cent of its inhabitants.[15] Those who stayed behind were
dispirited, poverty stricken and hungry. As well as instigating
preaching campaigns and parish missions, Rees spent a great
proportion of the following years contributing to the social needs
of his diocese. He opened the Bishop's Palace, which he had
renamed 'Llys Esgob', to parties of the unemployed and through
his chairmanship of the Llandaff Industrial Committee attempted
to put pressure on the politicians and industrial leaders to provide
work for the people. In November 1935 he led a deputation to
Whitehall to plead for government help in the rejuvenation of
south Wales. The second Special Areas Act of 1936 allowed for
limited investment in the Merthyr area, though in the main the
situation remained grim. The bishop also made available his
'Messengers', a small unit of young unmarried clergymen who
were dispatched to the most needy parishes in order to assist in
relief work. Despite his evangelical commitment and evangelistic
zeal, Rees was clear that the Church's social ministry was no
optional extra, rather it was essential to its fulfilment of the
demands of the gospel. 'Let us remember', he continued, 'that
Almighty God is just as interested in the doings of the Borough
Council as in the doings of the Diocesan Conference; that He is
just as interested in the problem of providing decent houses for
people to live in as in the problem of providing decent churches for
people to worship in.' The catholicism of social conformity was
giving way to a radical incarnationalism with which Welsh
Churchmen were hardly familiar. 'There is nothing secular', he
claimed, 'but sin.'[16]

The progressive deterioration of Timothy Rees's health from 1937
onwards caused grave anxiety to those who sought the spiritual
renewal of the Church in Wales and its full integration into the life

of the nation. The combination of his gifts was unique: a genuine evangelical faith (to which Nonconformists warmed) which manifested itself through a rounded catholic theology; an unblushing commitment to traditional orthodoxy tempered by sensitivity to the sincere doubts of an increasingly agnostic generation; the balancing of social concern with the call to individual repentance and conversion; a wide experience of the universal church wedded to a sincere and enlightened Welsh patriotism; and an ecumenical openness which, while never compromising Anglo-Catholic particulars, was nevertheless appreciative of all that was positive in Nonconformist faith. His death on 29 April 1939 following a protracted and painful illness deprived the Church in Wales of one of its most humble, endearing and impressive sons. The loss of Rees, compounded by the onset of war, led to the failure to materialize of the 'new epoch' in the Church's history.

The Second World War was not nearly as traumatic for either the Church or the Welsh nation as the previous conflict had been. Ecclesiastically life was put on hold for the duration as many of the clergy and even more of their parishioners served in the armed forces, the former chiefly as chaplains and the latter mostly in the ranks. There is little evidence of the war either disclosing a widespread hidden scepticism or conversely leading men to faith as it had done a generation earlier, or forcing people to ponder the age-old questions of suffering, evil or theodicy in a new light. The main difference between Anglican attitudes to the fighting and that of the Nonconformists centred on the issue of pacifism: the number of conscientious objectors from the Church in Wales was infinitesimally small, though at least one ordinand who was destined to hold high office, John Cledan Mears, later bishop of Bangor, refused to undertake military service, believing it to be incompatible with his understanding of the Christian faith.

The death of Timothy Rees a few years after that of Frank Morgan, the Church's seemingly inexpendable chief lay executive, followed in 1940 by Canon H. R. Johnson and Gilbert Cunningham Joyce, bishop of Monmouth and erstwhile principal of St David's College, marked the passing of a generation. Archbishop Edwards had died in 1937, aged eighty-nine, three years after his retirement, while Bishop Hughes, formerly of Llandaff, had passed on a year later having reached the even more advanced age of ninety-one. Each had been moulded by the disestablishment controversy and reflected the values and presuppositions of the Victorian era. Leadership within the province devolved to younger men, though Bishop Prosser, another ageing Victorian, continued to provide benign and increasingly feeble oversight in St David's, while neither the onset of years nor the contingencies of war dented in the slightest Archbishop Green's prelatical and dignified ways at Bangor. He died, aged eighty, on 7 May 1944. From 1939 Swansea and Brecon was served by the shy and introverted High Churchman Edward Williamson, formerly a well-loved but soft-hearted warden of St Michael's College; this fine scholar proved too reclusive and other-worldly to provide the sort of leadership from which the diocese would have best benefited. John Morgan, Williamson's predecessor in the see who was translated to Llandaff at the beginning of the war as Timothy Rees's successor, was quite different: small, fiery, unshakeable and a strict disciplinarian. He possessed few of Rees's gifts, however, and was felt to be rather prickly and over-critical.

W. T. Havard, at St Asaph since 1934, was a big man in all respects; tall, wide and brawny, he had played rugby for Llanelli, association football for Swansea Town and had shown sufficient valour to have merited the MC as a young chaplain during the First World War. Like Timothy Rees his background was rural, Nonconformist and linguistically Welsh, and his rapport with Christians of other traditions was substantial. Of all the Welsh bishops of this period he would become the most accessible and pastorally effective. Alfred Edwin Monahan, a spiky Irish High Churchman, had been elected to Monmouth in 1940. As monarchical and authoritarian as the diocese's first incumbent but lacking his tact and finesse, his quarrelsome and stubborn nature caused him and others much grief.[17] He died, aged sixty-six, in the summer of 1945. The situation at Lampeter, by then rather incongruously headed by its Australian principal, H. K. Archdall, had been soured by 'the well-nigh incredible dispute between the two Professors of Theology', Morris and Harris,[18] while from 1939 onwards Glyn Simon proceeded to stamp his influence even more indelibly on the Church in Wales and many of its prospective clergy as warden of St Michael's College during its sojourn to St David's where it had migrated to avoid the blitz.[19] The marriage of this abrasive, anti-Dissenting celibate in 1941 to Sheila Roberts, formerly a Baptist and still proudly radical and nonconforming, did much to assuage Simon of his antipathy to the proletarian chapel culture of Welsh Nonconformity. It also made him much more sensitive to the failings of less disciplined mortals than himself.

Despite the glimpses of optimism which Welsh Churchmen perceived amidst the gloom of the inter-war and wartime years, it was clear that even a financially stable and adequately staffed Church would not be immune from the encroaching secularization of the twentieth century. Baptisms throughout the province were decreasing steadily, from 25,454 in 1920 to 19,551 a decade later and 17,917 in 1939. Easter Communion, though, had become steadily more popular: 159,957 had partaken of the sacrament in 1920, 184,605 in 1930 and as many as 193,668 in 1939. Whereas Nonconformity was rapidly losing its influence, adult membership in the Church in Wales was becoming acceptable among a much wider range of the Welsh population than it had been in the past. People were no longer stigmatized for wanting to belong to what had formerly been regarded as a discredited organization. On the contrary, between the wars Welsh Anglicanism became a somewhat fashionable religious option. On Sundays parish churches and the cathedrals were, if not full, at least comfortably well attended and the ordained priesthood represented not only a calling but a respectable, fulfilling and reasonably well-paid career. The mild confidence perceptible throughout the Church and its increasingly positive attitude to the value of its own independence – in 1944 a calendar of Welsh saints was adopted to complement the feast days already included in the Book of Common Prayer – did not, however, belie the problems with which all the denominations would have to contend. The greatest obstacle facing the Church, as Timothy Rees had realized as early as 1934, was not active opposition or flagrant vice but 'the dead weight of sheer indifference'. This 'indifference to spiritual things which prevails in our parishes'[20] was no respecter of specific theological convictions, ecclesiastical traditions or individual persons. It would present the churches with their single most urgent challenge for generations to come.

Roman Catholic advance

On 13 April 1921 amid scenes of splendour and celebration, a vast congregation at St David's Cathedral in Cardiff witnessed the

enthronement of Francis Mostyn, bishop of Menevia, as archbishop of Cardiff and metropolitan of Wales. At the lord mayor's
reception which followed, a message was read from the prime
minister, David Lloyd George, who regretted not being able to
attend the 'historic gathering'. After his presence at the eucharist
at St Asaph a year earlier celebrating the establishment of the
Church in Wales (where, as a non-Anglican, he scandalized many
by taking Communion), the erratic Baptist was in danger of
becoming a fixture at grand ecclesiastical occasions which many
Nonconformists would have regarded with disdain if not horror.
In his message he noted that the appeal which Giraldus
Cambrensis had made eight centuries earlier for Rome to create a
specifically Welsh province had at last been heeded. Referring to
Mostyn's 'famed Welsh lineage' and 'loyalty to Welsh traditions',
he claimed that undoubtedly 'Welshmen without distinction of
creed will rejoice in today's ceremony'. The independent arch-
bishopric for Wales headed by a Welsh archbishop was a 'signal
indication of the enduring vitality of Welsh nationhood'.[21] It was
also a signal indication that the Roman Catholic Church would
henceforth be an inescapable and significant presence in the
religious life of twentieth-century Wales.

Not least among the things which illustrated the strength of
Catholicism in the archdiocese of Cardiff especially was the
annual Corpus Christi celebration. With its colourful procession
through the streets into the grounds of Cardiff Castle, this had
been the big event in the Catholic life of the town since 1874. By
the 1920s 6,000 children would take part annually with some
30,000 people visiting the grounds and even more lining the roads
to watch the parade. Similar scenes, though on a lesser scale, were
witnessed in Newport, Swansea, and from 1921, in Monmouth as
well. Although the Catholic population of the diocese of Menevia
was significantly less than at more cosmopolitan Cardiff, nevertheless it too could boast of well-attended public celebrations of
its own. From 1931 an annual and widely supported Corpus
Christi procession was held at Trefriw in north Wales's Conwy
Valley while, following a conference of the Catholic Young Men's
Society of Great Britain held at Colwyn Bay in 1935, over 4,000
Catholics attended an open-air mass described as 'the largest
religious event yet experienced at Colwyn Bay'.[22] Three years later
a Corpus Christi procession at Llandrindod attracted a large

concourse of the faithful from all over mid-Wales. During Mostyn's first ten years as metropolitan the number of Catholics in the Cardiff archdiocese rose by 27,471, from 59,640 to 87,111, an increase of 46.06 per cent made all the more remarkable by the fact that the population of Glamorgan and Monmouthshire fell by 2.14 per cent and 3.51 per cent respectively during the same period. The steady level of Catholic adherence between the mid-1930s and mid-1940s contrasted sharply with the general fall in population due to widespread emigration and with Nonconformist decline as well. Furthermore, between 1921 and Mostyn's death in 1939 the number of churches in the archdiocese increased by thirty-five, from 81 to 116, while the number of priests rose from 95 to 166. Between 1931 and 1939 the population in Menevia decreased by 2.16 per cent whereas Catholic growth reached a substantial 41.17 per cent and between 1931 and 1940 rose even higher to 51.25 per cent. Church planting went on apace, from 52 in 1921 to 91 in 1945 while the number of priests, both secular and regular, more than doubled.[23]

The growth of Catholicism, 1921–1945

Archdiocese of Cardiff

	Catholics	baptisms	conversions	priests	churches
1921	59640	2034	232	95	81
1930	89137	2992	441	127	99
1939	85580	2594	214	166	118
1945	84100	2269	244	152	120

Diocese of Menevia

	Catholics	baptisms	conversions	priests	churches
1921	9881	486	75	88	52
1930	13223	503	110	117	66
1939	15000	604	99	149	79
1945	21675	580	113	170	91

'The Archdiocese of Cardiff is on the way to becoming one of the most important Catholic strongholds in Britain', stated one contemporary observer. 'On all sides there are abundant signs that

Catholic activity is very energetic in both religious and social schemes.'[24] Although the overall impact of the Church was much less obvious in Menevia, there is no doubt that between 1920 and 1945 Catholicism perceived itself as a potent and growing force throughout Welsh life.

Catholic increase can be accounted for principally by birth, Catholic families being on the whole larger than average, and immigration (from Italy and Belgium to south Wales and from the Catholic heartlands of Lancashire into the coastal belt of the north), though every year a not insubstantial number of people came into the Church by conversion. Most conversions were the result of former non-Catholics marrying Catholics and wishing to profess their partners' religion. There were others, however, who chose Catholicism for specifically spiritual reasons. 'There have been some notable conversions in the last few years', wrote T. P. Ellis, 'of men and women, most of them young, wholeheartedly devoted to Wales, and the leaven of their example will spread.'[25] The Church was very zealous in endeavouring both to win new adherents and to prevent baptized Catholics from giving up on religious practice and drifting away. The Catholic Evidence Guild was perpetually busy proclaiming Catholic truth to a nation which, it was said, was anxious to listen. 'The spirit of enquiry is abroad with regard to the Church and her teachings', announced an observer in 1921, and the future was bright: 'The glorious Faith of which Wales was once beguiled is showing many signs of new life, and there is hope that she is slowly coming into her own again.'[26] Parish missions, such as the one led by Fr Filmer of the Catholic Evidence Guild in Cardiff's St Peter's parish in 1921, made an impact on both the faithful and interested outsiders, while five years later a Franciscan-led mission to the same parish drew over 1,000 to each session and was said to have caused 'a strong revival in fervour and devotion'.[27] A travelling mission replete with mobile chapel was operative in the Menevia diocese, otherwise all sorts of places were used as mass centres including a wooden hut at Llangollen, a dance hall at Benllech on Anglesey, a barn at Llanrwst in the Conwy Valley, a club room at Rhiwabon near Wrexham, a cottage in Harlech and a garage at Penrhyndeudraeth. Reflecting the ideals and practices of the evangelical street preachers, the outdoor activities of the Catholic Evidence Guild were especially prevalent in Cardiff during the inter-war years. After finding a pitch on a street corner or the edge of a town park, laymen as well as priests skilled in public apologetics would expound the faith from a soapbox. The Llandaff Fields and St Mary Street, West Wharf Bay, were particularly popular venues on Sunday evenings in the summer, while Fr Owen Dudley of the Catholic Mission Society became a favoured and effective open-air evangelist. On the parish level numerous confraternities such as the St Anne's Guild, the Children of Mary, the Catholic Institute, the Catholic Young Men's Society and the St Vincent de Paul Society thrived, while a plethora of activities were geared to preserving the loyalty of birth-Catholics and making parish life attractive to prospective converts. Since his translation from Menevia Mostyn had continued to act as the diocese's apostolic administrator, but the appointment of a successor in 1926 provided a further fillip to the Church's confidence. Like his archbishop, Francis Vaughan, nephew of Cardinal Vaughan, former archbishop of Westminster, was the scion of another of Wales's ancient landed families, the Vaughans of Courtfield, and became bishop of the diocese at the age of forty-nine. Since his ordination in 1903 all his parochial experience had been gained in industrial south Wales. Asked for his comments on being appointed to the hierarchy, he replied: 'What shall I speak of if not what is nearest to my heart, namely the restoration of its ancient faith to gallant little Wales.'[28] Henceforth in both the diocese and the archdiocese evangelization would be made a priority. With a zealous and effective indigenous leadership, well in tune with the current aspirations of the people, Catholic confidence was high. 'In His time and in His season, Wales will return to the Faith and to Catholic unity which were hers for a thousand years,' lyricized one commentator, 'Wales will be a Holy land; her wind-vext Tegid a Sea of Galilee, her headlong Dee a Jordan, her Snowdon a Mount of Transfiguration.'[29]

There is no doubt as to the attraction Catholicism held for a certain class of religiously minded people. Its faith was authoritative, supernaturalist, morally bracing, international in scope and (notwithstanding the rigidities of ultramontanism) intellectually rigorous. If Welsh Anglicanism was still tainted by its erastian past and Nonconformity was being dissolved by modernist subjectivism, the Rock of Peter remained steadfast and uncompromising. Both Mostyn and Vaughan were ultramontanist to the core: when Rome was at its most intransigent, loyalty to the Holy See was the bedrock of their faith. Mostyn ruffled not a few Anglican feathers in 1929 when he claimed that the old Welsh cathedrals 'stood as cold and empty shells awaiting the time when new life will be infused into them, and they would be once more used for the purpose for which they were erected'.[30] Like his friend and acquaintance, the Anglo-Spanish aristocrat Cardinal Raphael Merry del Val who, a generation earlier, had pronounced Anglican orders 'utterly null and totally void', Mostyn would have no truck with a heretical Church which had pretentions to catholicity and claimed falsely to be faithful to the apostolic creed. Having rejected duly constituted authority, it was guilty of schism and had cut itself off from the fount of divine blessing. The same was true of Nonconformity. In 1937 a Cardiff Catholic had contrasted 'on the one side . . . the Roman Catholic Church, founded by God, undivided now and forever; on the other side . . . the Protestant Church, founded by man, divided now and forever into many hundreds of different sects'.[31] It was the very starkness of the contrast that constituted Rome's strength and enduring appeal. Papal infallibility, devotion to the Blessed Sacrament, the doctrine of transubstantiation and the Real Presence, the Latin liturgy, the rejection of private judgement, homage to the Blessed Virgin and the complete trustworthiness of the Roman system were staple fare of contemporary Catholicism and as such made the Church hugely appealing even to some of the most subtle and brilliant minds. The 'notable conversions of men and women, most of them young, wholeheartedly devoted to Wales' to whom T. P. Ellis alluded included such intellectually distinguished individuals as Catherine Daniel, T. Charles Edwards (the grandson of Lewis Edwards, Calvinistic Methodism's greatest theologian) and Saunders Lewis. By embracing Catholicism they positively revelled in what had been, for those of their upbringing, its alien mysteriousness. What their parents and contemporaries found repellent, they found uniquely alluring. There was no doubt that this was part of the Church's potency during the inter-war era.

For most Nonconformists and Protestants generally, Roman claims and practices were, however, 'the essence of superstition, idolatry and error'.[32] They directly contravened reason and biblical teaching and led credulous people into darkness and perdition. 'The vast majority of Welsh people look upon Catholics as still "lying unmoved in the iron chains of Popery" ', noted one convert, 'and that Popery makes for everything that is vile, anti-Christian and of the devil.'[33] Sometimes paranoid at the Church's advance, Protestant polemics were testy and virulent. In their respective pastoral letters of 1927, Mostyn and Vaughan were compelled to counter criticisms of the sacrifice of the mass and clarify basic Catholic dogma. According to the archbishop, many were guilty of 'directly contradicting the word of our Blessed Lord Himself, speaking of His wonderful sacramental system as mere magic'.[34] The bishops' apologetic had little effect, however, as throughout the 1930s rather crass misunderstandings of the Catholic position persisted and Protestants were still wont to believe a parody of the Roman faith. Although one Monmouthshire correspondent admitted that the idea of transubstantiation was 'intended probably to simplify a mystery', nevertheless it was 'to the man in the street absurd, contrary to reason and opposed to the evidence of one's senses, of sight, taste and feeling'.[35] Sometimes this lack of comprehension drove Catholic apologists to despair. 'I do not complain that they reject [Catholic beliefs]' lamented Dr John Barrett Davies, the most erudite of Wales's parish priests, 'or that they criticise them vehemently, only that they do not understand them.'[36] Yet by standing so far apart from the Christian mainstream which still consisted almost exclusively of Nonconformists and Anglicans, and refusing to enter into detailed and constructive ecumenical dialogue, to a large extent the Church had itself to blame for such widespread misapprehension and ignorance. It was also quite obvious that the theological sophistication of a Barrett Davies would have hardly squared with the simple pieties of those ordinary Welsh Catholics who believed quite literally in Christ's real presence in the sacrament, that the Pope was unequivocally God's plenipotentiary on earth and that the Blessed Virgin did, in some way, share divine honours with her Son.

The fact that the Church stood aloof from the other Christian bodies clearly rankled with some, though there seemed little desire on the part of most Anglican, and even less on the part of Nonconformists to enter into a closer relationship with their Catholic neighbours. What caused most consternation was Rome's claim to absolute exclusiveness. Taking his cue from Pius XI's encyclical *Mortalium Animos* (1928), Mostyn castigated the 'breaking away from the Catholic Church by heretics and schismatics'. Though Christ had willed unity for his church, that unity would come about 'in no other way than the submission of those outside the Catholic Church to the teaching and authority of that Church. Without this the true unity of Christendom is merely a pious wish which can never be attained.'[37] Protestants were duly scandalized. Professor D. Miall Edwards of the Congregationalists' Memorial College in Brecon had already put forward the alternative ideal of ecumenical unity on the basis of a common confession of Christ and stated that 'the reunion of Christendom will come, not by one communion absorbing all the others but by large-minded mutual recognition'. True catholicity, he claimed, was 'inclusive and comprehensive and tolerant, not exclusive and narrow and excommunicative. Catholicity is a bigger thing than Catholicism.'[38] Catholics, of course, would have none of it; this was merely woolly sentimentalism born of indifference to revealed truth. 'The only unity that they [Protestants] seem capable of attaining', wrote one Catholic commentator, 'is unity in rejecting those very principles which are the foundation and indispensable basis of real unity.'[39] True unity could only be based on truth and the fullness of revealed truth had been vouchsafed by God to the Roman Church alone.

The man who succeeded Vaughan to Menevia in 1935 and Mostyn to Cardiff in 1939, the equally unbending Michael McGrath, made the same point during the 1940s. When German bombs were hitting Cardiff and decimating the centre of Swansea he reminded his flock to 'remember that Christ founded one Church . . . Her teaching is dictated by Her possession of Christ's doctrine guaranteed by the presence and direction of the Holy Spirit.'[40] Not even the spirit of national unity engendered by the war would induce the Welsh hierarchy to concede an iota of its claim to exclusiveness. McGrath disapproved vehemently of Cardinal Hinsley of Westminster's 'Sword of the Spirit' movement which had been launched in 1940 to demonstrate Catholic support for the war effort. The 'Sword's' cautious but daring approval of cross-denominational co-operation caused McGrath huge consternation. Instances of common prayer between Catholics and Protestants he found quite ignominious. They had led, he claimed, to 'the impudence of lay folk who, of course, do not know the implications of many of the acts they perform'. He told Hinsley that they had 'occasioned great scandal to our people. Both clergy and laity have been shocked.' Even the proposal that inter-denominational meetings should be prefaced by silent prayer was scorned. Simply by associating with non-Catholics the Church was brought 'on to the same level as heretical bodies', he claimed. McGrath strictly forbade the establishment of 'the Sword of the Spirit' in his archdiocese. 'The movement, carried on as it has been in England so far', he concluded, 'would prove a catastrophe to the Church in Wales.'[41] Throughout these decades Roman Catholicism, supremely confident in its possession of apostolic authority and divine truth, stood far apart from the other denominations, a constant, alien, though for some a strangely attractive, presence on the Welsh religious scene.

The strength and weakness of dogma

The Catholic world-view of the time was ordered, hierarchical and authoritarian. God had revealed himself clearly in his Church and provided for humankind both spiritual sustenance and objective truth. The Catholic doctrine of man and society was just as tightly formulated as the Church's teaching on grace, salvation and the sacraments. For the Catholic there was no such thing as private truth. This authoritarian temper had long made Catholicism suspicious of liberalism (and sometimes of democracy) and sympathetic to causes of the right. Quoting Pope Leo XIII, one Cardiff Catholic had stated unequivocally that the state would be 'unjust and cruel if under the name of taxation it were to deprive the private owner of more than is fitting'. The rights of private property were inviolable and state socialism, to say nothing of communism or Marxism, were in flat contradiction to the teachings of the Church.[42] Just as in south Wales laissez-faire Liberalism was giving way to the politics of Labour, the Church made quite blatant its opposition to the ideology of socialism and to all revolutionary movements of the left. At a rally of south Wales branches of the Catholic Young Men's Society in 1932, Mostyn quoted infidelity and socialism as being the Church's two greatest contemporary threats and four years later he denounced the 'pernicious doctrines' of communism whose aims were ultimately 'to obliterate the name of God'.[43] The persecution of believers in Soviet Russia, to which Mostyn

referred, had made Catholics even more resolute in their
opposition to what was quite obviously an inhuman and tyrannical regime. In an article published in the *Western Mail*, T. P. Ellis
explained that he had written *The Catholic Martyrs of Wales*
(1933) partly to rebut 'Communist teaching' which was 'spreading
in Wales'. He warned that 'if the Communist-Modernist
combination gains headway' such persecutions as had been
witnessed at the Reformation and were being repeated in modern-
day Russia would become commonplace in Britain once more.[44]
Far from being paranoid or a rabble-rouser, Ellis had been a
judicious and humane lawyer and high court judge who, before his
return to Wales, had served in colonial India with great
distinction. He was typical of virtually all cultured and educated
Catholics in being clearly alarmed at the spread of socialism not
least among his fellow countrymen: 'The Communist agitator has
been busy in South Wales', reported *The Tablet* in 1936, and was
clearly gaining a hearing and a following among the people,[45]
including, one would suspect, the many working-class Catholics in
Cardiff and the industrial south. The convert H. W. J. Edwards
looked with trepidation at the situation in his beloved Rhondda
Valley and saw the one possibility of redemption, both spiritual
and political, in the Catholic faith alone. Catholicism, he claimed
(not without a good deal of logical justification), was 'the only
coherent body of philosophy capable of contesting the teaching of
Marx'.[46]

As the Church expanded, fear of Catholicism's purported
divided allegiance between the Vatican State and the British
Crown intensified. The apparently totalitarian claim which the
faith made on its adherents caused Welsh Protestants (and
secularists) to mistrust its temporal power as much as its spiritual
claims. 'Christendom must have a headship' stated an Anglican
critic, 'and that must be Roman. Once that is definitely settled, it
inevitably applies the eventual control of the civil, or temporal,
power.'[47] 'The opposition of Protestants to the Roman Catholic
Church is not a matter of mere sectarian rivalry,' wrote another
commentator, somewhat disingenuously, '[but] is at bottom to the
dangers of political interference by foreign ecclesiastical rulers in
the affairs of this country.'[48] The immediate point under discussion was the state's financial support for Catholic schools, but,
as the international situation deteriorated, it had a much wider

political application as well. The 1930s was the decade of the dictators: Stalin on the left, Franco, Mussolini and Hitler on the right, yet the fact that the Church's wholesale opposition of communism was not balanced by an equally outspoken criticism of fascism only served to exacerbate Protestant suspicion. At a rally in Cardiff in 1936, J. A. Kensit, the bellicose Protestant propagandist, claimed that were it to convert to the Catholic faith, Wales would go the way of Italy and Spain, where democracy had been destroyed and the rights of conscience trampled underfoot. 'Wales would present a strange spectacle if it were converted into a Spain, an Italy, or an Austria . . . the larger the figure of the priest the smaller the figure of liberty.'[49] The Presbyterians, meeting at Llandrindod a few months later, countered 'the opportunist combination of Fascism and Roman Catholicism as movements opposed to religious thought and practice', and only as an after-thought saw fit to include communism in their critique.[50] Whereas for Welsh Catholics the greatest threat to religion and world order was Marxism, what Protestants and Nonconformists feared most was Catholicism and its softness towards fascist oppression and ideals.

The whole vexed question of Catholicism's tacit approval of dictatorships of the right found a focus in one of the most contro-versial political and literary figures of inter-war Wales, Saunders Lewis. Lewis, an academic on the staff of University College, Swansea, had returned from the First World War determined to fashion a new, neo-traditionalist, European Wales infused by the spiritual and cultural ideals of ultramontane Catholicism. A founder member of Plaid Genedlaethol Cymru, the Welsh Nationalist Party, he had been elected its president in 1926 and following his reception into the Church in 1932 he became 'the perfect target against which those who feared the political goals of Fascism could aim their accusations and anger'.[51] The somewhat alien and exotic tone of the nationalists' ideology (in the ears of Nonconformist Wales at least) arose in part from its borrowings, via Lewis, from such wholly unfamiliar sources as the papal encyclicals *Rerum novarum* (1891) and *Quadragesimo anno* (1931) which were, of course, in the mainstream of Catholic social teaching. Yet Protestant and Nonconformist distrust of the papacy generally and mounting criticism of the Vatican's stance on fascism particularly helped curtail the nationalists' political effectiveness and increase Lewis's reputation as a brilliant but slightly sinister outsider. As early as 1926 Professor W. J. Gruffydd, an unrepentant Protestant modernist and the doyen of Welsh letters, had berated 'the Neo-Catholic Movement' in Welsh literature (meaning Saunders Lewis and Ambrose Bebb) as embodying a wholly retrograde development intent on snuffing out free enquiry and taking Wales back to the Dark Ages. Worst of all was the neo-Catholics' active sympathy for the Action Française and other anti-democratic political movements. In his open letter of reply to Gruffydd, 'Llythyr ynghylch Catholigiaeth' ('A Letter concerning Catholicism') in the influential journal *Y Llenor* (1927), Lewis repudiated these accusations by claiming that, despite his cultural indebtedness to such conservative French intellectuals as Charles Maurras and Maurice Barrès, he disowned their politics unreservedly (as did the Vatican which had anathematized the Action Française some months earlier). This availed little and accusations that the nationalists were a front for a reactionary Catholicism of a most unpleasant kind persisted throughout the 1930s.

The nationalists' 1939 policy of neutrality in the face of war served merely to deepen popular suspicion, and in an attack of unprecedented bitterness, the Revd Gwilym Davies, apparently at the behest of his friend Dr Thomas Jones, a socialist supporter and president of the University College of Wales, Aberystwyth, claimed that 'in an independent, totalitarian, fascist and papist Wales, there will be but one party, one church and one language'.[52] What was ostensibly an attack on nationalist ideology was equally scathing about the supposedly reactionary nature of Catholic social dogma, it being obvious to the critic that one was a logical extension of the other. The campaign during the 1943 election for the University of Wales's seat at Westminster in which W. J. Gruffydd, standing as a Liberal, defeated Saunders Lewis, was equally virulent, with Lewis's Catholicism being as contentious as his nationalism, if not more so. It was only after 1945 with the collapse of Europe's totalitarian regimes of the right and his (Lewis's) withdrawal from public life that accusations of a Catholic-nationalist plot against democracy and individual rights subsided. After that the Welsh hierarchy's renewed attacks on communism and the totalitarianism of the left, led by Saunders Lewis's friend Archbishop McGrath, became much less contentious and in keeping with the mood of the Cold War.

The Catholic working class, centred upon the conurbations of Cardiff, Barry, Newport and the Greenhill area of Swansea, knew little of ideological battles between Welsh-speaking intellectuals and cared even less. Their roots were more likely to have been in Limerick than in Llanddewi-brefi and their concerns were with employment and a working wage rather than with the preservation of culture and national identity. Their natural sympathies were with Labour and they were far from immune to the appeal of socialism and its propaganda. The Catholic Social Guild routinely urged the faithful to take interest in social and economic matters and involve themselves in local politics in order to bring a Catholic view to bear on community life, while Mostyn and even more pointedly Vaughan criticized the excesses of capitalism as much as they feared the pernicious effects of communism. Mostyn's pastorals of the 1930s regularly mentioned the plight of the poor while Vaughan, in words which would be echoed by the South American liberation theologians fifty years later, berated 'the greedy concentration of wealth and power in the hands of a tiny minority'.[53] As inter-war south Wales faced economic collapse these concerns were far from theoretical, indeed in the Cardiff archdiocese poverty and hunger was so dire that in 1929 Mostyn exempted his flock from partaking of the usual Lenten fast. In 1936 three consecutive issues of *The Tablet* provided detailed reports on the hardships which ordinary Catholics and others were having to undergo in the south Wales valleys, quoting one local priest as saying: 'These people are enduring martyrdoms worse than any in the Roman Martyrology.'[54] Yet socialism as an ideology remained highly suspect to the clergy at least, nor was there any sign that hardship would be translated into outright political disaffection thus causing a rift within the Church.

Although Catholic advance continued throughout these years, the Church like all others had to contend with its share of problems. In the Cardiff archdiocese a growing trend towards intermarriage, social acceptance born of increasing familiarity and the development, in pockets, of a thriving middle class, served to integrate the Catholic community into the norms of everyday Welsh life, yet the price of assimilation was a weakening of community ties and spiritual boundaries. By as early as 1922 over 50 per cent of marriages in the archdiocese were 'mixed' (between Catholics and non-Catholics), and whereas this brought many partners into the Church, it was often the route which took others out. For every convert that was made, there were birth-Catholics who absented themselves from attendance at Mass and the other regular ministrations of the Church, many of whom simply drifted away from religion altogether. What was happening in Cardiff was being replicated in Menevia as well. In a letter to Bishop Vaughan in 1930, Lieutenant John McGuire of Brecon noted that 'our poor few Catholics are slowly slipping through [our] fingers . . . a good many do not come to Mass', while he reported that there had not been a single 'churchgoing convert' among the town's Catholic community for many years.[55] After their wedding 'marriage Catholics' would, as a rule, simply allow their religious affiliation to lapse. For Michael McGrath the whole situation was quite abominable. Mixed marriages were 'ever odious to the Catholic Church', he claimed, deeming them to be 'unlawful and pernicious',[56] while his observations from the archiepiscopal chair some years later were even more colourful. 'Continue to pour water into milk and eventually there is a nauseating liquid which is neither water nor milk', he claimed. 'So will a parish change and deteriorate under the influence of this evil.'[57]

Whatever the strengths of contemporary Welsh Catholicism and the appeal that its dogmatic certainties made to many religious-minded enquirers, it was far from immune from the pressures of secularism, spiritual apathy and worldliness which were affecting each of the different denominations at the time. Whereas some were clearly excited at the prospect of the nation's wholesale return to *yr hen ffydd*, 'the old faith', there were others who realized clearly that the creation of a Catholic Wales was, given present circumstances, far from being a feasible possibility. The rather bleak description of parish life in Menevia, where 'nearly all of its threescore and ten or so of churches and public chapels are served by lonely priests, living far from other missions and working bravely on the scantiest resources',[58] provided a truer picture of the Church's situation in inter-war Wales than the over-confident hyperbole of some of its apologists, as did the incidental comments of a correspondent in the *Western Mail*: 'Up in the hills there has been a struggle to keep certain oases of Catholicism alive in a desert of bigotry.'[59] Yet on the whole Welsh Catholics were in good heart between 1920 and 1945 and were certainly spared many of the traumas which their Protestant Nonconformist neighbours underwent during that same era.

4

Nonconformity 1920–1945: confessing the faith

Doctrinal reformulation among the Calvinistic Methodists

Of all the Nonconformist bodies it was the largest, the Calvinistic Methodists, which emerged from the First World War (and the Disestablishment campaign) most conscious of the need for reformation and change. Although the prevalent mood was hardly one of fervency, it was nevertheless widespread and deep and no one expressed it more clearly than the Revd John Morgan Jones (Cardiff), the patriarchal director of the Connexion's evangelistic wing, the Forward Movement. 'Recently and with virtually no warning', he claimed, 'the idea has gripped a host of our younger ministers that the [Calvinistic] Methodist constitution is outdated, that it is totally unsuited to meet the needs of the present and there have been direct calls for it to be reviewed and reformulated.'[1] The initial tentative suggestion for the setting up of a denominational commission for reconstruction had first been broached by the North Wales Association in November 1918 within days of the armistice, and by the spring of 1919 such was the momentum for change that five separate committees representing both Associations, north Wales and south, had been convened in order to deal with different aspects of connexional life: history and doctrine, church order, ministerial education, worship and mission, and finally social questions. The first committee's report, published to coincide with the Bala Association which met in June 1920, set the tone for the labours of the commission as a whole. It showed with exceeding clarity the state of religion in Wales and the seriousness of the problems which Nonconformity would have to face. There was no doubt in the minds of the report's authors that the nation was facing a crisis of faith which only a renewal of experiential Christianity founded on a credible doctrinal base could hope to resolve. The reasons for the present malaise were faced honestly: that religion was becoming peripheral to the interests and aspirations of the rising generation;

that urbanization and modernization were making Christian convictions seem obsolete; that the current post-war craze for entertainment, amusement and pleasure was playing havoc with the seriousness of purpose which used to characterize Nonconformity at its most thoughtful; that education had come to be regarded as a means of social and financial betterment rather than a means by which ordinary folk enriched themselves culturally; and that the mounting interest in social reform was being divorced from explicitly religious principles and the mission of the churches. Apart from the pressures of the outside world the report readily admitted the internal weaknesses of the churches themselves: that the profession of so many church members had lacked moral integrity, that religion had been allowed to be divorced from everyday life, and that doctrinal changes had deprived the churches' message of its immediacy and effect. 'The change in our understanding of the world and of life itself has modified our views of heaven, hell and the Day of Judgement so making it exceedingly difficult to express with any measure of conviction the moral reality which these concepts still embody.'[2] Whereas the preconceptions of the Enlightenment demanded that the church could never return to a pre-critical world-view, the claims of faith required that the moral truth of the eschatological doctrines be retained: 'Our forefathers made heaven, hell and judgement very real to their listeners; it is our task to make the transcendent reality of the spiritual world equally real.'[3] Following reinterpretation in the light of current thought, the great doctrines of the faith would have to be applied anew.

For a confessional body like the Calvinistic Methodists it was the question of reinterpretation which would prove contentious in the years to come. Since 1823 the Connexion's creed had been enshrined in its Confession of Faith. Strongly orthodox and incontrovertibly Calvinistic, it reflected the predilections of what many believed to be a bygone age. There was no doubt about its Reformed character or the high dignity of its cadences, yet even traditionalist connexionalists found some of its emphases disconcertingly narrow. For Dr John Cynddylan Jones, still the most engaging of the *Corff*'s conservative evangelical theologians and, though well into his eighth decade, as much a wag as ever, the Confession's chief weakness was its overdependence on a sterile and scholastic rationalism. 'Could any of you poor people list the

Five Points which made the Connexion Calvinist?' he asked the delegates to the South Wales Association, in best knockabout fashion, during their gathering in 1924. 'Of course you couldn't. Neither could I if I didn't have them written down!' The Confession, like the Five Points of the Synod of Dort, included unconditional election, limited atonement and mankind's total depravity through sin, yet Cynddylan was far from convinced of the scriptural justification for any of these propositions. Election itself was wholly biblical; it was the fatalistic way in which the Methodist fathers had understood the doctrine which gave him pause for thought. 'Let us keep to the essentials but dispute the details. Election is a fact, how it is worked out is a mystery.' Equally incontrovertible was Christ's atonement for sin in virtue of his sacrificial death on Calvary, yet the Confession's claim that he had died 'for the elect, and the elect alone' (Article 18) went far beyond the New Testament evidence and the conviction of the church catholic regarding the breadth of God's love. Though he contended for the historicity of humankind's fall in Adam, Cynddylan was less than happy with the wording of the Confession's eleventh article on human sinfulness, that 'by nature all are dead in trespasses and sins, enemies in their minds by wicked works, every imagination of the thoughts of their hearts being only evil continually, without desire to know the Lord or to obey him, and justly deserving eternal death'. How, then, could men and women be held accountable for their sins? Although a fallen creature, man's fall had been broken by a grace which had prevented him from reaching the most abysmal depths of corruption. 'I wonder', he mused, 'whether the Confession of Faith gives sufficient credit to the unquenchable light which is mentioned in the Gospel of John, " *That* was the true Light, which lighteth every man that cometh into the world" (1: 9).'[4] Yet ironically it was not Cynddylan Jones who argued that the Confession should be retained unaltered but the Reconstruction Commission itself, some of whose members were far less enamoured of the virtues of traditional orthodoxy than the learned and witty octogenarian divine.

The reason for the Commission's unpreparedness to countenance the replacement of the Confession of Faith had as much to do with the tenor of the times as with any intrinsic appreciation of the document itself. Theologically, philosophically and scientifically the world was in flux; it was hardly the time to draw up a new Confession in place of the old. 'Let it be kept as it is, and as a historical document it should remain inviolate' was the overwhelming view.[5] Yet it was widely accepted that it no longer truly expressed the Connexion's views. In the light of this conundrum the Commission's doctrine panel prepared a Declaratory Statement of Common Faith and Practice which was endorsed by both Associations at their annual meetings, the one at Rhyl in November 1922 and the other at Glyn-neath in April 1923. Its seven succinct paragraphs were liturgically elegant and scripturally based though direct references to the inspiration of scripture, the virgin birth, original sin and the doctrine of election were studiously avoided as were particular theories of the atonement and a specific eschatological scheme. What for some was a reasonable expression of catholicity and inclusiveness was seen by others, inevitably, as an exercise in statecraft and compromise. Although the personal integrity of its four authors was beyond reproach,[6] the situation boded ill for the unity of the Connexion and the future success of its mission. The next decade would be one of strife for the Calvinistic Methodists of Wales.

For the members of the Commission's doctrine panel and for the leaders of the denomination as a whole, the key reason for current uncertainty centred on the nature and authority of scripture. 'One of the chief needs of the present age', according to the Commission, 'is a powerful theological renewal. The dawn will not break on the cause of religion in our land until men once more turn their minds to the doctrines of the faith.' The problem, of course, was that in a critical age there was no agreement as to how those doctrines could be formulated. With the basis of Christian truth being assailed from outside the church and questioned unrelentingly from within, it was far from obvious how that theological renewal could be achieved. 'On considering the situation, it appears to us', continued the Commission's members, 'that the religious problems which assail most of our people have to do with the Bible and what constitutes religious authority, i.e. the question of Revelation.'[7] Biblical criticism had come to stay; for virtually all of the Connexion's leaders and its academy-trained ministers there was no question of reverting to pre-modern theories. This being the case, how could the scriptures retain their character as God's Word while being regarded simultaneously as a timebound, fallible and at times highly imperfect human construct? 'Having forfeited the old idea of the Bible without having had it replaced by anything new, many have found themselves without a strong foundation for their beliefs or an authoritative standard for their faith.'[8] Critical methods of interpreting the Bible had been employed in the denomination's seminaries at Bala and Trefecca for a generation or more and connexional literature such as *Y Drysorfa*, *The Treasury* and the more heavyweight quarterly *Y Traethodydd* regularly featured articles on biblical themes in which the results of the Higher Criticism were taken for granted. Yet it was not until 1920 that tensions between the traditional and modern interpretation of scripture created overt controversy within the churches.

The subject set for the 18–21 age-group throughout the Connexion's Sunday schools during the 1920–1 session was aspects of the Pentateuch, and the author commissioned to write the commentary was the Revd D. Francis Roberts, minister of the Fitzclarence Street Church in Liverpool. Roberts's theological training had taken him from the University College of North Wales, Bangor, via Bala to the universities of Berlin and Marburg. Prior to ordination he had spent some years as an assistant lecturer in Hebrew at the University of Glasgow. The short commentary, published under the imprimatur of the Welsh Calvinistic Methodists, contained nothing new.[9] Following the critical orthodoxy of the day he rejected the Mosaic authorship of the Old Testament's first five books in favour of the documentary hypothesis ('J E D P') dating them from the exile sometime in the sixth century BC. The creation story in Genesis was derived from Babylonian myth and much of the rest of the Pentateuch was highly primitive and unhistorical. Despite these ideas having been in the public domain for years, this was the first time that ordinary church members, at a highly impressionable time in their personal development (to say nothing of their unsuspecting teachers), were exposed to them in a systematic fashion in innumerable Sunday school classes throughout the land. The ensuing furore was huge; there were calls for the commentary to be withdrawn, for its author to be disciplined and the Connexion was censured by many of its most loyal members for allowing such heretical ideas to be circulated. Yet not all who objected to the commentary were unlettered fundamentalists. Of the critical reviews the most thoughtful came from the pen of the Revd R. S. Thomas, Abercynon, who had learned his theology not in the connexional seminaries but at Princeton at the feet of the Reformed giants Archibald Hodge and B. B. Warfield. Following Warfield's scholastic method of rational deduction, Thomas held resolutely to the factual infallibility and inerrancy of the biblical text as a corollary of the concept of inspiration. It was a sophisticated theory which Thomas defended with impressive erudition and much aplomb.[10] Yet to no avail. Thomas had absolutely no following within his denomination, not even among his fellow conservatives, but more to the point concepts such as inerrancy were being abandoned across the board. By the early 1920s it appeared that Calvinistic Methodists, like virtually all other mainline Christians in Wales, would have to make do with a fallible Bible and pick their way across the theological morass as best they could. There seemed no longer to be a guaranteed and dependable standard for religious truth upon which all could agree.

Highly conscious of the prevailing difficulties, the members of the Reconstruction Commission's doctrinal committee made a valiant attempt at providing a sound basis for contemporary faith. The theological renewal which they believed to be the key to Nonconformity's future regeneration could be founded on the New Testament witness to Christ as Saviour and Lord. 'We can accept wholeheartedly the assured results of Biblical Criticism', claimed the Revd R. R. Hughes, the principal author of the report, 'while being perfectly confident that they will never clash with the claims of Christ much less dethrone him.'[11] Christ's position in the church's faith was unassailable and his centrality to the biblical revelation was equally strongly assumed: 'When studied in the light of criticism the scriptures disclose a remarkable unity; and the key to that unity is Jesus Christ.'[12] The Old Testament, even when read according to the then fashionable evolutionary canons of historical progression, culminates in the coming of Christ, saviour of the world, and just as Christ is the centrepoint of scripture he too is the norm by which all subsequent doctrine can be judged. 'Our idea of God', claimed the panel members, 'must begin from our knowledge and experience of Christ.'[13] Rather than beginning with an abstract concept of God and applying that to Christ, which was said to have been the besetting weakness of the older theology, Calvinistic Methodists were urged to begin with Christ and derive their doctrine from him. Christ should be the judge of doctrine as well as its subject. 'As soon as we recognize the principle that each partial and incomplete revelation should be judged in the light of the perfect revelation in Christ', claimed a winsomely confident R. R. Hughes, 'all the problems immediately disappear.'[14] A christocentric religion was not inconsistent with a critical appreciation of the Bible and would provide a solid foundation for contemporary faith.

However sincere this doctrinal reformulation appeared, there were some obvious questions which would remain unanswered. The first had to do with the unassailable nature of the revelation in Christ. If biblical criticism were to be allowed free rein (as its connexional supporters universally demanded) what certainty was there that its claims would *never* clash with those of Christ? It was hardly surprising that the monumental and supremely scholarly Bible dictionary *Y Geiriadur Beiblaidd* published in 1926 under the auspices of the University of Wales's Guild of Graduates, would be at best ambivalent on the question of Christ's virgin birth, his unique deity and physical resurrection, and outrightly dismissive of the factual nature of his transfiguration and his coming again in glory.[15] Yet it was repeatedly implied during these years that Christ was exempt from the critical process and that the unique truth of his person would prevail come what may. Secondly, if scripture, judged critically, witnessed to a progressive revelation along evolutionary lines, on what basis could Christ be claimed to be its terminus and fulfilment? 'The principle governing our thoughts in these comments is divine revelation through ongoing human development', wrote the Revd G. Wynne Griffith, another leading member of the doctrine panel. 'That revelation reaches its goal and pinnacle in Christ.'[16] This, of course, was a dogmatic affirmation rather than a rational conclusion drawn from the logic of either biblical criticism or evolutionary theory. The inconsistency, though, was hardly admitted far less challenged during the early inter-war years. And thirdly, despite their sincere conviction that Christ should be the key to understand revelation and doctrine, the Connexion's reconstructionalists had virtually no recourse to any objective theological criterion beyond that of their own critical opinions. In a courteous and measured defence of his use of the critical method in his commentary on the Pentateuch, D. Francis Roberts repeated his appeal to Christ as the judge and norm of revelation and doctrine:

> The Christ, his life and teaching, is our only standard. From this standard we can judge the value of everything in the scriptures . . . Whenever our ideas of God and man fail to accord with the teaching of the Lord Jesus, they can never be an authority for us.

But when he proceeded to explain which Christ is authoritative, his preconceptions became immediately apparent: 'Christ within us is the highest revelation, and that revelation is forever expanding and developing.'[17] For Roberts, the immanent Christ was the final arbiter in matters of faith and not necessarily the Christ of apostolic testimony. Such orthodox formulations as the virgin birth and the physical resurrection could presumably be rejected if the canons of biblical criticism or the dictates of evolutionary dogma so ordained. If the biblical unorthodoxy which this theory implied would provoke most controversy during the following years, it was the element of subjectiveness which would prove its principal conceptual weakness.

There were those, though not averse to constructive biblical criticism nor believing in the wholesale infallibility of the Confession of Faith, who nevertheless protested vigorously against the pronounced liberal complexion of what was rapidly developing into the prevailing consensus among some of the Connexion's leaders. During these years liberal theology, with its downplaying of the supernatural and the uniqueness of Christ and its interpretation of revelation according to the categories of human experience and morals, tended to go hand in hand with what Francis Roberts and others termed 'the scientific attitude to the Bible'. R. R. Hughes, who was on the whole still fairly traditional in his theology, insisted on translating the uniqueness of Christ into moral rather than ontological terms and by so doing substantially compromised the concept of the miraculous. 'In this sense [namely, the ethical] His mighty works remain even for those who can no longer accept the supernatural', he claimed.[18] It was Christ's moral rectitude and his exquisite experience of the Fatherhood of God which made him divine. 'He is a perfect man', claimed G. Wynne Griffith, 'one who realized the ideal of humanity and so became the Son of God incarnate.' This frankly adoptionist christology chimed in perfectly with the theory of evolution: 'Christ teaches this doctrine explicitly in connection with the kingdom of heaven', he said, 'and is himself the most perfect example of the principle which has ever been seen.'[19] Such was the extent of his filial experience that through it his divinity shone forth. 'At the centre of Jesus' view of God is the experience of fatherhood', wrote the Revd Morgan Watcyn-Williams, 'and at the centre of his view of man is the experience of brotherhood.'[20]

Saunders Lewis, the son, grandson and great-grandson of Calvinistic Methodist ministers of repute and by then on the staff of University College, Swansea, was already moving in a Catholic direction when, in a widely reported analysis of contemporary Welsh life given at Llandrindod in 1923, he took Nonconformity to task for its doctrinal laxity. Nonconformity, he claimed, had forfeited the respect and loyalty of Wales's youth and its spiritual authority was in tatters. Theology proper, it seemed, had yielded to literary criticism and all certainty had been dissolved in subjectivism. 'It appears to me that the chief characteristic of theology today is the tendency towards the indefinite in matters of credo, – the state which is called "modernism".' The best antidote for such woolly-mindedness and doctrinal confusion, he claimed (with a wry humour), would be for all of Wales's theologians to read Pope Pius IX's 'Syllabus of Errors' and take its contents to heart! Nothing would become of Nonconformity until it returned to the certainties of classical orthodoxy and dogma.[21] D. Francis Roberts was quick to defend his fellow theologians; like virtually all of his colleagues of that generation, his contempt for popery knew no bounds and it was especially galling to see his tradition being criticized by one whose roots were so deep in the soil of Welsh Calvinistic Methodism. 'Neither the dogmatism of Pope Pius IX nor that of any other pope, Methodist or not, will succeed in turning back the tide of today's best and most enlightened theology', he claimed. Still smarting from the controversy over his handbook on the Pentateuch, he widened the field of his defence. His invective was unrestrained and his anti-semitic jibe was unfortunate to say the least:

> There are enough popes in Wales already, especially in South Wales . . . If Moses or some other Jew said that the whole of creation was completed in six days, then let the British Association and all the astronomers and geologists insist what they will, we couldn't possibly question Moses!

Having been released from the shackles of biblical infallibility, Nonconformity was now free to progress according to the genius of modern scholarship and contemporary culture. The last thing it needed was a lesson in obscurantism from those whose infallibility was vouchsafed by the bishop of Rome: 'The great weakness of those who call themselves theologians today is not a lack of dogmatism in matters of creed but a negative dogmatism which is quite irrational.'[22] In fact Roberts found Lewis's critique wholly bizarre. Lewis's reply was uncompromising. 'The Revd Francis Roberts, on the evidence of his own words, despises dogma', he wrote. 'Yet it is impossible to be a Christian without believing dogma. But Mr Roberts rejects dogma. That is, he rejects Christ.'[23] Saunders Lewis would repeat his critique, not so much of D. Francis Roberts but of the 'modernism' he saw afflicting Welsh intellectual life, in his 'Letter concerning Catholicism' published in W. J. Gruffydd's influential literary magazine *Y Llenor* in the summer of 1927.[24] It was a measure of the still considerable influence of Nonconformity and the Nonconformist pulpit that what was in fact a literary and aesthetic controversy among the intelligentsia should be fuelled by the contents of popular preaching which was yet appreciated by tens of thousands of ordinary people.

Though he would still occasionally attend services at his father's church in Swansea, by this time Saunders Lewis was on the very periphery of Welsh Nonconformity. (His actual reception into the Catholic Church would not take place until 1932.) Yet there was a considerable number of Calvinistic Methodists close to the centre of denominational life, on presbytery and local church level at least, who, though sharing Francis Roberts's abhorrence of popery, nevertheless had considerable sympathy with Lewis's criticisms of the Connexion's doctrinal drift. The move to defend theological orthodoxy found its focus in the campaign to preserve the link between the 1823 Confession of Faith and the Connexion's legal constitution. Since 1826, a decade and a half after the secession of the Calvinistic Methodist movement from the Church of England, the Connexion's legal status had been bound indissolubly with the Confession of Faith. When registered by the Court of Chancery as a separate and distinct Christian body during that year, the constitutional deed stipulated that 'no alteration in the Confession of Faith or the tenets or doctrines to be taught and maintained by the said Connexion shall be at any time allowed or even discussed'. In other words both the spiritualities and the temporalities of the Welsh Calvinistic Methodist body were henceforth and in perpetuity bound to the letter of the Confession of Faith. Despite there being little enthusiasm for the wholesale abandonment of the Confession, it was apparent that the situation which had served the *Corff* adequately for nearly a century had become seriously problematic. As was admitted readily by conservative and liberal alike the Confession no longer expressed the true opinions of the Connexion, and what was perhaps even more unsatisfactory in the light of more recent developments was the fact that (because of the constitutional deed) the final court of appeal in denominational matters was not the church itself but the House of Lords. After decades of agitating for the disestablishment of the Anglican Church in Wales, the Calvinistic Methodists had come to realize keenly the anomalous position in which they found themselves. It now struck them forcibly that as Protestant Dissenters they had forfeited their spiritual freedom for the protection and patronage of the state.

The report of the doctrine committee of the Reconstruction Commission had stated boldly: 'As Protestants and especially as Free Churchmen we declare unhesitatingly our belief in the right of our Church to review her creed when she feels that the circumstances so require.'[25] What was novel about this statement was the confidence with which the committee described themselves as being Free Churchmen. This had not always been the case. The Connexion had originally been a renewal movement within the establishment and it was with the greatest trepidation that Thomas Charles, leader of the Welsh Calvinistic Methodists and a clergyman of the Church of England, had presided over the ordination of exhorters in 1811 which sealed the movement's secession from the mother church. The breach had occurred not for theological reasons but for pragmatic ones. Had the bishops been more accommodating to Methodist convictions and catered explicitly for their spiritual needs, the secession would have never taken place. Between 1735 and 1823 their only standard of faith was the ecumenical creeds and the 39 Articles of the Church of England. For decades following, the Connexion's leaders refused to regard themselves as either Dissenters or Nonconformists: they were Calvinistic Methodists whose respect for the ideal of an

established church remained undimmed. They eschewed radicalism and were politically conformist. It was much later in the
century, not least in reaction to the catholicizing tendencies of
Tractarianism upon the Anglican Church, that the Methodists
came to regard themselves as Nonconformists and only by Victorian times that they embraced wholeheartedly Free Church principles. It was not for nothing, therefore, that when surveying the
reconstruction process the Revd E. O. Davies stated: 'Nothing
more important than this [the committee's declaration] was
uttered, in connection with the doctrine of the Denomination,
during the last hundred years.'[26] In order to practice this right the
stipulation of the 1826 constitution would have to be annulled and
this could only be achieved by an Act of Parliament. But as Free
Churchmen the Welsh Calvinistic Methodists now knew that there
could be no alternative: they should take the right to review and
renew their creed without having to seek permission from the
state.

There was, however, little enthusiasm even among the liberals
that this potential freedom should be used in order to abandon the
Confession in any way. 'We would not like to see any interference
with a historical document like the Confession of Faith', stated
R. R. Hughes.[27] But following the North and South Wales Association meetings of late 1923 and early 1924 in Manchester and Ty-
croes, Ammanford, respectively, the process of seeking the
presbyteries' permission for constitutional change commenced in
earnest. As the Reconstruction Commission's principal secretary,
E. O. Davies, the minister of Siloh Church, Llandudno, and
formerly professor of Christian doctrine at the Connexion's
seminary at Bala, was given the prime responsibility for overseeing
the process. A competent theologian and, as it would transpire, a
canon lawyer of genius, he knew instinctively what needed to be
done and how it should be achieved. The task was constitutional,
not one which had immediate bearing on the way in which the
Connexion confessed its faith. 'This question should not be
confused with another which is being asked at the moment, viz.
whether it is appropriate for us to review or change our credo', he
said. 'The use which is made of that freedom once it is gained will
depend on the Connexion itself.'[28] Davies was a cautious
theologian, sensitive to the intellectual challenges of the twentieth
century yet grounded in a liberal-tinged Christian orthodoxy. His

admiration for the Confession of Faith, which he expressed in a masterful survey of its formation and history from the presidential chair of the North Wales Association in 1923, was sincere: 'The least that we can say about it is that it is a masterpiece in all senses . . . It is one of the classics of our Connexion, and so it shall remain.'[29] Despite his receptiveness to biblical criticism, to the fact of comparative religion and to the prevailing theories of divine immanence, he remained basically an orthodox divine.

> My own opinion as to the way in which things will develop in the future is that neither the Shorter Declaration nor any other statement which the Connexion may devise will ever replace the Confession of Faith. The Confession will remain, and not merely as a historical document, but – subject to the ultimate authority of Holy Scripture – as the vital standard of connexional doctrine. Any further declaration made in the light of new-found knowledge and under the guidance of the Holy Spirit would only serve to augment and not supplant the present Confession of Faith.[30]

This conviction, from which Davies never deviated, would be of immense significance for the future unity (and orthodoxy) of the Connexion. There is no doubt that the *Corff* and its reformers were hugely fortunate in their man.

No matter how sensitive Davies was to the need for constitutional freedom, the call for doctrinal change, the spirit of the Confession and the scruples of the denomination's more conservative members, reaction against such a far-reaching development was bound to occur. It found a definite form early in 1925 in a series of articles entitled 'Torri'r Rhaffau' ('Cutting the Ropes') in the connexional weekly *Y Goleuad* and subsequently published in several editions in pamphlet form. Their author was the Revd W. Nantlais Williams, the popular and talented minister of Bethany, Ammanford, flagship church of the Connexion's conservative evangelicals in south Wales. Though not opposed to the principle of freedom nor to the idea of broadening the Confession of Faith in order to make it more scriptural and evangelical, he was nevertheless deeply suspicious of the trend towards reformulation and the motives of some of its keenest advocates. He was in fact quite convinced that the reconstruction process was being hijacked by the liberals in order to destroy the Connexion's biblical faith. As a

Christian body founded upon revealed truth, the Calvinistic Methodists were duty bound to guard the gospel and preserve the deposit of faith. Yet the present trend within the church was towards subjectivism, doubt, unbelief and heresy: 'Today doctrinal slackness is perceptible in all directions.' The objective authority of scripture was being eroded and the deity of Christ, his atoning sacrifice on the cross and the reality of his resurrection were being widely questioned if not openly rejected. Neither was Nantlais entirely happy with all the prevailing talk of freedom. The freedom which the New Testament mentioned was limited by the bounds of a specific revelation; it was not the freedom to transmute the gospel or to go beyond that which was written. And reminiscent of the constitutional subservience and quietism of the older Methodist tradition, he also doubted the wisdom of the Connexion's tinkering with the law of the land and seeking to be made free from its obligations to the state.

Yet the crux of his opposition to the denomination's reconstruction was not constitutional but doctrinal. Those who seemed most keen to change things were 'supporters of the new school' which had long exerted its influence in places of authority throughout the Connexion, in the seminaries, the ecclesiastical bureaucracy and some of the more fashionable pulpits. Having done their best to seize spiritual power they were now after the temporalities, the right to the Connexion's properties and possessions which were, under the present regime, bound tightly to the 1823 Confession of Faith. 'In fact', he claimed, 'the new school has already taken possession of everything except the right to the properties: and that is the meaning of the present endeavour – a subtle attempt to possess the possessions. Having taken the penny they now want the pennyworth.'[31] And finally he was suspicious of the incipient ecumenism of the present drive. Both the Reconstruction Commission and its principal secretary had emphasized repeatedly the need for denominational co-operation and church unity.[32] By loosening the bonds of the constitution and opening the way to reformulate the Confession of Faith there would be nothing to prevent the Connexion from embracing a church unity which would undercut theological orthodoxy. The present spirit of co-operation neglected traditional formularies in favour of a relativist inclusivism which would ultimately embrace Unitarians, Papists and even those of other faiths. For Nantlais 'the unity of the new

school', were it to ensue, would lead to ecclesiastical amalgamation and a spiritual tyranny which would stifle all dissent. 'In fact',
he claimed again, 'what is being aimed at is the unity of the new
school. In order to achieve this we are told that we must release
ourselves from the Confession of Faith and be freed from the
fathers' vision.'[33]

Nantlais was not at his best as a controversialist. By nature he
was genial and benign, wholly committed to the Connexion and in
this altercation his better judgement was in part clouded by suspicion and fear. Yet the fears he expressed were shared by a not
insignificant body of loyal connexionalists, especially in the
southern Association – it was the south Walians whom D. Francis
Roberts had singled out for specific criticism in his reply to
Saunders Lewis on the matter of dogma – and throughout Wales
as well. Neither were they totally unfounded. Liberalism was
gathering strength apace, diluting orthodox convictions, sometimes sowing dissension, and, in the view of its opponents, sap-
ping spiritual life. If Nantlais's critics like the Revd John Thickens,
minister of the church at Willesden Green in London, accused him
of missing the whole point of the reconstructionalist exercise, it
would have been highly naïve not to have seen the liberal stamp on
at least some aspects of the more recent developments: 'the subject
under discussion at present is not whether the Confession of Faith
should be abolished or changed, rather that the Connexion be
afforded the right to preserve the Confession if it so desires.'[34]
Although not disingenuous, in this matter it was Thickens and
others like him who were naïve, and not the apprehensive and
apparently reactionary pastor from Ammanford. The flurry of
correspondence in the denominational press throughout 1925
illustrates the sensitivities of the Connexion, its hopes and
trepidations, at this critical juncture in its history.

In the meantime debate on both the general propriety of constitutional change and the particular matter of the Confession of
Faith continued. After considerable discussion by both North and
South Wales Associations meeting in late 1923 and early and mid-
1924, the report of the Reconstruction Commission's committee
on church order and organization had been approved, and
thereafter a version of the Declaratory Articles (modelled on those
of the Church of Scotland) which would form the basis of any
Parliamentary Bill was circulated for consideration by the

presbyteries. The Articles' seven paragraphs contained a credal statement which, although much more succinct than the 1823 Confession, was nevertheless more detailed and doctrinally specific than the Shorter Declaration of 1922/3. This was followed by a historical description of the life of the Connexion and the way in which the Confession of Faith functioned as its doctrinal norm; a statement contending that Christ alone and not the state or any secular body is the one head of the church; a further statement making explicit the Connexion's right to change the way in which its faith is expressed though ensuring that all changes would be in accordance with the substance of Christian truth as enshrined in the Confession of Faith; and finally a paragraph committing the church as far as possible to inter-denominational co-operation and unity. Such was the significance of the putative change that the accompanying discussion by the presbyteries was inevitably protracted and slow. By the time the North Wales Association met in Caernarfon in September 1927 twenty-five of its presbyteries had approved the Articles and three were against, while at Treherbert, Rhondda, in April 1928 it was reported that nine of the south Wales presbyteries had affirmed the Articles, though again another three were against. It was against the backdrop of this still rather strained and uncertain situation that a further debate arose which had a direct bearing on social theology, the challenge of the secular and the way in which the Connexion formulated its creed. It was, in all, a curious matter not lacking in notoriety and came to be known as 'the Tom Nefyn controversy'.[35]

'The Tom Nefyn controversy' and its significance

The Revd Thomas Nefyn Williams had been inducted into the pastorate of the Ebenezer Church in the east Carmarthenshire village of Tumble in the autumn of 1926. His own faith had been forged in the heat of the Dardanelles, and before enrolling first at R. B. Jones's fundamentalist Bible school at Porth, Rhondda, and then at the denominational seminaries at Aberystwyth and Bala, he had gained a reputation as an itinerant evangelist of exceptional effectiveness. His first months of settled ministry were accompanied by marked success. He was popular both in the community and among his flock and managed for a time to stem the flow of newly radicalized young men from the church into the secular pursuits of socialist politics. A convinced evangelical before his arrival, his experience of social hardship among the west Wales anthracite miners during the year of the General Strike began to affect his thought and witness deeply. Like many of his contemporaries he tried desperately to bring the gospel to bear upon the secular concerns of the age. He instigated a spectacularly effective housing campaign in the village which led to vast improvements in living conditions being made. There was, however, a touch of theatricality about his ministry, characterized in part by such unconventional behaviour as placing lumps of coal instead of bread on the communion paten and allowing working men to smoke while on chapel premises. It was this rather than any theological disagreement which caused contention within his congregation though it soon became obvious that Williams's doctrinal opinions were undergoing a fundamental upheaval. Following disagreements between the minister and his deaconate, four of Ebenezer's elders resigned and the case was taken before the presbytery's monthly meeting. Thus began a process which would culminate in Williams's highly public suspension from the Calvinistic Methodist ministry and the expulsion of over 200 communicants from membership in the Ebenezer church.

Because Tom Nefyn Williams had refused, according to the erstwhile elders, to adhere to connexional rules, the presbytery transferred his case to the South Wales Association which met at Crickhowell, Brecknock, in June 1927. The association delegated three representatives including Williams's former college principal, Dr Owen Prys, to interview both him and the office-bearers when it transpired that the minister's views were no longer in accord with those of the Connexion as a whole. With his customary wisdom and tact Prys suggested that Williams temporarily withdraw from his pastoral responsibilities in order to reflect upon his ministry and the content of his faith. He had a high opinion of his former student's integrity and every confidence that, after due consideration, he would be in a position to accept the substance if not the wording of the Confession of Faith and return to his pastorate with a renewed social and evangelistic resolve. Williams, though, would have none of it, and in a letter to the South Wales Association meeting in London in October 1927 he demanded that the connexional authorities deliberate on the content of his creed and, were it to be found wanting, exercise ecclesiastical discipline. In order to assist them in the task he published a forty-page résumé of his current views entitled *Y Ffordd yr Edrychaf ar Bethau* ('The Way I Look at Things'). On perusal of the pamphlet Dr Owen Prys's heart must have sunk. Apart from some interesting, if eccentric, observations on the sacraments and the nature of Christian ministry in the contemporary world, Williams insisted on expounding points of doctrine. He was no theologian and this, in fact, would prove his undoing. The basic category for the understanding of God's relation with his world, he claimed, was one of immanence. No longer over and above creation as its redeemer and Lord, God was the force within creation which energized the evolutionary process. Neither was He the inter-personal Father, Son and Holy Spirit of classical trinitarianism: 'To speak of three Persons in the Godhead means sacrificing true unity', he claimed: 'We must, therefore, reject the notions of three persons in God.' Williams much preferred to describe God in nonpersonal terms like Creative Mind and Eternal Mind. The fact that God was inherent in the evolutionary scheme had rendered the supernatural redundant. 'Fact and fancy are often intertwined in the New Testament', and in the light of modern notions of physical laws and progress it was 'incredible' to think of Christ's miracles as being literally true. Christ's deity had given place to his unique sense of the divine which was defined in turn as an example of perfect humanity. Man shared this potentiality for human perfection in virtue of the divine nature which he too had inherited. Its plenitude would be experienced to the degree which men and women strived to overcome their own imperfections and experience unclouded fellowship with God. The resurrection, he claimed, is a metaphor for this unbroken harmony, it was the disciples' 'early method of declaring the victory and lasting value of Christ's personality, . . . it was a Jewish way of emphasising the conquest of life and goodness of Jesus over sin and destruction'.[36] It was quite obvious that this one-time near-fundamentalist had become a modernist of the most advanced kind. What is more he demanded to be judged not on the content of his social ministry among the needy of the Gwendraeth Valley nor on his zeal for the application of Christianity to everyday life but on his definition of the faith.[37] It was a foolhardy (if brave) venture in which the young and flamboyant minister from Tumble was bound to come to grief.

The connexional committee which had been convened to consider the affair made its report to the Treherbert Association in April 1928. Owen Prys, whose hands had been tied by the treatise *Y Ffordd yr Edrychaf ar Bethau*, had no choice but to list his former student's heresies. After having interviewed Williams it was apparent that he no longer held to the doctrines of the trinity, the incarnation, the deity of Christ, the atonement nor the concept of salvation in any recognizable form. What is interesting in light of the current controversy surrounding the constitution was that Prys did not fault him for failing to adhere to the letter of the Confession of Faith but stated that his views were 'fundamentally opposed to the standards of our Connexion and to the historical faith of the Christian Church'.[38] Yet the principal, far from relishing his position as doctrinal prosecutor, wished to interpret Williams's theology in as positive a way as was possible and to allow him an opportunity to defend himself before his brethren. But first the pamphlet would have to be retracted. Its contents were clearly irreconcilable both with the faith of the Calvinistic Methodists and that of the church catholic. Williams, whom the Association had treated with consideration, respect and sympathy throughout, was given a further year to respond to its deliberations: 'Should Mr Williams find himself unable to conform with our standards by that time it is expected that he will resign.'

It was with an impending sense of drama if not of doom that delegates attended the Nantgaredig Association in August 1929. Williams had already responded to the Treherbert decision by tending his resignation as minister of the Ebenezer congregation. 'It is evident that antiquated theological forms are considered more important than a forward-looking humanity', he wrote in his letter of withdrawal. His congregation responded by refusing outright to accept their pastor's resignation and resolving to stand by him come what may. Already their hero, he was about to become their martyr as well. At Nantgaredig he was asked by the moderator, the Revd Peter Hughes Griffiths, whether his views were now in accord with the Connexion's standards of faith. He inquired what exactly those standards were? Refusing to be drawn on this question, the moderator repeated the previous year's stipulation which required Williams to resign from the

Connexion's ministry (and not merely that of the local church in Tumble) if he was no longer in agreement with its creed, whereupon Williams replied that he repudiated the Treherbert decision and he would not willingly withdraw from ministry within the denomination as a whole. By now the tension had reached breaking point. It was then that Owen Prys, with all the gravity at his disposal, proposed: 'That we confirm the resolution which was passed at the Treherbert Association, and that, until the Rev. Nefyn Williams is enabled to conform to our standards, he be suspended from the work of the ministry in our midst as a Connexion.' It was passed almost unanimously. With sadness but obvious determination (and highly conscious of the media interest which the controversy had generated), the Association suspended Williams from serving in any capacity within the Connexion's churches. He was not formally excommunicated and neither did he lose his ministerial accreditation, but until he recanted of his errant beliefs and promised to uphold the Connexion's doctrines and abide by its rules, he was effectively barred from its pulpits.

Tom Nefyn returned to Tumble little knowing what the future held in store. He was by now exceedingly well known (if not notorious) throughout south Wales and sought after as a preacher, lecturer and speaker on political as well as religious matters. Rather than being dented, his reputation had been enhanced by the publicity he had received. He received more than one call to settle in pastorates outside his own denomination where he would be free from connexional rules and the requirements of a formal confession of faith. He had been allowed by the Association to remain at Ebenezer on the understanding that he concluded his ministry there on 9 September. Such was the size of the congregation for the final evening service that worship had to be conducted in the open air. Thousands attended in order to witness and partake of what was a very emotional and dramatic farewell. Yet the controversy was far from over. After the initial resignation of Ebenezer's four elders and a few other communicants who had been unhappy with the direction of his ministry two years before, the winsome and charismatic Williams had received almost total support from his flock. Before the Treherbert gathering the five remaining elders and 215 members had each put their names to a resolution that 'the attitude of the Association toward Tom Nefyn will decide the future attitude of the undersigned towards Welsh

[Calvinistic] Methodism'.[39] Their determination to follow their pastor and, if necessary, share in his suffering had made some of them contemptuous of the Connexion, its doctrinal standards, regulations and mores. The attitude of the church to connexional discipline was discussed at the local presbytery meeting on 2 October and it was decided, drastically perhaps, that the Ebenezer fellowship be dissolved. On the morning of Sunday 7 October the members found themselves locked out of their chapel building and were told by presbytery officials that they had all been ex-communicated. Those who were willing to sign the Confession of Faith and abide by the Connexion's rules would be received back into membership and the church would be established once more. Not surprisingly the excommunicants preferred to make their own arrangements. Within days they had established an independent congregation free of denominational attachment and unshackled by any confession of faith which would be open to all who were honest in their search for truth. After securing land for a new meeting house, this would become 'Llain y Delyn', home to the Tumble Christian Fellowship.[40] Although present in its opening services, by the time it was fully established Tom Nefyn Williams and his wife had returned to their native north Wales where (inexplicably for many), in March 1931, he would be received back into membership of the Calvinistic Methodist Church and within a year be reinstated into its pastoral ministry.

This curious and, for those who had remained loyal to him in Tumble, bitterly disappointing *volte face* was never explained satisfactorily,[41] especially as he would have been required to assent specifically to the Confession of Faith. It added to the mystique which would always be attached to the name of Tom Nefyn, though the man himself receded to comparative obscurity, spending the rest of his life fulfilling a conventional pastoral and evangelistic ministry among the quarryfolk and farmers of Gwynedd. The significance of his tortuous development, his relationship with ecclesiastical authority and the church's response to the challenge he posed was difficult to fathom at the time yet it encapsulated perfectly the spirit of the 1920s: doctrinal turmoil, the appeal of a 'practical' Christianity over and against official creeds, the question of orthodoxy, tolerance, and how to apply an ancient faith to a rapidly changing world, all of which occurred against the background of the industrial and economic strife. In

Tom Nefyn connexional radicals found an undoubted champion.[42] He was, though, much too intellectually unstable and spiritually restless to provide a lasting focus for a liberal rejuvenation within the denomination. Ultimately the Tom Nefyn controversy was a diversion rather than a turning-point in the history of Welsh Christianity during the inter-war years.

The future and status of the Confession of Faith

While the drama in the Gwendraeth Valley was drawing to its conclusion, the seemingly interminable move to complete the Connexion's constitutional transition rolled wearily along. Minor changes to the Declaratory Articles were still being made and following the spring Associations of 1930, the one in Wrexham and the other at Borth near Aberystwyth, it was decided to press ahead with the preparation of a draft Parliamentary Bill for further perusal by the presbyteries. Nantlais Williams, by now cast rather unwillingly in the role of the conservatives' champion, still held out against change. The sticking point remained the detail contained in the credal statement which formed the basis of the Declaratory Articles and Parliamentary Bill. Whereas E. O. Davies was happy with the loosely trinitarian formula used by the Church of Scotland, Nantlais was adamant that, in order to preserve the substance of the 1823 Confession, references to the virgin birth, the substitutionary character of Christ's atonement, his resurrection (which was not mentioned at all) and his coming again in glory would have to be included. Taking time off during the Connexion's General Assembly meetings in 1931, the Reconstruction Commission's principal administrator did his best to convince Nantlais of the doctrinal soundness of the Declaratory Articles without the additions which he (Nantlais) was so keen to include. 'Dr E. O. Davies tried to persuade me that not *all* these truths were essential though he himself professed to believe them fully', wrote Nantlais years later. 'We departed the best of friends. Indeed I felt him to be a true friend of mine, and a gentleman, throughout the years.'[43] Although they represented a minority view, the conservatives' support would be vital as unanimity was demanded in order for the process to be deemed valid in the eyes of the law. As one gentleman to another Davies was confident that, when the time came, even Nantlais could be prevailed upon to support the measure as it stood. What he had not bargained for was some heavyweight opposition from an unexpected quarter.

Discussion of the second draft of the Parliamentary Bill continued into the following spring with Nantlais as the only sectionally influential connexional leader courteously but tenaciously refusing to yield an inch. Then, much to observers' surprise, powerful figures including Ellis W. Davies, a church elder and barrister who was Caernarfonshire's MP, and two former Association presidents and moderators of the denomination's General Assembly, the Revds Peter Hughes Griffiths and R. R. Roberts, took up the cause on the conservatives' behalf. Sensing that at this late juncture the whole constitutional process was in danger of being derailed, E. O. Davies urgently convened a private meeting at Shrewsbury and invited each of the men to attend. The outcome was that references to the virgin birth, the substitutionary atonement, the resurrection and the second coming of Christ were included in the draft bill which was to be finally ratified at both Associations during the coming autumn. 'This changed the whole course of the conflict', reminisced Nantlais. 'I no longer felt any opposition to the Parliamentary Bill which would release us from the Confession of Faith.'[44] From then on the current ran swiftly. During the autumn of 1932 both associations approved the measure without demur with Ellis Davies proposing its acceptance at Caernarfon and R. R. Williams, seconded by Peter Hughes Griffiths, doing likewise in the south Wales gathering at Cardiff. 'Our freedom to understand these central doctrines more fully will not be curtailed', moved Roberts, 'nor our right to interpret them according to the promise of the Holy Spirit who will guide us to all truth.'[45]

Although this development was not devoid of ambiguities, it was nevertheless a clear victory for the conservatives. If Nantlais and others could now endorse connexional policy more or less to the full, varying degrees of liberalism remained so entrenched in denominational life that everyone knew that they would never be dislodged. The Tom Nefyn controversy had shown how messy disciplinary measures based on strict fidelity to doctrinal standards could be, while the continuing affirmation of the 1823 Confession of Faith (duly domesticated as a historical document) by all shades of opinion virtually legitimized theological pluralism within the Connexion. George M. Ll. Davies's ordination by the North Wales Association a few years earlier on the basis of his acceptance of the Shorter Declaration typified the continuing connexional view even after 1933. Davies, who had rejected formal Christianity soon after the First World War in favour of a spiritualized Jesus-centred humanitarianism, had been enticed back to church membership primarily by Dr E. O. Davies. Feeling called to the pastoral ministry he was ordained by the Rhosllan-nerchrugog Association in 1927 despite having made it known that he could accept neither the Confession of Faith (the virgin birth and doctrine of the atonement he found particularly problematic) nor the final authority of Scripture.[46] By the mid-1930s he had left the Connexion once more and for the rest of his troubled life he made his spiritual home among the Quakers. Yet the desire to allow full membership to all who could pledge their allegiance to Christianity no matter how widely it was construed, and to ordain elders, preachers and ministers on the basis of the Shorter Declaration rather than the Declaratory Articles or the Confession of Faith, remained widespread throughout the denomination. The Parliamentary Act finally became law in July 1933[47] which, to the relief of all, marked the virtual cessation of theological hostilities. For the remainder of the decade Welsh Presbyterians were content to confess the faith of their church according to a variety of inter-pretations, though the increasingly alarming international situa-tion drew their attention from internal matters to those that were brewing abroad. Twelve momentous years later in the history of Europe and of its Christian faith, the Revd Gomer M. Roberts noted the changes which had occurred in the Connexion's life: 'By today', he wrote, 'it can hardly be said that the great body of our members are very interested in doctrinal matters.'[48]

The voice of Karl Barth

It was not only the Calvinistic Methodists who were exercised with redefining the nature of the faith during these years. By the eve of the First World War Protestant modernism had affected to varying degrees each of the main Nonconformist denominations and none more so than the Independents. In fact liberal theology was rapidly becoming the received orthodoxy among the younger (and some of the not so young) leaders of Welsh Congrega-tionalism.[49] Liberalism of a most pronounced kind had already been introduced into Congregational circles by the Revd David Adams (1845–1923), minister at Hawen and Bryngwenith, Cardiganshire, and latterly at Grove Street, Liverpool, who, by 1913, 'had graduated from being a heretic into one of the denomination's oracles'.[50] By the 1920s what had been an aberration was fast becoming the norm with such distinguished preachers as the Revds Dyfnallt Owen, T. Eirug Davies, R. J. Jones and W. T. Gruffydd and seminary professors of the calibre of Thomas Rees and John Morgan Jones (Bala-Bangor), Thomas Lewis and D. Miall Edwards (Brecon), and J. Oliver Stephens (Carmarthen), staunch and unrepentant modernists. The sover-eignty of each local congregation and the fact that the denomina-tion was not legally bound to any specific confession of faith ensured that this far-reaching doctrinal shift did not engender nearly as much controversy as that which affected the Presbyter-ians. Yet not all Welsh Congregationalist leaders shared in this penchant for theological change and there remained a solid phalanx of ordinary church members who were faithful to the evangelical faith in which they had been nurtured and who found contemporary trends perplexing and disconcerting. There is little doubt, however, that during the inter-war years liberalism had replaced Calvinism as the accepted creed of the Welsh Independ-ents.

The most eloquent scholarly expression of liberal theology to appear during these years came from the pen of a Congrega-tionalist divine, Professor D. Miall Edwards of the Memorial College in Brecon. *Bannau'r Ffydd* ('The Pinnacles of Faith') was a 390-page systematic theology which distilled the essence of liberalism in a most attractive manner. What the 1926 *Geiriadur Beiblaidd* did for biblical studies, Edwards's *Bannau* attempted in the field of doctrine. The author marked out his ground rules clearly at the beginning. 'The mind of the present age is very cautious and unsure', he claimed, 'its spirit is restless, inquisitive, groping in the dark.' Whereas the authoritative status of all dogmatic assertions was being routinely rejected especially by the young, for most people the absolute truth of 'the scientific mind' (including the theory of evolution) had become a virtual axiom. The challenge for the Christian church was to reformulate the faith in such a way as to respond to the values of contemporary culture. 'On the whole', he continued, 'I believe it is a blessing to have discarded the crutches of authority in order that we should learn to walk on our own two feet as free spiritual beings.' The present need, he asserted, was not for 'a comfortable, infallible creed like a pillow to sleep on . . . but an adventurous, militant, personal faith, ever ready to learn afresh in the school of experience'.[51] The yard-stick by which faith was to be measured was experience, the believer's experience of the spiritual on the pattern of Jesus of Nazareth's experience of God as Father.

Rather than beginning with God in the manner of the older dogmatics, Edwards began with an analysis of humankind's spiritual experience, moving, logically, to the doctrines of salvation, the person of Christ and only finally to the doctrine of God and the trinity. In fact he turned classical orthodoxy on its head, the standard being not divine revelation but human experience. According to this scheme, Christianity was not about the formulation of objective or propositional truth but about experiencing the divine: 'It is apparent that we are working on the assumption that experience is the key to doctrine';[52] it followed, therefore, that Jesus' importance lay in the unique quality of his spiritual experience. In fact he was 'the first Christian', 'Christ is the principal expert that we have ever had in the realm of the spiritual. He is the chief authority today as ever in the knowledge and the experience of God.'[53] Far from being objectively true, each of the traditional formulations concerning Christ's person and his work, his divine pre-existence and the virgin birth, his sinless perfection and the miraculous quality of his public ministry, his sacrificial death as an atonement for sin, his resurrection, ascension and coming again in glory, expressed the church's doctrinal response to the spiritual impact he had made on his followers. Whereas theology in the past had formulated its faith according to the categories of its own age, the present challenge was to express the ongoing experience of God's fatherhood as exemplified by Christ according to the categories of the modern, scientific world. Doctrines such as the trinity (one God in three Persons) and Christology (two natures in the one Person of Christ) need no longer be normative for contemporary faith: 'I see no reason at all why we should consider ourselves restricted to the verdict of the Council of Nicaea (325 AD), the Council of Chalcedon (451 AD) or the Council of Constantinople (680 AD) on this important matter, though they claimed to speak the final word in the name of the whole Church.'[54] In fact such formulations had been rendered impossible according to the rules of contemporary thought. What was left was Jesus of Nazareth and his experience of the divine. Unlike many of his contemporaries, though, Edwards was too honest a thinker to avoid the implications of his reasoning. Every single aspect of classical orthodoxy would have to be rejected including, in the end, Christ's objective uniqueness. 'If in the future "evolution" produces one whose authority in the realm of the spiritual is higher than Jesus Christ, I would be obliged to pledge my most absolute loyalty to him.'[55]

Such was the blithe confidence of liberalism by the late 1920s that Edwards could forward these views with little sense of incongruity or fear of being contradicted or even challenged by any of his peers. Yet there were Congregationalist theologians of substance – Keri Evans in Carmarthen and Vernon Lewis, at the time a pastor in Brynaman – whose views were diametrically opposed to his. It was neither of these but J. E. Daniel, the twenty-eight-year-old professor of Christian doctrine at Bala-Bangor, who responded to Edwards's volume with most verve and by so doing marked virtually a new chapter in the development of theology in Wales. In an extended review in the Welsh Student Christian Movement's magazine *Yr Efrydydd*, he mounted what was by any reckoning a devastating critique of his colleague's work. Every single thesis which Edwards forwarded he rejected outright: the axiomatic status of the 'scientific mind', the use of experience as the sole criterion for religious truth and the attempt to begin theological reflection on the basis of human perception rather than with God's revelation of himself as Father, Son and Holy Spirit. For Daniel this was not theology but anthropology. In an understandable though wholly misguided attempt at contemporary relevance, what the Brecon professor had done was to shear God of his radical otherness and make Him a virtual projection of the religious spirit of humankind. A flood-tide of doctrinal romanticism was attempting to wash away the citadel of objective faith. In an amusing change of metaphor (all the more risqué given the teetotal predilections of contemporary Nonconformity) he wrote, 'A man may get drunk on gin and soda, brandy and soda or whisky and soda, but it's not the soda which will have inebriated him!' Experience is fine, but men and women are not saved in virtue of their religious experience, however delectable, but solely by faith. By such an emphasis on man's experience of the divine, man himself had been made divine. There was little wonder that such ideas 'had led to the theological and spiritual bankruptcy of Protestantism'.[56]

Having disposed of Edwards's initial presuppositions, Daniel proceeded to deal with specifics, especially the doctrines of Christ's person and his work. If Jesus of Nazareth was no more than a spirit-filled or God-intoxicated man, different in degree though not in kind from all other religious individuals, anything resembling an objective salvation would be rendered impossible: 'The Modernists' Christ could not perform an objective redemption even if they believed such a thing existed.' Yet humankind's spiritual dilemma was such that this redemption was essential in order to reconcile him to God. God and man were not one: God was God, the Creator and transcendent Lord; man was man, finite and sinful to boot. Man could never arrive at a saving knowledge of God through his own striving, far less through the quality of his spiritual quest. Man's guilt was a metaphysical fact which needed to be assuaged. His need was not for an example – an 'expert . . . in the realm of the spiritual' – but a saviour who was actually divine. 'For me atonement is something which has been wrought for us, independently, a fountain opened *before* we drink from its waters.' Despite its pious talk of Jesus' fellowship with the Father and his experience of the divine, what liberal theology did, claimed Daniel, was to posit an unbridgable ontological gap between the Father and the Son thus rendering salvation impossible. On the basis of Edwards's theology the church could no longer claim that *God* in Christ had reconciled the world to himself. Despite its elegance, attractiveness, and undoubted appeal, this was in fact a theology of despair. For the sake of its present doctrinal integrity and its future spiritual health, Nonconformity should 'with the undivided tradition of the Church, reject the concept of experience and return once more in the concept of revelation'. What was needed was a restatement of classic orthodoxy according to a rejuvenated theology of the Word of God.[57]

Following this *tour de force* it was obvious that Congregationalism's modernists were not going to have it all their own way.

What was significant about Daniel's critique was not only its incisiveness but its indebtedness to the thought of the Swiss theologian Karl Barth. Vernon Lewis had already alerted his fellow Nonconformists to the immense impact which Barth was currently making on continental Protestantism[58] but it was Daniel who made Barth's spirited anti-liberal polemic his own. Unknown to him, Daniel's critique of Miall Edwards was strikingly reminiscent of Barth's own confrontation with Adolf Harnack, the doyen of Germany's liberal theologians, six years previously.[59] The ideals of Harnack, the friend and mentor (as it happened) of John Morgan Jones, Daniel's colleague and by then the principal of Bala-Bangor, were all-pervasive among senior Congregationalist theologians and there was little sign of their popularity and influence abating. Traditional conservative evangelicalism was pre-critical, inward-looking, and pietistic; it possessed no leaders of first-rate doctrinal ability and was powerless to meet the intellectual challenge which the most scholarly of the liberals posed. Its literalist biblicism and reactionary mind-cast had little appeal for inter-war Christians (except in some parts of the industrialized south). Yet there was a latent sense of unease with the prevailing liberal consensus. It was left to a younger generation of continental Protestants led by Barth, Emil Brunner and Rudolf Bultmann to rediscover the concept of revelation and reformulate it in a contemporary guise.

What the 'crisis theologians' had been doing in Europe, Daniel attempted in the Welsh context: he sought to place popular Christianity under the searing judgement of the Word of God. His growing reputation as a theological *enfant terrible* was compounded a year later when he addressed the annual conference of the Union of Welsh Independents on the topic of the Church. His paper, 'The Church of Christ Essential for the Gospel of Christ', was a direct rebuttal of Professor W. J. Gruffydd's 'A Layman's Ideas on the Church' given two years previously. For Gruffydd the concept of the church was hardly necessary at all. Christ had preached universal brotherhood and the coming of the Kingdom which he interpreted as the forward march of humankind towards perfection. At best the church was a chance collection of earnest souls bound together for mutual encouragement, at worst an active impediment to the aims of Christ. In any case it was a dispensable extra and real Christianity was as likely to be found outside its structures as within. No matter how radically these ideas departed from the high ecclesiology of classic Independency, the fact that Gruffydd's address elicited such a rousing response among delegates indicated how far Welsh Congregationalism had drifted from its theological moorings.[60]

In the same incisive fashion as before, Daniel proceeded to demolish this myth as well. Reflecting the views of Schweitzer and Weiss, the Kingdom, he claimed, was an apocalyptic concept, vouchsafed by God for the end of time. It was not a moral ideal, something towards which men and women could strive. Rather it was only God's to give according to his sovereign design. As for the church, it was the creation of God's Word through the Holy Spirit. It was a divine, supernatural community brought forth by the proclamation of the gospel. Its essence was unique. It existed not so much to serve humankind (though this was indeed part of its function) but to bear witness to the mighty acts of God in Christ. Entry into its fellowship was only possible by the miracle of regeneration. 'The Gospel', claimed Daniel, 'needs an institutional form and it is only self-deception or hypocrisy which underlie the profession so common today that there is just as much religion on the golf-links as there is in chapel.'[61] The interest this short address generated was considerable. For nearly three months the correspondence columns of the Congregationalists' weekly *Y Tyst* were filled with a plethora of conflicting responses, some puzzled, others approving, many mystified and still more wholly repudiating Daniel's thesis. 'The heartfelt instinct of many of us, under the definite teaching of our childhood and youth, is that this is where the emphasis should lie', wrote the Revd Arthur Jones, Ystalyfera. 'The paper will have done a singular service if it were just to check the speed in which we have been travelling along these extreme and dangerous paths.'[62] Conversely, in a series of articles the Revd James Evans, Saundersfoot, claimed: 'If this paper was meant to be a counterblast to the Machynlleth address, it has failed miserably.' If enlightened Protestantism were to prevail in modern Wales he argued, its docetism, its Paulinism and its outdated ecclesio-centrism would have to be rejected at all costs.[63]

As the 1930s progressed doubts about the validity of the prevailing liberalism would steadily gather pace. J. E. Daniel's critique of theological modernism within his own denomination would be echoed elsewhere and a younger generation of Nonconformist ordinands and ministers began to be drawn to 'the strange new world of the Bible' and its unfamiliar emphases on the transcendence of God and his sovereign, gracious condescension in Christ, the divine redeemer.[64] The liberal reply was vehement: 'At the moment we are in the midst of a reaction (short-lived, I hope) against all the late nineteenth century movements towards enlightenment', retorted John Morgan Jones, Daniel's colleague at Bala-Bangor. 'We are being called back to a uniform, medieval system in politics and theology. In my opinion this is nothing but panic, the attempt to erect a buttress of sand against the rush of the incoming tide.'[65] The tide, in fact, was flowing in the other direction and before long it would be James Evans, John Morgan Jones and others who would be on the defensive while the rising generation of Nonconformist preachers would find hope and inspiration from the renewal of neo-Calvinist orthodoxy.

Evangelical entrenchment and the fundamentalist impulse

There were evangelicals in all the churches who, though standing squarely on the essentials of biblical faith, were none the less committed to their own denominational traditions. There were others who sat very loosely to traditional structures and whose loyalty was to one another and to their own particular interpretation of Christian truth. They tended to be (sometimes highly) suspicious of the institutional church and, especially during the early inter-war years, progressively assertive in their defence of evangelical Christianity. The most forceful personality among them was the Revd Rhys Bevan Jones, a native of Dowlais and minister of the Baptist churches at Ainon, Ynys-hir (1904–19), and Tabernacle, Porth (1919–33), both in the Rhondda. Like Nantlais Williams, 'R.B.' was a smooth-talking popular preacher whom the 1904–5 Revival had transformed, in his case into a craggy prophet of the divine wrath. Unlike Nantlais, he chose not to contend for evangelical truth within the existing structures (though he never, in fact, repudiated his Baptist affiliation) but worked principally through a network of conventions, campaigns and non-denominational missions. He represented not just evangelical Christianity as a conservative force but a Christianity which was reactionary in its primitivism and harsh in its denunciations. The conservative evangelicals' chief platform during these years was the monthly magazine *Yr Efengylydd* ('The Evangelist') jointly edited by Nantlais and R. B. Jones, and their main focus for teaching and fellowship was the annual Llandrindod Convention, 'the Keswick of Wales'.[66] The influence of American fundamentalism was patent in both.

The series of booklets *The Fundamentals* (1910–15) had served as a rallying point for conservatively minded American Christians who believed that liberal theology was threatening the vitality of the Protestant churches. Although scholarly, sound and respectably orthodox, they soon became equated with a belligerent attitude to all aspects of secular culture and thought. By the early 1920s fundamentalism's militant temper and its polemical defence of biblical inerrancy was being replicated in south Wales, and the more dizzy the rate of change in society and the church, the more uncompromising and reactionary its stance became. Along with an unshakeable faith in biblical infallibility, the deity of Christ including his omniscience and omnipotence (which confirmed the Davidic authorship of the Psalms, the single authorship of Isaiah as well as his virgin birth and the veracity of the miracles), and the substitutionary nature of the atonement, Welsh fundamentalism was resolute in its literalistic interpretation of scripture (a six-day creation, Adam and Eve and the serpent, the historicity of the Book of Jonah), a Keswick-type holiness doctrine and dispensationalist eschatology.[67] No matter how wooden and unimaginative, the literalism was an understandable response to the tendencies within much mainline teaching which seemed to be undermining the trustworthy nature of scripture as the Word of God. The holiness teaching was also a reaction to the apparently low level of personal sanctity prevalent among members of the visible church. 'Full consecration' or 'victorious Christian living' had been a hallmark of Protestant pietism since the late Victorian era, and not only did it stress the need for an experience of the renewing power of the Holy Spirit but it guaranteed that such an experience was attainable, subsequent to conversion, by all. 'All that believers can do is discard what God has already slain', claimed R. B. Jones. 'In daily experience he casts away his old nature which God has doomed. By the power of the Cross the whole body of flesh – the inclination, habits and desires – can be deprived of power to obstruct the Holy Spirit.'[68] For those who had experienced a vision of God's holiness during the 1904–5 Revival and who longed for a deepening of their spiritual lives, the promise of a further baptism of the Holy Spirit had undoubted appeal. The concept of 'full surrender' became an additional badge of identification among those who would have no truck with a worldly or carnal church.

Dispensationalist teaching was equally novel and served to particularize further Welsh fundamentalists during these years. According to the dispensationalist reading of biblical apocalyptic (Daniel, Mark 13, 1 and 2 Thessalonians and Revelation) Christ would return to earth in person before the millennium in order to inaugurate the resurrection of the saints and their rapture to glory. Far from being a merely speculative abstraction, this premillennialism had a practical effect on the attitudes and practices of those who held to it. Among the signs of the Lord's imminent advent would be lawlessness, tribulation and social unrest in the secular realm and the apostasy of the visible church. Social amelioration would be pointless; it betokened an unspiritual emphasis on the well-being of the flesh over the immortal destiny of the soul. The task of the church was the winning of individuals to Christ in the short time available before his coming again in judgement. Intimations of doom were in plentiful supply during the inter-war years: the distressing social situation in the south Wales valleys, labour unrest, political upheaval, talk of class warfare and the like. For some millennialists the 1917 Bolshevik uprising in Russia had been prophesied in the Book of Daniel and Revelation and was another sign that the end of the world was at hand. R. B. Jones was convinced that south Wales and the country at large were sliding into anarchy, and that the secularism and spiritual declension which he witnessed all around was a prelude to the second coming and as such part of God's sovereign plan. He was unsparing in his criticism of worldliness: smoking, gambling, the cinema, and he was suspicious of the League of Nations, believing its pretensions to be at best naïve and at worst Satanic. In the course of an exposition of 2 Thessalonians he interpreted the 'Man of lawlessness' as a combination of the higher criticism, cubism, radical politics and jazz music.[69] His most pointed criticisms, though, were reserved for the church. 'It is wholly clear', he wrote in his commentary on the Epistles to the Thessalonians (the first and only exposition of premillennialism in Welsh), 'that Paul expected the visible church to finish its course as Israel did of old, in apostasy; that is, a rejection of the Christ of New Testament Christianity.' The signs of this apostasy were manifest: 'Virtually all the periodicals, seminaries and official positions of the denominations are in the hands of those who mock the infallible authority of the Bible and the supernatural conception, atonement and resurrection of Christ.'[70] Premillennialist eschatology, so characteristic of contemporary American fundamentalism, provided R. B. Jones with a key to interpret the gloomy state of church and society in the south Wales of the 1920s.

As well as providing a lead for the more extreme among conservative evangelicals in south Wales,[71] during the 1920s R. B. Jones spent more and more time among fundamentalist fire-brands in England and the United States. During a preaching tour in Pennsylvania he was referred to as 'the Welsh Billy Sunday' and he returned to Porth enthusiastic to instigate vast American-style rallies in his church. Among those whom he invited to his monthly Bible conferences were the separatist Baptist leader T. T. Shields from Toronto, W. B. Riley, the initiator of the World Christian Fundamentalists Association, and the scholarly J. Gresham Machen who was later to secede from Princeton Seminary to form the theologically more sound Westminster Seminary in Phila-delphia. Both the South Wales Bible Training Institute, based initially in his chapel vestry in Ainon, Ynys-hir, before transferring to Tynycymmer Hall in Porth, and the Bible College of Wales, established in Derwen Fawr, Swansea, in 1924 by Rees Howells (another highly idiosyncratic Welsh evangelical much influenced by transatlantic fundamentalism), were inspired by the American example of fundamentalist Bible schools, the Moody Institute in Chicago most of all.[72] What with the capitulation of denomina-tional colleges to the prevailing liberalism, there was no choice but to establish fresh seminaries where the Word of God would be honoured and ministerial training provided in accordance with the genuine spiritual needs of the saints. It was a separatist ideal wholly in accordance with the mores of contemporary fund-amentalism.

The pages of *Yr Efengylydd* were redolent with a sincere though narrow pietism which saw sin exclusively in terms of personal shortcomings, usually of the flesh, and was highly dubious of anything resembling a social gospel. Testimonies to conversion gave the impression that the new life in Christ was a matter of rejecting football, the theatre and politics as though they all belonged to the kingdom of Satan.[73] Speaking from Psalm 139, 'Search me O Lord', at the Llandrindod Convention during the mid-1920s, Dr Charles Inwood, an Irish Methodist pietist, listed self-abuse and adultery, theatre-going and dancing, card-playing and smoking, strife-making and tale-bearing, self-made plans and the breaking of vows to the Lord as things which quenched the Spirit.[74] One student at Rees Howells's Bible College of Wales was summarily expelled for having the temerity to ask permission to compete in a local eisteddfod.[75] Worldliness and sin were interpreted in exceedingly narrow terms which left the most intractable problems of human motivation virtually undisturbed and the structures of society intact. Yet there is no doubt that piety of this type made a genuine appeal and that there were thousands of men and women, mostly in the south Wales valleys, who found its virtues satisfying and its teaching ennobling. At its best it produced winsome Christian believers whose personal testimony to the redeeming power of the gospel was salutary and authentic.

Yet the manifest weaknesses of fundamentalism – its censoriousness, its theological naïvety and often serious lack of balance – militated against it ever becoming an adequate interpretation of the evangelical faith. Whereas Nantlais Williams's rootedness in mainstream Nonconformity and his doggedly persistent loyalty to the Calvinistic Methodist Connexion helped him preserve a sense of wholeness and proportion, R. B. Jones became more and more alienated from the main body of Welsh Christianity. No longer at home in a fast secularizing world, he took to denouncing it and laid the blame for change squarely at the feet of the preachers. Whereas he could declare in 1919 'that the Baptist Churches of Wales are solid for orthodoxy', such was his disillusionment a decade later that he spoke of 'the wholesale abandonment by the Welsh pulpit of evangelical belief'.[76] The standard of perfection that he demanded from his flock – many of whom idolized him – was so high that by 1929 dissension within his own congregation had become inevitable and when he died in 1933 his ecclesiastical isolation was almost total.[77] Yet there is no doubt that he personified, for many, all that was heroic in the church militant. For all his limitations he remains a figure of significance in the history of Christianity in twentieth-century Wales.

If fundamentalism was gaining a hearing in the churches, the 1920s also witnessed the beginnings of an explicitly conservative Christian grouping among the students of the University of Wales. With the liberal drift it was timely and inevitable that some within the student community would take a stand for the fact that 'Christ died for our sins according to the scriptures' and the need for the appropriation of that message through costly repentance and personal faith. Burdened by the conviction that 'God requires not men *interested* in religion, but men who *know* Jesus Christ as Saviour and Lord', D. J. Thomas, an earnest young man from Brynaman, posted notices throughout the University College of South Wales and Monmouthshire at Cardiff inviting 'those who know that their sins are forgiven and have thus accepted the Lord Jesus Christ as their own personal Saviour' to contact him.[78] Seven did so, and in a prayer meeting convened on 12 January 1923 the Cardiff Evangelical Union was formed.

Beginning in Cambridge in 1910, then in Oxford, London, Bristol, Edinburgh and Glasgow, evangelical believers had separated from their universities' principal religious body, the increasingly liberal-dominated Student Christian Movement (SCM), in order to preserve the integrity of the biblical gospel. Since 1919 representatives from the new grouping had met annually at what they called the Inter-Varsity Conference,[79] and during the Easter vacation 1923 they were joined by D. J. Thomas, the secretary of the Cardiff Union. By the 1923–4 session the Union had expanded to twenty, and in an article in *Yr Efengylydd* its president, T. G. Thomas, explained its *raison d'être* as a separate religious grouping:

> There was, and still is in our midst, a movement known as 'the Student Christian Movement' but (and we say this quite charitably) it was found, that, owing to its attitude and outlook upon certain truths, it did not meet the needs felt adequately, and, that whilst appreciating that there are amongst its members those whom we respect for their integrity and motives, it was found to become clearer and clearer that a basis for co-operation could not be found.[80]

The formation of the Evangelical Union in opposition to the SCM both reflected the growing rift between liberal and conservative within the churches and perpetuated what would be a permanent and significant division of Christian life within twentieth-century Wales: the contracting out of conservative evangelicals from wider Christian communion and, in many cases, the main structures of denominational life as well. It was not, principally, a matter of ideological fundamentalism (though the influence of Keswick and R. B. Jones on that whole generation of south Wales evangelicals can hardly be denied), but of a deep conviction concerning the nature of revealed truth and the need for spiritual fellowship which would edify young and sensitive believers rather than sow the seeds of doubt. By 1930 three of the four University colleges – Cardiff, Aberystwyth and Swansea – possessed Evangelical Unions, and although the Swansea grouping preserved its links initially with the SCM, they all became fully integrated with British Fellowship of Evangelical Unions and, following its establishment in 1928, with the Inter-Varsity Fellowship (IVF). Just as fundamentalism was regarded somewhat as an American phenomenon, the presence of such IVF luminaries as Hugh Gough (later to become archbishop of Sydney), Dr Basil Atkinson of Cambridge, Cedric Harvey and Professor Rendle Short as regular speakers in their meetings tended to confirm the suspicion that evangelicalism was an English import. It was only with the establishment of the Evangelical Movement of Wales after the Second World War that an uncompromisingly conservative brand of Christianity coalesced with the classic spiritual traditions of Welsh Protestantism once more.

Despite the initial verve which the formation of the Evangelical Unions generated, during the 1930s they tended to languish. The SCM was still by far the most visible Christian presence in the University, and although it suffered from the nominalism and flabbiness of all conventionally religious bodies, it continued to provide a focus for intellectual challenge and social engagement which the evangelical groupings lacked. It was not until the advent of the war and the arrival at Cardiff of a new and impressive generation of evangelical students, that the fortunes of the IVF in Wales began to revive.[81] The 1930s was a lean decade for evangelicalism as a whole. With the death of R. B. Jones in 1933 and the withdrawal of Nantlais Williams from the front line of connexional affairs following the passing of the Parliamentary Act of the Presbyterian Church of Wales, evangelicals tended to retreat into their own ghettos. Already old men by the 1920s, the former generation of mainstream conservative leaders represented by Dr J. Cynddylan Jones among the Calvinistic Methodists and Dr William Edwards, former principal of the South Wales Baptist College, had long withdrawn from the public arena, while the Barthianism of the younger generation was too accommodating of biblical criticism and non-sectarian in outlook to attract much conservative support. The Llandrindod Convention declined severely and inner tensions wracked both the Bible College of Wales and the South Wales Bible Institute, Welsh fundamentalism's two most visible inter-war manifestations.[82] By the later 1930s *Yr Efengylydd* was long past its most creative phase, its articles having become repetitive and its contents commonplace. Ironically there were no intimations as yet that what would become one of the most powerful forces in Welsh evangelicalism, the ministry of Dr Martyn Lloyd-Jones, regarded itself as being partisan in any way. Lloyd-Jones was quite content to work within the structures of his own communion, the Presbyterian Church of Wales, and enjoy fellowship with those of divergent doctrinal views. The highly sectarian evangelicalism with which his name came to be linked belonged to a much later phase in his theological development. Whereas the appetite for biblical preaching was on the increase and the need for a more orthodox basis for Nonconformist faith was becoming more and more apparent, the more conservative evangelicalism was still regarded generally as being too pietistic and negative, too denunciatory, anti-intellectual and fundamentalist, to provide a wholly fulfilling option for widespread Christian commitment and faith.

The Word of God and the advent of war

By the mid-1930s the victory of the traditionalists in the matter of the Calvinistic Methodist Parliamentary Bill and the deepening interest which was being shown in the neo-Calvinist orthodoxy of the Barthian school marked a change in the climate of thought among mainstream Welsh Nonconformists. Although this affected only a minority and the underlying trend was still towards institutional decline, Christian conviction was not extinguished. There were signs, in fact, that Protestant Dissent was taking stock of its faith and steeling itself for the battle ahead. Economic and social hardships at home and the threat emanating from political crises abroad characterized religious as well as secular life, and as the decade drew to a close it was obvious that a second world war was moving inexorably closer. Whereas the First World War had done little to dent the Welsh people's faith in inevitable progress, the extreme hardship of the inter-war years and the seemingly intractable social and economic problems which prevailed engendered a new realism that was not inimical to faith. Concepts such as sin and redemption, the sovereignty of God and the divine judgement on human folly gained a fresh potency. Suddenly the unbounded optimism of liberal theology and its faith in the potentiality for human goodness seemed rather threadbare and glib. What did engage congregations' interest was the uncompromising challenge of the gospel. Preaching as proclamation and not just moral uplift became a creative possibility once more.[83] Though the days of popular Nonconformity were numbered, it was increasingly apparent that orthodoxy, not liberalism, possessed the wherewithal best to withstand the pressures of the day. John Morgan Jones's assertion that the theology of Karl Barth was 'the death gasp of the old Protestant orthodoxy before finally expiring'[84] would prove to be embarrassingly premature.

In 1936 Moelwyn Merchant, a Calvinistic Methodist from Port Talbot and a graduate student in the University at Cardiff (he was later to become an Anglican parson and professor of English at Exeter University), attended the conference of the World Student Christian Federation in Geneva. The keynote conference speaker was Karl Barth. 'In one week of astringent discussion the vaguely liberal theology of early undergraduate days was sharpened into "crisis theology",' he recalled. 'Barth, Niebuhr and Brunner were invoked to interpret my history studies. It was at least a purgative experience.' Faced with the challenge of grace and judgement, he was forced to reassess his preconceptions and alter course radically. 'Liberal Protestantism was no longer an open possibility; there was', he claimed 'only one way forward.'[85] When the Revd Ivor Oswy Davies returned from his studies on the continent, he had no illusions as to the depth of the crisis engulfing the Christian church. The situation in Germany, Switzerland and in Wales demanded an uncompromising witness to God's sovereign will in Christ. 'The witness of the prophets and the apostles to the Word of God must be transformed ever anew into God's living,

mighty Word to us, *today*.'[86] In an address to the English assembly
of the Presbyterian Church of Wales in June 1938, only a few
months before Neville Chamberlain's last attempt at appeasing
Hitler at Munich, the note he struck was uncompromisingly
positive. At a time when many speeches were gloomy and doom
laden, Davies spoke of the victory of Christ's Kingdom. Despite
the manifestation of the divine wrath in the judgement of the
nations, God's victory was assured. He was still at work in the
church of faith, the fellowship of true believers, in grace and
redemption. God would use the encircling darkness, as he had
done at the cross, to bring forth his unquenchable light.[87] On the
eve of war this was a message to which Welsh Christians could
assuredly respond.

The declaration of war in September 1939 was neither unexpected nor especially traumatic. Unlike August 1914, there was
little triumphalism, absolutely no jingoism and a much more
realistic sense of the justice of the cause. Inevitably perhaps, given
the obscene rate of the carnage a generation or so earlier and the
feeling of betrayal which many still harboured against the politicians and the state, pacifism was a much more acceptable option
than it had been a quarter-century before. It was especially so
among Welsh Nonconformists, a high proportion of whose ordinands registered as conscientious objectors despite being officially
exempt from the draft.[88] At home and abroad, for those Christian
believers who had joined the forces and the (much smaller) band
who had refused to bear arms on the grounds of conscience, the
claims of faith retained their relevance. By now the theology which
undergirded this faith was frequently orthodox in tone. Although
not universally welcomed, it was typified by the popular volume
Sylfeini'r Ffydd ('Foundations of the Faith') published by what
had been the staunchly liberal Student Christian Movement. 'As
believers in Wales we must recognise once more the authority of
the Bible as the Word of God . . . and listen in humility to what
God has to tell us.'[89] J. E. Daniel's wartime essays such as 'The
Emphasis in Theology Today' (echoing Barth's earlier tract
Theologische Existenz Heute) and 'The Secular Assessment of
Man' were extremely powerful and especially arresting.[90] Among
many the church regained its unique character as God's ordinance
and sacrament of his presence in the world. 'The Church is as
necessary to the Gospel as the Gospel to the Church', declared the

Revd T. Glyn Thomas. 'There is today a widespread attempt to believe the principles of Christianity while disbelieving in the Society where alone they can be incarnated. Christianity is thus made an individual relation between a man and Christ.'[91] Although Glyn Thomas never divested himself of all the characteristics of the older liberalism, it was clear that the extreme antipathy to the church as the Body of Christ and concomitant emphasis on faith as a purely subjective, internal phenomenon, was falling progressively out of favour. During the immediate post-war years the call would increasingly be 'Let the Church be the Church!' Many of the younger ministers who would assume leadership roles – Gwilym Bowyer and W. B. Griffiths among the Congregationlists, J. Ithel Jones and Lewis Valentine among the Baptists and others among the Presbyterians and Wesleyans as well – were forsaking liberalism (or in Ithel Jones's case, biblical fundamentalism) for a renewed orthodoxy. The church of God animated by God's Word through the sovereign grace of Christ in the Spirit would be deemed worthy of respect once more and a focus for renewed faithfulness and commitment. No longer the preserve of doctrinal antediluvians or of the eccentric sects, by 1945 the theology of the Word had taken centre stage.

5

Nonconformity 1920–1945: responding to the secular challenge

The formulation of a social message

By the time of the Calvinistic Methodist Connexion's bicentenary in 1935 the doctrinal crisis within the denomination had been averted. A *modus vivendi* had been achieved allowing liberals full right of interpretation of the doctrinal articles contained in the Parliamentary Bill, while the conservatives could rest assured that the Presbyterian Church of Wales (the alternative name by which the Connexion, following the passing of the Bill, came formally to be known) had not departed from the orthodox and evangelical faith. Much the same was true of the other denominations with radicals and traditionalists maintaining a sometimes uneasy truce over contrasting readings of the same doctrines though maintaining fellowship within the same body. Each tradition aspired to maintain its own specific witness while contributing to the wider Nonconformist identity. This did not always prove easy. With almost touching self-assurance the Revd Benjamin Humphreys, the Baptists' foremost guardian of denominational orthodoxy, could state that 'the Baptists are the best type of Christians and certainly they are the most original'. For Humphreys, genuine Christianity was synonymous with the Baptist faith, no more, no less: 'We believe that our faith and practice are wholly in accord with the New Testament.' There was no doubt that (for him) his interpretation of the Baptist faith – individualistic, anti-sacramental and rankly Arminian – was incontrovertibly true.

> It is to do us an injustice to accuse us of being narrow-minded, prejudiced and bigoted. There may be some such like among us: we do not claim to be perfect. But if there is a bigot in the camp it is not because he is too much of a Baptist but because he is too little of one. Intelligent, enlightened Baptists can never be bigots.[1]

Such an invincible lack of self-doubt was almost endearing in its sincerity. There were those in each of the denominations who believed in the infallibility of their own tradition with a vehemence which would put the most ultramontane papist to shame. The fact is, though, that that which united the Nonconformist bodies outweighed by far those elements which divided them. During these years Welsh Nonconformity was routinely seen as one. It was the undisputed prevalence of this very unity which prompted the churches' most zealous partisans often to overstate grossly denominational features and convictions.

For all that, the problems which still beset organized religion whatever the denomination seemed just as intractable as ever. At home the social and economic situation remained bleak. The depression had lasted for years. In 1930 unemployment had affected 27.2 per cent of the insured population, the brunt being borne by the working men of the south Wales valleys. Of the adults of Rhondda and Pontypridd, 30 per cent were unemployed while the proportion in Newport was as high as 35 per cent. By August 1932, when the slump reached its lowest point, 42.8 per cent of all Welsh insured workers had been made idle. The cost of maintaining the unemployed was itself crippling. In September 1931 state benefit was cut and all prospective claimants were means-tested. Those who were in a position to leave did so, in their thousands and tens of thousands. Between 1925 and 1931 an estimated 297,000 people emigrated and in 1935 alone a staggering 292,000 left the country. Welsh families flocked to Slough, Cowley and the great conurbations of the English Midlands in order to find work. The rest had no alternative but to stay, whiling away their time in despondency, hunger and despair. In her report on Brynmawr, Brecknockshire, Hilda Jennings described a scene which was replicated in countless communities throughout the valleys:

> Visits to the Exchange . . . take up part of two half-days in the week. For the rest, some men stand aimlessly on the Market Square or at the street corners, content apparently with a passive animal existence, or with the hour long observation of passers-by, varied by the occasional whiff of a cigarette. Others work on allotment or garden, tend fowls or pigs, or do carpentry in the backyard or kitchen, making sideboards out of orange boxes stained brown with manganate of potash, while

their wives cook and tend the children in a restricted place round the fireplace, uncomplaining . . . On wet days the Miners' Institute offers papers and a shelter, although shop doors and street corners satisfy many . . . In these and other ways the unemployed man drags out his time and, whether he expresses it lucidly or not, in almost every individual there is an abiding sense of waste of life.[2]

The trauma this left on the national psyche was immense and its recollection would remain emotive for years to come. Many of the churches tried to alleviate some of the suffering as best they could. In Merthyr Tydfil Morgan Watcyn-Williams's ministry at Penyard and the Tydfil Forward Movement Hall, and later at Twyn-yr-odyn, was geared specifically to provide spiritual and material relief to those in need, while from his headquarters in the Central Hall, Tonypandy, the Revd Rex Barker blended Christian commitment with effective social concern. His brotherhood meetings, craft workshops and debating forums and the practical measures he initiated in order to relieve hunger and physical hardship typified Wesleyan piety at its best. It was said that 'Many of those who had been hit hardest by the distress . . . have confessed that if it had not been for Rex Barker's work they would have joined the Communist Party.'[3] Like Watcyn-Williams, Barker was a left-leaning pastor whose theology of the divine immanence led directly to social involvement and a Christian humanitarianism.[4] The same was true of the Quakers who made the Rhondda a special field of mission. Maes-yr-Haf in Trealaw was established in early 1927 as an educational establishment and centre for relief work and soon became a focus for such varied activities as music, drama, weaving, quilting, embroidery, woodwork and pottery, along with more cerebral pursuits such as lecture courses on moral philosophy and Plato's *Republic*. The centre also sponsored many self-help schemes and clubs for the unemployed.[5]

It was partly in response to the catastrophic hardships of the period that Nonconformists were keen to develop a social strategy and elucidate a political theology. It had already become obvious that the future of Welsh Nonconformity would depend, in part, on its response to the incipient challenge of labour politics and the social movement with which it was allied. In 1917 the army medical orderly Alfred Jenkins had told Principal Owen Prys that, on the basis of numerous contacts with ordinary Welsh soldiers already half-alienated from the chapels, 'a plainer declaration of the churches' sympathy with Labour and a fuller dedication of its resources to social betterment, in co-operation with various branches of the social movement' would be essential for the future success of Christian witness in the principality.[6] The Calvinistic Methodists' Reconstruction Committee's fifth report was on 'The Church and Social Questions'. This in itself was remarkable. Never before had any of the Christian bodies issued a specific set of guidelines on the social application of faith and it was apparent that the Presbyterians were treating this matter with urgency. Among the themes with which the report dealt were home and family, citizenship and politics and industrialization in both rural and populous areas. 'There is but one Governor of the universe, and the believer is a free man in his Father's world . . . That is where the possibility of a social gospel lays', it claimed.[7] This was followed two years later by the Congregationalists' report *Cenadwri Gymdeithasol yr Efengyl* ('The Social Mission of the Gospel'), while each of the denominations expended much ink and contemplation on COPEC, William Temple's Conference on Christian Politics, Economics and Citizenship, which was held in Birmingham in April 1924.[8] In fact, the 1920s transpired to be a golden age for the so-called 'social gospel' in Wales because of these ventures and the Welsh School of Social Service, a forum convened annually at Llandrindod in order to disseminate Christian social concern, the activities of the Welsh Christian youth movement Urdd y Deyrnas ('The League of the Kingdom'), the Student Christian Movement and its lively magazine *Yr Efrydydd* ('The Student') with its outlets in the colleges of the University of Wales and the various teacher training colleges at Barry, Wrexham, Carmarthen and Caerleon, and the preaching, lecturing and journalism of such notable proponents of Christian humanism as the Revds Gwilym Davies, Herbert Morgan and others,[9] as well as the line taken by the influential monthly *The Welsh Outlook*.

Yet there were ominous signs looming on the political horizon which threatened all that was positive in this approach, while the grave weaknesses in the theology itself did much to vitiate its ultimate effectiveness. The inter-war years marked the ascendancy of the Labour Party with each successive general election seeing the consolidation of Labour's power to the detriment of the

Liberals. For the 21 Welsh Liberals returned in Lloyd George's 'coupon election' in 1918, Labour gained 10 seats; the party won nearly 10 per cent of the Welsh vote – before the First World War its active support had been derisory. Following the collapse of Lloyd George's coalition government in 1922 the Liberals went into steep decline; only 11 members were returned for Welsh seats in 1922 and 12 in the election a year later, 11 again in 1924 and 10 in 1929. This contracted further to 9 in 1931 though four National Liberal members were returned, thus indicating a splintering of the Liberal cause which worsened in the election of 1935 with a three-way-split between Liberal (3 members), Independent Liberal (4 members) and National Liberal (3 members). Wracked by inner tensions and largely discredited due to Lloyd George's propensity to political opportunism, by the 1930s the Liberals' situation had become dire; the party had become virtually moribund, the preserve of the unadventurous, the rural and the old. Labour, on the other hand, was well on the way to making Wales a fiefdom of its own. From 18 Parliamentary members in 1922 to 25 in 1929, the drop to 18 in 1935 was less severe than it appeared. In an election which saw a general fragmentation in each of the major parties' support, Labour retained its hold on the industrial south in which it won every seat, polling nearly 400,000 votes or over 45 per cent of the Welsh total. By the 1930s Wales had, on the whole, rejected the individualism of its Liberal past in favour of a collectivist, socialist and more class-based Labour future; south Wales especially had become a Labour Party stronghold. Nonconformity's zeal for social Christianity coincided with this sea-change in political loyalty.

For generations Nonconformity and Liberalism had been virtually twinned. Ever since the widening of the franchise in 1870 Welsh chapelgoers had seen no incongruity in combining Christian piety with sometimes the most radical of Liberal politics. However, by about 1910 a reaction against this synthesis had set in and chapel leaders felt not a little guilty about the implications of their formerly uncritical support of the Liberal cause. The disestablishment campaign had left a bitter legacy which served to underscore the dangers in excessive political zeal in ostensibly a spiritual cause. So just as the group consciousness of Labour developed, its political aims were crystallized and the workers of south Wales were beginning to transfer their allegiance *en bloc* to the socialist cause, Nonconformity, fearing that its moral and spiritual mission was being compromised, withdrew from overt political involvement. Despite the publication of reports, the holding of conferences and a theoretical zeal for a Christian understanding of social ills, the majority of ministers, elders and denominational leaders fought shy of direct political engagement. Whereas working people as a class were becoming more politically conscious, the chapels were becoming less so. In fact Welsh Nonconformity 'sought to be less political at a time when the working class was claiming its political rights'.[10]

There were also huge deficiencies in the sort of social gospel being advanced. Although the Presbyterians' report did mention the social implications of the doctrines of the incarnation, trinity and the atonement, the governing concepts were not so much these as the fatherhood of God, the brotherhood of man and the kingdom of God as an ethical construct. 'Our Lord taught the two great doctrines which are to govern the history of mankind – that God is the universal Father and that all people are brothers and sisters to one another.' Given the deep problems of industrial Wales at the time, the Committee's simplistic faith in the coming of God's kingdom by the exertions of men and women of goodwill was culpably naïve:

> We are quite convinced that the Kingdom of God can have an impact on all aspects of our duties, and that Emmanuel's salvation is as wide as the lives of all mankind. A realization of this will bring an end to all greed and covetousness, impurity and deceit, thus ensuring that fairness and justice, purity and honour will blossom forth once more.[11]

The Independents' report was even more utopian. The application of Christian values, it maintained, would do much to usher in God's kingdom, and although the words of Jesus did not offer a blueprint for social regeneration, general principles gleaned from his teachings, especially the concept of God's fatherhood and the eternal value of the individual soul, were conducive to establishing an effective social scheme. Mutual respect between worker and manager was called for and the need for the profit motive to be curbed and profits channelled into improving working conditions was urged. Yet it was not the state nor even the institutional church which was charged with making this change but the enlightened individual. Once convinced of this fact there was little doubt that substantial improvements in the social fabric could be effected.[12]

Apart from an incipient Pelagianism, both reports (and the ideology which undergirded them) suffered from an individualistic concept of sin and redemption and a patent lack of practicality. Whereas socialists and Marxists were applying their own compelling analysis of the entrenched structural imbalances of south Wales's society and its economy, Nonconformity, still in thrall to the dogmas of human perfectibility, inevitable evolutionary progress and the sovereign value of the individual, offered a salvation which seemed superficial in the extreme. The optimistic humanism of liberal theology was blind to the vested interests and intractable economic evils which the politicians had so starkly revealed, and whereas the trade unions and labour movements put forward concrete proposals for social improvement, the churches would not commit themselves to anything but bland generalities. For all their social gospelling rhetoric, it had become a matter of principle that the churches should remain aloof from political partisanship even when injustice was rife. This social theology had no preferential option for the poor, nor was God seen in any practical way to be in favour of the downtrodden or the dispossessed. Despite the Hegelian Idealism that governed the doctrinal thinking of the most advanced among Nonconformity's leaders, social solidarity and a structural concept of sin yielded to an individual salvation reminiscent of evangelicalism at its most pietistic. Moreover, the insistence that worker and owner should strive together in harmony for the common good did nothing to disabuse the working population of industrial Wales that the chapels were, in fact, bastions of a discredited political Liberalism and guardians of the status quo. The fact that the churches refused to take sides during the widely supported General Strike of 3–12 May 1926, and that they were silent in the face of the harsh treatment meted out to the miners following their forced return to work nine months later, boded ill for their future. Religion, indeed God himself, was seen to be on the side of privilege and the ruling class. By the late 1920s Welsh Nonconformity, which had prided itself so long on having retained the loyalty of working men and their families, seemed no longer to have anything constructive to contribute to the social and political debate in Wales.

When chapel leaders finally responded more uncompromisingly and realistically to the needs of the people, alienation had already occurred: it was, unfortunately, too little too late. The Revd T. Alban Davies had commenced his long and distinguished pastorate at Bethesda Congregational Church, Ton Pentre, in 1925. Although he had done what he could to alleviate hardship both within his congregation and in the community at large, initially his ministry had been conventional; he fought shy of social radicalism or direct political involvement of any kind. His values were typically Nonconformist: thrift, sobriety and a profound respect for individual freedom. By coalfield standards his church members were comfortably well off. Although the majority of the menfolk were miners, few families lived in rented accommodation but owned their own homes. Ironically it was this very fact which served to politicize their pastor so thoroughly. The rules governing the means test, which was introduced following the extreme hardship of the 1931 depression, stipulated that home-owners were exempt from any financial assistance whatever. This meant that those who had exemplified all the staunchest virtues of traditional Dissent, thrift, self-reliance and honesty, were penalized the most. On enquiring, during a pastoral visit, as to how one of his families was managing to make ends meet, he was shaken deeply by the (albeit good-humoured) reply: '*Rŷm ni'n gorfod b'yta'r tŷ!* ('We've got to eat the house!'). The only way out for that particular family, and others like them, was to sell the home in which they had invested so much of their time, capital and aspirations. 'It was at that moment that I became a rebel', he later recalled.

> This provided me with a kind of impetus that this could no longer be endured . . . I did feel that something had to be done, that there should be some persons with something definite to say in a crisis like this. I felt that the churches were silent.[13]

It was through Alban Davies's influence that the Union of Welsh Independents at last called for practical measures to create work and redress the scandal which denied thousands of unemployed workers and their families access to medical treatment because they could no longer afford to pay their health insurance contributions.[14] A year later, in 1935, he was appointed secretary to the

United Churches Committee for Social Welfare. It was in this capacity, accompanied by the Revd Dr John Roberts representing the Presbyterian Church of Wales and Dr W. T. Havard, bishop of St Asaph, that he sought a meeting with Ramsay Macdonald in order to plead for the economic rejuvenation of south Wales. The reception which he received from the member for Aberavon, formerly Britain's first Labour prime minister, did nothing to stem his radicalization: 'What disturbed me was that Ramsay was not really interested.'[15] Whereas Macdonald asked the committee to forward 'some practical suggestions', all that the home secretary, Oliver Stanley, could suggest was that the workers left their home communities in order to seek work elsewhere. He was apparently oblivious of the fact that as many as 292,000 Welsh workers and their kin were in the process of doing so during that very year. Nothing concrete having been achieved, a second deputation met with the prime minister, Neville Chamberlain, in 1937. 'We found, to our dismay, that he was as cold as an iceberg, unresponsive, even indifferent.'[16] The government, he claimed, had no control over market forces. His suggestion was just as creative as the home secretary's had been two years before: that the dispirited and dejected dregs who were left in the valleys should leave to find employment in England where the situation was not nearly so grim. 'The result', recalled Davies, 'was that for me Plaid Cymru was inevitable . . . that Wales ought to see (*sic*) for itself.'[17]

Nationalism, pacifism and Christian faith

He was not the only Welsh Christian during the 1930s who would come to the same conclusion. A year previously Saunders Lewis, Lewis Valentine (who was by then a Baptist minister in Llandudno), and a Presbyterian layman D. J. Williams, had set fire to a hut at the RAF bombing school at Penyberth near Pwllheli and been given a nine-month gaol sentence at the Old Bailey for their pains. It was the first time in centuries that Welshmen had used an albeit tiny measure of physical force in order to defend their nation's heritage against what was seen as English militarism in a build-up to war. The stand they took was deeply principled and incontrovertibly Christian.[18] Since its inception in 1925 Plaid Genedlaethol Cymru, the Welsh Nationalist Party, had attracted a small minority mostly of the intelligentsia, academics, school-teachers and ministers of religion, who were deeply concerned about the erosion of the Welsh language and current threats to Welsh nationhood generally. The underlying philosophy of the party owed much to the social teaching of the Catholic Church and despite accusations of hierarchical, anti-democratic (and sometimes pro-fascist) sympathies, following the Penyberth incident especially it became a vehicle for Christian idealism of a much more ecumenical nature. Apart from Saunders Lewis, its principal leaders had been Ambrose Bebb, a francophile historian and littérateur whose Calvinistic Methodism had been unexpectedly reinforced by his growing acquaintance with the works of St Thomas Aquinas via Jacques Maritain and Etienne Gilson, and the Barthian theologian, Professor J. E. Daniel. But when Gwynfor Evans, a young lawyer recently down from St John's College, Oxford, proposed in the annual Assembly of the Union of Welsh Independents in 1938 that Wales should take charge of its own affairs,[19] there were signs that a much less ideologically restrictive Christian nationalism would soon come to the fore. It fell to J. E. Daniel to lead the party during the Second World War, but just as his renewed contribution to the theological debate coincided with this political responsibility, his 1944 sermonic essay 'Gwaed y Teulu' ('the Blood of the Family') would prove to be a milestone in the development of a specifically biblical philosophy of Christian nationalism in Wales.[20]

It was not only Saunders Lewis, Bebb and other devotees of European civilization who were conscious of developments on the continent during these years. If the situation at home was bleak, the rise of fascism in Mussolini's Italy, news of the civil war between the republicans and Franco's nationalists in Spain, an ominous crackdown against political dissent in Nazi Germany soon followed by Hitler's most alarming expansionist policy of *Lebensraum*, indicated the way in which events were progressing abroad. While studying in the Protestant faculty of the University of Bonn during the winter semester of 1934, Ivor Oswy-Davies had witnessed Nazi thuggery at first hand. Having graduated in the University of Wales and at Oxford, Davies spent his final year of ministerial training on the continent first at Zurich under Emil Brunner and latterly at Bonn attending the lectures and seminars of Karl Barth. By then the Church Struggle in which the German

Confessing Church actively opposed the Nazi regime's ecclesiastical tyranny was in its first stage. The neo-Calvinist Barth, who was even then being fêted as the most celebrated European theologian of his generation, was in the vanguard of the opposition and his refusal to bow to Hitler's pressure led in the spring of 1935 to his being dismissed from his post. Davies, who was present when the University's vice-chancellor issued his most celebrated professor notice to quit, relayed the news to friends at home.[21] It was patent that the German situation could only deteriorate, yet the memory of the previous war remained so raw, and the collective guilt Nonconformists carried for having so gullibly supported Lloyd George's propaganda was still so painful, that even to contemplate another conflagration was, for most of them, simply inconceivable. If the undergraduates of the Oxford Union could vow in February 1933 'that this house will, in no circumstances, fight for its king and country',[22] representatives from among Welsh chapelgoers had pledged repeatedly during these years that they would never allow themselves to be implicated again in war.[23] The extraordinary (and unrealistic) level of hope which was invested in the League of Nations reflected this dread-laden aspiration. Support for the League, most concretely through its own peace society, the League of Nations Union, was universal and constituted a principal plank of each of the denominations' social witness. The Calvinistic Methodists had taken a stand for peace and the principles of the League as early as 1921: 'It is our conviction that universal disarmament should be established immediately',[24] yet it was the older, more radical, Dissenting traditions who ultimately took an uncompromisingly pacifist line. In their Caernarfon Assembly in 1930 the Independents proclaimed their 'opposition to war, root and branch' as being completely contrary to the gospel, 'and we henceforth covenant to abstain from all things which tend towards war, or which support war in any way',[25] while the Welsh Baptists' announcement two years later made much of their supposedly Anabaptist past:

> After discovering the cruelty, obscenity and uselessness of war . . . we wish to declare our emphatic conviction that war in all its forms and under any circumstances is completely incompatible with the teaching and example of our Lord and Saviour Jesus Christ, and that our undoubted responsibility as Baptists is to honour our profession by

1. (above) Lloyd George in the company of the Revd Thomas Charles Williams, Menai Bridge, one of the keenest ministerial supporters of the recruitment campaign during the First World War.
Photo: Presbyterian Church of Wales

2. (left) A soldier carrying a St Patrick's banner during a Corpus Christi procession in Cardiff, *c.* 1915.
Photo: Cardiff Libraries and Information Services

3. Archbishop A. G. Edwards and the bishops of the Church in Wales
at the consecration of Bishop Timothy Rees, Llandaff, in 1931.
Photo: Community of the Resurrection, Mirfield

4. Francis Mostyn, Roman Catholic archbishop of Cardiff, blessing the
cornerstone of a new church in Grangetown, 1928.
Photo: Cardiff Libraries and Information Services

5.a The Revd E. O. Davies, Llandudno, who was deeply involved in the
controversy surrounding the reformulation of the Confession of Faith
of the Welsh Calvinistic Methodists during the late 1920s.
Photo: National Library of Wales

5.b The Revd R. B. Jones, Porth, 'the Welsh Billy Sunday'.
Photo: National Library of Wales

6. 'A hero of the people': the Revd Tom Nefyn Williams with a group of
Caernarfonshire fishermen, 1928. *Photo: National Library of Wales*

7. Bryngolwg church soup kitchen, Miskin, Mountain Ash,
Glamorgan, during the depression.
Photo: courtesy of Bernard Baldwin

8. The campaign for the Sunday opening of cinemas, Merthyr Tydfil, 1956.
Photo: Merthyr Tydfil Libraries

9. Archbishop Edwin Morris and the bishops of the Church in Wales
at the Lambeth Conference, 1958.
Photo: Church in Wales Publications

10. Corpus Christi procession in Cardiff, 1960.
Photo: Cardiff Libraries and Information Services

11. (above) The disaster at Aberfan, 1966.
Photo: Merthyr Tydfil Libraries

12. (left) The Revd Kenneth Hayes, whose remarkable ministry during the Aberfan disaster and its aftermath did so much to rebuild community life.
Photo: courtesy of Mona and Gwilym Hayes

13. 'Remember Jesus': a young people's evangelistic campaign in Gwynedd, 1972.
Photo: National Library of Wales

14. A representative of the youth of Wales at the presentation of the New Testament, Y Beibl Cymraeg Newydd, the New Welsh Bible, Bangor Cathedral, 1975.
Photo: National Library of Wales

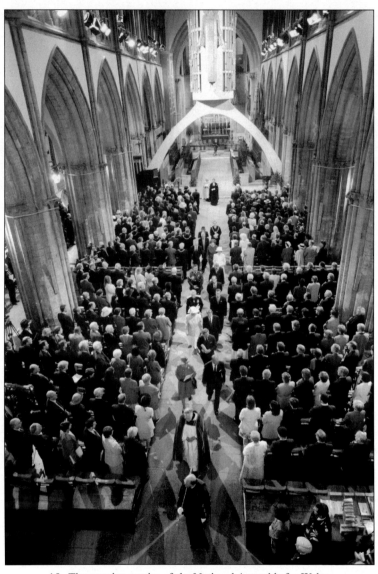

15. The opening service of the National Assembly for Wales,
Llandaff Cathedral, June 1999.
Photo: Western Mail

refusing to bear arms of destruction as our fathers did during the early years of the Christian Church and at the outset of the Protestant Reformation.[26]

That this affirmation drew the ire of the *Western Mail* as an act of treachery merely confirmed radical Dissent in its prophetic stance. 'Allow us to inform the *Mail*', wrote the Revd E. K. Jones, the most vocal of a knot of Denbighshire-based Baptist pacifists, 'that the standard and rule of our faith is not the newspapers but the New Testament.'[27]

Throughout the 1920s and 1930s it was the searing memory of the horrors of the Somme rather than a realistic appraisal of the incipient evil of totalitarianism which governed Welsh Nonconformists' attitudes to war. Pacifism was seen as a panacea, and not only among members of the older Dissent. The individualist, absolute and near-Mennonite ideal of the Baptists merged with the more pragmatic, politically grounded policy of the supporters of the League of Nations to create a consensus in which refusal to take up arms became an imperative. Few questioned the pre-conceptions which prevailed: that international disputes could be eliminated without undue recourse to force, that governments acting in good faith could curb wars of aggression, that political leaders no less than the man and woman in the street were basically rational beings who, when faced with undeniable facts, could be depended upon to act in an enlightened manner, and that conflicting national interests could be ultimately harmonized in order to forward the common good. What is more there was an implicit, and often explicit, belief among Welsh Nonconformists that the churches had it within their power to affect public opinion, that individual Christian discipleship included the call to put away the sword and that a prophetic faith would have a salutary effect on government policy.

The restless freelance radical George M. Ll. Davies, the grandson of John Jones, Tal-y-sarn, one of the Calvinistic Methodists' most renowned nineteenth-century preachers, and by now Wales's best-known pacifist idealist, personified these principles perfectly. After experiencing a spiritual awakening reminiscent of Tolstoy's during the First World War, this lieutenant in the Territorial Army had registered as a conscientious objector and turned his back decisively on the bourgeois values of his life thus far. Following the war he became a full-time (and penniless) propagator of the pacifist faith and in 1923 was elected on a Christian Pacifist ticket to represent the University of Wales seat at Westminster. His victory marked the extent of anti-war feeling among graduates and the middle-class intelligentsia generally, and during his (albeit short) parliamentary career Davies sought to combine the conviction of an exceedingly sensitive individual conscience with a coherent political policy. 'In the end social peace and order must be thought out and not fought out', he had stated in his election address, therefore 'Come let us reason together.'[28] This note of optimistic reasonableness persisted throughout the decade and even as late as Christmas 1937 the Revd Gwilym Davies, the Welsh secretary of the League of Nations Union and an untiring and high-profile advocate for conciliation and disarmament, could perceive something positive in the midst of the present crisis:

> As far as I see it, we are in the midst of a great drama which is being played out on the world stage – the greatest drama in the history of mankind . . . And what is that drama? Human society transforming its basis from one of competitive nationalism – its foundation for centuries past – to one of international co-operation.[29]

Even after Neville Chamberlain had returned from his fateful meeting with Hitler at Munich in September 1938 thus sealing the fate of Czechoslovakia, George Davies's message would remain the same: 'Our Lord's method was arbitration, conciliation and reconciliation.'[30]

The chill winds of realism first began to cool Welsh Nonconformist ardour for peaceful change following the Abyssinian crisis in 1935–6. The fact that both Italy and Abyssinia had signed the League of Nations covenant did nothing to prevent Mussolini's troops in October 1935 from entering the ancient African kingdom, and by the following May from sacking its capital Addis Ababa and deposing its ruler Haile Selassie. Even ordinary people were outraged, as much by the pathetic ineffectiveness of the League of Nations as by the Italian dictator's blatant aggression. The deepening trouble-filled situation throughout Europe – in Spain, Italy and Hitler's Germany – forced people to face the question of how to oppose effectively dictatorial tyranny, yet the ideals of rational discussion and conciliation were so ingrained that Welsh Nonconformity could only respond by redoubling its pacifist zeal. In 1936 the Anglican parson Dick Sheppard's Peace Pledge Union received the backing of thousands of young Welshmen who vowed that in the event of a second world war they would never take up arms, while a year later Cymdeithas Heddychwyr Cymru, 'The Fellowship of Welsh Pacifists', was formed with George M. Ll. Davies its president and Gwynfor Evans its secretary. Following the declaration of war in 1939 it did much through its literature and network of personal support to publicize the pacifist standpoint,[31] yet the most pressing point, namely, whether pacifism was an appropriate Christian response to the entrenched evil of Nazi domination or fascist tyranny, was never seriously faced. Although Chamberlain's return from Munich was heralded as a triumph, only the most credulous believed that Hitler's word could be trusted; 'peace in our time' was more a pious hope than a copper-bottomed promise. By that time even Gwilym Davies had lost faith in appeasement though, refusing to contemplate going to war, he had nothing to put in its place. Nevertheless his reluctant acknowledgement of the failure of the League of Nations revealed the intellectual feebleness of political pacifism when faced with a regime of Jew-baiting, concentration camps and the build-up of naked force:

> In its political aspect the League of Nations has failed. Why? Because none of the great nations was ready for it. Fellowship between the nations, and consequently world peace, will be impossible until each country is willing, in the spirit of the New Testament, to suffer for one another, the large for the small, the strong for the weak.[32]

A deficient theology had once more betrayed Welsh Nonconformists badly. An inability to come to terms with the complexity of evil, an overly optimistic, evolutionist view of human nature, an incapacity to comprehend the disturbing, the irrational and the demonic, a naïve assessment of the ambiguities of power and a failure to differentiate between personal morality and collective evil, all militated against their responding to the challenge of the hour in a realistic manner. Believing the Augustinian doctrine of sin to be a hangover from the primitive past, many of the older Nonconformist leaders were at a loss as to how to face the inevitability of war. In the main it was those who partook of the

renewal of orthodoxy who could face the situation with a degree
of equanimity. 'For me Germany is *la barbarie*', Ambrose Bebb
told his Breton nationalist friends in late August 1939, 'do you
really think that she will leave you alone?'[33] Conciliation,
appeasement and all that constituted pacifism as a political
strategy had failed: for those who could not conscientiously bear
arms only pacifism as an individual and prophetic vocation
remained. 'From now on', stated the Calvinistic Methodist
minister, the Revd J. P. Davies, in July 1939, 'we shall have to base
our campaign for peace on the Gospel alone.'[34] In fact this had
been Christian pacifism's only valid justification all along.

Preaching, spirituality and the churches

By the eve of the Second World War institutional Christianity was
in obvious decline. Following its statistical high-point in 1926 of
approximately 530,000 communicant members in the four main
Nonconformist bodies, by 1939 it had fallen to 510,600.[35] Even at
their highest these statistics concealed the true level of commitment and development within the church. Children were being lost
from the Sunday schools at a much steeper rate than the actual
figures indicated, while the previously numerous class of adherents, those who would attend services though not committed to
formal membership, was in danger of disappearing altogether.
Formerly it had been from among these that the churches had won
their converts and replenished their sources. As well as preaching
'to the converted', sermons had been aimed at the thousands who
were on the periphery of chapel life but who were sufficiently
interested to attend Sunday schools or worship services in order to
consider the claims of faith. Yet, in an analysis of life among the
Calvinistic Methodists published in 1927, the Revd Dr John
Roberts bemoaned what was becoming a trend. 'Our preaching
has improved vastly. There is far better preaching in all our
churches on every Sunday than ever before, but the old giant breed
is almost extinct.' The standard of preaching was, in fact, still
high, from the Geneva-gowned dignity of the Connexion's most
prestigious English-language pulpits such as Trinity, Wrexham,
Cathedral Road in Cardiff, and Castle Square, Caernarfon,
through to the homely, proletarian exhortation which was

common in the most unassuming Forward Movement halls. In the Welsh-language churches, which were by far the most numerous and best attended, preaching was still regarded as the climax of public worship but both as a social event and evangelistic tool it was losing its edge. 'It avails little today', continued John Roberts, 'to say "come and hear John Jones preach".'[36] On reflecting upon the situation among the Baptists, Lewis Valentine drew similar conclusions:

> I returned from the Association meeting deeply convinced that rarely before had Wales heard better preaching . . . I believe that our preaching today is more scholarly, that the pulpit is more honest, there is an unprecedented attempt to get to grips with the problems which afflict people in their everyday lives . . . But, alas, I am equally convinced that never before has our preaching been less effective, though I hardly know why. I would give a fortune to discover why Welsh preaching, which is currently so excellent and strong, is having so little impact on its hearers. Somehow men and women today are not allowing themselves to be convicted by the proclamation of the Word.[37]

The standard of preaching could hardly be faulted: Peter Price, D. J. Lewis (Tumble), H. Elvet Lewis ('Elfed'), Joseph James and R. H. Williams (Chwilog) were household names among the Congregationalists, John Roger Jones, D. Tecwyn Evans and E. Tegla Davies among the Wesleyans, J. Williams Hughes, J. M. Lewis (Treorchy) and Jubilee Young among the Baptists, and the Presbyterians could boast such talents as T. C. Williams, M. P. Morgan and Phillip Jones, Porthcawl. Even such a notably effective preacher as Dr Martyn Lloyd-Jones, the former Harley Street specialist whose ministry at Bethlehem Forward Movement Hall in Sandfields, Port Talbot, was creating such an impression during these years,[38] was unable to turn the popular tide. Describing a packed meeting in a Rhondda chapel during 1936, the novelist Rhys Davies recounted how Lloyd-Jones had issued an appeal at the close of his sermon. 'The difficult exit began. I was one of the last to leave. No one remained behind. The air was as thick as glue . . .' Despite the preacher's earnestness, spiritual attractiveness and exquisite oratorical gifts, the vast and eager crowd was not engaged. 'Something more is needed than the old pleasures of surrender, however seductively they are painted.

These Welsh are new people now.' Whereas the faithful were still gleaning spiritual sustenance from the churches' ministry generally, the uncommitted were attending public worship less and less and those who did were not, on the whole, being converted. 'In these industrial regions, where the clumsy feet of the modern world have intruded', continued Rhys Davies, '[the chapels] are becoming moribund. Only a celebrity like Dr Martin (*sic*) Lloyd Jones can attract a crowd, and even then the old ardour is not evoked.'[39] A less hostile commentator had regrettably to concur. The day of the popular preacher and his vast and expectant congregation seemed to be numbered. 'There is an absence that haunts our most crowded assemblies', wrote John Roberts during the Connexion's bicentenary year, '*Everyman* comes no more.'[40]

Neither did everywoman. There is no doubt that the trend, which would later become the norm, of worship being a female rather than a male preserve began during the inter-war years, though even the womenfolk became less numerous in chapel gatherings. Among mainline Dissenters it was taken for granted that the eldership and ministry were confined to men. There was virtually no opportunity for women to take a leading role in church affairs, and among the Presbyterians the deaconess's league and the foreign mission board were the only connexional organizations which afforded women an opportunity for full-time Christian service. When those with a vocation for ministry were set apart for the work they were invariably sent to the most difficult and least rewarding spheres.

At the outset of the First World War Sister Kate Jones had begun work among the street girls of Swansea: 'I saw that the Devil was riding high and that, without Jesus Christ, precious souls were moving rapidly towards perdition.' During her first year she made 4,397 pastoral visits, conducted 241 meetings and attended 544 more. 'I am quite sure', she wrote after six years of unstinting labour at Cwmbwrla and Swansea's town centre, 'that many of those whom the world had written off as hopeless cases Jesus, in his infinite mercy, saved to be eternally his own.' From Swansea she was sent to pastor a congregation of two dozen munitions workers in Hereford who were too poor to own a chapel building of their own and thence, after six more years of quite heroic exertions, to take charge of Trinity Forward Movement Hall in Trethomas, Monmouthshire, which had a total complement of nine members. At no time was she allowed to administer communion, the sacraments being the preserve of the ordained, male ministry, nor once was she known to have complained of her lot. 'I believe the strength of our little church has sprung from the prayer meeting', was her poignant testimony. 'My privilege has been to preach on the sabbaths.'[41] There was virtually no feeling of the unfairness of sending such obviously gifted Christian workers to face such arduous tasks virtually unaided, yet occasionally some women (invariably those who had been afforded higher education) struck an enquiring if not discordant note as to the status of the female's role in church life. 'With a multitude of outstanding opportunities for social service and leadership', wrote Miss Florence Grey, a headmistress from Mold, 'can we expect them [women] to be content with a sphere which consists largely, if not altogether of the sewing of garments, the preparing of meals, and the decorating of the church buildings . . . with Sunday School and Band of Hope work as their highest achievements?'[42] Her main concern was that talent was being wasted, not that women were having a raw deal. As the century unfolded feminism would not be a subtext let alone a text in the history of mainline Christianity in Wales.

The shortcomings of Nonconformity

If more and more people absented themselves from public worship during these decades, criticisms of Nonconformity's shortcomings became so common as sometimes to reach crescendo pitch. The most prevalent accusation among the burgeoning band of Labour supporters was that the chapels were becoming increasingly bourgeois institutions, reactionary and otherworldly, as well as being intellectually obscurantist. For Herbert Morgan, who sometimes gave the impression of being a fifth columnist for socialist humanism within the chapel milieu, the case against popular religion could be summarized in two words: indifference (to the labour cause) and insincerity.[43] (Labour's indifference to the gospel was, apparently, acceptable and its altruism invariably beyond reproach.) Although Morgan was still nominally commit-ted to the Nonconformist faith, criticisms made by others, whose loyalty to the chapels was beyond suspicion, carried more weight. Spirituality was waning and the cleft between a profession of

Christianity and true discipleship had become too common by far. Worshippers, it was said, 'come to listen to the preacher not because he is sent of God, but often because he is an able man or talented or that he is entertaining to listen to'. Hymn-singing too was in danger of having more to do with the flesh than the spirit: 'The singing, if the Spirit is absent, can become mere self-indulgence rather than a means of worshipping Almighty God.'[44]

With self-assessment as acute as this, there was little wonder that outside criticism could be intemperate and extreme. The Catholics, empowered by a sense of ultramontane triumphalism, were not averse to making capital from the perceived weaknesses of the chapels. Because ministers were dependent on their congregations 'for daily bread and for the still sweeter morsel of popularity' the people were being pandered to rather than served. Having made 'the pulpit more important than the altar' and investing 'authority in the pew', such degeneration had become inevitable.[45] With its inveterate pulpiteering and liturgically uninformed spirituality 'Welsh religion has in its centre the creature rather than the Creator', claimed the august Catholic weekly *The Tablet* in 1925. Frenzied preaching, popular hymnody and even pulpit-led prayer too frequently appealed to that which was base in people's religious nature: 'Too many "services" in Welsh chapels are services rendered to men and women rather than to almighty God.'[46] Four years later some mischievous observations on contemporary Welsh life made by 'a Mr Saunders Lewis' were quoted with obvious satisfaction. 'Hundreds of thousands of Welshmen go to what they call "places of worship" on Sundays when they are really going to places of entertainment', ran the report. There was little idea of true worship and it was patent that the chapels were not fulfilling the nation's religious needs.[47] The complete text of Lewis's paper was not quoted, but the original hardly served to endear him to Welsh Nonconformists generally:

> Wales today has without question the ugliest religious architecture and the poorest villages in western Europe, and they have affected even our religious habits. Welshmen in their chapels do not kneel in prayer. They bend down sitting as though they were vomiting. It is sadly appropriate![48]

Although Lewis said this with a glint in his eye, severe denunciations of the spiritual inadequacy of Welsh popular religion became commonplace among Catholic commentators during the inter-war years. For De Hirsch-Davies Nonconformity lacked 'stability, authority and cohesion' which was no match for the Church of Rome. Catholicism was attracting 'intelligent, cultured and highly educated men who, with the "obsession of God" weighing on their souls, are tired of the negations of Protestantism, of the nebulosities and barren abstractions of "Modernism" in all its forms'.[49] Doctrinal declension combined with a moralistic rigidity had absolutely nothing to commend it to the present generation. 'Nonconformity, through the death-dealing influence of modernism, has ceased to be a religion and has become an affair of village politics', asserted Fr Eric Green in 1935. The Welsh longed for spiritual fulfilment yet 'going to their chapels to ask for bread they are given the stone of respectability, Sunday observance, with a long face and a big black book, and total abstinence where one is known'.[50] Catholic censure of Nonconformity reached a climax a year later with J. T. F. Williams's comments in the Jesuit publication *The Month*. Chapel people, he claimed (from personal experience), were 'woefully ignorant of the nature of God – Father, Son and Holy Spirit'. God, for them, was the *Bod Mawr*, unknown and impersonal, while Christ was 'not the second Person of the Trinity but a man of the Jewish race born of the woman Mary by her spouse Joseph'. The concept of sin, he claimed, was virtually non-existent, and 'far more heinous if it brings the good name of *Capel Salem* into disrepute than as a breach of an eternal law of God'. With further echoes of Caradoc Evans, Williams also claimed that chapel prayer consisted of the 'ability of addressing beautiful phrases to the Great Being for the edification of an admiring congregation'.[51] Despite its malevolence, the caricature bore sufficient resemblance to the truth to be unnerving.

Yet the chapels were losing out far more to secularism and irreligion than to the Catholicism of the Church of Rome. The novelist Caradoc Evans, the *bête noire* of chapel culture, had already given a lead which the inter-war adversaries of Nonconformity would follow. 'We are as Welsh Nonconformity has made us. Not until the last chapel is a cowhouse and the last black-coated worker of abomination [the minister] is hanged shall we ever set forth on our march to the light.'[52] His censure may have been as exaggerated as the grotesque characters in his short stories

but it did serve to illustrate the perceived shortcomings of Welshness as it had evolved under the aegis of a formerly overconfident
Nonconformity. 'Chapels are the signs of our poverty and perfid-
ity', he continued, the preacher 'is the hangman of our liberties
and the enemy of God'.[53] For Caradoc the essence of Welsh
culture was in its religion which was for him a joyless, repressive
puritanism, contemptuous of art, good literature and the imagination, dismissive of human feeling and which undermined the true
welfare of the people. 'Wales would be brighter and more Christ-
ianlike if every chapel were burned to the ground and a public
house raised on the ashes thereof.'[54] Amidst the outcry these
excesses wrought, there were those who realized that beyond the
hyperbole Caradoc was making a valid point. Nonconformity *had*
become conformist and too often did cloak hypocrisy and petty
tyranny. 'My quarrel is not with religion', he said. 'It is with the
promoters of what is known as Nonconformity, a strong, powerful
body . . . which has substituted God for the black-coated figures
that oppress the people and drain them of their substance.'[55]

Evans was altogether too strident, too much of a *poseur* and a
buffoon, to be considered anything more than an irritant on the
body of inter-war Nonconformity in Wales, yet the narrowness of
puritanism, its repressiveness and world-denying character did have
the effect of alienating a considerable number of its more
thoughtful children. If some were attracted to Anglicanism or
Catholicism, many more were lost to religion altogether. Owen
Griffith, Welsh national secretary of the Student Christian Movement, lamented that every year dozens of students refused to join
the SCM, stating that Christianity made life cramped and unbearable and expunged all colour, romance and adventure.[56] Thomas
Jones of Rhymney, secretary to the Cabinet, sometime editor of *The
Welsh Outlook*, the inspiration behind the establishment of the
adult education centre Coleg Harlech and one of the most influential figures in Welsh public life, had (privately) forsaken
Christianity for 'the religion of humanity'. Although he had once
been a candidate for the Calvinistic Methodist ministry, his deepening agnosticism was fuelled partly by a distaste for the puritanical
dogmatism of chapel culture. Jones remained the sort of unbeliever
that only Welsh Nonconformity could produce: 'Although his faith
in religion and politics had weakened and waned, he retained an
absolute belief in the power of popular education. It was to him,

beyond question, a moralizing agency, perhaps a surrogate for his lost religion.'[57] However, the chapel itself, and the Christianity it represented, was clearly insufficient to retain his loyalty.

The same was true (but in a more flamboyant way) of Goronwy Rees, the hugely gifted son of the Revd R. J. Rees, formerly the pastor of Tabernacle Church, Aberystwyth, and latterly superintendent of the Calvinistic Methodists' Forward Movement. A bookish young man, he decided to pursue a career as a writer. Although his upbringing had inculcated in him finesse, wide culture and a deep appreciation for the things of the mind, its drawback was its Nonconformity which made life 'cramped and constrained'. Like Caradoc Evans, that other renegade Cardiganshire native, for Rees Welshness and Nonconformity were inextricably bound. The 'Welsh way of life', he claimed was that of 'a dying peasant culture which had its face resolutely turned to the past'. A brilliant undergraduate career at Oxford during the 1920s and a fellowship at All Souls singularly failed to provide some objectivity to his view of the culture which he determined to reject: 'since after leaving Wales I had thought of it as the land of a dying language and culture which could no longer satisfy anyone except the very young and the very old'.[58] The company of Guy Burgess and a life of unbridled worldliness was obviously preferable to the values and virtues of his upbringing in a Calvinistic Methodist manse.

Whereas agnosticism hardly featured in Welsh life before the First World War, it became an undoubted presence in cultural and intellectual circles during the inter-war decades, not least among those who had been brought up within the orbit of the chapel. Quietly, unsurreptitiously, but deliberately none the less, poets of the stature of T. H. Parry-Williams and R. Williams Parry, politicians like Morgan Phillips and Megan Lloyd George, journalists like Wynford Vaughan-Thomas and many more, rejected Christianity in favour of agnostic humanism and in so doing broke irrevocably with their Nonconformist past. This rejection became a recurring theme in contemporary literature, especially among the Anglo-Welsh: 'You Welsh!', exclaimed a character in Rhys Davies's powerful first novel *A Withered Root* (1927):

A race of mystical poets who have gone awry in some way. Alien and aloof in your consciousness of ancient austerity and closing your eyes to the new sensual world . . . Your brilliant children leave you because of the hopeless stagnation of your miserable Nonconformist towns; the religion of your chapels is a blight on the flowering souls of your young.[59]

Davies's alienation from his Congregationalist roots in Rhondda's Clydach Vale was exacerbated by his homosexuality. His pilgrimage took him eventually to full-blown secularism by way of Anglo-Catholicism, Bloomsbury bohemianism and exile on the European continent. Yet his loyalty to Wales, especially to the hard-done-by people of the suffering valleys, proved endearing and sincere. In his opinion Nonconformity had done the nation a grave disservice. It had stultified its creative potential by laying upon it an intolerable burden of repression and guilt.[60] 'Puritanism and its ugly sister Nonconformity', he wrote in his literary portrait of Wales of 1937, 'have worked damage and mischief and become, not liberating influences, but deadlocks and dungeons of the genuine Welsh spirit.'[61]

Blatant atheism was infinitesimally rare. Most agnostics drifted away from Christianity and the chapels rather than wishing to overturn them in revolutionary style. Wales experienced nothing of the militant anti-clericalism which typified the socialist atheism of the Mediterranean countries. Even most south Wales Communists frequently viewed their conversion to Marxism as a development of, rather than a declension from, Christian faith. The only recorded instance of a Welshman embracing Communism for explicitly anti-religious reasons was that of the Aberdare miner Edward Greening. He joined the Communist Party in 1931 in a gesture of solidarity with the Russian government's persecution of the Baptists.[62] Although there were other examples of atheism – Lilian Price, arrested for riotous assembly in support of the Bedwas strike of 1933, refused to swear an oath on the Bible claiming that she had no religious beliefs, while the funeral services held for Welsh members of the International Brigade killed during the Spanish Civil War were invariably secular in nature – not a few Welsh Communists conjoined their political convictions with active membership in their local chapels. David Phillips, the secretary of the Ferndale lodge of the National Union of Mineworkers, and Howell Davy Williams, a leading member of the Rhigos lodge, remained regular chapelgoers throughout their lives.[63] The poet Idris Davies was never a

Communist, yet (apart from Gwenallt) it was he more than any-one else who encapsulated in verse the excruciating experience of industrial Wales during the inter-war years. Though he bowed to family convention in attending Penuel Baptist Church in his home village of Rhymney, his contempt for Nonconformity and all its mores became formidable. 'What I believe is one of Wales' greatest needs is this,' he told Keidrich Rhys in 1936, 'an eradica-tion of Christianity within her borders . . . I want a Wales of the Mabinogion not the Wales of Christmas Evans or of the *cymanfa ganu*.'[64] If there was a God, He was certainly not the God of conventional Christianity: 'I refuse to believe', he wrote in 1938,

I have refused for years – that the Creator of the universe . . . the God who created all the wonder and the beauty and the terror of earth and sea . . . had ever had anything to do with the local tent-squabbles and blood-orgies of the Old Testament or the sickly, nightmarish stories of the New Testament. No intelligent person, in his heart of hearts, believes in such stuff, whether he goes to chapel or not. He knows it is all ridiculous.

Nonconformity was despicable for having institutionalized such nonsense: 'In Wales religion is a fungus which spread rapidly after the semi-lunatic Methodist revival, and which spawned still coarsest after the crudities of the 1904–5 Revival.'[65] Yet, for all his railing against the narrowness, hypocrisy and intolerance of a decadent religion, his atheism was tinged with a nostalgia for the innocence of childhood in which the virtues of piety were remembered with a grudging respect. During his London exile in the depression he could still sing:

> To Castle Street Baptist chapel
> Like the prodigal son I went
> To hear the hymns of childhood
> And dream of a boy in Gwent
> To dream of far off Sundays
> When for me the sun would shine
> On the broken hills of Rhymney
> And the palms of Palestine.[66]

His wistfulness was never more apparent than in his diary entry
for Christmas Eve 1939:

> I believe Christianity will have withered away in another 200 years. It is
> dying now – now on this silent Christmas morning . . . Christianity, as
> we know it, is undoubtedly one of the weeds of human history. It must
> go. It will go. And yet, tomorrow morning, sometime between
> breakfast and Christmas dinner, I will probably read again the second
> chapter of St Luke – for my childhood's sake, 'hoping it might be so'.[67]

The renewal of hope amidst despair

By the eve of the Second World War it was obvious that Christianity was losing its grip on the bulk of the Welsh people not only
as a social phenomenon but as a spiritual conviction and living
faith. The mounting criticisms being made against its principal
manifestation in Nonconformity, its waning evangelistic influence
and steady numerical decline, all reflected a loss of inner certitude
and belief. 'It is often said that our young people are ignorant of
the true meaning of religion and have never experienced its power'
was a complaint noted by the Calvinistic Methodists' Reconstruction Commission as early as 1921.[68] By 1929 Lewis Valentine
reported complaints of 'deadness, impotence and lethargy' among
the north Wales Baptists. 'Personally I see very little hope of a
swift recovery. As Christians we have become too appallingly
materialistic and indifferent, and the churches too dead and
dumb.'[69] As though to prove that the malaise was not confined to
any one tradition or any single part of Wales, in a meeting of the
Union of Welsh Independents' council in February 1930 the Revd
Dr H. M. Hughes, pastor of Ebenezer Church in Cardiff, voiced
his concern over the state of the denomination's Sunday schools:
'This apathy has arisen from the fact that the spiritual life of the
churches is weak, the fire is burning low and the climate is getting
colder all the time.'[70] One of the few Congregationalist leaders of
the period not to succumb to the appeal of liberal theology,
Hughes was adamant as to the main reason for the all too
prevalent spiritual declension. 'When religious leaders rule out the
possibility of the supernatural', he declared at his denomination's
Assembly in 1931,

and avoid or explain away the miracles and the cross and the resurrection as they were quite obviously understood by the Apostles and the Early Church and by Jesus himself, then the significance of revelation is changed and the Gospel loses its meaning. It is hardly surprising that the rising generation no longer finds it arresting or worthy of respect.[71]

A liberal gospel, bereft of saving power, no longer had the ability to challenge or transform human life. The virtues of contemporary Nonconformity were many: its still impressive size and breadth of influence over a whole swathe of Welsh life, its wide provision of church fellowship in every town, village and hamlet, the undoubted quality of an ordained ministry which was still attracting some of the most talented young men of their generation, the unassuming devotion of many of its faithful, its adherence (despite everything) to the orthodox faith along with a liberality of interpretation which was now guaranteed to all, its social and humanitarian commitment as well as its dedication to Christian mission abroad; but there was still a consciousness of decline and a nagging feeling that little could be done to halt its relentless progress. 'There is no sign of any mass movement towards religion', wrote Morgan Watcyn-Williams in 1937. 'There has been a drift away from it. The road back is the long, slow road of personal evangelism, but a great incoming may yet reward the faithful who refuse to faint.'[72] Alas, it was not to be. Denominational apologists did their best to emphasize all that was positive, yet the basic dilemma remained:

> The old fires may have died down, [wrote Dr John Roberts at the centenary of the Calvinistic Methodist Connexion] and our people today know less of the heights and the depths of religious experience through which their grandfathers passed, but our churches today have a greater number of loyal, conscientious, kindly men and women than ever before. There are more Christians among us now, if fewer saints.[73]

Few would begrudge John Roberts the comfort of whistling in the dark, but even he knew that in order to ensure its long-term survival the church needed to nurture not only kindliness but genuine spiritual experience and faith. Even the Welsh Presbyterians needed their saints. Yet throughout the 1920s and 1930s all that many people could hear was the melancholy, long, withdrawing roar of the sea of faith not so much on Dover beach but on the sands of Cardigan Bay, Llandudno, Barry and all the promontories between.

And yet this was not the whole story, nor, in fact, the most important part of the story. The gospel was still being preached, prayer was still being offered to God and the faithful dared to keep the faith despite manifold temptations to despair. Just as Nonconformity was being despised by the intelligentsia for its philistinism, dismissed by the socialists for its otherworldliness and increasingly ignored by ordinary men and women who believed it to be irrelevant to their lives, there were those who, having trod the path of agnosticism and rebellion, were finding their way back to its fold.

David James Jones, the poet Gwenallt, was born in Allt-wen in the Swansea Valley, the son of a steelworker and his wife. His parents' roots were in rural Carmarthenshire and although they lived within sight of the blast-furnaces and earshot of the clanking of the crane's gantry, he was nurtured in the Calvinistic Methodism of his parents' home:

> The chapel where I used to go stands in an industrial village. I went every Sunday to morning service; to Sunday School in the afternoon; to the five o'clock meeting where the young were taught to pray aloud in public; to the evening service; to singing practice; to the prayer meeting and the *seiat* each week; to the dawn service on Christmas morning; to a whole week of prayer meetings at the beginning of January; to sit the Scripture examinations; and in summer I would go to the Sunday School trip to the seaside.

Yet it was not the chapel but the verve of industrialism all around which fascinated an impressionable boy, an industrialism in which hardship and suffering were intrinsic:

> I'd ride a bike pilfered from scrap, or with a pig's bladder
> Play rugby for Wales; and all the while,
> Little thought I'd hear how two of my contemporaries
> Would spew into a bucket their lungs red and vile.

Initially such things were deemed inevitable: death by accident, 'the leopard of industry leaping sudden and sly', the widows, mute and brave, chopping firewood and turning to their Bibles for consolation, the graves garlanded with 'silicotic roses and lilies pale as gas'. But with the years of discretion the consciousness of injustice became unbearable as did a desire to know what was at the root of such inequity:

> And there we learnt, over lids screwed down before their time,
> Collects of red revolt and litanies of wrong.[74]

It became obvious to many of his generation in industrial south Wales that their grievances could only be redressed through the implementation of socialist policies, policies of which the chapels were dubious:

> Keir Hardie gave us the explanation in his speeches and in his Socialist newspaper *The Labour Leader*. The economic system was a capitalist system, based on competition; its purpose was to amass wealth for a few people to keep workers in slavery. Under the system, unemployment and war were inevitable. The Christian churches accepted it all passively and justified it. We were shocked and disillusioned . . .
>
> The true Christians were outside the Church, in the Labour Party and the movements for social reform. I saw the difference between my father as a worker and my father praying in the chapel; I saw the gap between the steel works and that chapel.

If the first influence was Keir Hardie's ILP socialism, there were others as well: Tolstoy's pacifism and his 'Christian anarchism' and Dostoyevsky's 'Messianic rebellion' (there was nothing in a Welsh-speaking, chapel-going, working-class upbringing during the first decade of the twentieth century to prevent an intelligent lad from reading widely and imbibing influences which were international in scope); the prim Anglo-Saxon atheism of Bradlaugh, Ingersoll and Blatchford; James Frazer's *Golden Bough*: 'There was no historical basis for the Bible. It was mythology. No, the Grand Inquisitor was right. There was no such thing as sin; only hunger.' Yet for a restless mind in the throes of adolescence, there was the incessant need to travel farther. When weighed in the Marxist balance, Hardie's democratic socialism and Tolstoy's idealism were too tame, too compromising, to be ultimately effective in the battle to free the working class from its thraldom. The next stage in this youthful development ('We reacted easily to every theory and influence because the passion and depth of our feeling was much greater than our reason') was the idea of the class war:

> Marxism became our gospel, a much better one than Methodism. It was a religion, a social religion, for which we were prepared to live and die and make sacrifices; but we would not have raised a finger to defend Calvinism. Capitalism was something that we knew in our lives. We saw the poverty and hunger, the hovel-like houses, mothers growing old before their time, the cruelty of soldiers and policemen during the strikes, doctors putting tuberculosis instead of silicosis on the death certificate to avoid the paying of compensation to relatives, and the bodies coming home after the accidents. Years later my father's body came home after he had been burnt to death by molten metal, and that unnecessarily. When, in the funeral sermon, the minister said that it was God's will, I cursed his sermon and his God with all the hauliers' swear-words that I knew, and when they sang the hymn *Bydd myrdd o ryfeddodau* at the graveside, I sang in my heart *The Red Flag*.

By the time Gwenallt read for his degree at Aberystwyth (he had spent two years in Dartmoor and Wormwood Scrubs as a conscientious objector during the First World War) both his espousal of class politics and his break with Christianity were complete. Yet his spiritual odyssey was not at an end. There was a further move towards aestheticism: 'There was at that time in the College a whole nest of poets – . . . Our favourite poets were Keats, Rossetti, Swinburne, Oscar Wilde . . . and Baudelaire. Walter Pater was our master and teacher in English prose, and his book *The Renaissance* was our Bible.' So pagan was this aestheticism that it would have no truck even with the agnosticism present in the poetry of T. H. Parry-Williams, R. Williams Parry and Gwynn Jones:

> It was a weakness to mention the Galilean. Since he was just a myth, far better let him be. If we were to have paganism, then let it be real paganism, not some mash of Christianity and paganism. I loathed Puritanical paganism. What Welsh poetry needed was to get rid of every single image or simile that was Christian, not only because they

were ridiculous but because they were trite; and to create instead new images that grew from contemporary life, especially industrial life.

So far Gwenallt's development was typical of the artistic intellect-ual during the 1920s: atheism, revolutionary politics, bohemian-ism, a contempt for the past. The decade was calamitous for the reputation of Christianity in England;[75] as a member of the *avant garde* his experience was running true to form. But as the years went by disenchantment set in, not with Christianity this time, but with both materialism and aestheticism. Further reflection posed fundamental questions about the human condition with which neither politics nor culture were equipped to deal. 'Marx', he wrote,

> showed that self-interest lurked behind bourgeois ideals, and he was right, but could not self-interest lurk behind Communist ideals? . . . Rousseau and others taught us that human nature was fundamentally good, and that man could, on the basis of his own power and knowledge, build a just society. But I saw that one thing was common to capitalists and Communists – self-interest.

The unions existed to bargain for more pay. They did not strike to establish socialism or even to increase the old age pension. The division between the skilled and the unskilled worker remained, and only a small and able section of the workers took an interest in union politics. A miner or steelworker who was a good speaker became an official, and moving further and further from the coalface or the works floor he would eventually find himself in Westminster. Thinking of the 1924 Labour government, Ramsay Macdonald and the ignominious end of the General Strike: 'It was the workers' leaders in Parliament who betrayed the workers at the time of a strike.'

Slowly, painfully, but very surely, Gwenallt found himself being drawn once more to the Christian analysis of the human condi-tion, to the doctrine of original sin and divine redemption, as the only way of making sense of the inter-war world. It was not just the politicians who attempted to use ideals to cloak their self-interest, it was true of the poets as well. The one thing which marked Baudelaire out from the other Romantics was his dis-covery of sin and guilt: 'Anyone who perceives his own sin is half-way to becoming a Christian.' Gwenallt's earliest poetical works, the national eisteddfod odes 'The Saint' (1926), 'The Monk' (1928) and 'The Poet's Dream' (1931), although ostensibly on religious themes, were marked by a rabid – and somewhat vapid – romanticism, but by the mid-1930s it was obvious not only that he had found his voice but that he was intent on reinstating Christianity in a sophisticated, pertinent and highly contemporary way.

> Woe to us if we know the words without knowing the Word
> And sell our soul for toffee and fairground confetti,
> Following every drum and dancing after every flute
> And drowning the hymn of the Intercession with the rhyme of the
> Absolute.[76]

By 1936, with the publication of his poem 'Ar gyfeiliorn' ('In error'), he had thrown in his lot with the Christians and had begun worshipping once more among the Calvinistic Methodists, the denomination into which he had been baptized and raised. He found now that he could affirm the rural piety of his parents' generation while still holding to the radical social critique of his socialist days. Unlike T. S. Eliot, C. S. Lewis and Rosalind Murray, the literary converts to orthodox Christianity from among the 1920s generation in England, Gwenallt's faith did not take him away from involvement in the world, rather it sharpened his engagement with the evils of the day and gave him added verve and spirit. For him pietism was never a valid option, neither did the nebulosities of liberal theology hold any attraction whatever.

Following his conversion he spent years searching for a radically satisfying orthodoxy. Though he found the hymns of Williams Pantycelyn, with their emphasis on sin and redemption through the cross, refreshing, he was repelled by their otherworldliness – 'the wilderness of [industrial] south Wales stood between us' – and though he found Karl Barth's theology vastly superior to the usual trite modernism, it was lacking, in his view, in a full-orbed Christian humanism. He was drawn to Thomism and its synthesis between nature and grace – which would take him, years later, into the Anglican fold, though he returned to Nonconformity and evangelical Calvinism in the end. What was remarkable was that someone who was in the vanguard of contemporary life, the epitome of modernity, wholly committed to the social, political and cultural life of his nation, would find his way back to a Christianity which more superficial critics were currently rejecting as being effete, moribund and pathetic. It was Christian faith and not secular humanism that would provide him with a means of understanding, and overcoming, the malaise of his generation: 'As Socialists and Communists we wanted to reform everyone and everything except ourselves. We could not see that old Adam lives in Moscow. The Communist revolution is a mere flea-bite beside the Christian revolution.'

The essay in which Gwenallt related his spiritual journey *Credaf* ('I believe'), from which the above prose quotations have been taken, was published in 1943.[77] By then the theological renewal connected with Barth, Brunner and the American Reinhold Niebuhr was taking its effect and Nonconformists were looking beyond the end of the war to a new Wales and a new Europe. Optimism may well have vanished but there was little sign of despair. If conventional religion was in decline, Christianity retained its validity to challenge the status quo and provide a persuasive analysis of the human condition. 'In the disorder, misrule and poverty which will follow this war', concluded Gwenallt, 'we shall have to chose between mechanistic totalitarianism and constructing a civilisation upon Christian foundations.' The choice itself was invigorating. Having been deeply chastened, the churches retained their faith and nurtured hope.

The striking difference between the quiet Christian confidence of the mid-1940s and the liberal optimism which had emerged a generation earlier was its note of realism. The older individualism had given way to a richer, more corporate analysis of human society, while it was readily admitted that human structures as well as the individuals who composed them had been effected by the blight of sin. In a compelling critique of secular humanism made in 1943, J. E. Daniel echoed St Anselm's sentiment *nondum considerasti quanti ponderis sit peccatum* ('you have not considered how weighty sin is') with his own observation on the unique effect of the proclamation of the gospel. It was the insidious nature of this original corruption which grows through each social construct and blights every single improvement that humankind has ever made which still calls forth for 'the Sacrifice between the nails of steel'.[78] At the end of the war secular humanism would still be popular in Wales as elsewhere, but now Christians were no longer ashamed to admit their belief in human corruption rather than humankind's perfectability. Not believing in the doctrine of sin, secular men could never build a better world, claimed the Revd J. E. Meredith, by then the minister of Tabernacle in Aberystwyth (the church Gwenallt attended): 'They reject Christianity's realistic way of considering humankind: she rejoices in man's value, his dignity and his possibilities, but she also declares his sinfulness and calls upon us to face honestly the demonic power of the evil which is in the world.'[79] No self-respecting Nonconformist theologian would dared to have spoken of the demonic even ten years earlier, but the tragedy of Christian Europe overtaken by tyranny, the unspeakable horror of Belsen and Buchenwald soon to be revealed and in the east the unleashing within months of the bomb upon Hiroshima made the biblical categories relevant once more. By 1945 the faith still retained its efficacy and its capacity to transcend man-made dualities:

> The span of the Cross is greater by far
> Than their Puritanism and their Socialism,
> And the fist of Karl Marx has a place in his Church:
> Farm and furnace are one together in His estate;
> The humanity of the pit, the piety of the country:
> Tawe and Tywi, Canaan and Wales, earth and heaven.[80]

~ 6 ~

Reconstruction and crisis, 1945–1962

Confidence within the Church in Wales

The Church in Wales entered the post-war years in a spirit of considerable confidence. Having reached its twenty-fifth year as a disestablished body, it was at last feeling comfortable in its role, free of Canterbury, as an independent church serving the Welsh people. D. L. Prosser, the elderly bishop of St David's, succeeded Charles Green as archbishop in November 1944, while David Edwardes Davies, the vicar of Swansea – whose church of St Mary's had been severely bombed during the blitz – had been consecrated bishop of Bangor a few months earlier. In September 1945 Alfred Edwin Morris, the conscientious but unbending professor of theology at Lampeter, was elected bishop of Monmouth. Yet the change of key personnel was not the most important aspect of Anglican life in Wales at the time. There was a marked increase in optimism and a renewal of hope at the grass roots, among younger parish clergy and the laity, that in the reconstruction of a post-war Wales, the Church would come into its own. 'It may be fairly said that there is among Welsh Churchmen at the present a widespread mood of expectancy', wrote the Revd Ewart Lewis in 1945,[1] and eight years later the warden of Llandovery College spoke of 'a growing conviction that it is to her [the Church in Wales] the future belongs'.[2]

The plethora of committees and commissions which were instigated between 1945 and 1953 witnessed not so much to a mania for institutionalization as to a rejuvenated zeal: the Reconstruction Committee of 1945 charged with financial reorganization; the Commission for Religious Education in Wales of 1945 which made its report to the Governing Body a year later; the Commission of 1947 on the Nation and Prayer Book which published its highly significant report two years subsequently; and the Commission for Cathedrals in 1949. Such was the dervish-like freneticism of these years that a breathless Bishop John Morgan of

Llandaff (who succeeded Prosser as metropolitan in 1949) called for a year of grace during 1950 in order for the Church to recuperate and return to normality! Activities associated with the Standing Liturgical Commission and the Provincial Evangelistic Council, both of which were founded in 1951, culminating in the Welsh Church Congress at Llandrindod in 1953, showed that the respite was only temporary. Undergirding much of this sense of expectancy was the work of 'Cymry'r Groes', the Church's youth movement which had been formed in 1944, and the activities of the Provincial Council for Youth, established a year later. The same vigour and enthusiasm was apparent in the Church's publications of the time, the highly stimulating monthly magazine *Cymry'r Groes* edited initially by Moelwyn Merchant and then Derrick Childs (it was renamed *Province* in 1949) as well as the Welsh language *Y Gangell*, and in the substantial and scholarly *Journal of the Historical Society of the Church in Wales* the first issue of which appeared in 1947. A renewed and popular catholicism, doctrinally orthodox, in continuity with the Christian centuries, positive and world-affirming, was catching Church-peoples' imagination and firing them with a fresh commitment. For many, post-war Welsh Anglicanism was to provide a counterpoint to what was perceived as a decaying and oppressive Nonconformity on the one hand and the aridity of secularism and irreligion on the other.

The generation of leaders and prospective leaders which came to the fore during the late 1940s and early 1950s was of exceptional quality. They were, according to one of their number, 'all friends and of a similar age, and determined to establish a thoroughly Welsh and Catholic Anglicanism in a tradition which we knew united us with the rich literary, artistic and liturgical tradition of medieval Wales'.[3] Dr H. Islwyn Davies who had taught philosophy at Lampeter before becoming vicar of Llanbadarn Fawr, then Llanelli and thereafter dean of Bangor; Gwilym O. Williams, warden of Llandovery College and from 1956 bishop of Bangor (and like Davies and Moelwyn Merchant formerly a Calvinistic Methodist); Eryl Stephen Thomas, the vicar of Risca who would become dean of Llandaff and afterwards its bishop; H. J. Charles, later bishop of St Asaph; John James Absolom Thomas, vicar of Swansea, archdeacon of Gower and from 1958 bishop of Swansea and Brecon; and John Gwynno

James, who moved from a tutorial post at St Michael's College, Llandaff, to be the vicar of Roath, the archdeacon of Llandaff and eventually dean of Brecon. All were relatively young, able – intellectually Islwyn Davies and G. O. Williams were quite outstanding – and possessed of style, administrative skills, and in some cases considerable panache. The 1949 *Report* of the Nation and Prayer Book Commission expressed many of their priorities. Whereas in the past the Church had been defensive, theologically complacent, liturgically derivative and divorced from the Welsh mainsteam, the time was now ripe for a confident affirmation of its maturity and rightful place at the centre of the nation's life. No longer would the Church in Wales turn in upon itself or stand apart from the social, economic and cultural concerns of the day. Neither would it depend theologically or liturgically on the Church of England. Social reflection, broadly according to a Welsh version of the Christian Sociology of the Anglo-Catholic 'Christendom' group, and Prayer Book revision would be instigated immediately. 'Wales today is a nation losing its vision of God', wrote Ewart Lewis, 'under the influence of false trends in her religious development combined with the present crisis in men's affairs.' The progressive weakening of Nonconformity and its failure to retain the commitment of the rising generation had created a vacuum which Welsh Anglicans were confident that they alone could fill: 'Nor could that nation be brought back to the vision of God till the Church in Wales, the only agent among us capable of the task, sets herself in grim earnest to recall it to belief in the full Catholic faith.'[4] By 1950 there were signs that that mission was beginning to be fulfilled.

It was obvious during these years that it was catholicism rather than evangelicalism or broad-churchmanship which was proving compelling. Evangelical churchmanship had all but vanished. 'By the 1950s,' according to its historian, 'save for a few men here and there, the evangelical tradition had virtually died out in the Church in Wales.'[5] Even in St Mark's, Gabalfa, Cardiff's only evangelical parish church, it was at a low ebb.[6] The absence of an Evangelical Union at St David's College, Lampeter, during these years[7] was illustrative of the trend throughout the Church. Neither did the doctrinal liberalism which had vitiated the testimony of Protestant Nonconformity for so long hold much attraction for Welsh Churchmen. When Sir Idris Bell, a president of the British

Academy and soon to become an exceedingly valued lay member
of the Church in Wales, found his way back to vital Christianity in
the years immediately after the war, it was to a doctrinally
orthodox creed that he returned. 'It was, indeed, the gradual
realisation, in the course of my own work, that the historical
evidence for the Gospel narrative, and particularly for the
Resurrection, was very much stronger than I had supposed, which
was among the first steps in my own change of direction,' he
recalled. He was now convinced that the liberal Christ, non-
miraculous, moralistic, a great religious teacher transformed by
his credulous disciples into a divine figure, was a fiction. 'If Jesus
of Nazareth was not what he claimed to be, the Son of God, the
Redeemer of the world, then he was either a charlatan or a self-
deluded fanatic.'[8] Modernism was bankrupt, discredited and
lacking in saving power. For Bell, like the 1950s generation
generally, liberalism was not a valid option; it was either the rich
dogmatism of classic Christianity or nothing.

By that time there was evidence of pockets of renewal throughout the province. In Monmouth the 1951 mission, meticulously
prepared for by Bishop Morris and his team, quickened the
worshipping life of the parishes considerably and that year's
Tintern Abbey festival was an obvious spiritual highpoint for
many.[9] At the opposite end of the land, in the diocese of Bangor,
Bishop John Charles Jones's prayerful dedication and inspiring
leadership was helping to deepen the spiritual life and corporate
worship of numerous parishes. Jones, another distinguished Welsh
Churchman to have been brought up a Calvinistic Methodist (at
Llansaint near Carmarthen), had spent eleven years as a
missionary in Uganda before returning in 1945 as vicar of Llanelli.
A transparently godly Anglo-Catholic, his appointment to Bangor
in 1949 marked what some perceived to be the beginnings of a
widespread religious awakening. The diocesan pilgrimage to
Bardsey, the 'island of the saints', in 1950 and activities associated
with the 1400th anniversary of the founding of the see two years
later became foci for considerable rededication. 'The Church in
Lleyn had come alive;' it was reported, 'the Church in the diocese
had seen the beginnings of spiritual revival'.[10] By then Jones had
become the most popular of the bishops and his unexpected death
at the height of his powers in 1956, when he was aged fifty-two,
was a catastrophic loss to the diocese and to the Church in general.

Such confidence and growing vitality, especially when viewed against the backcloth of pessimism which was besetting the chapels, bred triumphalism. The orthodox tended to the view that the Church was flourishing due to its grasp of catholic truth in its fullness. This being the case there was no possibility of co-operation with other Christian bodies whose validity, in some cases, was called seriously into question. This was stated most boldly (and with the greatest degree of logical consistency) by the bishop of Monmouth in his *Primary Visitation Charge* (1946) and, following the furore which it caused, amplified and reiterated three years later in *The Church in Wales and Nonconformity*. 'The Church in Wales is the Catholic Church in this land, and we cannot without denying our very nature, yield one iota of this claim.'[11] Although he was a Prayer Book Anglican rather than an Anglo-Catholic, Morris held firmly to the belief that there was but one Church commissioned by God to minister Christ's gospel in its entirety, and just as in England that church was the Church of England, in Wales it was the Church in Wales. For the bishop it was as much a matter of legally constituted authority and order as a channel of divine grace. While preaching at the consecration of Daniel Bartlett as bishop of St Asaph in 1951 he stated the logic of his position with customary clarity:

> A bishop is to bear rule in the Church, not because men have created the office to satisfy a social need, but because our Lord himself chose to exercise his authority through his Apostles, who, in turn . . . chose to pass on the authority of their office to the Order of bishops.[12]

The apostolic tradition was one of unbroken succession having originated in the will and purpose of God. The Catholic Church with its threefold ministry of bishop, priest and deacon were all of a piece: 'God Himself has made known the way of salvation, and has appointed One, Holy, Catholic and Apostolic Church to be the guardian of that way.'[13] Neither Protestant Nonconformity, which had rejected both the form of ministry and in many cases the substance of the faith enshrined in the creeds, nor the Roman Church, which had signally failed to reform itself at the Council of Trent adding a multiplicity of new errors (culminating in 1951 with the dogma of the assumption of the Blessed Virgin Mary), could claim validity as the Church Catholic. In Wales that privilege belonged to the Church in Wales alone.

What had galled Nonconformists (and Welsh Roman Catholics) was not so much the unpalatable doctrinal assertions contained in the bishop's charge but the accusation that they had no rights or spiritual jurisdiction in their own land. 'Both the Roman clergy and Nonconformist ministers are, strictly speaking, intruders. There may be historical reasons for their being here, but we cannot recognise their right to be here.'[14] The single word 'intruders' put paid to any serious attempt at rapprochement between the Church in Wales and the other Protestant denominations for a generation or more. But the fact is that throughout the early and mid-1950s Welsh Anglicans were so secure in their position that the need to forge ecumenical links hardly arose. For all his popularity and charisma, Bishop J. C. Jones was not a whit less uncompromising than his colleague at Monmouth. 'There are strains and tensions', he remarked in 1954. 'It would be mischievous to try and ignore these and pretend that there are no differences among us.' Co-operation in any activity which would jeopardize the Church's integrity as the sole valid representative' of the Church Catholic in Wales was inconceivable. 'The fact that we cannot meet together at the sacrament of the Body and Blood of our Lord is caused by honourable and conscientious reasons to which we must cling.'[15]

Bishop Morris, for his part, prohibited his clergy from joining with Nonconformists in joint services and evangelistic work: 'We and Nonconformist ministers use the same word Evangelism, but we do not understand it in the same sense', he claimed. Whereas for Free Churchmen the simple preaching and believing of the gospel was the essence of evangelism, for Churchpeople belief could never be complete were it not accompanied by sacramental incorporation into the One Body of Christ which was, for him, synonymous with the Church in Wales: 'We cannot consistently with our own doctrines join in a campaign which by its very nature would suggest that it does not really matter to which of the various denomination a man may attach himself.'[16] Even as late as the 1960s, by which time the ecumenical tide was running fast, Glyn Simon reiterated the Anglo-Catholic standpoint which had become the accepted norm in the Church in Wales: 'The Apostolic Ministry . . . is thus not an optional extra, or something to do with the fullness or *bene esse* of the Church; it is essential to the being of the Church as founded by the Lord Himself through his ordaining and sending of his Apostles'.[17] A few years earlier, on

the tercentenary of the 1662 Act of Uniformity which had simultaneously introduced a revised *Book of Common Prayer* and
created modern Nonconformity, he had made plain the mutual
incompatibility of Chapel and Church:

> Henceforth there were to be two religions, for though the Dissenters
> differed considerably among themselves . . . there was, and is, about
> them a similar ethos, a rejection of Church Order and sacramentalism
> which makes it possible, and indeed accurate, to speak of Church and
> Dissent as two broadly opposite conceptions of institutional
> Christianity.[18]

If, by the mid-twentieth century, toleration between the different
traditions of Christendom was both desirable and essential, a
coming together on the basis of a shared Christian conviction
remained out of the question:

> I am inclined to think that there are certain opposed beliefs about the
> Christian religion, about the Church and Grace, which, in the last
> resort, are different beliefs about the Person and Work of Christ and
> about the nature of God, which, in this world at any rate, seem finally
> incompatible.[19]

Even after the Anglican Communion's commitment, following the
Lambeth Conference of 1958, to visible unity between the
separated branches of the church, Simon remained a reluctant
ecumenist. The only bishop wholly to endorse the ecumenical ideal
of a full reunion between Wales's disparate religious bodies which
would not involve a wholesale capitulation to Anglican claims was
Gwilym O. Williams, from 1956 J. C. Jones's successor at Bangor.
His vision, however, only came to be shared more widely during
the late 1960s and 1970s. In the main the only reunion which Welsh
Churchmen envisaged between 1945 and 1962 entailed the
dissolution of Nonconformity by the return of all 'separated
brethren' to the bosom of *Yr Hen Fam*, the mother church.

Conflict within the gates

The mid-1950s saw the generation of younger leaders of whom so
much was expected, come into positions of authority. In 1954,

Glyn Simon, already dean of Llandaff, was appointed bishop of Swansea and Brecon before being translated to Llandaff three years later. Along with Edwin Morris, his was the most forceful (and angular) personality on the bench of bishops and perhaps the most impressive. His initial unpopularity had been dissipated not only by the effects of a happy married life, but by parochial responsibilities during his time at Llandaff. 'In general', noted his biographer, 'he exuded cheerfulness and friendliness.'[20] He would combine his high and authoritarian episcopal doctrine with a surprising lightness of touch. G. O. Williams, having returned in 1956 from the wardenship of Llandovery College to his native Caernarfonshire, made plain from the beginning his patriotic, if not nationalistic, credentials, and even more disconcertingly his newly disclosed ecumenical convictions. His first visitation charge contained the words: 'It must be confessed at the outset that in Wales we have been belated and slow in working our way into the tide now running so strongly throughout the world in the direction of Christian unity.'[21] He would do more than any to take the Church in Wales into the inter-ecclesiastical mainstream and remedy the effect that Morris's 'intruder' remarks had made a decade earlier. In 1953 Eryl Thomas had succeeded Simon as dean of Llandaff; in 1957 H. J. Charles left St Michael's College for the deanship of St Asaph; Gwynno James had become one of Llandaff's archdeacons before proceeding to the deanship of Brecon Cathedral; while 1958 saw John J. A. Thomas's election as bishop of Swansea and Brecon. Perhaps the most unexpected appointment to the hierarchy during this time was that of an older man, John Richards Richards, who, in 1956, followed W. T. Havard as bishop of St David's. Richards, a Cardiganshire man, had spent two decades as a missionary in Iran before returning to the less than cosmopolitan parish of Skewen an acknowledged expert on the Baha'i faith. It was ironic that during the comfortable, insular, triumphalist 1950s, the Welsh bishops had among them a first-class expert on inter-faith dialogue.

   With a high calibre of leadership, a confidence born of the conviction that it possessed the full catholic faith, and an apparent determination to take its place at the heart of Welsh life, the Church of the 1950s exhibited much vibrancy and *élan*. 'My own impression', stated Sir Idris Bell in 1953, ' . . . is that the Church has in recent years improved its position relatively to that of other denominations'.[22] Statistics for Easter attendance bore that perception out. Whereas Nonconformity was in obvious decline, on Easter day in 1945, 155,911 communicants partook of the eucharist at the Church's altars, 170,338 did so on the same occasion in 1959 and as many as 182,864 communicated in 1960.[23] The pattern was more or less uniform throughout each of the six dioceses:[24]

Easter attendance in the Church in Wales

	St Asaph	Bangor	St David's	Llandaff	Monmouth	Swansea and Brecon
1945	33888	15866	29323	38144	18141	20549
1959	37177	19008	28632	44426	20308	20787
1960	37756	20137	33775	46142	21353	23701

The trend of church attendance everywhere was upwards. It would seem that the Church was shedding its alien image and drawing more and more Welsh people into its orbit. Following the *Report* of the Nation and Prayer Book Commission and labours of the Standing Liturgical Commission, it was certainly doing much to revise its worship services in a way which accorded with both catholic practice and contemporary needs. In 1956 a new table of Lessons and Psalms for Sunday worship was introduced; new forms for infant and adult baptism were issued two years later and a new edition of the marriage service in 1960. As well as partaking of the gains of the Liturgical Movement which was having such a marked effect on Western Christendom at the time, it also marked the province's resolve to free itself from over-dependence on the Church of England's 1662 *Book of Common Prayer* which not even disestablishment had managed to supplant.[25]

Beneath the smooth surface of assurance and advance there were other currents running deep which would soon cause sharp turbulence. However confident the Church seemed, it singularly failed to provide the wherewithal or to inspire sufficient loyalty in its own clergy to prevent them from transferring from its ministry in droves. Stipends had not been raised since 1939, consequently there was an exodus to the Church of England whose benefices were better paid than those within the province. For the first time since disestablishment the Church was neither recruiting clergy in sufficient numbers nor keeping hold of those it already possessed to staff fully all of its parishes. Despite the success of the Layman's Appeal of 1952 in raising £1.5 million from the parishes apart from the required annual quota, salaries were slow to rise and the exodus continued unabated. Between 1947 and 1954 276 priests left Wales in order to take up office in the still-established Church of England. By 1962 600 Welshmen were said to be serving in the provinces of Canterbury and York.[26] This often irked those who chose (or had no alternative but) not to 'cross Offa's Dyke' causing inevitable resentment and bitterness. There were other problems. No matter how keen the younger, more patriotic leaders were to emphasize the spiritual vitality and theological soundness of the Church, in their more candid moments even they had to admit of much formalism, conservatism and social snobbery within Welsh Anglicanism. Neither the layfolk nor the clergy were exempt from these blights. 'The Churchpeople of Wales are not as a general rule intelligently aware of their membership of the Catholic Church',[27] wrote Ewart Lewis with an air of resignation, while the same author, as secretary of the Nation and Prayer Book Commission, reported the low standard of theology and learning common among his fellow priests. 'The possession of a fixed liturgy is undoubtedly a great help to a Church in preserving orthodoxy and unity of belief', he stated, yet the Church had remained sound not so much due to the way in which the clergy had made orthodoxy their own, but through 'a refusal to wrestle with the great issues of faith and the bearing of modern thought upon them, [rather] than in a common conviction of the truth tested by theological debate'.[28] When all was said and done, intellectual indolence and doctrinal inertia were not wholly uncommon in Welsh vicarages during the 1950s.

The underlying disquiet came to the fore most forcibly early in 1958 with the election of Edwin Morris, bishop of Monmouth, as archbishop, and with the appointment soon after of the much revered John J. A. Thomas as bishop of Swansea and Brecon. Neither man was Welsh-speaking, indeed Morris was an Englishman whose roots were in Worcestershire; this was to prove contentious in the extreme. Despite the move towards fuller integration into the life of traditional Wales and its culture, the

Church still had much to do to reassure people that it was not the church of the squirearchy, the landowners or the Anglicized Welsh Tories. Less than a decade before, the Nation and Prayer Book Commissioners had admitted as much:

> We cannot deny that in Welsh-speaking Wales the Church is widely held to be isolated from Welsh life and that her alleged lack of interest in the preservation of Welsh culture and tradition is being interpreted as a sign of total lack of care for the well-being of the people.[29]

Morris's appointment on 5 November 1957 was uneventful, but the lobbying that accompanied Thomas's election three weeks later left at least one of the bishops very disconcerted indeed. The electoral college, composed of the bishops, a dozen representatives from the vacant diocese and six from elsewhere within the province, had to choose between J. J. A. Thomas, Eryl Thomas, Dr H. Islwyn Davies and Gwynfryn Richards, the rector of Llandudno and a leading figure in the Bangor diocese. What galled Glyn Simon was not so much the election of 'Jack' Thomas (the only non-Welsh-speaker among the candidates and a man whom Simon liked and admired) as the prejudices which governed the electoral college's choice. For Simon was convinced that Thomas had been elected solely to keep a Welsh-speaker out. Although he indicated as much in a private correspondence with the new archbishop, what ignited the controversy were his frank and undiplomatic remarks in the January edition of the *Llandaff Diocesan Leaflet*: 'These recent elections, and utterances both before and after them, have revealed an anti-Welsh and pro-English trend and, in some cases, a bigotry as narrow and ill-informed as any to be found in the tightest and most remote of Welsh communities.'[30] G. O. Williams, though less inflammatory, was just as perturbed. 'The recent elections have thrown a sharp light on the ambiguous attitude of our Church to the Welsh language', he wrote. As a bilingual Church in a bilingual nation, he had assumed that all its leading clerics would be able to officiate in both languages when required, and that Welsh would be given full parity with English: 'Both assumptions have been proved wrong.'[31] These comments, and the considerable press coverage they engendered, served to widen the electoral debate and raise questions concerning the exact nature of the Church's attitude to Wales as a national entity.

The confidence, vitality and apparent desire to integrate fully into ordinary Welsh life which had been so apparent a decade earlier, seemed now to have begun to dissolve. Already disillusioned by current attitudes, some Anglicans felt they had no alternative but to leave the Church altogether. The poet D. Gwenallt Jones, whose most mature and enduring verse had reflected catholic orthodoxy at its most forceful,[32] was fierce in his denunciation. 'The Church in Wales has tied itself to royalty, the landowners and the Tories', he claimed. Rather than showing solidarity with the Welsh people in their manifest imperfections, the Church had sided once more with privilege, status and the forces of Anglicization. Its much vaunted Anglican 'middle way' was a compromise which would always favour the strong over the weak. The Church in Wales, he said:

> does not have the mass like the Roman Catholics; nor preaching and hymns like the Nonconformists . . . The Church of Rome has the symbols, the pictures and visual icons which reach into the dark recesses of human nature; and Nonconformity, in its preaching and hymns, especially the hymns of Ann Griffiths and Pantycelyn, possesses the symbols and verbal images which can penetrate the same depths . . . Anglicanism is a middle way between Rome and Geneva, but it is the Englishman's middle way.[33]

Gwenallt promptly left the Church for his former Nonconformist denomination, the Calvinistic Methodists. Another prominent layman to register his protest (though he was never tempted to forsake Welsh Anglicanism) was the broadcaster and litterateur Aneirin Talfan Davies. Responding to the way in which he believed the bishops of Llandaff and Bangor had been vilified in the press, he stated: 'If there was any doubt before about the anti-Welsh bias and bigotry of *some* Welsh Churchman, there is no doubt about it now.'[34] The dean of Monmouth, the Very Revd R. E. Evans, and Canon Thornley Jones of Brecon, were singled out for particular opprobrium, nor did the bishop of St David's escape unscathed. The spectacle was hardly edifying. Yet, however offensive, Davies was fixed in his resolve to disclose how the situation seemed to him and those like him: 'There are at least two reactions to any mention of Welsh and Wales in Welsh Church circles. The first ranges from dull apathy to a not unfriendly embarrassment. The other ranges from a faintly disguised hostility to open anti-Welsh belligerence.'[35] In either case it hardly boded well for the Church's unity or its mission to reconcile the different linguistic and cultural communities which it sought to serve. There was an obvious tension between the universal nature of the gospel and Church and its particular manifestation in terms of Wales's culture, he claimed, yet it was his opponents who were guilty of narrowness and parochialism; his appeal was for a true catholicity:

> It is a good thing for a small province such as Wales to receive the services of men from outside. All that we ask is that whether he be an Englishman or a Hottentot he should become sufficiently acquainted with the Welsh language to enable him to take part in the full life of the *whole* Church. Is this too much to ask?[36]

The controversy simmered on throughout the following months and whereas most of the clergy carried on with their duties regardless, relations between the archbishop and the bishop of Llandaff became so strained as never to recover. Simon, who had not previously been outspoken in his support for the Welsh language, was unrepentant: he refused to withdraw his accusations of bigotry and intolerance, while Morris refused his offer to officiate at Llandaff: 'I do not think that I could happily pay an official visit to your Diocese at present. You have told the world in effect that you think that I am not qualified to be the Archbishop of Wales, and I do not see how you could welcome me as Archbishop.'[37] Whereas John J. A. Thomas said nothing so retaining widespread sympathy as well as episcopal dignity, it was not in the new archbishop's nature to be silent. He pressed his Llandaff colleague relentlessly: 'It will clarify this point if you tell me whether or not you think I ought not to have been elected.' Simon's reply, dated 10 March 1958, was unequivocal: 'My answer is that I do not think someone unable at least to minister in Welsh should have been elected Archbishop of Wales.'[38] Responding to a rebuke from the bishop of St David's, who despite being Welsh-speaking had sided with Morris throughout, Glyn Simon explained the vehemence of his stand:

> It is a matter of knowing something of the history and the ethos of Wales, and being familiar with leading Welshmen of today, and

knowing something of the new situation which has developed with the revival of Welsh in the last quarter of a century. The Electoral College [did] not begin to be aware of this.[39]

It was this sensitivity to the changing cultural patterns of post-war Wales which would make Glyn Simon (unexpectedly) a major force in the modernization of the Church's attitudes during the 1960s. For Edwin Morris, however, despite his manifest virtues of honesty, clarity of thought and a searing sense of duty to the Church which had called him to its service, this cultural sensitivity was absent. In the words of his biographer, 'the Welsh dimension was missing'.[40]

By 1962 much of the expectancy displayed by Welsh Anglicanism a decade earlier had evaporated. Materially Welsh society had improved drastically. Employment was higher than at any time since the First World War and the trauma of the depression had effectively been assuaged. Following the end of austerity and rationing in 1951, people's standard of living rose substantially, and, with more money available, men and women were free to take advantage of technological advance. By the mid-1950s television sets, washing machines and cars were becoming the rule rather than the exception, distances were decreasing due to the revolution in means of transport and Wales was being opened to the world at an unprecedented rate. Slum clearance in some of the urban areas – Merthyr Tydfil's 'China' district and Cardiff's Tiger Bay for instance (Hitler had done the corporation's work for them during Swansea's blitz in 1941) – had been complemented by huge housing schemes, and both council and private home building proliferated. The establishment of the National Health Service in 1945 coincided with the general improvement in the population's health, and this, along with the soon-to-be-nationalized coal industry, marked a period of new and popular optimism. Eden's and Macmillan's 'you've never had it so good' Conservatism consolidated rather than destroyed the immediate post-war Labour government's earlier changes, and during the 1950s Wales entered a phase of stability and growth.

The strength of the Church remained in the rural heartland and increasingly in the older urban communities. Its ministrations and outreach were markedly less successful in the newer suburbs and the vast housing estates which, by the 1960s, appeared so bleak. By

1962 it sponsored no specialist ministries in hospitals, colleges or the University (apart from the Church Hostel in Bangor and St Teilo's Hostel in Cardiff) though since August 1960 an experimental industrial mission (in the person of the Revd David Lee) had been established under the auspices of the Llandaff diocese in the huge Port Talbot steel complex. With industrialization on this scale came unprecedented secularization. If Victorian and Edwardian Wales had combined religious affiliation with industrial progress, the situation in the new Elizabethan age was not nearly so propitious. 'The man-in-industry is no longer the man-in-church, in-chapel, in the worshipping community', remarked the bishop of Llandaff in 1961. Recent social and economic changes 'have largely destroyed the supernatural context, the religious setting in which his fathers saw the meaning and end of their natural life and work . . . "Industrial man" does not go to church'.[41] And there were other fears as well: the nuclear threat laid waste to even the most chastened post-war optimism about creating a better, more equitable world, while the rather comfortable catholic orthodoxy which seemed so satisfying in 1945 was becoming rather jaded and ineffectual in the face of rampant secular materialism. Within a year Bishop John A. T. Robinson's *Honest to God* and the secular and 'death-of-God' theologies would affect the Church in Wales just as they reverberated through British theology generally, upsetting the older certainties and questioning radically the doctrinal status quo.

Whereas in 1950 there were signs of church growth and spiritual renewal, by 1962 Welsh Anglicanism was, according to Glyn Simon, merely 'holding its own'. If figures for Easter Communion were still fairly encouraging, significantly fewer parents brought their children for baptism and the rate of confirmations had declined even further. Not only in Llandaff but throughout the province the Church would have to face unpalatable facts: 'There is no room at all, not even an inch of room for complacency and self-satisfaction.' The trend away from organized religion would soon register even in the most flourishing parishes. The signs were not promising: 'What this means is that the major traditional religious forces in Wales, the main instruments for the conversion and evangelisation of our country, the Free Churches and ourselves, are losing their grip.'[42] In a sermon of a year earlier, the bishop had spoken for Christian pastors and leaders everywhere:

> First of all we have to realise, and probably most of us do, that the
> Church is working in a world where it is not hated but regarded as
> irrelevant; as having nothing new to offer. It simply seems to the men
> and women of today either to have nothing to say to their
> circumstances, or to say them in a way that has no sort of meaning for
> them. The biblical symbols themselves . . . do not speak at all to the
> great part of our industrial and technological society.

The spiritual atmosphere was chilling believers to the bone: 'Better
far the open hostility; better far hatred and persecution than the
numbing embrace of this amiable but total indifference.'[43] Whereas
the social and economic reasons for the Church's failure to
evangelize were not to be discounted, what was especially disconcerting was the low standard of spirituality among the believers
themselves. Was not 'the main explanation of the inefficiency of
the Church', 'the dullness of its message, the apathy of those who
hear it, the sparseness of vocations, the passivity of most of her
children?'[44] The sight of thousands making their annual
appearance at Easter Communion was one thing; costly Christian
discipleship was quite another: 'Were all of them converted
practising Christians we should again begin to find the Church
once more a real force in our society.'[45] Before the Church
converted society, it would first have to be converted itself. Given its
spiritual ebullience during the late 1940s that seemed not to be
impossible; by 1962 such a prospect was very remote indeed.

Roman Catholic consolidation

It was not only Welsh Anglicans who felt elated by the prospect of
advancement and growth following the Second World War; the
same was true of the Roman Church as well. Speaking at the
centenary celebrations of St David's parish in Swansea in 1947,
Cardinal Griffin of Westminster caught the mood of the period
perfectly. 'Signs are not wanting that the age of transition has
arrived', he claimed, 'and that the call of the past is likely to come
with overwhelming power to a people so deeply attached to their
ancient faith which they have loved long and lost awhile.'[46] Some
months earlier, at the consecration of John Petit as bishop of
Menevia, Archbishop McGrath had been even more upbeat.

'Wales is not Catholic but it is fast becoming Catholicised . . . It is more than a dream of life that the future is with the Church of Rome in this country.'[47] Officiating at a pilgrimage to the shrine of Our Lady of Pen-rhys in the Rhondda following its rededication in 1948, he struck the same triumphalist chord: 'Today hundreds of pilgrims are demonstrating the return of the Faith; this is revival.'[48] Whereas Anglican hopes tended to dissipate as the years went by, Catholic ebullience persisted. 'You cannot speak of "converting" the Welsh so much as "reconverting" them', wrote Francis H. Poyer in 1957, 'and please God, that day is fast approaching.'[49] Baptisms were on the increase, conversions were up, church building and school extension were progressing steadily and the Church was making headway not only in its older strong-holds of Cardiff and Newport but throughout Nonconformist and Protestant Menevia as well. With the triumphant return of the Cistercians to the abbey of Valle Crucis in 1947, the re-establishment of the pre-Reformation shrine of the Virgin at Pen-rhys in 1948, the founding of the Lamp Society's travelling mission to the rural parts of Menevia in 1949, the procession through England and Wales of the statue of Our Lady of the Taper of Cardigan in 1956 and the reintroduction of the Corpus Christi festivities in Cardiff in 1960 when 30,000 Catholics filled the castle precincts, Catholicism in Wales appeared to be going from strength to strength. 'It may well be tiresome and disquieting for some folks', wrote a correspondent to the *Western Mail* in 1960, 'but there is little doubt the "Faith of the Fathers" is rapidly returning to the "Land of our Fathers".'[50]

Diocese of Menevia

	secular clergy	regular clergy	churches	Catholics	baptisms	marriages	conversions
1945	68	102	91	21675	580	361	113
1950	68	118	115	23000	924	371	179
1955	72	122	83	26400	927	434	170
1960	78	112	103	31500	1105	419	187

Archdiocese of Cardiff

	secular clergy	regular clergy	churches	Catholics	baptisms	marriages	conversions
1945	97	55	120	84100	2269	1156	244
1950	110	64	126	90600	2781	1145	324
1955	124	70	125	88700	2724	1157	424
1960	128	73	130	95500	3102	1278	429

Total[51]

1945	165	157	211	105775	2849	1517	357
1950	178	182	241	113600	3705	1516	503
1955	196	192	208	115100	3651	1591	594
1960	206	185	233	127000	4207	1697	616

The main increase in numbers was due to the unusually high birth-rate within the Catholic community, but the Church was also very zealous in its approach to pastoral ministrations and keen to stem leakage by retaining its hold on the faithful. Many were brought into the fold by a discipline which required those who married Catholics to undergo instruction which not infrequently led to their converting. Neither had the moral and spiritual appeal of an authoritative church replete with sacramental ministry vouchsafed by the successor of St Peter lost its capacity to attract. Both McGrath as metropolitan and Petit from his base at Wrexham were staunchly ultramontane, their authoritarianism frequently breeding deference from within and admiration from without. 'The Protestant interpretations of the promises to Peter as set forth in the scriptures have produced a chaos of conflicting opinions', wrote one convert in 1950, 'while the Roman interpretation has in fact resulted in a world-wide church with authority and at unity with itself.'[52] The stream of converts, reaching the 700 mark by the late 1950s and including many who became Catholics through conviction rather than convenience, were clearly attracted by unambiguous teaching which they believed to be faithful to all the tenets of orthodox Christianity and in accordance with their needs.

Often it was the very strangeness (for non-Catholics) and alien character of the faith which proved to be most potent and enticing to potential converts: the infallible nature of the Petrine office when expressed *ex cathedra*, the sacrificial element in the mass and the fascinating unfamiliarity of Marian devotion. Recounting his own conversion decades before, Saunders Lewis emphasized the abiding pull of Catholic particularities. It was not so much the preaching of the Word which was essential to Christianity's witness he claimed, but the sacrifice of the mass.

> That is why I am a sort of unprofitable Catholic or Papist [he told Lewis Valentine in 1962]. That which drove Luther and Calvin out of the Catholic Church is the very thing which drew me in. They were humanists; the humanism of the Renaissance refashioning the Faith is what I perceive in their teachings. To me our Lord's saving mission is of *secondary* importance. The primary element is His presenting to God on man's behalf the worship which only Calvary could offer. To me that's the only thing which makes Christianity possible in the second half of the 20th century.[53]

The significance which the Church afforded to the Blessed Virgin Mary also exerted a pulling power of its own. Not a few converts owed their new allegiance partially to the influence of her cult.[54] Marian devotion had been rising within the Church for decades, reaching a climax in November 1950 with Pius XII's promulgation of the dogma of the Virgin's bodily assumption into heaven. The controversy the decree engendered was enormous, the issue virtually taking over the Welsh religious press until well into 1951. Yet for all the claims and counter-claims made, many of which were rooted in crass ignorance of the Catholic viewpoint, the newly promulgated decree, what the hierarchy called 'the last jewel in Our Lady's crown',[55] caused obvious satisfaction to the faithful and provided one more unique feature in the Welsh Catholic identity.

It was not only doctrinal matters which singled out Catholics from among their compatriots and often their fellow Christians, but frequently ethical concerns and questions of conduct as well. Much Catholic moral teaching centred on the family and it was partially in order to preserve family life intact and ensure the passing on of the faith from one generation to the next that the

Church was so heavily involved in the establishment and upkeep of
its own schools. 'We Catholics are indissolubly bound to our
schools', stated Petit in 1954 at the opening of the Blessed Richard
Gwyn School in Flint, 'because they are for us the extension of
that Catholic family life before which we eternally place the
everlasting example of the Holy Family of Nazareth.'[56] Following
the Butler Education Act of 1944 which made non-fee-paying
education possible for all children up to the age of fifteen, a huge
programme of school extension had to be undertaken by local
authorities. Whereas extant Catholic secondary schools retained
their denominational status, teachers' salaries and running costs
being provided by the LEAs, Catholics themselves were required to
pay 50 per cent towards all improvements and alterations and to
contribute total funding for yet-to-be-established schools. As they
already paid the same amount of taxes as their non-Catholic
neighbours, what they perceived to be the unjust bias of the Act
not surprisingly irked them considerably. In response to the Act's
demands, in 1951 McGrath imposed a penny-a-week schools levy
on all Catholics which he increased to five shillings per head per
annum a year later and ten shillings per head in 1956. This enabled
him to found a relatively strong secondary school system within
his Archdiocese. Yet in Menevia resources were scarce and the
problem consequently much more acute. In order to provide
adequate Catholic education Petit estimated that £750,000 was
needed, a sum which threatened to stunt the Church's progress
within the diocese. He too imposed a levy of £1 per person on
each Catholic, and although the 1959 Education Act increased
grant aid to denominational schools, the burden was still felt to be
quite excessive. Canon John O'Connor spoke for all Welsh
Catholics in 1963 when he claimed that 'with building costs all the
time on the increase, the financial burden for the building of
denominational schools still remains a crushing one for the
promoters'.[57]

As well as providing children with a grounding in Catholic
mores, the Church's schools also had their part to play in inculcating sound Catholic social doctrine. Whereas social concerns were,
in principle, independent of specific political commitments, this
never included a toleration of doctrinaire socialism or communism. 'I hope the Government, in its fight against Communist
infiltration in this island, will realise that in the Catholic children

of England and Wales it has close on 500,000 allies, to say nothing of their parents and families', said Petit in 1948.[58] Neither he nor McGrath tired of warning their flocks of the communist threat and they were quite explicit that the Church's schools should champion their view. In 1955 the bishop of Menevia charged his diocesan schools to be 'the training ground for anti-Communists'.[59] Despite his fiery anti-communism, Petit was equally critical of unbridled capitalism and sensitive to the need to uphold workers rights, encouraging involvement in trade union activities and other social concerns, if possible through the Catholic Young Men's Society, the Young Christian Workers and the Catholic Social Guild.

McGrath, for his part, was progressively less keen on such ventures. Unlike his colleague at Menevia, he was suspicious of the Welfare State, seeing it as tending to undermine personal responsibility and giving the government absolute powers over individual citizens. Politically he veered to the nationalist persuasion and approved the rather patrician, élitist policies of Plaid Cymru during its earlier pre-war phase. By the late 1940s and 1950s, though, he inclined to eschew politics altogether and emphasize instead moral absolutes. Divorce, he had claimed in 1941, was 'an unmentionable crime against God's institution',[60] and remained, in the post-war world, 'an everspreading plague' which was 'paganising society'.[61] 'Divorce', he reiterated in 1953, 'is rotting our civilisation'.[62] His puritanism was oddly reminiscent of the Nonconformist Conscience, a fact underlined by his championing, in the face of secularizing forces, of the Welsh sabbath. Both men were opposed to the morally debasing influence of the cinema, many of its most popular films serving to 'pander to the lower instinct of man'.[63] McGrath, in more colourful language, characteristically indicted the cinemas of south Wales for discharging 'moral filth into the faces of their audiences'.[64] Ever the moral policeman, a decade later he enjoined upon the faithful to report media culprits forthwith: 'If you see anything undesirable or immodest on your television screens you are to switch it off immediately and make a report to your parish priest'![65] The older McGrath grew, the less enamoured he became of a world which seemed to be careering towards moral destruction. Even Petit, during a pilgrimage to Bala in 1954, stated that 'prayer and penance now alone can save the world from disaster to which it is running in headlong fashion'.[66] Yet surprisingly for such innately conservative prelates, both were implacable opponents of nuclear weapons. 'Few of us', they stated at the height of the Cold War, 'have any desire to be blasted to incandescent dust by the atomic weapons of a godless science.'[67] The evils of communist totalitarianism notwithstanding, the crass stupidity of the potential war-mongers of the west was just as menacing for the future of God's good creation.

Whatever a rather pliant and expanding flock actually thought of the Church's uncompromising ultramontane orthodoxy and moral conservatism, there were those outside the Catholic pale who found its attitudes unpalatable in the extreme. For them the Roman Church was intolerant, tyrannical, unscriptural, super-stitious, idolatrous and oppressive. A reasoned and informed critique of Catholicism was rare during these years while the Church's own dismissive attitude towards ecumenism and dialogue did little to improve its standing among Nonconformists and Protestants generally. Catholics were routinely forbidden to attend non-Catholic services, and were certainly not to join with Protestants in common prayer; indeed even on the eve of Vatican II Petit was still making it clear that Catholic presence at Protestant worship afforded legitimacy to what was, in his eyes, blatant error and grievous schism. The Catholic mayor of Aberystwyth was sharply rebuked in 1962 for causing 'scandal' by attending a civic service in a Nonconformist chapel. He was guilty, according to his diocesan, of showing 'a bad example to fellow Catholics and the higher the office that is held, so much the worse is the bad example'.[68] There is no written evidence of the existence in Wales of the sort of tension between an inclusive and exclusive Catholic-ism which was apparent in England at the time,[69] but there can be little doubt that there were those among the clergy and laity who found current attitudes unnecessarily harsh and who would be mightily relieved by the *aggiornamento* which Pope John XXIII's Council would before long put into practice.

Despite a growing post-war weariness with religious contro-versy and polemic, the residual Protestant distrust of the Catholic Church persisted, outside Cardiff and Newport at least, well into the 1950s. Barrett Davies's measured apologia for the dogma of the Assumption which appeared in the *Western Mail* on 1 November 1950 was met with a barrage of opposition, some of it valid but much of it vitriolic and crude. For Nonconformists the whole process, from its original announcement by the Vatican a few months previously to Pius XII's actual *ex cathedra* deliberation in November, comprised 'a huge stride on the part of the papacy to deify Mary'.[70] From the Anglican polemic of the bishops of St David's and Monmouth that the dogma, being impossible to prove from 'Holy Scripture which alone containeth all things necessary for salvation', distorted the balance of truth putting paid to any prospect of pan-Christian union, to the more populist criticism of many laypeople and clergy in the religious press, the main thrust of opposition was the same: that by turning an unsubstantiated tradition into an unconditional truth, Rome had afforded the Virgin an unwarranted and at least semi-divine status. As they reasoned from different premises, the *sola scriptura* of classic Protestantism versus the progressive development of doctrine within the Church under the tutelage of the Holy Spirit, reaching a common mind was patently impossible, yet even potentially informed critique was often clouded by deep hostility.

Professor T. Ellis Jones of the Baptist College in Bangor betrayed an extravagant perversity in his claim that 'the papacy has deified Mary because of its failure to believe in the incarnation itself'. His riposte, that 'we [Protestants] respect his mother but it is He *alone* whom we worship, and reject anyone, be he the Pope himself, who places between [Christ and] us priests, saints, martyrs or Mary',[71] did little justice either to the subtleties or the truth of the Catholic position. Catholics routinely and wearily rebutted such claims. It was 'a cruel falsehood' asserted Petit 'that we Catholics put Our Lady in the place of God';[72] and he reiterated a few years later, 'the honour we pay to Our Lady is the highest honour we can pay to any creature of God, but no more than that'.[73] Given the rationalist presuppositions of some of the more liberal critics of the dogma, Saunders Lewis may not have been too wide of the mark in his claim: 'The belief in Mary's corporeal assumption to be united with her soul is regarded as superstition and blasphemy for the simple reason that we do not seriously, from a true intellectual conviction, believe in the incarnation of God.'[74] Sustained and reasoned theological dialogue, though, was rare indeed, and what could have provided the basis for insight and reflection degenerated, in the main, to innuendo and effrontery. In the words of one recent authority: 'There remained a thin line between justifiable debate and criticism which was born out of hostility and prejudice. The latter, unfortunately, was undoubtedly far more common than the former.'[75]

Almost all public discussion surrounding Catholic beliefs was characterized by a measure of bigotry. For Anne Lodwick Lewis, the Church's faith was 'a substitute for Christianity. The Pope claims to be a substitute for Christ. The sacrifice of the Mass is a substitute for our Lord's sacrifice on Calvary. Mary and the saints take the place of Christ in the hearts of Roman Catholics', she said. Wales's most dire need was 'for another Martin Luther'.[76] The naïvety of many of these attacks was revealed by another letter from a Mrs T. Thomas, a Baptist: 'We do not need candles or beads to help us; a few minutes in silent prayer can make us feel God is very near. We do not need anyone to intervene between God and ourselves; the minister is there to show us the way.'[77] Much popular Protestantism was not only ignorant of the fundamentals of Catholic belief but oblivious to the shortcomings of its own faith. It replicated its own versions of those Catholic errors which it abhorred: the authority of tradition (its own), the infallibility of the Church (or denomination or sect to which its adherents belonged) and the absolute power of the priest (or in its case minister, preacher or elder). Often its much vaunted freedom was as restrictive as ultramontane papalism at its narrowest. Yet for all that ignorance, prejudice and bigotry were far from being a Protestant monopoly. Just as some Nonconformists believed the Pope to be God and Mary as sharing deity with Christ, so 'Catholics have been convinced that Protestants worship only one day a week, that they are usually hypocrites, or that they knowingly misinterpret the Bible in order to bolster their false claims'.[78] Even Christopher Dawson, the widely respected Catholic historian, was compelled to respond to derogatory remarks about Welsh Protestants which had appeared in *The Tablet* and intercede on their behalf: 'I do not see how Catholics can hope to convert Wales to the faith so long as they remain blissfully ignorant of the religious forces that have had such a profound influence on Welsh culture and the mind of the people.'[79] The Church was fortunate to have some apologists – H. W. J. Edwards, J. P. Brown and the Oxford-based Dominican Illtud Evans being foremost among them – whose allegiance to Rome never blinded them to the virtues of chapel culture and the type of popular Nonconformity which had moulded Welsh nationhood over the previous century and a half.

Although Welsh Catholicism was not riven by the tensions which afflicted the Church in Wales during the later 1950s, the triumphalist note struck by the hierarchy disguised at least a measure of failure and uncertainty. For all its numerical expansion, it was clear that cradle Catholics were turning away from the Church in alarming numbers. 'There is appalling leakage', admitted H. W. J. Edwards in 1952. 'There are thousands of lapsed Catholics in Wales.'[80] After the war mixed marriages became the norm and whereas many partners were won to at least a nominal affiliation to the Church, it was apparent that by marrying outside the faith others were contracting out of Catholic commitment for good. The missionary enthusiasm and financial zeal expended in Catholic education was failing to bring commensurate returns. As was true of Christians in the other traditions, indifferentism and spiritual decline were striking at the heart of the Roman faith as well. Whereas the optimistic had believed that the Church was poised to mount the pedestal which Nonconformity seemed set to vacate, there were others who counselled caution and restraint. Describing the state of the Church in Menevia, Illtud Evans pictured 'a handful of Catholics lost in a world that was Protestant until yesterday and today is fast drifting to total unbelief'.[81] Far from paving the way for the triumph of Catholicism, the retreat from the chapels, and, by 1962, from the parish churches as well, signified the ascendency of secularism, atheism and total worldliness. 'Some think we should wait for Protestantism to collapse, when its disillusioned adherents will flock to Catholicism', remarked J. P. Brown in 1957. 'Unfortunately the evidence shows that the vast majority of them turn to modern materialism.'[82] In the increasingly barren atmosphere of mid-twentieth-century unbelief, no church or tradition was safe from its baleful effects.

The crisis of Nonconformity

Despite the secularization which had gone on apace since the late nineteenth century and which had begun seriously to register in the popular consciousness following the First World War, post-Second World War commentators could still refer to Wales as predominantly a Nonconformist nation. 'By the end of the first quarter of the nineteenth century', wrote Professor W. J. Gruffydd, 'Wales had become what it substantially is today, a nation of Evangelical Christians.'[83] 'Today', for Gruffydd, meant 1951. Yet it was obvious to everyone at the time that Welsh Nonconformity was facing a crisis of huge proportions. Its malaise was deepened by the fact that its former ascendancy had been so absolute. The extraordinary success of chapel culture meant that its demise would seem almost calamitous. By the 1950s it had begun to dawn upon the faithful not only that their formerly assured place in Welsh society could no longer be taken for granted, but that institutional Christianity as such was being called seriously into question. Of all forms of faith which would suffer during the subsequent years, it was Nonconformity that would suffer most.

Notwithstanding the despondency which characterized much chapel life after 1945, Nonconformity retained a more than residual hold on the Welsh population as a whole. In 1946 for instance, the Calvinistic Methodists could still boast a membership of 173,000, the Congregationalists 156,000, the Baptists (including those both in fellowship with the Baptist Union of Wales and the London-based Baptist Union of Great Britain and Ireland) 111,000, and the Methodists, who since 1932 had consisted of Primitive and United Methodist congregations as well as Wesleyans, as many as 51,000. In all nearly half-a-million Welshmen and women (491,000) remained communicant members of their respective (principal) denominations. The total Welsh population at the time was some 2.5 million. In some parts of the country, especially the predominantly Welsh-speaking areas of north and west Wales and the heavily urbanized area around Swansea, Nonconformity remained a significant force. The large chapels throughout the eastern valleys of Glamorgan and Gwent and in the highly populated Anglicized conurbations of Cardiff, Newport and Wrexham also witnessed to the continued pre-valence of Dissent. Yet Aneurin Bevan's graphic description of the chapels as being so many 'extinct volcanoes' seemed woundingly accurate. Post-war Nonconformity was fast losing its empire and had not yet begun to find its role.

Amidst the sweeping social transformation which affected the nation after 1945 one element of continuity was the political hegemony of Labour. Its capture of Caernarfon in 1945 and of Brecon and Radnor and of Anglesey in 1951 marked its predominance throughout Wales, both Welsh- and English-speaking, industrial and rural. Yet despite the presence of such committed Nonconformists as George Thomas, Cledwyn Hughes and Tudor Watkins within the parliamentary ranks, most of the Welsh Labour MPs seemed more in tune with the humanist secularism of an Aneurin Bevan than with the chapel-bred radicalism of a James Griffiths. The post-austerity affluence and economic stability over which the 1945–51 Labour government, and its Tory successor, had presided was universally appreciated, yet by the early 1950s there were other aspects of everyday life which some were beginning to find disturbing. Socially and culturally if not economically and financially, this new Wales seemed poorer than the old. Older, more communitarian values, often bound to language and focused in communities of faith, were finding themselves under increasing strain. The 1951 population census showed an alarming decrease among those who could speak Welsh; from 830,000 in 1931 to 715,000, over 100,000 in two decades. More ominous still, the steepest loss was in the industrialized areas and among the young. Welsh was ceasing to be a first language throughout significant areas of Wales, especially in urban districts. Neither was there any sustained policy to halt the decline. Welsh Wales's sense of helplessness and frustration reached its lowest point in 1957 with the decision of Liverpool Council, despite repeated appeals and wholesale and all-party opposition, to drown the Tryweryn Valley and the community of Capel Celyn near Bala, in order to provide the city with drinking water. Tryweryn would become a symbol of the expendability of the older Wales, its culture, values and religion, within a blander, more 'progressive' world. (Along with the creation of the Welsh Language Society in 1962, it would also provide the catalyst for the rejuvenation of nationalism during the later 1960s.)

Yet even where the 'language question' was not foremost in the public consciousness, there was a feeling that the quality of modern life was declining despite all material gains. In south Wales, drinking clubs proliferated, becoming, in Pennar Davies's memorable phrase, 'the Devil's parody on the chapels'. Older cultural forms were either forfeiting peoples' loyalty or being otherwise discontinued. James Griffiths, MP for Llanelli and Wales's first secretary of state, reminisced thus:

In the social and cultural life of the valley communities the most notable change is to be found in the decline in the membership of the nonconformist chapels. In my boyhood days the chapel was the centre of the life of the community. We all grew up under its wing. We learnt Welsh at the Sunday School, took our part in the cantata, joined the choir and cultivated our gifts at the Young Peoples Guild. All of these are still there but their influence has weakened, whilst the 'clubs' multiply. There seems to be ample resources available to build palatial club buildings, and these are full every evening and crowded on Sundays. Even the miners welfare institutes . . . now find that they can keep going only by adding a bar to their other attractions. The local clubs provide good fellowship, they give generously to local causes and help the afflicted and distressed. Whether they will produce leaders for the community, as the chapels did in my time, remains to be seen.[84]

The close link between chapel culture and these seemingly increasingly redundant cultural forms posed a huge challenge for Nonconformity during the 1950s. The denominations' response to the challenge was disappointing at best.

The most pressing problem which faced Welsh Nonconformity between 1945 and 1962, the tercentenary of the religious separation of 1662, was how best to respond to the challenge of decline. Certain key characteristics of Nonconformist life were failing to evoke any positive response among Nonconformists themselves, much less among the population at large. A leading Congregationalist minister, R. Ifor Parry, listed these marks in his able but gloomy study *Ymneilltuaeth* ('Nonconformity') published to coincide with the 1962 celebrations. The current *Zeitgeist*, he claimed, militated against the perpetuation of Welsh Nonconformity, much less its future expansion. Its first debilitating characteristic, he claimed, was, curiously, its Welshness. The very fact that Nonconformity had become so much entwined with Welsh, and especially Welsh-language culture, meant that when one was under threat, the other was bound to suffer. What had been a strength during the nineteenth century when Welsh had been the common speech of the ordinary people, had by the Anglicized 1950s become a glaring weakness. 'As a rule', he wrote, 'wherever people hold fast to Welsh, they remain wedded to the chapel . . . In many areas the fate of Nonconformity is bound up with the fate of the language'.[85] Although each of the principal Welsh denominations had English-language churches while the specifically English bodies were all well represented throughout the land, for a still vast number of people, Welshness and chapel culture were virtually synonymous. The demise of one meant the end of the other. Its second perceived weakness was its particular social morality. The 'Nonconformist Conscience' had coincided with English Nonconformity's Victorian triumphalism at its most bourgeois. Developed during the closing years of the nineteenth century, it had stipulated that social ethics should not only reflect the private morality of the individual chapelgoer, but that a Nonconformist puritanism should be enforced by official legislation. The century-old Welsh Nonconformist consensus meant that puritan mores were perfectly acceptable socially, yet with the weakening of the consensus, the idea of enforcing those mores was to become highly problematic and contentious. For instance, when the people of Swansea voted by a small margin in 1950 that the borough's cinemas should be opened on Sundays, the chapels were vehement in their response. 'The people of Swansea have this week delivered a more serious blow to the moral and spiritual life of the town than the worst of Hitler's bombs could achieve', retorted a local Free Church leader.[86]

Such a disproportionate, though sadly characteristic, response showed how the gap between older, more pietistic, attitudes and present realities was widening. This was highlighted even more by the Licensing Act of 1960, which, in deference to the perceived popular strength of Nonconformity, stipulated that the Welsh people should be allowed to vote on the propriety or otherwise of the Sunday opening of public houses. The result of that vote, which took place in autumn 1961, revealed the starkness of the sabbatarian–non-sabbatarian divide: the eight Welsh-speaking and predominantly Nonconformist counties of the west all voted against Sunday opening while the six more populous and Anglicized counties each voted in favour of change. Yet even then the vote was felt to be an anachronism. A younger generation, less enamoured of the values of puritanism and highly sensitive to the ambiguities of the Nonconformist Conscience, its tendency to censoriousness, smugness and hypocrisy, and its obliviousness to broader social and economic questions, were even then rejecting its morality as repressive and stifling.

Along with these features, Nonconformity's appeal to the internal was increasingly being seen as detrimental to its success.

Whereas both Catholicism and Anglicanism were gaining ground in post-war Wales, Nonconformity, being wed to a dour puritan aesthetic, was thought to be drab and lifeless. Chapel religion was the religion of the Word, not of the senses; its spartan rejection of colour, ceremony and liturgy was losing it appeal. The cerebral character of its piety and its harsh, didactic emphasis was out of step with the world-affirming trends of the time. But for Parry the most threatening challenge which Welsh Nonconformity faced in 1962 was the current fashion for superficiality. The 1950s was a time of release from former disciplines and repression. The idea became prevalent that the post-war world was less morally serious than previously, and that this perceived superficiality would have a detrimental effect on Christianity generally and would sound the death knell for chapel religion in particular. 'This lack of seriousness is fatal for Nonconformity', he claimed. Dissent had triumphed in adversity, when it had gone against the grain of human weakness. Alas, during an era of increasing self-indulgence, the call for self-discipline was falling on deaf ears. 'This is the atmosphere in which Nonconformity is forced to exist and today it is fighting for its life.'[87]

What Parry did not mention expressly but what he and others assumed throughout, was that contemporary Nonconformity's principal problem was spiritual. The word which was used incessantly, almost *ad nauseam*, to describe the state of chapel religion during this period was 'crisis'. The Bangor historian Ambrose Bebb's last testament was entitled *Yr Argyfwng* ('The Crisis'), a volume which more than any other encapsulated the bleak despair of the times. For Bebb the problem was not chiefly social nor psychological nor economic; it was theological, that ordinary church members' faith had become a sham, that their Christianity was no more than a pious charade, that they had apostasized from God and that the Lord was wreaking a wrathful revenge. Other assessments, though less dramatic, were frequently no less pointed. 'It is exceedingly difficult to get our people to realize that what the Gospel has to offer is a matter of life and death', wrote one Presbyterian minister. 'Too many of them are too self-satisfied and self-assured, too comfortable in Zion. Words like "sin" and "grace" mean virtually nothing to them; spiritual realities are a closed book.'[88] A survey of one un-named south Wales chapel, well served by its pastor and outwardly flourishing, revealed a most depressing state of affairs. Of its 324 communicant members, as many as 142 (44 per cent) had not attended public worship for a whole year. The reasons they gave for their absence were:

- that they gleaned no benefit from the sermon (27)
- that they treated Sundays as a day of rest (!) (25)
- that they were too ill to attend (though none had seen a doctor throughout that period) (21)
- that they had quarrelled with fellow worshippers (19)
- that they had tired of the constant requests for money (17)
- that they claimed to be either atheists or agnostics but had never bothered terminating their membership (14)
- that they were unable to attend because of genuine illness (11)
- that they had fallen out with the minister (8)

Even more disconcerting were some of the reasons given by those members who *had* attended services during the previous year:

- 62 attended 'through force of habit'
- 34 attended 'for the sake of the children'
- 34 attended 'in order to worship God'
- 27 attended 'out of respect for the minister'
- 12 attended because they enjoyed the singing
- Of the young people, 12 attended because obliged to by their parents.

Such was the spiritual state of one well-established Nonconformist chapel in south Wales in 1955. 'The sad probability', wrote Iorwerth Jones, editor of the Congregationalists' monthly magazine *Y Dysgedydd* which had published the survey's findings, 'is that the vast majority of our churches are in a similar situation.'[89] Lewis Valentine wrote in similar vein: 'We are witnessing Welsh Wales becoming progressively more irreligious each year, and her grasp on Christianity becoming more tenuous', he claimed, and spoke of 'these recent withered and surly years . . . these days of indefinite faith, of hazy half-belief, of lukewarm, occasional worship, of icy listening and blatant neglect of responsibility.'[90] Despite there still being nominally nearly a half-million chapel members left, and despite their being served by a generation of ministers of high intellectual and spiritual calibre, Welsh Nonconformity seemed to be suffering from a sickness to death.

> It became sick unto death [wrote another thoughtful commentator] for
> want of fresh air. Conventionalism in its way of worship and conduct
> and thinking enclosed it as in a tomb. Each church stood in isolation –
> withering often on its own feet. No vivid sense of contact with a living
> Head, no glow of fellowship with the Church Catholic, or even with
> neighbouring churches, no missionary ardour. One thinks of the valley
> of dry bones.

The words were F. J. Powicke's describing eighteenth-century
Nonconformity in England. Not for nothing did the Revd Trebor
Lloyd Evans, minister of Morriston's Tabernacle, the 'Cathedral'
of Welsh Dissent, deem them highly appropriate to describe the
state of Nonconformity in 1960.[91]

By 1962 the downward trend in chapel affiliation had registered
sharply. Membership within the Presbyterian Church of Wales
had been reduced to 131,000; the Congregationalists were down to
125,000; the Baptists to 90,000 and the Methodists to as few as
16,500. By then more and more of the ministers were questioning
their role and the nature of their calling. 'The ministry as we know
it today is a failure', wrote one of the more restless and imaginitive
of her younger members. 'The partition between ourselves and the
divine has become so solid', he continued, that 'the bare walls of
our chapels, the set-piece greyness of our services and the fear-
driven ordinariness of our ministry can no longer rekindle the
fire.'[92] Badly paid and seemingly little appreciated, many had
sought to fulfil their calling outside of the system, principally as
schoolmasters or in the social services:

> It must be admitted [stated Ifor Parry] that a host of ministers have
> become broken-hearted at their flocks' conservatism and apathy . . . For
> each minister who has left the ministry to become a school teacher, it is
> certain that at least a further half dozen have applied for that same post.
> The question of salary is not the chief consideration but rather bitter dis-
> appointment in the face of the indifference and laxity of their people.[93]

R. S. Thomas's radio poem 'The Minister', broadcast in 1952, expressed their anxiety with exquisite perceptiveness and unique force:

> They chose their pastors as they chose their horses
> For hard work. But the last one died

> Sooner than they expected; nothing sinister,
> You understand, but just the natural
> Breaking of the heart beneath a load
> Unfit for horses. 'Ay, he's a good 'un',
> Job Davies had said; and Job was a master
> Hand at choosing a nag or a pastor.[94]

In his magisterial study of the Welsh Independent tradition, R. Tudur Jones concluded that, by then (1966), 'Christianity itself is under siege. We are facing a crisis of belief.'[95] Yet, despite the despondency, the discouragement and the despair, attempts were being made to forge a future for the Welsh Free Churches.

Attempts to allay the crisis

Broadly speaking the first solution to the crisis within Nonconformity was the evangelical one. Since the end of the war there had been much evangelical activity in the University Colleges, at Bangor and Cardiff especially. This revolved around the Inter-Varsity Fellowship whose doctrinal emphases were the great Protestant truths – justification by faith alone on the basis of Christ's atoning sacrifice for sin – and the infallibility of scripture, and whose experiential emphasis was on the need for personal conversion or being 'born again'. Whereas earlier conservative Welsh evangelicalism had been of the pietistic type characterized by R. B. Jones, Nantlais Williams and their monthly magazine *Yr Efengylydd* ('The Evangelist'), the newer evangelicalism was more scholarly, doctrinally robust and outward-looking. Its focus was *Y Cylchgrawn Efengylaidd* ('The Evangelical Magazine'), initially published on a shoestring budget in November 1948, and soon to become the rallying point for a group and a movement (predominantly of young people), the Evangelical Movement of Wales (EMW). Through its network of fellowship meetings, its annual conference, its ministers' fraternals and, from 1955, its English-language publication *The Evangelical Magazine of Wales*, the EMW struck a new, sometimes strident and soon influential chord in the religious life of the nation. By the mid-1950s the growing crescendo of equally strident opposition to its activities is ample evidence of the effectiveness of its witness.[96] The armchair

Christianity of a still too self-satisfied Nonconformity was being severely rattled by the so-called 'intolerance' of the young evangelicals.

Running parallel with and complementary to this post-war conservative evangelicalism was the Barthian theology of the Word of God. Liberal Protestantism, though still an undoubted factor in Welsh Nonconformist life, had long been felt to have become dated and old-fashioned. The reaction to its utopian optimism which had been registered on the Continent following the First World War was only recorded in Wales after the Second. Lewis Valentine's regular appeals that his fellow Nonconformists return to 'the main thorough-fare of strong doctrine and sound theology'[97] was characteristic of the Barthian ethos. Those deeply indebted to Karl Barth's theology were less biblically conservative than the new evangelicals and usually less intransigent; their emphasis on a renewal of doctrine rather than a specific conversion experience (which was implied rather than explicit in their theology) made them suspect to those on the right wing of the Evangelical Movement. Nevertheless that which evangelical and Barthian held in common – a commitment to the revealed doctrines of orthodox Christianity and a passion for the proclamation of the gospel – was much greater than that which held them apart; their opposition to theological liberalism was total. By the mid-1950s those who held to the theology of the Word of God had arrived at positions of influence within their denominations: Gwilym Bowyer, Isaac Thomas, W. B. Griffiths, J. Ithel Jones, Lewis Valentine and others. Valentine's comments were characteristic of evangelical and Barthian alike:

> It is claimed by the most perceptive commentators that our peoples' ignorance of Christian doctrines is abysmal and even among our most faithful hearers that we dare take nothing for granted. For many Christians the Bible has become the most unfamiliar book in the world, while the preacher's words have become practically unintelligible . . . The reason why the language of Christ's servants has become so unfamiliar to our people today is because Christ the Lord has become a stranger in their midst.[98]

The evangelical solution to Nonconformity's malaise was in a return to the Word of God preached in the convicting strength of the Holy Spirit. Only thus would Welsh religion be revived and restored to its former glory.

Yet this was not the only solution which was offered at the time. Whereas in the England, and to an extent the Scotland of the 1950s, a robust, orthodox theology of revelation was wholly compatible with a zeal for ecumenism (as the careers of such luminaries as Stephen Neill, Lesslie Newbigin, Daniel Jenkins, T. F. Torrance and a host of others confirm), the tendency in Wales was for evangelicalism and ecumenism to be seen as being mutually exclusive. For the evangelical the crying need was for the *individual* to be redeemed whereas the ecumenist emphasized the renewal of the *church*. There was much talk of the Ecumenical Movement being 'the great new fact of our time', and since the Edinburgh Missionary Conference of 1910 the vision of one, undivided Protestant Church had gained considerable momentum. The formation of the British Council of Churches in 1942, followed by the establishment of the World Council of Churches in 1948 and the Council of Churches for Wales in 1956 illustrated the pace of ecumenical development. For Welsh ecumenicals the concept of the 'denomination' had served its purpose; God was now calling upon each single Christian grouping to forgo its historical distinctiveness and merge into a single visible Christian communion 'that the world may believe' (John 17).

There was much in the ecumenical vision that was wholly commendable. The New Testament concept of the church is undoubtedly 'high'; the idea of the community of the redeemed is central to the gospel and not an optional extra. Neither is there any doubt that interdenominational divisions in Wales had been deep despite the underlying oneness, sameness even, of the Nonconformist ethos, a fact which militated against the manifestation of unity as a 'mark' of the church ('We believe in One, Holy, Catholic and Apostolic Church'). 'To know where this Church exists is not a secondary matter', claimed Huw Wynne Griffith, 'or who today is in the apostolic succession.'[99] The continued existence of separate denominations, all of which were professedly Christian and in open competition with one another, was seen increasingly to be a negation of the gospel.

There are six denominations at work in this tiny community of Blaendulais [wrote Erastus Jones], each with its own regular and occasional ministry, its collections, its councils, its literature and its study schemes. This is an ideal system to keep each flock apart but completely inadequate to reclaim the inhabitants of this part of the world which has been entrusted to the care of Christ's church in Blaendulais . . . In the past our diversity, under different historical circumstances, contributed to the glory of our witness. Now it is a hindrance.[100]

To such ecumenical stalwarts as Huw Wynne Griffith and Erastus Jones the need was not for fraternal co-operation between churches and denominations but a wholesale merging into a new unified body: 'In the New Testament church union is organic union', stated Huw Wynne Griffith.[101] 'Each denomination should undergo its own denominational crucifixion', claimed Erastus Jones, 'in order to be resurrected as an organic part of a new and wider church communion.'[102] The initial support of the proposed scheme of union *Tuag At Uno* ('Towards Unity') by each of the principal Nonconformist bodies late in 1962 was thought to mark a tentative beginning of the end for Welsh denominationalism.

But the end was not to be. Even at the time this support in some quarters was half-hearted, and when the practical implications of the unity scheme were realized, popular enthusiasm for ecumenism waned considerably. (The offer made by the Cardiganshire millionaire Sir David James to share a million pounds between the four denominations on condition of their becoming one only served to worsen the situation. Iorwerth Jones, a leading Congregationalist, expressed the feelings of many: 'The sight of a rich man . . . trying to lay down the law . . . by waving his chequebook rather turns my stomach.'[103]) Denominations, by their very nature, are conservative bodies, but there was more than a desire for self-perpetuation in the growing scepticism which accompanied the union discussions. On reflection not everyone was wholly convinced that the day for denominational crucifixion had arrived. Organic union begged serious questions as to the nature of the church; should the proposed 'United Church of Wales' ('Eglwys Unedig Cymru') be governed according to Presbyterian rules, or should it be a loose confederation of separate congregations, or should it appoint its own bishops? And did not the emphasis on organic union presuppose an all-embracing unity which would threaten legitimate diversity and stifle dissent? It transpired that neither theological liberals nor conservative evangelicals were keen to join a monolithic and presumably bureaucratic church structure where the importance of the individual – his intrinsic value in the first instance, her need for redemption in the second – would be compromised. The evangelicals were especially critical; they suspected the Ecumenical Movement of compromising the gospel in a worldly desire to create a 'super-church':

> Every true Christian abhors the narrow spirit of denominationalism and sectarianism [wrote Martyn Lloyd-Jones], but our greatest tragedy today is not the lack of unity within the church but the fact that all parts of the church are so dead and that each denomination is so bereft of the strength and power of the Holy Spirit. Spiritual life does not belong to the realm of mathematics, and were we to make all the denominations into one . . . that would not secure spiritual verve. The fact that more than one dead body is buried in the same cemetery will not lead automatically to resurrection! Life is far more important than unity.[104]

By 1962 attitudes had hardened considerably and Martyn Lloyd-Jones and the Evangelical Movement of Wales were in the vanguard of anti-ecumenical opposition which would intensify as the decade progressed. Yet there were others, although far from virulent in their anti-ecumenical stance, who felt by the mid-1960s that ecumenism and church unity were secondary matters at best. After 1962 the ecumenical vision faded; the crippling secularism of the later 1960s made union schemes seem quite beside the point.

There were other developments within Nonconformity during these years which did not conform to either of the above trends. Pentecostalism, which although doctrinally fundamentalist had little in common with traditional Welsh evangelicalism, became an accepted feature of the life of south Wales if not of the rural areas or the north. The witness of the hierarchical Apostolic Church from its headquarters in Pen-y-groes, Carmarthenshire, had been augmented before the war by the congregationally based Assemblies of God and the more centrally run Elim Four Square Alliance. By the 1950s there was no doubt that a millenarian Christianity which prized vibrant worship and the practice of such spiritual gifts as prophecy, healing and speaking in tongues had the ability to attract converts among the working class. Another minority concern was Quakerism. Unlike Pentecostalism, its appeal was to a more culturally sophisticated middle class. The one Quaker whose influence on subsequent Welsh spirituality would be enormous was the poet Waldo Williams who had been brought up as a Pembroke-shire Baptist. His single volume of verse *Dail Pren* ('The Leaves of a Tree') published in 1956 would become a classic, its simplest lyrics:

> Gwyn eu byd tu hwnt i glyw,
> Tangnefeddwyr, plant i Dduw.
> (Blessed are they beyond earshot,
> Peacemakers, the children of God.)

and its most profound expressions of mystical prayer:

> O ba le'r ymroliai'r môr goleuni
> Oedd a'i waelod ar Weun Parc y Blawd a Parc y Blawd? . . .
> Diau y daw'r dirháu, a pha awr yw hi
> Y daw'r herwr, daw'r heliwr, daw'r hawliwr i'r bwlch,
> Daw'r Brenin Alltud a'r brwyn yn hollti.
> (Where did the sea of light roll from
> Onto Flower Meadow Field and Meadow Field? . . .
> Surely these things must come, and what hour will it be
> That the outlaw comes, the hunter, the claimant to the breach,
> That the Exiled King cometh, and the rushes part in his way.)

both witnessing to a sense of the ineffable which was yet earthed in the reality of brotherhood, human community and the joys of everyday life. Pennar Davies, principal of the Brecon Memorial College, was neither a Quaker nor a Pentecostalist, and, although he lived actively at the heart of post-war Welsh Nonconformity, he was much too singular a personality to be equated with either evangelicalism or ecumenism as such. Yet his spiritual journal *Cudd Fy Meiau* ('Hide My Sins') which appeared in 1958 showed that prayer, contemplation and a wondrous sense of God's nearness were still richly possible even in the context of institu-tional decline.[105] For all the talk of crisis, spirituality remained a vital factor in the ongoing witness of Welsh Dissent.

If the 1950s marked the end of an era, the 1960s marked the beginning of a new phase in British, European and American history. Pop culture and the youth revolution, Vietnam, the assassination of J. F. Kennedy and Martin Luther King, the Profumo scandal, John Robinson's *Honest to God*, Pope John XXIII and the Second Vatican Council, they each made an impact upon Wales or had their parallels within Welsh society. Christianity in Wales would find itself carving out a niche for itself in this new world of change, bewilderment and not a little excitement as well.

7

Uncharted waters, 1962–1979

The lure of the secular

By the early 1960s there were signs that the explicitly churchly concerns of Welsh Christians in the decade and a half following the Second World War were being eclipsed by the novel predilections of the age of the secular. Suddenly the focus of God's activity was said to be not the church but the world. Having been faced with institutional decline, believers sought evidence for the divine presence beyond the ecclesiastical structures and in the political and social ferment of the day. It was certainly an exciting period in the history of the West. Such was the effect of globalization that the nuclear threat and the Cold War were ever-present realities even in the remotest parts of Wales. The conflict in Vietnam, the assassination of John F. Kennedy in 1963 and the shooting of Martin Luther King five years later impinged upon the consciousness of the young everywhere, while pop culture had its exponents not only in Chelsea's King's Road but in Cardiff's Queen Street as well. Expressly Welsh concerns, not least a resurgent nationalism which affected urban, English-speaking Wales as well as the rural heartland, meshed comfortably into the wider pattern, while the searing tragedy of Aberfan not only drew sympathy from around the world but left its indelible mark on the spiritual psyche of the native population as a whole. The theological ferment represented by Bishop Robinson's *Honest to God* (1963) and the transient doctrines of the 'Death of God' school also had their parallels within Welsh Christianity. During the late 1960s it was clear that attitudes towards institutional religion were undergoing a transformation, while by the mid-1970s there had been a sea-change in the public's perception of the faith itself. The Christianity which had been a defining characteristic of Welsh nationhood since the age of the Celtic saints had become the concern of an ever-shrinking minority.

The change in focus from church to world affected Churchmen and Nonconformists alike and was reflected in the somewhat surprising evolution of Glyn Simon, bishop of Llandaff and between 1968 and 1971 archbishop of Wales. Although he could still claim, not without justification, to be an old-fashioned Anglo-Catholic clergyman resolute in his orthodoxy, nevertheless by the 1960s he was moving in an increasingly radical direction. For one thing, he came to reject the traditional theory of the Just War, even feeling that the war against Hitler with its aerial attacks against unarmed civilians had degenerated into something quite barbaric. 'Then', he said, 'came the Bomb.'[1] Simon became outspoken in his support for the Campaign for Nuclear Disarmament, even believing that in a nuclear age pacifism was the only viable Christian option, an opinion which had already been championed by his colleague, Gwilym O. Williams, the bishop of Bangor: 'I consider', said Williams, '. . . that to possess nuclear arms and be prepared to use them is so incompatible with Christian morality that we must renounce war altogether, in all circumstances, and take the consequences.'[2] This was a highly unusual position for any Anglican bishop at the time. As for the bishop of Llandaff, neither was he enamoured of America's role in Vietnam. In a letter to *The Times* in 1965, Simon wrote: 'I am sure that I speak for very many Christians who are horrified by the use there of napalm bombs and gas . . . Napalm bombs in Korea roasted whole villages and left people alive, blind and skinless. These are horrific and inexcusable weapons to use.'[3] What would have been unexceptional from the pen of a Nonconformist still struck some as being dangerously subversive from a senior bishop in the Church in Wales. In fact as Nonconformity atrophied, the older distinction between Dissenting radicalism and Anglican conservatism broke down. If the bishop of Monmouth, Simon's predecessor as archbishop, remained staunch in his defence of the nuclear deterrent and the establishment's attitude towards the concept of the Just War,[4] others on the Welsh bench were becoming much more explicit in their radicalism.

Yet it was in his attitude to the urban, industrialized, ever more rootless Wales that the bishop of Llandaff displayed the evolution of his thought most openly. Already in his Primary Visitation Charge of 1961 he had stated that 'the man-in-industry is no longer the man-in-church, in-chapel, in the worshipping community'. Whereas formerly in the south Wales valleys the industrial working class had not been alienated from institutionalized religion, that was obviously no longer the case. However, instead of bemoaning the fact he decided to act: 'Since men do not come to the Church, the Church is making an effort to go to them.'[5] The reference was to the Industrial Mission inaugurated in August 1960 at Port Talbot's Abbey steelworks. By 1962 the Steel Company of Wales employed a workforce of 17,000 at Port Talbot while newly opened Llanwern near Newport, Gwent, would soon expand to a comparable size. Whereas the industrial chaplaincy had been initially a joint venture between both Nonconformists and Churchmen, by 1965 only the Anglican chaplain, the Revd David Lee, remained, a fact which irked the bishop enormously. 'The combined efforts of about a dozen Free Churches have failed to provide a Free Church chaplain', he announced, 'so we are left with one man at work amongst fourteen to sixteen thousand men.' Ever the Anglican, Simon berated the 'deficient theology of "the Gathered Church"' for the fault.[6] In fact the store he set on the concept of a professional chaplaincy was, in Free Church terms, much overstated. For Nonconformity, Christian presence had always been most efficiently manifested by the *laos*, ordinary church members bringing their witness to bear in the workplace and among their fellows. Yet by the 1960s the most pressing problem for both chapel and church was the encroachment of secular values upon the population as a whole and a decline in active Christian commitment by working-class men especially. Social structures were in flux and the break-up of the older, more static communities in which all shared a single workplace, language and limited range of economic opportunities presented 'a baffling pastoral problem: everybody moves about'.[7] The authors of the survey of the industrialized zone in south-west Wales, *The Church in a Mobile Society* (1969), were exercised with the same phenomenon: how could a still static church serve both gospel and community in a rapidly changing society? The survey revealed

a preoccupation with women's work, a shortage of youth, a preoccupation with buildings, and a general picture of being out of contact with the community . . . The church in the zone is very largely a collection of individual congregations, unevenly distributed, inadequately co-ordinated . . . to their wider missionary task, and certainly with no purpose or plan with which to serve the community as a whole.[8]

Christian renewal, though, was still a possibility, but not through traditional revivalism or the replication of conventional church-centred patterns. The conference of the Council of Churches for Wales entitled 'the Church in Industry', held at Rhoose in the Vale of Glamorgan in July 1962, had already suggested that the most apposite form of Christian witness in the new Wales was not proselytization or active evangelism but costly solidarity with the unchurched in order to learn from them. The gospel note was muted. 'The pattern of Christian mission in the secular world must be one of constant encounter with the real needs of our age', deliberated the Council's Industrial Committee in 1965. 'Its form must be dialogue, using contemporary language and modes of thought, learning from the scientific and social categories, and meeting people in their own situations.'[9] The confident orthodoxy of the late 1940s and 1950s whether Anglican, evangelical or Barthian, which presupposed that the church knew the truth and only needed to apply its message to society's needs, had given way to a much more halting, questioning and insecure stage in which the secular realities of contemporary life were given prominence over God's objective revelation whether in scripture or in the church. The Council of Churches for Wales's 'People Next Door' campaign, a six-week programme lasting between January to May 1967, was equally circumspect in its evangelistic content. 'It will not be so much an attempt to draw outsiders into the Church as an earnest attempt by the Church itself to understand the world and God's activity within it . . . In *People Next Door* we shall be more concerned with converting the Church so that it can be more effective as part of God's answer to men's needs.'[10]

By the mid-1960s mainstream Christianity in Wales had imbibed many of the attitudes and dogmas of the Ecumenical Movement in its most overtly secularist phase. There was Welsh representation at the World Council of Churches Geneva consultation on Church and Society in 1966, the most serious attempt by the WCC to understand the revolutionary realities which were shaping the modern world, and at the Uppsala Assembly in 1968, the high point of the Council's developing politicization. The Movement's ideals and ideas were mediated in part by the Blaendulais Ecumenical Centre, located initially in Seven Sisters in the Dulais Valley, Glamorganshire, under the dynamic directorship of the Revd Erastus Jones, while from 1966 the Commission of the Churches

on Industry, chaired by Port Talbot's David Lee, and from 1967 the
Gwynedd Ecumenical Forum, also helped popularize current WCC
thinking. According to their ideals, the boundary between church
and world had become blurred and the difference between Christian belief and human goodwill was frequently inconsequential. In a
reaction against the biblicism and church-centredness of the
previous generation, the emphasis tended now towards 'anony-
mous Christianity' and signs of transcendence were sought within
the secular sphere. 'It cannot be said too much', said the authors of
the churches' survey in south-west Wales, 'that the Church must
work out afresh in each age not the meaning of the Christian
religion but the Christian meaning of the world.' That world was
comprised of 'men of goodwill from all denominations or none'
while the Christian mission therein should not be confined to
committed church members alone.[11] Whereas there was much in
this which was salutary and sound, current trends did little to
reassure ordinary churchgoers of the validity of their traditional
faith or its relevance to a secular society. If a great deal of effort
was expended on trying to understand contemporary life, little
time was taken to explain how the gospel could meet the challenge
of the time. In fact, with secular, political and a demythologized
theology now in vogue, doctrinal minimalism was in danger of
becoming the norm. The impression gained during the 1960s was
that prayer and spirituality had become increasingly problematic,
that only a secularized gospel would commend itself to technological man, while worship was superseded more and more by a
religiously tinged activism. All in all they were, in the words of
Glyn Simon, 'days of uncertainty and difficulty and change'.[12]

The theological ferment

Christianity's fascination with the secular during the 1960s was
inextricably connected with the influence and appeal of radical
theology. In his Second Visitation Charge of 1966, Llandaff's
bishop bemoaned the fact that vocations for the priesthood had
declined due, in part, to 'the theological ferment of our days'.
If, in the wake of John Robinson, the bishop of Woolwich's
phenomenally popular paperback *Honest to God*, doctrine and
theology had found their way back into the everyday conversation

of ordinary people, the drawback was that 'men have been made to feel unsure of the Scriptures, the Creeds, the Church, the Ministry, even Christianity itself'. If the focus for God's presence was no longer the church but the world, it was thought that in order to be effective the gospel needed to be reformulated according to the mundane and non-miraculous thought-patterns of contemporary man. It was obvious, therefore, that older certainties would be called into question in a fundamental way. 'In their efforts to do this many writers have used misleading and sometimes wild phrases such as "the Death of God", "the Abolition of Religion", "the End of Religion", and "our Image of God must go" and so forth, which have caused great confusion.'[13] Despite his growing openness to change in both society and the church, Simon retained his belief in the historicity of the gospel narratives and would have no truck with doctrinal reductionism. He was not unduly perturbed by the challenge which the secular theologians posed: 'It will pass and leave behind it whatever is of permanent value for our better understanding and use of the riches of the Gospel.'[14] There were others, however, who were much less complacent.

If the ferment did not directly affect most ordinary church members, the rapidity of social change which characterized the decade helped engender bewilderment and gave the impression that all formerly accepted truth was being shaken to its very foundations. Those who were directly involved in the exposition, proclamation and defence of the Christian verities – ministers and the clergy, teachers of religion in the schools and colleges, seminary tutors and ordinands – could hardly avoid facing the new theological issues squarely. The tensions between secular and sacred, the experimental and the familiar, erupted in the theological colleges and in the theological (and philosophical) departments of the University of Wales. Under the wardenship of the Revd O. G. Rees, St Michael's College, still set firmly in its rather baroque Tractarian mould, experienced something of a crisis. Following his appointment in 1958, the first thing Rees did was to take the college into the University College of Cardiff's Faculty of Theology thus ensuring that it would no longer be sheltered from the influences of the academic mainstream. As the 1960s progressed, the pressures of modernity rendered some of the older spiritual disciplines obsolete while there developed an escalating retreat from earlier positions of obedience and authority. What had been the norm in the 1950s came to be felt as unreal, precious and cloyingly pious a decade later. Questions were asked about the place of prayer, worship and semi-monastic spirituality in a world come of age. Rather than retreat from the challenge, Rees, who had been an intellectually distinguished and exemplary High Church priest, responded creatively not only to such Anglican trends as Joseph Fletcher's 'Situation Ethics' and the bishop of Woolwich's 'South Bank Theology' but to the weightier issues connected with the much more powerful thought of Rudolf Bultmann, Paul Tillich and Dietrich Bonhoeffer. There was 'a growing unwillingness on the part of the Warden to be trammelled by the Tractarian legacy of the Founding Fathers'[15] which resulted in a liberalization of the regime and an opening up not just to newer trends in critical theology but to spiritual traditions besides Anglo-Catholicism. Bishop Simon, in whose conscience conservative and radical forces seemed to be constantly at war, did not approve of this widening of the gates, especially when it involved the appointment of a conservative evangelical to the staff. Yet the warden stood his ground and by the 1970s St Michael's was representative of a much more open Anglicanism than had hitherto been the case.

It was not only among the ordinands and clergy of the Church in Wales that theological contention raged, in fact the one single figure who generated the most controversy was neither an Anglican nor a clergyman but a Calvinistic Methodist layman employed by the University of Wales in Swansea. Since 1952 J. R. Jones, a diffident, eminently respectable and highly able north Walian, had been professor of Philosophy at the town's University College. Although he was relatively unknown beyond the world of academic philosophy, by the mid-1960s the twin crises of nationhood and Christian identity had forced him on to a more public platform. Not previously renowned for political partisanship, he suddenly championed the cause of Welsh cultural nationalism in its more militant guise, becoming the house philosopher of Cymdeithas yr Iaith Gymraeg, the Welsh Language Society. The Society had been formed in 1962 following Saunders Lewis's epoch-making BBC annual lecture 'The Fate of the Language' in which he urged immediate political action to preserve Welsh as a living language into the twenty-first century. Jones became one of the few senior academics who immediately supported the Society's civil disobedience campaigns and it was knowledge of this unexpected radicalization, oddly characteristic of certain other middle-aged western intellectuals during the 1960s, which gave his pronouncements on religious matters publicity which otherwise they would not have been afforded. His powerfully expressed pamphlet *Yr Argyfwng Gwacter Ystyr* ('The Crisis of Meaninglessness') (1964) caught the temper of the times perfectly and stimulated discussion in the Welsh-language press and media for months on end. Like *Honest to God* its content was derivative and imprecise and its rejection of classic Christianity was cavalier in the extreme. What it did convey was passion and moral earnestness made all the more striking by its vigorous prose style.

According to J. R. Jones both conventional and orthodox Christianity were based on the supposition that man's sinfulness induced guilt which needed to be assuaged by the divine forgiveness. Consequently, for traditional Nonconformity the doctrines of atonement and redemption were both deemed essential. These ideas, though, had been thoroughly discredited by modern people whose current existential need was not so much for the divine forgiveness but for meaning, the assurance that life was purposeful. Traditional religiosity assured men and women of succour and comfort through God's personal redeeming presence in their lives, a concept which, for Jones, belonged quite definitely to humankind's infancy. What modern, technological people needed was not some superstitious mythology about salvation but a religion which would give them strength to live their lives in a world in which the traditional God was dead. The most pressing problem for secular people was that of power, how to live with dignity without being crushed by impersonal forces within a post-religious world. Though shorn of its metaphysic, Christianity still provided the answer to this problem in the cross. The cross of Christ had no atoning value but was symbolic of the paradoxical nature of the divine power, a strength perfected in weakness. 'Jesus died as he did to *teach* us – to teach mankind truly to understand the most awesome and dangerous possession which has been given him, that of power.' In order to learn the lessons of power, men and women needed to be convicted and converted, not in the evangelical sense but in the sense of actively appropriating the reality of contemporary godforsakenness. Whereas formerly justification was by faith, in a godless age justification could only possibly be by *un*belief: 'This is the only faith possible for thousands in an age devoid of meaning.' The God who accepted modern people on these terms was not the God of orthodoxy but 'the God beyond God', 'Being itself', the depth and ground of all existence. The way out of the crisis of meaninglessness was by justification through radical unbelief, 'the justification by faith beyond faith', or, in words quoted from Tillich, 'Simply accept that you are accepted'.[16]

The response to J. R. Jones's reflections was fast and furious. Dr R. Tudur Jones, professor of church history at the Congregationalists' seminary at Bala-Bangor, already a towering intellectual and then becoming a Christian leader of wide influence, was characteristically blunt: 'If Rudolf Bultmann, Paul Tillich, Dietrich Bonhoeffer (in his teaching on "religionless" Christianity), Dr J. R. Jones and the Bishop of Woolwich are correct, then for twenty centuries Christianity has been built on a lie.'[17] But it was H. D. Lewis, like J. R. Jones a Calvinistic Methodist layman and professional philosopher, holder of the chair in the philosophy of religion at King's College, London, who was the most outspoken in his critique. 'It appears to me', he wrote, 'that there are some elements in the living faith which are essential for it to be Christian faith at all. One is the objective existence of God and the other is that Jesus Christ is both human and divine . . . It appears that J. R. Jones accepts neither.'[18] One by one he challenged each of the Swansea professor's contentions stating, instead, that God was an objective, personal, self-revealing reality and not the abstract, impersonal ground of human existence; that the essence of religion was a reasoned and mature response to the mystery of the divine and not a childish cry for transcendental succour; that there was nothing unbecoming in Christianity's character as a redemptive faith replete with doctrines of atonement and salvation, neither was this out of place even in the secular environment of a technological world. The crisis of meaninglessness, although undoubtedly a fact, was but one aspect of a wider crisis which could not be detached from questions of forgiveness and belief, questions which could still only be answered adequately by a full-bodied gospel which presupposed God's personal and saving involvement in the world: 'If we truly understand our present predicament . . . we will soon realise that there is no remedy apart from God having shared our lives as indeed he did in the person of Jesus Christ.' Far from being justified by their inability to believe, modern men and women would only find salvation in the God who had made this redemption possible. 'I would not be at all surprised to see a revival of religion', Lewis concluded, 'in which perceptive preaching and earnest prayer will play a most prominent part. At its heart will be a consciousness of the glory of Jesus Christ and the wonder of what he has achieved on our behalf.'[19]

By the mid-1960s J. R. Jones had achieved a reputation among the orthodox for being a troubler of Zion and among the liberals as a martyr for the truth. There is no doubt that there was much in his religious thought which was eclectic and crude; theologically he lacked both balance and breadth and he seemed wholly ignorant of the riches and subtleties of the historic faith. But what he lacked in doctrinal finesse he made up for in moral seriousness. If anything he was *too* serious; nowhere in his work is there a lightness of touch or a feeling of the joy of redemption or of the openness of the Holy Spirit. It would be easier to agree with D. Z. Phillips's criticism of the harsh response of 'the Welsh theological establishment' to Jones's theories, a response which 'brought little credit on it intellectually or spiritually',[20] had his colleague and predecessor in the chair of philosophy at Swansea shown a less superficial grasp of Christian orthodoxy and been less biting in his contempt towards its practitioners. 'Pay no heed to the "salvation mongers",' he had said. 'All they will do will heap a load of guilt upon your shoulders – they are utterly devoid of the love of Jesus. You will leave their services with your intellectual integrity insulted and impaired.'[21] This bitter disdain for the deeply held conviction of others did as much as anything to vitiate any positive contribution which J. R. Jones might have made to the development of the Christian mind in Wales.

The evolution of Jones's thought between 'The Crisis of Meaninglessness' in 1964 and the end of the decade took him even farther from Christian truth, and though he bore a fatal illness with immense fortitude and dignity, his final work *Ac Onide* ('And Were it Not') (1970) showed clearly the extent of his disenchantment with traditional faith. Whereas he had formerly held fast to the person of the historical Jesus, by the end even that seemed to have disappeared: 'In the light of the confusion and bewilderment of the New Testament evidence, I cannot but believe that *it has all been only a dream.*[22] His later essays are gloomy and stoical, characterized more by what he felt he had to reject – especially God's providence and personal presence within the world – than that which he could positively affirm. But by that time his religious influence if not his political prestige through the ever more active Cymdeithas yr Iaith Gymraeg had waned. Jones, though, was a figure of the 1960s more than of the 1970s, whose seemingly prophetic daring, so exciting and challenging when the optimism of the decade was in full flow in 1964, had coalesced with the post-Vietnam, post-Kennedy and post-Luther King pessimism which so marred its conclusion. And of course in the interim there had been Aberfan.

The Aberfan disaster

The Aberfan disaster was a defining moment in the history of Christianity in twentieth-century Wales. Like the senseless slaughter of the Somme and the Holocaust for the Jews, it called into question virtually all the truths of people's conventional understanding of the divine: God's involvement in creation, his providential ordering of the world and above all the suffering of the innocent. The problem of theodicy was made even more emotive by its context in the historical development of south Wales. Coal, which had been the mainstay of the Welsh industrial economy for nearly a century, capitalism and human rapaciousness as well as questions of faith and meaning were all seen to have a bearing on the calamity of 21 October 1966. Yet if the cry of dereliction was heard on that misty autumn morning, in the midst of tragedy there was evidence too of the divine pity and, haltingly but unmistakably, the hope of resurrection as well.

The village of Aberfan, a community of some 3,000 inhabitants, is situated five miles to the south of Merthyr Tydfil towards Cardiff on the western bank of the River Taff. Of the 850 miners employed at the Merthyr Vale Colliery, a large number were local, many from Aberfan itself. Since the early decades of the century, the colliery had disposed of its waste in seven pyramid-like tips to the west of the old Glamorgan Canal on the side of Merthyr Mountain. The 111-foot No.7 Tip, which was directly above the

Pant-glas area of the village, had already suffered substantial slippage in 1963, yet despite local protests nothing was done either to secure it or to prevent further waste from being disposed on the site. Following heavy rainfall, at 7.30 on the morning of the 21st, a squad of workmen arrived at the tip to find that it had subsided overnight by some 10 feet leaving a crane in danger of falling into the newly created depression near the tip's summit. One of their number reported back to the colliery with this information and, on his return in the company of the chargehand responsible for work on No.7, found that the crater had expanded by another 12 feet. While the other workers were in a shed nearby, the crane driver, Gwyn Brown, surveyed the scene and was amazed to see slag, slurry and waste welling up from the hole which, in a huge wave, began pouring volcano-like down the mountain's side. A second wave, some 30 feet across and 30 feet high, burst out after it with tremendous force and the whole tip broke away careering down the slope and disappeared into the mist below. Two farm cottages directly in its path were engulfed, killing their occupants instantly, while the thousands of tons of wet rubble sped across the canal, the railway embankment and through Pant-glas Junior School, damaging the adjoining senior school and smashing into eighteen terraced houses in the village's Moy Road. It happened in a matter of minutes between 9.15 and 9.20 a.m. and the noise it made was said to be like the screech of a jet plane crashing into the mountain side.

At the Pant-glas Junior School the day had begun as usual at 9 a.m. (activities commenced half an hour later in the senior school next door thus preventing the disaster from being even more calamitous than it actually was). The black avalanche hit the unsuspecting pupils, all of whom were between four and eleven years old, at their desks less than twenty minutes later. The head-mistress, Miss Ann Jennings, died in her office; the deputy headmaster was killed along with his class of thirty-four; the body of another master was found shielding in vain three small children – the whole class of thirty-three had perished. In another room only one child survived from a class of twenty, their female teacher having died, while another mistress perished along with her whole class of thirty-three. The body of the dinner lady was found still clutching a pound note in her hand. Of a staff of nine, only three survived. Apart from the sixty-four-year-old headmistress, all the teachers were in their twenties and one in her early thirties. The rescue services arrived swiftly to find a scene of horror and utter devastation. The mountain of slurry was ice-cold, black and lethal. It was littered with boulders, uprooted trees and masonry from the buildings which had lain in its path. A waterpipe had burst in the village adding to the mayhem. By the time the first ambulances came, miners from the Merthyr Vale Colliery were already at work frantically digging for survivors. By 10 a.m. sixty bodies had been recovered; by 2 p.m. the total was eighty-three and by 6 o'clock that evening it had risen to 100. After 11 a.m., hours before, no one was brought out alive. All the children were laid to rest in Bethania, the Welsh Congregational Chapel, a few hundred yards along the road. Throughout the coming days distraught parents would queue outside its doors before entering the sanctuary in order to identify the bodies of their little ones.

Among the parents who arrived at the school almost immediately was the Revd Kenneth Hayes, pastor of Zion Baptist chapel in neighbouring Merthyr Vale. His manse was in Moy Road next to the school where his sons, Gwilym and Dyfrig, were pupils. Seven-year-old Gwilym was at home, recovering from an operation, but Dyfrig, two years his senior, was among the Pantglas juniors when the calamity struck. Their mother, a teacher at the adjacent senior school, had already arrived at work when that building was partly demolished by the onslaught of slurry and muck, though she emerged unscathed. Her husband was to remain among the buried classrooms for the rest of the day searching in vain for their eldest son before returning home to begin a sorrowful pastoral round comforting the bereaved. Seeing the need at hand he began compiling a list of the missing. The school registers were buried so he went round the parents, most of whom he knew, to ask which of their children had not been found. A provisional list was compiled. It was 11 p.m. before he joined the queue outside Bethania to see whether the body of Dyfrig had been brought in. The village had been inundated some twelve hours earlier by police, the rescue services, hundreds of miners from the surrounding pits and volunteers from the Salvation Army and the WVS, and by lunchtime by the media. 'The valleys of Wales have seen their tragedies', said the president of the National Union of Mineworkers at midday, 'but never one like this.'[23] By late afternoon Cledwyn Hughes, secretary of state for Wales, had arrived by helicopter from his Anglesey constituency, and on inspecting the scene of devastation was shaken to the core. He reported immediately to the prime minister, Harold Wilson, and described the disaster's scale. By then, twenty miles away in leafy Llandaff, Glyn Simon had already drafted a letter to the *Western Mail*. 'I write with a full heart, which I share with countless thousands, face to face with this terrible tragedy, as I prepare myself to go tomorrow to Aberfan to give what help I can to stricken families.' It contained no pieties or explanations but, in very clear and forthright terms, a call for immediate action to clear the valleys of tips.

> Many will feel embittered and enraged at a disaster the causes of which some will ascribe to the ruthless exploitations of the past, others to the procrastinations and carelessness of the present . . . All over South Wales are old tips full of potential danger. The task of removing them or making them safe is vast, far beyond the means of any local authority. I call upon all to support me by every means in their power to have this terrible problem solved at once by the Government which alone has the resources to deal with it . . . As a first step please write at once in tens of thousands to the Prime Minister, the Minister for Wales and your own Member of Parliament, demanding action now. In this way, though we cannot bring back the dead nor heal the sorrows of the bereaved, we can at least secure that these children shall not have died in vain.[24]

They were brave and timely words and that afternoon the bishop found himself spokesperson for the whole of Wales and beyond: 'He had put into words what millions were going to feel when the evening television and the morning papers had added their reports to those already carried by the evening papers and radio.'[25] By 9 p.m. the prime minister had arrived at the village from the RAF base at St Athan having flown from the north of England; he proceeded to the rescue headquarters which, earlier in the day, had been established at Merthyr Tydfil. Lord Snowdon, husband of Princess Margaret, sister of the Queen, came by at 2 a.m. and spent hours with the sleepless, bereaved and still waiting parents while the digging continued under arc lights throughout the night. But it was the bishop whose onerous task it had been late that evening, on television, to convey the sympathy of the Welsh people, to provide comfort and some semblance of meaning to the whole affair.

Sorrow brings us all together, and bitter as its lessons are, they do more to help us understand our fellow-men than any others we can learn. That understanding we give you, and you have seen it at work in the rescuers of every kind that are with you now.

I would like to share with you some words of scripture from Isaiah 43, that have often helped me much: 'Fear not . . . I have called you by name, you are mine. When you pass through the waters I will be with you; and through the rivers, they shall not overwhelm you'. And now a prayer: 'O Lord Jesus, whose heart was pierced with a spear and by Thy love left open for all who enter in: bring us thither in the hour of trouble, and hold us there for ever'.

Many of those who died today were children: they went straight from their prayers to the Father with whom they had just been speaking. God help you who love them so to live that with them you may go to Him and see: 'With the morn, those angel-faces smile, which we have loved, and lost awhile'.[26]

On Saturday it rained steadily. The duke of Edinburgh visited, Glyn Simon spent the day in the company of the rescue services and the bereaved while the local clergy went about a multiplicity of pastoral tasks. In the evening, belatedly, Lord Robens, chairman of the National Coal Board, put in an appearance. Such was the weight of traffic, activity and drenching rain that by nightfall the site was a quagmire. The body of Dyfrig Hayes had been recovered during the afternoon. By midnight the official figure of those who had died had reached 118.

On Sunday morning the faithful, along with assorted rescuers and newspaper people, turned out to worship. No services could be held in Bethania which still held the dead, or in Capel Aberfan, the Welsh Presbyterian chapel, which had become a second mortuary. Smyrna, the Welsh Baptist chapel, had been commandeered as a rest centre as had the meeting house belonging to the Churches of Christ. Each of the Sunday schools and those in Merthyr Vale had lost children in the landslide, the Church of Christ suffering most heavily with twenty-two fatalities and the Methodists with sixteen. Yet in the remaining churches and chapels services were held, prayers were offered to God and the comfort of the gospel was applied. Kenneth Hayes's ordeal was perhaps the worst. He had had virtually no sleep since Thursday night having worked incessantly as a member of the rescue team, organizing relief and comforting the bereaved. He was also carrying the burden of grief at the loss of his own young son. Despite everything he was in his pulpit at Zion chapel promptly at 11 a.m. He read from Psalm 90 and the closing verses of Romans 8, 'Nothing will separate us from the love of God', while prayer was offered by one of the church's deacons. The pastor himself made a plea for an end to the tipping of coal waste throughout the valleys, then he said: 'Let us thank God that things are not worse. We must not be bitter but must approach it with a spirit of love. Let us be thankful for miracles and thank God for those who survived.' When the congregation sang 'Safe in the arms of Jesus', he broke down and wept.

The role which Aberfan's churches played both during the tragedy and subsequently was considerable. As the servant church its members were at hand to fulfil a practical ministry and as the representatives of God within the community they did their best to offer some rationale for what had happened. 'Faith isn't dead', remarked the Methodist minister the Revd Irving Penberthy, 'but glows as a flickering flame to be coaxed and fed with friendship and kindness.' Like all communities in the valleys, the chapels and churches had suffered from a decline in membership for some two or three generations at least, but equally typically there was little anti-religious feeling and Christianity and the institutions which embodied it still engendered widespread respect. 'The community has accepted that the church has a mission and a message', said Kenneth Hayes, 'and can offer leadership. We in the church have discovered that there is more latent faith outside the Christian fellowship than we would have previously acknowledged.' Remarkable and perhaps unexpected was the lack of resentment or hostility towards God. 'Two or three people did ask me in the first days, "Why did God allow this tragedy to happen?" but I have not heard it since then', the Revd Hayes recalled. 'From my correspondence I would say that this question has been asked much more by people outside Aberfan.'[27] There was no cynicism; only unbelievers blamed God for the tragedy. If there would be no evidence of a widespread revival neither was there any renunciation of faith. As for the chapels and the churches, their contribution was revered even by the uncommitted: 'They were respected and they proved, in the days of trouble, a strength, a pillar of a veritable old order that still stood reliably among the human debris.'[28] Faith, if shaken, had once more stood the test. By Sunday evening the death toll stood at 122.

Arrangements for the burial of the dead began to be made on
Monday. Apart from those families who wanted individual funerals,
it was decided that there would be a communal burial in the
village's single hillside cemetery on the following Thursday. Miners
began cutting two vast strip graves 60 yards across. The service
would be conducted by Glyn Simon representing the Church in
Wales, the Most Revd Dr John Murphy, archbishop of Cardiff,
representing the Roman Catholic Church, while the
Nonconformists chose to be represented by the Revd Stanley Lloyd,
the village's senior pastor who had served the Bethania
congregation since 1945. On Thursday afternoon, which was
bitterly cold, the small coffins of eighty-two children along with
that of one adult were brought slowly in a fleet of hearses and made
their way to allocated spots on the hillside above the village. Some
5,000 had congregated to pay their last respects to the dead. The
thousands of flowers and wreaths which had arrived from around
the world were set in the shape of a huge cross 130 feet wide and 40
feet across and laid beside the graves. For the first time in a week all
clearance work stopped and silence descended. At 3 o'clock the
service commenced. Glyn Simon announced the first hymn and read
from Isaiah and St Luke and verses from Zachariah and Malachi:
'And the streets of the city shall be full of boys and girls playing . . .
and they shall be mine, saith the Lord.' The archbishop of Cardiff
led the intercessions and led the congregation in the words of the
Lord's Prayer. (The ecumenical significance of both the archbishop's
presence at an inter-denominational service and his leading joint
prayer was striking. Only a few years previously such a gesture
would have been impossible given the rigid discipline of the pre-
Second Vatican Council Catholic Church.) The words of the
committal were announced by the Revd Stanley Lloyd: 'In the name
of Almighty God and his Son, Jesus Christ, we tenderly commit the
bodies of our dear children to the ground. Earth to earth, ashes to
ashes, dust to dust, but the spirit returneth unto God who gave it.' A
closing hymn was sung and the benediction was given. The
mourners stood huddled together with dignity and restraint. The
service had taken fifteen minutes. No one noticed the cold. The final
total of those who had died was 154, eighty-two of whom were
buried in this service while forty-one were buried in separate
services in the same cemetery. There were eighteen cremations and
three were buried elsewhere.

It was during the months after the disaster that the complexity of the tragedy really registered. The burgeoning disaster fund, whose 90,000 contributions had already reached £1,607,000 by January 1967, threatened to create a second Aberfan disaster so potentially contentious was the financial aspect of rehabilitation. The government tribunal, which was commenced on 29 November 1966 and lasted a record seventy-six days, was also a likely source of strife. Its report, published in August 1967, was not the feared whitewash but placed the blame squarely at the door of the National Coal Board for having no overall plan for the disposal of colliery waste or for the regular checking of existing tips. Although blame was apportioned, a move which the community welcomed, there was no attempt at recrimination or vilification. The Board and its officers had acted through ineptitude rather than wickedness. One journalist at the inquiry had been oddly prophetic: 'What may emerge is a picture not of callously indifferent men but of a multitude of ordinary individuals discharging their jobs with honesty but without imagination.'[29] Yet the Board was clearly culpable for allowing Tip No.7 to be erected over the source of a stream the existence of which was well known within the village. Following the inquiry came the task of physical reconstruction and psychological rehabilitation to which the community responded with commendable resolve. Aberfan did not slip back into the apathy, inertia and indifference which was beginning to blight the older communities of industrial south Wales. Following grief there was the inevitable self-reproach, but from the guilt and anger came a sense of purpose and pride. There is no doubt that by 1968 a new sense of community, togetherness and mutual co-operation had been born. The village of Aberfan, refashioned by a shared experience of incomparable intensity, discovered hope, new concerns and a wholly unexpected spirit of rejuvenation.

The first sign of a creative communal response came as early as 29 October 1966, the day after the mass funeral. On realizing that only officially constituted societies would be allowed to give evidence before the tribunal, Kenneth Hayes called a meeting of concerned parents in Zion chapel; 600 turned out, and soon the Aberfan Parents' Association, later to merge with the Residents' Association, became the focus for rehabilitation and renewal. Hayes was unanimously elected joint-president of the new body.

Throughout those months his reputation for wisdom, humility and absolute rectitude served the bereaved parents splendidly. To the watching world he was, without doubt, 'the right man in the right circumstances with something worthwhile to say – and a Christian-hearted man too.'[30] There were other Christian-hearted men, and women, clergy and laypeople, whose contribution to the rehabilitation process was highly significant. Indeed, 'From the beginning it was the church which diagnosed the problem of Aberfan as being fundamentally one of community, and it was the church that provided the answer.'[31] The smallest denomination present in the village, the Churches of Christ, allocated a minister to serve as a community pastor, but of more lasting significance was the decision, made by the Merthyr Council of Churches, to instigate an ecumenical pastorate funded by the substantial collection made towards the disaster fund by the Welsh churches of Canada. Thus began 'Tŷ Toronto' (Toronto House), situated initially in a centrally located caravan, which became the office and headquarters of Aberfan's community worker, the ecumenical stalwart Erastus Jones, who, along with his wife, would serve the village and many of its needs for the next eight years.

From its beginning in December 1967 the Tŷ Toronto project co-ordinated village conferences and extensive community development and planning. Not the least of the post-disaster gains was the overcoming of the traditional division between Aberfan and Merthyr Vale situated on the opposite bank of the River Taff. The older designation for the area was Ystradowen, and the decision to call the community school which replaced Pant-glas after the traditional name greatly assisted the healing process. Soon a community centre, a youth centre and a new building for Bethania Chapel had arisen while the Anglican church of St Mary's, which had been damaged by subsidence even before 1966, had been reconstructed as the church of St Mary's and the Holy Innocents. The Parents' and Residents' Association, which had been so potent a medium for good, was superseded in 1968 by the Aberfan and Merthyr Vale Community Association with Erastus Jones as its secretary, and by 1970 the village, replete not only with new buildings but vibrant with social and cultural activities including a male voice choir and drama group, had become not the object of pity but a sign of hope. A wider process of renewal reached its culmination in 1974 with 'the Year of the Valleys', an incentive which began with Tŷ Toronto and its staff calling upon all the people of the south Wales valleys to work towards the economic and social rejuvenation of the whole region. 'The Valleys Call' was made in a conference held at Aberfan on 17 March 1973: 'We call upon the people of the Valleys to join with us in observing 1974 as a "year of the Valleys" . . . We invite the people, during that year, to examine themselves, to go back over their own story, to rediscover what has made them what they are, to choose together in a new age what they are going to be.' Between March 1973 and March 1975 a total of fifteen major study conferences had been held, mostly in the new community centre but others in Pontypridd and the Rhondda, which helped restore a sense of pride in the unique identity of the industrial valleys and point the way forward for the region as a whole. For Erastus Jones and his team this was proof that the people had been able 'not only to cope with the disaster which threatened to shatter them, but to extract from it a new attitude, a new confidence in themselves and their future . . . 1966 was a watershed, with its BC and AD. This side of it is resurrection.'[32]

A resurrection it undoubtedly was, though not one which was devoid of ambiguities. By 1975 the miners' strike had paralyzed much of Britain, and the three-day week had fatally injured Edward Heath's government, putting Harold Wilson's Labour Party into power once again though this time more with reluctance than with overwhelming conviction. The change of government had not solved the energy crisis, there was massive inflation, while the devolution debate was causing friction and dissension throughout Wales. The theological stimulus for Tŷ Toronto's involvement in the rejuvenation process had been that of the secular 1960s. 'God's part in the activity of the world', as Paul Ballard had said, 'is not simply to be found in one place, however that is defined in terms of Christian authority, but in the living interplay of historical existence.'[33] In other words, God had not returned to the churches but was still to be found in the non-religious world. Despite the Tŷ Toronto team's wholehearted commitment to the Christian faith as they interpreted it, their doctrinal presuppositions prevented them from calling for explicit conversion or overt faith. 'The role of helping people to search for meaning, for purpose and direction in personal life' was the closest that they came to defining the churches' missionary task.[34]

That might have sufficed at the height of the secular 1960s but by
the mid-1970s the emphasis upon a much more clearly delineated
and content-laden faith had been restored. The decade of the
secular had given way to that of the Spirit; now it was worship,
prayer, the need for a specific religious experience and above all a
relevant spirituality which exercised Christian leaders in Wales as
elsewhere. It was no coincidence that the one public religious event
which caused the greatest positive impact on Aberfan in the years
after the disaster was the visit of Dr Martyn Lloyd-Jones to the
annual preaching meetings at Capel Aberfan in November 1967.
'The whole series of services, culminating in your visit, has
sparked a flame among the churches of Aberfan', remarked one
local minister. 'Since the disaster everything has been so utterly
dormant that it is wonderful to see a reawakening. After our
experiences of the past week there is more of a spirit of unity, and
care for the work of the church and the work of Christ, than has
existed for many a long year.' It was a feeling shared by many,
including the village's Anglican vicar.[35]

It was also a portent of what was to come. The 'Call to the
Churches' of May 1973, the one specifically religious event
arranged by Tŷ Toronto during the valleys initiative, expressed the
nature of the current dilemma acutely. Whereas 'the age of
individualism is over and the gospel must be expressed as
thoroughly corporate, as it is in the Bible', it was a message
challenging, and comforting, the individual which was proving
evangelistically effective in this post-religious era. If ecumenicists
shook their heads at the narrow religiosity of 'the successful
fundamentalist sects,'[36] they at least had a vibrant message with
sufficient saving power to attract at least some from among the
rising generation. This was hardly the case with conventional
religion, whether emanating from chapel or church. Notwithstanding the rich lessons in communal development which post-
disaster Aberfan had bequeathed to the older industrialized areas
of south Wales, by the mid-1970s their need was for a much more
clearly defined and spiritually satisfying message than the abstractions of secular religion could supply.

If Aberfan was a searing tragedy which, through the quiet
dignity of its bereaved inhabitants and the fortitude of its young
survivors, became a beacon of hope in a darkened world, what
remains striking even today is the quality and depth of Christian

reflection which it so widely engendered. It was a catastrophe which forced believers to examine the very basis of their faith. The Revd Derwyn Morris Jones, a young Congregational minister in nearby Dowlais, was chaplain to the mayor of Merthyr Tydfil at the time. 'Any cheap faith we had has been shattered by this terrible weekend', he said, in a civic service, following the accident. 'The God who is but a projection of our prevailing mood of well-being is surely dead this day, but through our tears we must look to Jesus Christ. I know of no other but this Man of Sorrows who was acquainted with grief who can bring faith and hope to us this sad day.' As the secretary of the Union of Welsh Independents, Jones would become a Christian leader of singular sagacity and graciousness whose spirituality of suffering found its key and meaning in the crucified God. 'Those of us who falteringly seek to learn Christ came to the discovery that we were meeting Him in Aberfan, and doing so in the strangest places and often in the most unlikely people.'[37]

D. Gwenallt Jones, by then nearing the end of his distinguished career in the University College of Wales, Aberystwyth, and still among Wales's foremost Christian poets, was one of the few who had the courage to look the tragedy straight in the eye. No stranger to suffering himself, it was he more than anyone who, since the 1930s, had given voice to the anguish – and the faith – of the ordinary working people of industrial south Wales. The most striking piece in *Y Coed* ('The Trees'), his final volume of verse published posthumously in 1969, was the prose poem entitled 'The Aberfan Disaster'. The description of the tragedy was withering in its intensity: the landslide, the junior school like a living dam and the eerie, solid silence which followed; the rescue and retrieval of the small bodies and their being washed and laid to rest in Bethania:

Was there ever in a Welsh Chapel, in the sanctuary and in the gallery,
Such a strange congregation, and in its Schoolroom such silent pupils?

It was in Jerusalem, following the nativity, that Herod had killed the innocents and in Ramah that Rachel had shed tears for Benjamin, the dearest of her children, yet at least some reason could be gleaned from those ancient barbarities. No such comfort was forthcoming for the mothers of Aberfan. Theirs were 'the twentieth century's most bitter tears'. South Wales had experienced tragedies before, its coal being red from the spilt blood of generations of men who had lost their lives underground. But this was different; these were children, the bearers of hope for a better future, a hope which had been crushed by the dead weight of man's greed.

When Jesus of Nazareth had returned with Mary and Joseph from Herod's clutches, he had grown and become a man, and in the fullness of time had been called upon, in Gethsemane, to drink the cup, 'the cup which was filled with man's wretchedness and God's wrath'. On the cross, crucified between two criminals, wearing his blood like a garment with his grief-stricken mother looking on, 'He too was forsaken by his Father in the three-hour darkness after the eclipse'. His was the horror of innocent, vicarious suffering and godforsakenness at its extreme: 'He plumbed to the depths which are deeper than the suffering of Aberfan, man's demonic depths and the eternal depths of God'. The only comfort which can be gleaned from such senseless, innocent suffering is that God himself is intimately involved in it, has taken it upon Himself and through that costly empathy can strengthen and console the bereaved and provide them with the assurance of redemption and resurrection.

> From his wounds
> And the blood of his brow flowed to us, sinners, righteousness and pity,
> Forgiveness and love; and our hands strengthened by grace we can clutch
> The bond which binds us to him; a bond that tragedy will never break.[38]

Before the advent of the contemporary German theologian Jürgen Moltmann's 'Crucified God', Gwenallt's poem pointed to a theodicy which was true to the biblical revelation and spoke so powerfully to the bitterest experience of industrialized Wales. Once more it was through the age-old comfort of the gospel that the community's suffering found a focus and the anguished questioning of the whole generation found at least an oblique answer. In the history of twentieth-century Christianity in Wales Aberfan remains as both a challenge and a hope.

A faltering ecumenism and a renewed evangelicalism

The initially vigorous attempts between 1960 and 1975 to bring unification to Wales's disparate ecclesiastical bodies were Byzantine in their complexity and in the main fruitless as to their fulfilment. Of all the movements in mid- to late-twentieth-century Welsh Christianity, Christian union was the one on which the most energy was expended and whose dividends turned out to be the least profitable. Beginning with the highest of hopes, it brought forth the most acute sense of frustration, disappointment and failure. There were, broadly speaking, two movements towards unity during this period, the first encompassing the main Nonconformist denominations and the second which included the Church in Wales. Not infrequently the one militated against the success of the other. Despite the covenant entered into by the Anglicans, the Presbyterians, the Methodists and some others in 1975, neither movement amounted to much. Yet a decade and a half earlier there was nothing on the ecclesiastical agenda which engendered so much enthusiasm, expectancy and verve.

The first tentative scheme for church unity, *Tuag at Uno* ('Towards Unity') was published by the Committee for the Four Denominations in 1963, the denominations being the Presbyterians, the Union of Welsh Independents, the Baptist Union of Wales and the Methodist Church. The positive response which this produced led two years later to a more ambitious plan for a single non-episcopal Welsh Free Church, *Cynllun Uno: Eglwys Unedig Cymru* ('A Unity Plan: the Free Church of Wales'). The Committee canvassed the denominations' views asking them to formulate their reply by no later than 1967. The first squall of cross-winds came from the direction of the Baptists who felt that they could not, in conscience, forgo the necessity for believers' baptism, in order to join a single Free Church and in 1966 the BUW withdrew from the scheme though they retained their position on the Committee for the Four Denominations. During that year the Independents too noted their reservations but wished to persevere towards a church union which was 'in accordance with God's Word and [was] more acceptable than the present scheme'. Reformation according to the Word of God was shorthand for a more congregational form of church government. By 1967 it was obvious that the scheme had failed to generate sufficient

confidence to become a blueprint for a new denomination but it
was retained by the Committee as a basis for further discussion. It
was then that the Cardiff and Swansea District of the Methodist
Church announced their inability to proceed with a pan-
Nonconformist plan as they were in parallel unity talks with both
the Church of England and the Church in Wales. This hardly
boded well for the future of either the original scheme or any
alternative. 'By now', recollected one Welsh ecumenical leader, 'it
was obvious that all enthusiasm had been dispelled and the
general opinion was that the plan had no future.'[39] The Committee for the Four Denominations met in December 1968 to
survey the wreckage. Both the BUW and the Baptist Union of
Great Britain and Ireland (which was heavily represented throughout south Wales especially) reiterated their opposition to the sort
of scheme which had previously met with tentative approval by the
other denominations, and by the end of the decade it was clear
that ecumenical ardour among many mainstream Nonconformists
had cooled almost to freezing point. By 1970 discussions about
church union had become quite passé.

If the non-episcopal churches had failed to agree on a common
scheme of unity, there seemed scant hope for Nonconformists and
Anglicans to acquiesce in a joint unity plan. Yet the same verve
which had captured the imagination among chapel-going ecu-
menicists during the early 1960s had registered among Churchmen
as well. Its context was wider than that which prevailed among the
Nonconformists. Following the Third Assembly of the World
Council of Churches at New Delhi in 1961 the secretary of the
British Council of Churches' Faith and Order Movement had said:
'There is a real possibility of an ecumenical breakthrough in
Britain in our time.' It was at the Nottingham conference of Faith
and Order in 1964 that this conviction registered most forcibly, the
call being issued that all the (non-Roman) churches should come
together in organic unity by Easter 1980. There were Welsh
Anglicans and Nonconformists who were mightily affected by the
heady spirit of the time, and an extremely successful preparatory
conference for Nottingham entitled 'The unity we seek' was held
at Carmarthen's Trinity College in September 1963. What with
this and the concurrent work among the Committee of the Four
Denominations, for a time the ecumenical wave seemed unstop-
pable. The Council of Churches for Wales (which had been

established in 1956 and included the Anglican Church in Wales) issued its own call for unity, *Yr Alwad i Gyfamodi* ('The Call to Covenant') in 1965, which elucidated a positive response from the Church in Wales, the Presbyterian Church of Wales, the Union of Welsh Independents and the Methodist Church. The Baptists, who were having serious problems at the time agreeing on a common basis of polity with their fellow Nonconformists, could hardly have responded positively to a call to covenant with an episcopally governed church so they steered clear of the current plan. Within a year a Joint Committee for Covenanting had been established and the four denominations were joined by a fifth, the Wales district of the Congregational Church of Great Britain. In 1968 the Joint Committee issued an interim report entitled *Covenanting for Union in Wales*. The purported covenant for a united church body included seven articles on faith, membership, the nature of the church, its ministry and governance and was heavily weighted in favour of a non-congregationalist form of government and 'a pattern of ordained ministry . . . which shows its continuity through the ages and is accepted as far as possible by the Church throughout the world'. In other words the united church would be episcopalian. The document took it for granted that its ministry would embrace the historic threefold pattern of bishop, priest and deacon. The unyielding conviction of the covenanters was that, were unity to be achieved, it would be on Anglican terms alone.

The fact that many Congregationalists, Presbyterians and Methodists were happy to forgo their ecclesiastical distinctions in order to be integrated into an episcopalian body was patent by their still keen response to the covenanting plans, and in 1971 the Joint Committee's further two-part report also entitled *Covenanting for Union in Wales* was issued. This stipulated that the churches who wished to be part of the covenant should state their intentions by 1974 after which time each body would enter a solemn and binding agreement to move towards full organic unity. The Presbyterian Church of Wales, the Methodists, the United Reformed Church (which in Wales had superseded the Congregational Church of Great Britain following the 1972 merger between the Presbyterian Church of England and the Congregationalists), the Church in Wales and, curiously, a dozen congregations in the Cardiff area belonging to the Baptist Union of Great Britain and Ireland, all agreed to embrace the covenant. Apart from the few highly atypical Baptists, it was noteworthy that each of these bodies was centrally governed – by now the congregationally based Welsh Independents and the great bulk of both English- and Welsh-speaking Baptists would have nothing to do with the plan – and that the Church in Wales made crystal clear that its condition for joining was that none of its specific ecclesiastical and theological convictions were to be in any way compromised. Everyone else was expected to change, the Anglicans did not intend to budge; it was a curious approach to Christian co-operation. However, the covenant was ratified in a solemn service in Seilo Presbyterian Church, Aberystwyth, in January 1975, followed by similar services in eighteen other centres. Representatives of each of the denominations stated their intentions: 'We enter into this solemn covenant before God and one another, to work and pray in common obedience to our Lord Jesus Christ, in order that by the Holy Spirit we may be brought into one visible Church to serve together in mission to the glory of God the Father.' And that, in effect, was that.

What should have been the beginning of a new and vibrant phase in the ongoing story of Welsh Christianity in fact marked its end. Despite the huge commitment of a host of able, devout and exceedingly conscientious Christian leaders, it had become embarrassingly clear that the ecumenical dream (in its church unity form) had faded almost to nothing. By the mid-1970s church union was failing lamentably to engage the imagination and the ecumenical movement generally was seen as a somewhat bourgeois preserve of middle-aged and institutionally minded males. Renewal, spiritual sustenance and Christian excitement were now being sought elsewhere. In 1976 the Joint Committee for Covenanting evolved into the Commission for the Covenanting Churches which appointed its first full-time secretary, the Revd Noel A. Davies (who happened to be a Welsh Independent), a year later. It was his responsibility to help devise a scheme of union based on the covenant to which each constituent church could agree. It was an unenviable task. Although in 1975 the Welsh bishops allowed members of the Church in Wales to partake of the communion in churches of the covenanting denominations and cautiously welcomed covenanting members to share the eucharist at the altars of its own parish churches, specific permission had first to be sought and even then there was no guarantee that it would be granted. Despite all the pious talk, there was virtually no movement towards full ministerial parity within the covenant. It seemed as though the public, binding and sacred nature of the covenant service counted for little after all. 'It is clear', wrote the Revd D. Huw Jones, an ecumenically earnest senior Welsh Anglican, 'that the Covenanting movement has . . . run into the doldrums.'[40] The gains of ecumenism, which would be significant in terms of local projects such as joint and neighbourhood ministry schemes, a much needed scholarly translation of the Welsh Bible, humanitarian service through Christian Aid and not least the breaking down of ancient prejudices against Christians of other traditions, would evolve independently of the church union plans. By 1979 it was emerging that the main contribution which ecumenism could play in the future development of the faith in Wales was by facilitating mutual enrichment of Christians by introducing them to one another and to the treasures of each others' spiritual, liturgical and theological traditions.

If ecumenism was running out of steam there was no doubt that evangelicalism was going from strength to strength. In the colleges of the University of Wales, the teacher training establishments and the senior schools, the focus for Christian commitment had transferred from the liberal Student Christian Movement or conventional chapel or church attendance to the specifics of a fairly rigid and sometimes pietistic Protestant orthodoxy and an explicit experience of evangelical conversion. The fate of the SCM, which for generations had been one of the most potent forces in the lives of Welsh undergraduates, was illustrative of the change which was being undergone in the nation's religion generally. Its commendable policy of critical enquiry, openness to contemporary challenges and social involvement, once so appealing, now seemed both commonplace and bloodless. Because it was so accommodating to the latest intellectual trends it seemed no longer to stand for anything at all. Years earlier it had removed as a condition for membership either belief in God or a pledge to Christian practice. The intention, of course, was to attract the uncommitted in the hope of influencing them for good. The inevitable result was that, while the unaffiliated stayed away, Christians and serious seekers after truth gravitated towards the flourishing Christian Unions of the Inter-Varsity Fellowship. The university colleges at Aberystwyth, Bangor, Cardiff, Swansea and (since 1971) Lampeter, the training colleges at Cartrefle (Wrexham), Bangor (the Normal and St Mary's), Barry, Cyncoed, Caerleon, Carmarthen and Swansea each had its burgeoning Christian Union which could often attract crowds of 100 or more for Saturday evening bible expositions or even formal preaching services. The annual Welsh gatherings of the IVF (latterly the University and Colleges Christian Fellowship) reached new peaks of popularity: 'Conferences in these years were eagerly attended. In 1965 attendances passed the 100 mark for the first time; in 1967 numbers rocketed to 178. One remarkable address that year lasted well over two hours, the speaker being encouraged several times by his hearers to "carry on".'[41] Much of this verve was reflected in the churches. Whereas mainline congregations were contracting, evangelical churches could usually count on extensive support from all ages not least hosts of young people, men as well as women. If ecumenism appeared tired, jaded and (truth to tell) rather boring, evangelicalism was vibrant, youthful and excitingly relevant to the myriad challenges of the new Wales.

The fact that ecumenism and evangelicalism could be expressed in such mutually exclusive terms pointed to a characteristic of Welsh Christianity which was not apparent elsewhere. It also pointed to a weakness which would become glaring as time went by. By the mid-1960s the brand of evangelicalism which was in the ascendancy was linked to the Evangelical Movement of Wales. Its tendency was Calvinistic and separatist and it had become strongly judgemental of other forms of Christian faith. Such a proclivity to condemnation alienated not only obvious opponents but prospective allies and friends. It reflected the growing intransigence of one of the most powerful religious personalities in Welsh Christianity, Dr Martyn Lloyd-Jones. Although he had left Wales as far back as 1939 for Westminster Chapel, a huge Congregational church within a stone's throw of Buckingham Palace, 'the Doctor' had been utterly faithful to the land of his birth and had kept his links intact. As a visiting preacher he would invariably command vast chapel congregations on weekday afternoons and evenings in all parts of Wales and listeners were kept spellbound by his scintillating expositions of gospel truth. He remained, well into the 1970s, the last of the prince preachers, a formidable presence who did more than anyone to rehabilitate the authority and dignity of the Nonconformist pulpit. His legacy, though, was strangely flawed. For evangelicals of the Lloyd-Jones stripe, it had become virtually impossible to regard many within ecumenical circles as Christians at all. 'There is an irreducible minimum, without which the term "Christian" is meaningless and without subscribing to which a man is not a Christian', he had said in 1962. 'If men do not accept that, they are not brethren and we can have no dialogue with them.' What is more, conscientious affiliation with the World Council of Churches, the British Council of Churches and, by implication, the Council of Churches for Wales, was irreconcilable with the evangelical faith which was the sole embodiment of Christian truth. It was an impossible position to hold; bitter strife was bound to follow. 'Those who question and query, let alone deny the great cardinal truths that have been accepted through the centuries,' he continued, 'do not belong to the church and to regard them as brethren is to betray the truth.'[42] This reversion to strict separatism ventured farther than the older fundamentalism of R. B. Jones ever dared go. It would have the most unfortunate immediate consequences for evangelical unity and for the future of Welsh Christianity as a whole.

By 1965 Lloyd-Jones's trend towards exclusivism had become a fixed conviction, so much so that to insist on remaining in fellowship with the 'official churches' of the mainstream denominations, which he had come to regard as corrupt and apostate, was tantamount to schism. True unity could only be among those who were 'in Christ' which was construed as holding to the doctrinal convictions of an unalloyed and rigid evangelicalism. In England the controversy which this engendered came to a head at the National Assembly of Evangelicals, convened by the Evangelical Alliance at the Central Hall, Westminster, in October 1966 when Dr Lloyd-Jones issued his call for evangelical believers to forsake their present denominational loyalties and 'come out from among them' in order to regroup in a doctrinally pure association. John Stott, rector of All Souls, Langham Place, and the Church of England's foremost evangelical statesman, who was in the chair, immediately and openly dissociated himself from the call stating that both scripture and history were against it. The most immediate effect in Wales was in the spring of 1967 when seven Presbyterian ordinands at the United Theological College,

Aberystwyth, very publicly resigned their candidature for ministry
and left the denomination forthwith, while a small network of
new independent evangelical churches, each of which consisted
solely of members recently seceded from mainline congregations,
came into being. The Evangelical Movement of Wales (EMW),
which had previously consisted of individual supporters alone, at
once allowed full constitutional membership to these new
churches and to others which were in the process of severing their
denominational links. Cardiff's Heath Presbyterian Church of
Wales under its pastor the Revd Vernon Higham, an influential
preacher of narrow views, was perhaps the most significant of
these. It was far from clear that everyone associated with the
EMW was keen to sever their denominational ties or to unchurch
those who may have been deficient in certain aspects of
evangelical faith, but so overbearing was the influence of Lloyd-
Jones that their view was never seriously challenged. The fact that
the Movement's widely revered general secretary, the Revd J.
Elwyn Davies, was such an unwavering apologist for the secessionist line also carried weight. We are, he said, 'under a solemn
obligation to dissociate ourselves from all those who, though
avowedly Christian, deny our Lord'. In days of such acrimonious
polarization it was altogether too easy to equate commitment to
the ecumenical cause with a denial of Christian truth. 'Evangelical
churches who are associated with an ecumenical council of
churches', he continued, 'are required to terminate that association as a condition of affiliation [to the EMW].'[43] For an
evangelical to secede, dissociate from and condemn the historical
churches and their ecumenical ties seemed for a time to be the only
authentic Christian choice.

By the late 1970s evangelical popularity seemed not to have been
affected too adversely by the vitriolism of the secessionist debate.
The annual and sectional conferences of the EMW were still
drawing substantial congregations and the Movement itself was
expanding into the sphere of religious publishing and theological
education. Yet the death of Martyn Lloyd-Jones in 1981 marked
the end of an era. His eager disciples, now bereft of their leader,
possessed no one of comparable authority to plead the secessionist
cause. It had become clear by 1979 that the complete regrouping of
evangelical forces in Wales along sectarian lines would not, in fact,
take place. Evangelical renewal was beginning to be felt outside

secessionist circles and in places which traditional conservative
evangelicals would have deemed highly dubious indeed. The
Evangelical Fellowship of the Church in Wales, which rejected
secessionism and the sectarian mentality totally, was founded in
1967 and within a dozen years had become one of the most lively
bodies on the Welsh religious scene. Charismatic renewal had
brought more and more people into an experiential appreciation of
the fundamentals of the New Testament gospel, while all the
themes dear to the evangelical heart – justification by faith alone,
the supreme authority of scripture as the Word of God, the need
for personal faith and repentance, and salvation on the basis of the
finished sacrifice of Christ's cross – became the staple fare of much
mainline, denominational preaching. By 1979 few could claim,
with any conviction, that the gospel was not being preached in
Welsh pulpits. The influence of evangelical leaders who had never
been enamoured of the need to secede or averse to ecumenical
concerns as such – Principal R. Tudur Jones of Bangor being a case
in point – had become as widespread as that of Dr Lloyd-Jones,
and the more EMW congregations contracted out from the mainline concerns, the less influential they would become. Whatever the
weaknesses of current ecumenism – its doctrinal faddishness
(especially in the 1960s) on the one hand and its overemphasis on
the institutional unity on the other – there was nothing in the
ecumenical creed with which conscientious evangelicals need take
exception. Freed from the narrow constrictions of a fundamentalist
literalism and a sectarian temper, by the late 1970s evangelicalism
of this type proved to be of immense benefit to the health of Welsh
Christianity.

Continuing concerns

Whatever the gains and losses made by the ecumenical and
evangelical movements between 1962 and 1979, the Christian
mainstream was still represented by the principal Nonconformist
denominations, the Church in Wales and, increasingly, the
Catholic Church. Nor were the smaller Protestant bodies,
Pentecostalist sects like the Elim Four Square movement, the
Assemblies of God and the Apostolic Church, and the decidedly
non-Pentecostal Brethren in their 'mission halls', nearly as

negligible as 'official' Christianity may have liked to imagine. If classic Pentecostalism, and to a lesser extent Brethrenism, was undergoing a minor resurgence in industrialized, urban Wales during these years, membership statistics within historic Nonconformity had begun to nose-dive. Between 1962 and 1972 the Presbyterian Church in Wales lost 17,000 members, the Welsh Independents 25,000, the Baptists 22,000 and the Welsh Methodists 5,000. [44]

Nonconformist membership: Wales, 1962–1972

	Presbyterians	Congregationalists	Baptists	Methodists	Total
1962	131316	125612	89855	16279	363062
1972	104316	100398	67720	11491	283925

Denominational institutions had reached crisis point. In 1964 the doors of the Presbyterian College at Bala finally closed; they had been open since 1837 when Lewis Edwards left the University of Edinburgh intent on providing Welsh Calvinistic Methodists with a learned ministry. Another college whose name was redolent of the Methodist past, Trefeca, closed at the same time. From now on the Connexion would concentrate its ministerial education at the United College at Aberystwyth; Welsh Presbyterianism was quite obviously a contracting force. Despite the huge intellectual acumen of some members of their respective staffs, by the mid-1960s the Congregationalists' two remaining seminaries, Swansea's Memorial College (an amalgamation of the Brecon and Carmarthen colleges) and Bala-Bangor at Bangor, were struggling to survive, as was the Bangor Baptist College if not its sister foundation in Cardiff. Perhaps even more worrying than the slump in numbers was the decline in intellectual ability among those seeking ordination; having lost its social and financial status, the ministry was no longer attracting young men of calibre to its ranks. (There were, thankfully, prominent exceptions.) Nonconformity did not lack leaders of conspicuous academic eminence or preachers of still-great distinction – Pennar Davies, Tudur Jones, T. Glyn Thomas, Emlyn G. Jenkins, Walter P. John, to pick names at random – but they were, in the main, middle-aged at least. Traditional Nonconformity was fast losing its hold on the loyalty and imagination of the Welsh nation. Chapel culture was in an advanced state of decay and the stereotypical identification between Nonconformity and 'the Welsh way of life' was coming to an end. Except in a few enclaves here and there, by 1979 Nonconformist Wales was dying a lingering death.

Neither did Anglican Wales emerge to take its place. The seemingly boundless confidence of the Church in Wales during the early 1950s had long since evaporated though, ironically, there were signs that Anglicanism was coming to represent, in the public's perception at least, the official face of Welsh Christianity. Following the half-hearted acceptance of the covenant for unity in 1975, ecumenical activities faltered, smitten by the same enthusiasm fatigue which had paralysed the unity movement generally. 'The Church in Wales has, on the whole, shown little zeal for ecumenical activity', admitted one of its prime historians nonchalantly.[45] There were flashes of innovation, though, which showed that in some things the Church was ahead of the Anglican Communion rather than lagging behind. The Governing Body decided as early as April 1975 that there was no fundamental theological objection to the ordination of women to the priesthood though, characteristically, it refused to act upon this conviction until the time was right. By 1980 the time was right and the first ordinations of women to the diaconate took place, much to the chagrin of some curmudgeonly Anglo-Catholics in Llandaff who claimed, of the candidate in their diocese, that 'this attempt to give Holy Orders to a woman who is by nature incapable of receiving Holy Orders' was wholly invalid.[46] Elsewhere the ordinations were carried out without demur. It would be some years before the Anglican churches in the rest of the British Isles would follow the Welsh example. Yet the prime problem which the Church in Wales, like mainline Nonconformity, had to face was the general falling away in public worship and overall Christian commitment. John Poole-Hughes, formerly Anglican bishop of south-west Tanganyika, had returned to Wales in 1975 and was swiftly and unexpectedly elected bishop of Llandaff. (His predecessor, Eryl Thomas, had been found guilty of homosexual improprieties and forced to resign his see; it was a severe and embarrassing blow for a Church which was already suffering a failure of nerve.) The difference between the situation which he had left in the 1950s and the one which he would inherit could not have been starker. 'We seem to have a tremendous organisation, with committees and sub-committees, synods and conferences, but the result in terms of preaching the Gospel, forwarding God's Kingdom, and producing saints seems minimal', he remarked. 'We are a church in retreat, grouping parishes, closing down churches, and paying more and more for fewer and fewer priests.'[47] It was already a familiar litany and would become even more so during the years to come. Between 1962 and 1974 Easter communicants in the six Welsh dioceses fell by some 45,000. The pattern was uniform throughout the province.

Easter attendance in the Church in Wales, 1962–1974

	St Asaph	Bangor	St David's	Llandaff	Monmouth	Swansea and Brecon	Total[48]
1962	36978	20644	32746	46199	21569	22959	181095
1965	33312	18841	31446	41259	19030	21391	165273
1974	27303	15555	27042	32739	15743	16848	135228

Just as worshippers were becoming ever more scarce, so it became increasingly difficult to recruit candidates for ministry. In 1976 Bishop Burgess Theological Hall, the training foundation which was left following the secularization of St David's College, Lampeter (as St David's University College it had become the fifth constituent college of the federal University of Wales in 1971), itself closed down leaving St Michael's College, Llandaff, the only remaining full-time institution in Wales for the training of Anglican clergy. Whereas previously Lampeter and Llandaff were constantly over-subscribed, by 1979 St Michael's was down to a mere few dozen. As always, though, many prospective candidates for the priesthood of the Church in Wales attended theological colleges in England. In his final Visitation Charge to the Llandaff diocese, Glyn Simon, formerly the embodiment of the Church's ebullience and hope, was noticeably despondent. He spoke not so much of faith and confidence as of frustration and disappointment. The fact was that for many 'there is really no need to take the Church or the Christian Faith seriously any longer.'[49] Six years later Bishop Poole-Hughes had found it 'terrifying that there are vast areas and classes of people who seem untouched by our witness',[50] and that within the diocese over which Simon had presided so conscientiously for fifteen years. Some years earlier, commemorating the fiftieth anniversary of the Church's disestablishment, Simon himself had written: 'There exists a great spiritual vacuum in Wales and someone or something sooner or later will certainly fill it. Will it be the ancient Church of the land?'[51] Whereas in 1950 the answer might conceivably have been 'yes', a quarter-century later that prospect was well beyond the imagination of even the most fervent Anglican zealot.

It was equally clear that the fond dream of Wales's return to 'the Old Faith' which patriotic Catholics had nursed fitfully since the creation of a separate Welsh province in 1916 would not materialize either. The most immediate task which faced the Welsh bishops after 1965 was the implementation of the reformations of the Second Vatican Council, begun in 1962 by Pope John XXIII and recently concluded under the presidency of Pope Paul VI. There is little evidence that either the Most Revd John Murphy, archbishop of Cardiff since 1961, or the long-serving John Petit, bishop of Menevia, had much enthusiasm for change and even less sympathy with the Council's frankly radicalizing agenda, but with typical Roman efficiency and an ingrained deference to authority they instigated the modifications swiftly. The effects of this transition were deep-seated and in some cases traumatic and bitter. The vernacular had been encroaching slowly on territory once held by Latin since the cautious liturgical emendations made by Pius XII in the late 1940s, but from the end of 1964, following the instructions of *Sacrosanctum Concilium*, the Council's document on liturgy, the Epistle, the Gospel, the Gloria and the Credo were now to be said in the ordinary language of the people. In 1967 the whole mass was at last allowed to be celebrated in the vernacular. There were some who were deeply dismayed and scandalized. Saunders Lewis, for one, was severely shaken. For thirty-five years his spirituality had been moulded by the Latin cadences of Western Christendom at its most classical. To abandon this was to abandon so much of that which gave Catholicism its uniqueness. What compounded the tragedy was that, for twenty-four Welsh Catholics out of every twenty-five, the vernacular was English. Lewis, the poet and calligrapher David Jones and the conservative stalwarts of the Cylch Catholig, so traditionally loyal to papal authority, were deeply disenchanted. In a letter to his fellow nationalist, Lewis Valentine, Lewis wrote: 'Changes in the Blaid [Plaid Cymru, the party which Lewis had helped found in 1925] and in the Church, especially the abolition of the Latin Mass, have left me a very bitter old man.'[52]

Yet what for highly educated, middle-class, conspicuously Welsh-speaking Catholics of an older generation was a disaster, others found invigorating and exciting. Having been de-latinized, the liturgy became demystified, and with the celebrant facing the congregation rather than the altar during celebration and now audibly enunciating the words of institution, the nature of the Mass as the Lord's Supper became clear and the link between a formerly highly sacerdotalized priesthood and ordination to minister the Word of God was made explicit in terms which Protestants could at least begin to comprehend. There is little doubt that the changes of Vatican II helped enormously to bring Catholicism into the Welsh Christian mainstream, and the Council's *Decree on Ecumenism* opened the way for the Church to seek observer status on the Council of Churches for Wales. The Welsh Catholic bishops' own statement on ecumenism in October 1967 marked a huge shift in attitude (if not yet in basic doctrinal conviction) which began this process: 'The Holy Spirit calls upon us to put away doubt and bitterness and to come together in the love of Christ . . . We see that God's grace has been at work mightily in each of the Christian bodies, and we value the means and devotion through which their members have responded to his grace.'[53] Following exploratory inquiries in January 1968 the officers of the Council of Churches for Wales, including the Revd M. J. Williams, the inveterately Protestant secretary of the Baptist Union of Wales, met with a deputation from the Catholic Church's Welsh Ecumenical sub-Commission to 'review the existing situation', and on 24 May declared that 'wherever conscience does not forbid us to do so', co-operation would henceforth be essential.[54] By October the Church was duly granted observer status by the Council. Although the ecumenical ice had been broken, Catholic participation in inter-church ventures would remain minimal throughout the next decade despite the eagerness of such senior Welsh Catholics as Bishop Langton Fox and Fr James Wickstead, the abbot of the Cistercian house at Caldey off the coast of Tenby in west Wales, to play a fuller part in cross-denominational activities. Yet by the 1970s Catholic parishes were beginning to be involved in such ventures as Christian Aid Week and the week of prayer for Christian unity and, in the Menevia diocese at least, there was significant Catholic participation in the 1975 evangelistic initiative 'Wales for Christ'. Yet there was still a dead weight of conservatism and apathy apparent from within the Church itself, and very few parish priests seemed to have been fired with a new enthusiasm following Vatican II. Such was the indifference that the response to Pope Paul's 1968 encyclical *Humanae Vitae* on artificial means of birth control, which caused a furore elsewhere, hardly registered at all in Wales. Having been almost totally accepted as an indigenous element within Welsh society, the Catholic community was content to go about its business quietly and unsurreptitiously, savouring its long-awaited respectability.

If the 1960s began with a flush of worldwide optimism, the 1970s drew to their weary close in considerable gloom marked, in Wales, by the protracted aftermath of the miners' strike, prospective and actual social dislocation, continuing union militancy and the fractious debate about devolution. Since Saunders Lewis's powerful 1962 appeal for revolutionary measures to be applied in order to restore the fortunes of the Welsh language and Gwynfor Evans's election in 1966 as Plaid Cymru's first MP, nationalism had entered a new, energetic and remarkably populist phase. Although some of it ran in tandem with a genuine Christian communitarianism which was culturally motivated, expressly nonviolent and internationalist in outlook, other aspects were much more secular in tone. Whereas the older identification between chapel culture and Welshness was already disintegrating, some of this new pride in things Welsh consciously rejected religious values and eschewed Christianity altogether. This new Welsh (and Welsh-speaking) secularism would register most forcibly by the 1980s and 1990s but its beginnings were apparent in the youth movement of two decades earlier. 'In some areas of Wales', announced a 1973 report of the Youth Section of the Council of Churches for Wales, 'the whole question of what it means to be Welsh is of more concern to young people than what it means to be a church member.'[55] For the first time in a millennium and a half, Christianity and Welshness seemed to be going their separate ways. There were, however, others whose patriotic zeal was inseparable from their Christian discipleship. Despite Vatican II and the mounting

grumpiness of old age, Saunders Lewis remained a loyal Catholic
to the end; indeed from the perspective of the end of the century
what remains most striking about his phenomenal contribution to
the social, cultural and artistic well-being of twentieth-century
Wales is his unswerving Christian conviction. For Gwynfor Evans,
pacifism and Welsh nationalism were aspects of a single vision
whose key ideal was the coming of God's kingdom in Christ. The
militancy of Cymdeithas yr Iaith Gymraeg, the Welsh Language
Society, had more of Gandhi and Martin Luther King about it
than Malcolm X or the IRA, and it was quite patent that Christian
faith meant a great deal to Dafydd Iwan and Ffred Ffransis, two of
the society's most charismatic leaders.

The fact that Glyn Simon, who succeeded Edwin Morris in 1968
as archbishop of Wales, stated that 'there is nothing unscriptural
or un-Christian in nationalism as such',[56] illustrated how the
movement had affected people at all levels of life. Simon's three-
year tenure of the archiepiscopate coincided with the Welsh
roadsigns campaign and the call for improvement in the language's
status generally as well as with the beginnings of the devolution
debate. The archbishop affirmed all these things strongly. 'Wales is
not a region but a nation, and a nation without political institutions of her own.'[57] This was an anomaly which needed to be
redressed. Ill health prevented him from playing a fuller part in
these matters than he did. He was already suffering from Parkin-
son's Disease and died in 1972, only a year after having been
forced to resign office, the most revered archbishop in the history
of the Church in Wales. His successor, Bishop Gwilym O.
Williams of Bangor, maintained his concerns and by so doing laid
to rest the old aspersion that the Church lacked sympathy with
specifically national issues. One of the most interesting aspects of
the renewal of Christian concern which accompanied the
nationalist upsurge of the early to mid-1970s was the way in which
it engendered fresh theological thinking. From the quasi-Pelagian
biblicism of Pennar Davies to the pan-Calvinist vision of R. Tudur
Jones and Professor R. M. 'Bobi' Jones, a lively and specifically
Welsh liberation theology was forged which engaged the interest
of younger Christians especially. This liberation and the theology
which underpinned it 'was concerned with releasing the creative
energies of the Welsh people so that they may live a fuller, more
humane, more democratic life and so contribute responsibly to the

making of history', wrote R. Tudur Jones. 'Such a renaissance of national creativity cannot be inspired by acts of parliament, not even a Cardiff parliament. That can only come by a rediscovery of our Christian faith.'[58]

However affirmative the ideals of national renewal, by 1979 the question of language had become divisive while the devolution debate generated quarrels and bitterness. There was no single Christian mind on these matters, and among the politicians in the forefront of the anti-devolutionist campaign were such high-profile believers as George Thomas, formerly the secretary of state of Wales and latterly Speaker of the House of Commons, and Donald Anderson, MP for Swansea West. The failure of the Devolution Bill following the referendum of 1 March 1979 put paid to any further development of political nationalism for the time being, while the fall of James Callaghan's minority Labour government in the following May signalled the end of an era and the beginning of something new: Thatcherism. There were also signs of a termination in Christian circles as well. Institutional religion was increasingly under strain and traditional formulations of faith were being found wanting. Whereas the Council of Churches for Wales's evangelistic campaign 'Wales for Christ' (1975) came to little, less conventional renewal movements created significant local interest. The 1979 'Swansea for Christ' initiative, a wholly ecumenical affair led by the Anglican Charismatic leader David Watson, made an impact on the local Christian community across the board. According to one local Catholic, 'David Watson was something very special and I felt that we had been listening to a prophet for our time.'[59] Charismatic renewal and the search for spirituality was displacing both tradition and doctrinalism within the churches; not even the evangelicals would emerge unaffected. The British Council of Churches' 'Dayspring' celebration at St David's Cathedral in August 1977 which brought together over 1,000 young people from all over Britain characterized the sense of change. 'Dayspring' was 'a search for a meaningful spirituality, true to the insights of prayer and the struggle for involvement in the world', but like Taizé, charismatic renewal and the sacrament-alized pan-religiosity which emerged during the 1980s, it was disparate, individualistic and non-institutional. If prayer was on the agenda once more, it would not automatically lead to a rejuvenation of the churches. By then the uncharted waters into which the barque of faith had ventured in 1962 hardly seemed any less dangerous. The old Wales was rapidly being transformed into something else and it was far from clear whether Christianity would have any significant part to play in its further development at all.

8

Towards the new Wales, 1979–2000

Religion and society in the 1980s

The 1980s were not propitious years either for Welsh society generally or for the churches which both formed part of its fabric and sought to serve it. For decades the south Wales coal industry had been forced to yield its primacy to activities ancillary to steel production especially those connected with car manufacture. Yet by the 1970s even Welsh steel was being priced out of the market by foreign produce especially from Japan and the USA. With the contraction of the steel industry in Shotton in the north-east and in Glamorgan and Gwent in the south and south-east, the previously large though static population of the southern coalfield both declined and became more mobile. Rhondda, Pontypridd, Merthyr and the eastern valleys became dormitory areas for Cardiff and Newport; greater economic independence and choice served further to erode the stable community life which had underpinned traditional forms of religion well into mid-century. Rural Wales was also suffering a metamorphosis. Mechanization, and soon computerization and huge technological advance, coupled with the fiscal advantages of the European Common Agricultural Policy ensured a significant increase of output based on far fewer though much larger farms. The need for farm labourers and occasional workers disappeared. Service industries which were much less labour intensive than agriculture, became the economic mainstay of many rural localities. Perhaps the most marked cultural change was linguistic and even, in part, ethnic. As the urban areas were happily adapting to the presence of Asian immigrants replete with their (usually Muslim) faith systems, rural Wales became far more comprehensively peopled by an un-precedented influx of English incomers many of whom were disenchanted with city life and usually alienated from all forms of institutional Christianity. By the early 1980s it was estimated that 40,000 English people were settling in Wales annually and finding their way even to its remotest locations, while as many as a quarter of the inhabitants of Clwyd were English born. The Welsh language and culture including their religious manifestations were in danger of being wholly engulfed. It was, without doubt, a period of intense anxiety for those committed to the continuance of traditional forms of Welsh identity.

It was those who valued that identity most highly who were most disappointed by the defeat of the Labour government's devolution referendum by a five-to-one margin on St David's Day 1979. With a vast majority of the Welsh people seeming to reject decisively even a modicum of self-rule, it was felt that the notion of Welshness itself was being terminally eroded. This impression was reinforced by the general election result of May 1979 which turfed out James Callaghan's ineffectual Labour administration, replacing it by the Conservative government of Margaret Thatcher. What was most disconcerting was the fact that Wales, for so long staunchly radical, seemed now to be simply replicating the values, preferences and political norms of England. For the first time since 1874 the Tories possessed as many as eleven Welsh seats while Labour won only twenty-one, its lowest count for fifty years. The application of Thatcher's brash monetarist capitalism spelt the end of Wales's traditional industrial base: within a short time steel production had been abandoned at Shotton, Ebbw Vale and Cardiff. By 1980 unemployment, previously at the 7.5 per cent mark, reached 13 per cent rising three years later to 16 per cent. In the face of such a calamitous crisis, church leaders found it impossible to be silent. 'There is need . . . for the "prophetic word",' commented Erastus Jones, 'which has its sources in something deeper than current economic political ideologies and which can see further than the pundits'.[1] It was the prospect of the destruction of communitarian values and a way of life in which popular religion had once flourished which, for the Christian conscience, made the current changes so traumatic. Although some of the most baleful effects of the Thatcher revolution would be vitiated in part by the interventionist influence of Peter Walker and David Hunt, successive secretaries of state for Wales who were not wholly enamoured of their leader's economic ideology, the 1980s remained a gloomy and bewildering period in the more recent history of the Welsh people.

Yet even then this did not reveal the whole story. Whereas in some spheres national particularity was being undermined by an acute acculturalization to Anglicized norms, in other spheres Welshness was being reinforced remarkably. This was most obviously the case with the establishment in 1982 – following widespread pressure especially by Gwynfor Evans's threatened hunger-strike – of S4C, the Welsh-language television channel which soon gained popular approval. Even more significant, though virtually imperceptible at the time, were changes in the constitutional realm with the progressive (and highly ironic) devolution of powers to the Welsh Office and its secretary of state. By 1979 Cardiff was responsible for the administration of local government, road building and maintenance, primary and secondary education, industry, agriculture and all higher education (apart from that under the aegis of the University of Wales). The setting up of the Welsh Land Authority, the Development Board for Rural Wales and the Welsh Development Agency all served in an unselfconscious but nevertheless very real way to underscore Wales's separate identity within the existing structure of the British state. Even Cardiff, with its most attractive Cathays Park institutional complex at its centre, began (very slowly) to shed some of its nervousness at being regarded as the nation's capital in order to appreciate the potentiality of metropolitan status. Although few were conscious of it at the time (least of all, one suspects, the Conservative government which both approved and accelerated this process), it would only be a matter of time before direct democratic answerability through some sort of national forum or assembly would become probable.

The results of the 1983 general election, which followed on from the Falklands war, and that of 1987 revealed a tripartite divide in Wales's political map with the Welsh-speaking areas of Gwynedd returning Plaid Cymru MPs, the older and still densely populated former industrial areas centring on the south Wales valleys still solidly Labour, while the Marcher districts of the border and south-eastern Wales tending to the English pattern of Thatcherite Toryism. In this new Wales the old maxim that Labour owed more to Methodism than to Marx had become increasingly archaic; the comment of Glenys Kinnock, wife of the new leader of the Opposition, that 'Neil and I used to be Methodists but now we're atheists', gave a truer insight into the character of the time. Mainstream Christianity continued to contract, with the results of the 1982 survey on church affiliation reflecting the continuance of previous trends as well as characteristics commensurate with current social developments. The largest of the mainline denominations was still the Church in Wales with approximately 137,600 communicants in its six dioceses. Whereas three of its sees, between 1978 and 1982, showed a slight increase in church attendance, on the whole the trend was downwards, especially in the less populated rural areas and the older industrialized zone:[2]

Approximate attendance in the Church: Wales, 1978–1982

	St Asaph	Bangor	St David's	Llandaff	Monmouth	Swansea and Brecon
1978	17000	22200	23900	21800	30800	15500
1982	15700	21800	29600	21800	32000	15900

The fact that the Roman Catholic Church had evolved into the second largest Welsh ecclesiastical body came as a rude shock to some. Not only was Nonconformist Wales a thing of the past, the realities of the day were now challenging even the concept of a Protestant Wales as well.[3]

Welsh Catholic statistics, 1975–1985

	Catholics	receptions (previously listed as 'converts')	churches
1975			
Cardiff	103083	220	139
Menevia	41419	77	120
1980			
Cardiff	106515	263	136
Menevia	44052	109	124
1985			
Cardiff	186491	182	136
Menevia	44644	86	127

It was, however, the traditional long-established Nonconformist denominations which continued to suffer most grievously. Although each denomination possessed some thriving (middle-class) congregations almost exclusively in the larger towns and their suburbs, on the whole they were failing lamentably to replenish their membership from among their youth. In the rural areas chapel religion seemed to be dying and everywhere it had become predominantly the preserve of the middle-aged and the elderly. Membership numbers in all of these denominations were plummeting, while the fact that on average less than half of those who were listed on membership rolls would be present at worship indicated how deep the spiritual decay had penetrated.[4]

Nonconformist membership: Wales, 1978–1982

	Presbyterian	Congregationalist	Baptist	Methodist	Total
1978	85400	70100	54000	28300	237800
1982	79900	65200	50200	25300	220600

'To what direction is God calling us,' wrote one of the Presbyterian Church of Wales's least cynical servants, 'to oblivion and death or else to renewal and a new beginning? The present signs all point to death as the most likely outcome. It will not be a sudden death; not a heart attack but a slow and lingering cancer. The process has already begun and before long will have reached an irreversible stage where recovery will be impossible.'[5] The fact was that Wales had become a mission field in which very few of the faithful had the slightest idea how to cope with a new situation in which hard-nosed atheistic materialism had become the unquestioned assumption of everyday life. This was equally true of the more traditional 'evangelical' congregations who had always depended on a residual knowledge of religion and a familiarity with Christian terminology and norms as a supposition for conversion. It was as though the Welsh now inhabited a post-Christian world, the unfamiliarity of which was as unnerving for Anglicans and even for Catholics as it was for chapel-bred Nonconformists. According to the 1982 church survey, dynamic growth was restricted to the smaller Pentecostal denominations and to the newer independent evangelical churches, yet despite the undoubted verve and commitment which was found there (an increase in membership from 33,400 in 1978 to 35,300 four years later throughout a range of bodies including the Elim churches, the Assemblies of God and a handful of others[6]), it was hardly sufficient to offset the losses within the mainstream.

Statistics, of course, could not reveal all. There were positive developments during these years in each of the principal denominations. In 1981 the *Book of Common Prayer for Use in the Church in Wales* appeared, replacing, at long last, the 1662 *Book of Common Prayer*. Thus, sixty years after disestablishment, Welsh Anglicanism declared its liturgical independence from Canterbury. Stylistically, and for some theologically, the new prayer book was less than perfect but by placing the eucharist at the centre of worship it faithfully reflected the thought and practice of the vast majority of Welsh Churchpeople. By 1985 it had been generally accepted in the parishes and, according to the Governing Body, it alone and not the Church of England's *Alternative Service Book* was henceforth to be used within the province. In 1981 the Governing Body began its practice of meeting twice yearly in Lampeter thus perpetuating the Church's historical link with St David's College, which had by now become a secular liberal arts college within the federal University of Wales. The fact that the Church established its Board of Mission in 1985 headed by a full-time director with a wide remit including evangelism, education, social involvement and ecumenism meant that the Church in Wales was serious in its resolve to fulfil its mission in the context of contemporary society; how this could effectively be accomplished was another matter. The recruitment of new ordinands, which was around the fifty mark both at the beginning and the end of the decade, was not sufficient to replenish clergy who were retiring, meaning that more and more parishes had to be grouped together. Ordinands who were fluent in Welsh were very scarce indeed, though some of the younger clergy who were English by birth proved themselves adept at learning the language and in some cases provided an exceptionally effective ministry through their second tongue. Following the retirement of Gwilym O. Williams in 1983, the archiepiscopate was transferred to the Rt Revd Derrick Childs, bishop of Monmouth, a man who was well known within the Church for the role he had played in education not least during his years spent at Trinity College, Carmarthen. He was hardly in his post long enough to make a deep impression as archbishop (he died, tragically, in a car accident in 1987 a year after having retired) and was replaced, in 1986, by George Noakes, the bishop of St David's. The fact that such a pastoral bishop, utterly devoid of pretension and rooted so firmly in the soil of Cardiganshire, could reach the highest ecclesiastical office showed how far the Church had succeeded in shedding its establishment image. Noakes, whose qualities even as archbishop were basically those of an unassuming parish priest, typified those of the bench as a whole: Cledan Mears at Bangor, Roy Davies at Llandaff (who followed John Poole-Hughes in 1985), Alwyn Rice Jones at St Asaph and, following the retirement of B. N. Y. Vaughan in 1986, Dewi Bridges in Swansea; each was a modest, competent diocesan, in stature far removed from an A. G. Edwards, a Charles Green or even a Glyn Simon. By the 1980s there were few towering personalities left in either the Church or the world.

Although the rate of Catholic increase was upward both in the archdiocese of Cardiff and in the diocese of Menevia, as the decade progressed there were signs that the drop in mass attendance which would be such a stark characteristic of Catholic life throughout Europe was affecting Wales as well. The much publicized visit of Pope John Paul II to Wales in 1982 sparked no significant anti-Catholic protest but, while it put heart into the Catholic faithful and helped cement ecumenical goodwill, it made little impression on those outside the Church. Following steady growth Catholic Wales was seen to be holding its own rather than expanding considerably though even its growth was no longer keeping pace with the general increase in the population. Yet Catholic confidence was nevertheless expressed in the establishment of a third Welsh diocese, that of Wrexham, in 1987. The new see covered the counties of Gwynedd, Clwyd and Montgomeryshire in Powys, while Menevia was reorganized to include Dyfed, that part of Powys which included Brecon and Radnorshire, and the most westerly part of Glamorgan including Wales's second city of Swansea. St Joseph's Church at Greenhill in the city became the diocese's cathedral. John Aloysius Ward, OFM Cap, bishop of Menevia since 1981, was translated to the metropolitan see of Cardiff in 1983, his former place being taken by James Hannigan. Four years later he, in turn, left to become Wrexham's first diocesan while the reorganized see of Menevia welcomed as its leader another Irishman, the auxiliary bishop of Cardiff, Daniel Mullins. Mullins, though, was an Irishman with a difference. By far the best-known Catholic priest in Wales outside his own communion, he, like his mentor the former Archbishop McGrath, was (and remains) a learned, Welsh-speaking cleric wholly committed to the reconciliation of Catholic faith with all that is best in the life of the Welsh nation. Unlike McGrath, he was (and is) unencumbered by an ultramontanism which seeks to anathematize Christians of other traditions. His enthronement at St Joseph's on 19 March 1987 was a joyous and ecumenical affair in which many Welsh Anglicans and Nonconformists, to say nothing of Catholics themselves, took particular pride.

If traditional Nonconformity seemed to be in terminal decline, both ecumenism and non-sectarian evangelicalism served as foci for a sectional renewal within Welsh Christianity in which even the older Free Churches could share. After the failure of earlier reunion schemes the idea of organic union had been abandoned to be replaced by a much less grandiose but arguably more profitable ideal of grass-roots Christian collaboration. There had been signs for some time that the Catholic Church and some of the smaller more conservative Protestant bodies on the UK level were keen to draw closer to other Christians by emphasizing those elements of the faith which all held in common. In 1984, following the World Council of Churches significant report *Baptism, Eucharist and Ministry*, the British Council of Churches, the Catholic Bishops Conference of England and Wales and representatives of thirty other denominations decided that the time was ripe for a further move towards co-operation which resulted in the inter-church process entitled 'Not Strangers but Pilgrims'. During Lent 1986 some 70,000 local groups of ordinary churchgoers throughout Britain and from all points on the denominational spectrum met weekly for prayer, bible study and reflection on a common theme entitled 'What on Earth is the Church For'. The exercise turned out to be very fruitful. Whereas in the past ecumenical zeal had tended to come from the top down, this time it was a journey of discovery and mutual learning among ordinary church members from the bottom up. The scale of its impact in Wales was shown by the 20,000 participants in the Christian festival 'God's Family' held at Builth Wells on 24 May 1986. Having studied and prayed together during Lent, they responded to that opportunity to display their unity in corporate worship and celebration. It was clear that a new phase of ecumenical activity had dawned in which prayer, bible study and mutual enrichment among ordinary Christian believers would take precedence over schemes for organic unity. It was equally obvious that the faddishness of the 1960s and the doctrinal reductionism masquerading as radical faith were things of the past.

The Council of Churches for Wales's confident involvement in unity plans which included such a healthy dose of spirituality and mission came in the wake of another unexpected but exceedingly significant occurrence which, ostensibly, had nothing to do with Christian celebration or church matters at all: it was the miners' strike of 1984–5.

In March 1984 Arthur Scargill, president of the National Union of Mineworkers, called on his men to strike against the policy of the government, devised and implemented by Ian MacGregor, director of the National Coal Board, radically to restructure the mining industry by the wholesale closure of uneconomic pits. Realizing the parlous (and frankly unprofitable) state of the industry in south Wales and that government policy would spell the end of coal production throughout the principality, the Welsh miners responded almost unanimously to Scargill's call. Although the strike was to last a year, what was special about the Welsh response was its very high degree of solidarity, its communitarian character and the emergence of the miners' wives as spirited and articulate defenders of their endangered communities. In comparison with other British coalfields, very few men were tempted to break the strike, while popular opinion, from the slate-quarrying north to the rural west, was, on the whole, with the colliers. Yet the NCB refused to yield to the miners' anxieties about the future of their industry by instigating any negotiations to bring the dispute to an end.

Such was the background on which four Nonconformist ministers, Derwyn Morris Jones and Noel A. Davies from the Union of Welsh Independents, and John I. Morgans and Douglas Bale of the United Reformed Church, approached Emlyn Williams, secretary of the South Wales area of the NUM and Philip Weekes, South Wales director of the NCB, requesting a meeting to discuss the possibilities for reconciling the dispute's two sides. The six men came together, in secret, on 19 November 1984, in what was to be a very productive meeting. The suggestion which emerged was that an independent body should be established with the remit of planning the future of the south Wales coal industry in a way which would be economically responsible and show concern for social values and cohesion. Despite the fact that neither Scargill nor the NCB centrally were interested in any scheme which demonstrated a spirit of compromise, those involved determined to do what they could to forward the plan.

The death of David Wilkie, a taxi-driver who was killed on 30 November after transporting strike-breakers to and from work, sent shock waves throughout the coalfield. It was in his funeral service at Glyntaff Crematorium that John Poole-Hughes, the bishop of Llandaff, first made public the idea of an independent board to review the industry's future as a means of breaking the deadlock between the two sides. The *Western Mail* of 13 December was quick to publicize 'a major church initiative' which was gathering momentum to end the deadlock 'and could be taken up at the highest level'. What had begun as a private initiative by four concerned individuals had quickly gained the support of all the mainline denominations, the leader of the Opposition whose constituency was in the coalfield, the South Wales NUM and a growing body of public opinion. Yet the government remained as intransigent as ever. 'It is vital that hopes of a negotiated peace in the coal industry should be kept alive', commented the *Western Mail* on 8 January 1985. 'These hopes have had their biggest stimulus in months from initiatives by the leaders of the churches in Wales.'

Not only was this a highly significant step in the history of the strike but also, under the circumstances, in the mission of the Welsh churches. Having been so long marginalized and written off as irrelevant to modern life, churchmen found themselves at the heart of the conflict in which they could provide a genuine ministry of reconciliation and a prophetic voice as well. Christian witness was still valid in late industrial Wales. Time, though, was not on the side of those who sought an equitable peace. By then the strike had reached its tenth month and despite the tenacity and resolve of the mining communities, day by day hardship was deepening. Although the secretary of state for Energy agreed in February to meet with a deputation of churchmen including three of the original four instigators of the process, and both the Welsh archbishops, Catholic and Anglican, by then the strike was collapsing. The government's demand, to the end, was for the men's unconditional return to work. The most poignant image of the whole confrontation was that of the men of the Maerdy pit, where support for the action had been 100 per cent throughout, returning to work at dawn on 5 March with banners waving led by their brass band, knowing that both their pit and their community were destined for destruction. Within a few months coal production in the Rhondda ceased entirely and a specific way of life had become a thing of the past. As it happened, the economic crisis of south Wales was not as dire as it could have been due to the relative success which Peter Walker, as secretary of state for Wales in Margaret Thatcher's 1987 government, had in attracting inward investment especially from Japanese firms along the M4 corridor. Yet the fight for the coal industry was not so much for the perpetuation of outmoded and wasteful modes of production but against an ideology which exalted the individual to the detriment of society as a whole and was so insensitive to anything which refused to yield to the sovereignty of market forces. 'It is indeed a dangerous trend', remarked a paper which emerged from the Council of Churches for Wales's Industrial Committee, 'when those who claim the moral right to govern are knowingly involved in subverting moral values and standards of behaviour, turning them upside-down and saying that bad is good.'[7] For a century and more the moral values of the coalfield had been social and communitarian, and the Christian conscience had no choice but to defend those communities when threatened with unemployment, poverty and despair.

It was through the Council of Churches for Wales that the different denominations had proffered their unanimous witness during the strike. The one major Christian body which was not a member of the Council was the Catholic Church, but following the 'Not Strangers but Pilgrims' process and the Bangor ecumenical conference in March 1987 in which it was fully involved, and the conference of British Church leaders at Swanwick in the following September, it pronounced itself eager to align itself with the official ecumenical movement. The new ecumenical instrument (to use the parlance of the time) which would replace the CCW and include the Catholic Church and some of the smaller churches as well would be 'Cytûn: Churches Together in Wales'. After much discussion and not a little trepidation in which fears were voiced about the loss of denominational distinctives and, among the Baptists especially, anxieties about compromising Protestant convictions, a dozen denominations agreed to join the new alliance inaugurated on 1 September 1990.

Just as ecumenism had been rejuvenated during the mid-1980s, evangelicalism was also going through a creative phase at the time. If there were ecumenical parishes, such as Pen-twyn in Cardiff and the Pen-rhys initiative on a bleak, exposed hillside estate between the Rhondda Fach and the Rhondda Fawr, which indicated a creative and salutary missionary verve, there were explicitly evangelical causes that were in a flourishing state. The Glenwood Church in the eastern suburbs of Cardiff, the Linden Fellowship in Swansea and the Assemblies of God congregation in Newtown, Powys, all mushroomed during this time. Unlike most churches they were not tied to the past but were wholly in tune with the culture of the age: they prized spontaneity over tradition, immediacy over formality and experience over cerebralism. Doctrinally they were charismatic, practising such spiritual gifts as prophecy, healing and speaking in tongues. All of this conformed perfectly to the norms of a post-modern culture; it was visual, celebratory and experientially based, rather unreflective and wholly unencumbered by a sense of history. It was in pointed reaction to the sterility of a rationalist world-view. What these churches also had in common was a clear commitment to biblical authority and its application to everyday life. Where the more liberal churches continued to decline, this combination of unambiguous, not to say naïve teaching and colourful, exciting worship, had an undeniable appeal for many people. Less spectacular though nevertheless solid growth was felt in such Anglican parishes as St Michael's, Aberystwyth, and St Mark's, Gabalfa, Cardiff, and among the Baptists of Blackwood, Gwent, where these emphases were shared though in a less blatant and more nuanced way.

Despite their commitment to biblical truth, the attitudes and mores of these churches were much more open than those of the older conservative evangelicalism as a whole. By 1986 the non-sectarian Evangelical Alliance, which was much broader in scope and in sympathy than the Evangelical Movement of Wales, was established to provide a platform for a more variegated, world-affirming and socially involved evangelicalism than had hitherto been common in Wales. That its first full-time secretary was Arfon Jones, previously best known as a Welsh-language activist and the youth officer of the Union of Welsh Independents, illustrated the nature of the change. No longer would evangelicalism necessarily be equated with pietism, fundamentalism or a reactionary stance to the political realm.

The one undoubted triumph of the decade if not of the century in the field of scholarship, was the publication in 1988 of *Y Beibl Cymraeg Newydd*, the new Welsh Bible. Begun in 1961 by a team of scholars centred upon the University of Wales in Bangor, it was to provide an authoritative translation of the Bible in accessible modern Welsh. The New Testament had been available since 1975, but the appearance of the whole Bible, along with the Apocrypha, was timed to coincide with the 400th anniversary of Bishop William Morgan's 1588 Bible, the one book more than any other which had shaped the life of Wales and throughout the vicissitudes of history preserved its national identity. An undoubted popular success, it sold 75,000 copies during the first few months. So as the 1980s drew to a close Christians were left to appreciate the positive elements in their recent past while at the same time pondering the somewhat parlous state of their future.

Approaching the millennium

Whatever developments occurred during the Thatcher era, by 1990 (when Margaret Thatcher was replaced by John Major as prime minister) the political map of Wales remained relatively static. What had changed enormously in ten years were social patterns which reflected radically transformed perceptions of what was morally acceptable or otherwise. Since the Divorce Act of 1971 divorce statistics had crept steadily upwards; whereas they were only a few thousand in the 1960s, by 1990 it was being said that one in three Welsh marriages would end in dissolution. This being the case there was little surprise that young people rejected convention by cohabiting rather than committing themselves to a path which seemed to lead more and more, almost inevitably, to separation and the pain of divorce. Worrying as this was for those who still held to the Christian ideal of life-long commitment and holy matrimony, even more serious in terms of social cohesion was the growing proliferation of one-parent families. John Redwood, the prime minister's 1992 appointee as secretary of state for Wales, burned his fingers badly when he chose Cardiff's vast Ely council estate, where unattached single mothers were to be found in abundance, as a venue for castigating the decline of contemporary morals. If he was denounced for having scapegoated a particularly vulnerable section of society, there was little doubt that the disastrous absence of young men in stable, not to say married, relationships, contributed to the sense of moral dislocation of the period. Whatever gains had been made in the realms of personal freedom and gender equality, the signs of disruption within the areas of personal, marital and sexual morality were plain for all to see. This, along with the rise of crime, the spread of alcoholism and drug abuse and the ready availability of pornography in corner shops and video outlets to an extent which would have made an earlier generation blanch, had become a recognized characteristic of the times.

Yet for all that, the 1990s was not nearly as pessimistic a decade as its predecessor. Amid the evidence listed above, there were numerous signs of rejuvenation and verve. A now diverse economy was slowly growing stronger not only along the M4 corridor in the south but along north Wales's A55 as well. There was now a Welsh film and media industry which, although stimulated by S4C, was broadly based and international in scope. Cultural life in both languages was dynamic while the Welsh Language Act of 1993 not only safeguarded the rights of both linguistic communities but enhanced substantially the status of Welsh. Welsh-medium educa-tion was burgeoning having secured significant cross-party and government support, while generally there was a feeling of youthfulness and quiet optimism. The 1997 general election which swept Tony Blair's New Labour Party into power decimated the Tories: in Wales, as in Scotland, the Conservatives no longer held a single seat. And it was New Labour's commitment to constitu-tional change which many found particularly exciting. Although the 1997 devolution referendum was won by the most slender of margins (though support throughout the older industrial areas of the south and in the rural west was rock solid), the change in tone, opinion and general support for self-determination since the debacle of 1979 was stunning. The transfer of democratic power from Westminster to Wales which accompanied the establishment of the National Assembly in June 1999 has created a new situation whose social and psychological implications have only begun to be assimulated. What seems true is that even Cardiff, its bay area having been wholly transformed, is set to relish its status as a major European city, home of the Assembly and much else beside.

As far as the life of the churches was concerned, on the macro-level institutional decline continued very much as before, yet on the micro-level signs of hope were persistently visible. It may have been true that 'institutionalization has killed the spirit of enthusiasm that was the lifeblood of Welsh Nonconformity',[8] yet most of the formerly popular older Welsh institutions – the trade unions, the labour movement, working-men's clubs, voluntary societies, male voice choirs – were suffering from the same internal decay; if patent, the malaise of the chapels was hardly unique. New enthusiasms tended to be individualistic and sometimes ephemeral, reflecting the privatized and highly pluralistic culture of the day. This was equally true of the one serious popular concern of the period, ecology and the preservation of the environment, for which Celtic spirituality provided a convenient and highly dubious religious underpinning. The survey of church attendance which was carried out in 1995–6 revealed detail of what most observers had already discerned in part: that 731 churches had closed their doors for the last time since the previous survey in 1982, that the rate of decline was highest in the older Free Church denominations from the Wesleyans (28 per cent) through to the Baptists (12 per cent), that the Church in Wales had declined by 9 per cent and that, apart from the Roman Catholics, it was the newer charismatic and evangelical congregations which were experiencing growth but that these represented a very small percentage of the whole, less than 5 per cent in fact.[9] The very fact that the list of churches in the survey had extended to include the Congregational Federation, the Associating Evangelical Churches of Wales, the Fellowship of Independent Evangelical Churches, the Church of the Nazarene, the Lutherans and Orthodox as well as house church networks such as Pioneer and Covenant Ministries, not to mention the 125 non-aligned congregations, said much of the post-modern tendency to revel in diversity and plurality at the expense of an underlying coherence in which all orthodox Christians could share. This too was a sign of the times.

The forward march of progress went on apace – if, indeed, that was what it was; there was a vocal minority who strongly disagreed – with the decision of the Governing Body of the Church in Wales by a comfortable majority in October 1996 to ordain female deacons to the priesthood. Full equality between men and women within the Church was at last achieved; whether this was on the basis of a secularized, feminist agenda as opponents of the move argued, or on a gospel-based agenda as its proponents claimed, was not fully clear. It did mean that Churchwomen of great academic distinction like Dr Margaret Thrall of Bangor, and of obvious leadership skills such as the Revd Enid Morgan, director of the Board of Mission, were no longer barred from the full sacramental ministry of the Church. It could hardly be said that Welsh Anglicanism possessed weighty, decisive leadership, though Barry Morgan, the bishop of Bangor, latterly of Llandaff, and the one outstanding intellectual to grace the Welsh bench since Connop Thirlwell a century and a half previously, namely Rowan Williams at Monmouth, provided impetus for a liberal trend within the Church. Both are men of charm and influence, in sympathy with feminist and other radical causes and proponents of full rights for homosexuals within their communion.

In more than one way the 1990s were the end of an era. Not only was a new millennium within sight, but the old order was drawing to a close. Gwilym O. Williams, the former Anglican archbishop of Wales, died in 1990, the extraordinarily gifted Pennar Davies who possessed perhaps the most creative and fertile mind within Welsh Nonconformity passed away in 1996, and the giant-like figure of R. Tudur Jones died suddenly in 1998. All three were men of great presence and strength of character who had been at the centre of Wales's Christian life for, between them, well over fifty years. The poet-priest and Nobel Prize nominee R. S. Thomas, though still in full creative flow, is in his eighties. (It has been the poets as much as the theologians who have responded with most sensitivity to the spiritual concerns of the century; Thomas, whose oblique, ironic muse and consciousness of God's fleeting absences, speaks powerfully to the brokenness of the age:

It is this great absence
that is like a presence, that compels
me to address it without hope
of a reply. It is a room I enter

from which someone has just
gone, the vestibule for the arrival
of one who has not yet come . . .

What resources have I
other than the emptiness without him of my whole
being, a vacuum he may not abhor?[10])

For all their greatness these were men of yesterday; the question with which we must end this narrative is, what of tomorrow? Some commentators have been gloomy to the point of despair. 'Humanly speaking, at this rate of decline . . . it seems as if the end of distinctively Welsh expressions of Christianity may be in sight', lamented Sir Glanmor Williams, doyen of Welsh historians and himself a devout Baptist layman, 'as those religious values dearest to earlier generations are being more and more abandoned in a lingering but painfully inexorable process'.[11] Now that we have reached the twenty-first century, does Christianity in Wales have a future?

From the standpoint of faith, the believer has no right, nor does this author have any inclination, to be despondent. There is no place for pessimism in the divine economy, only hope which is beyond both optimism and pessimism and vouchsafed by the divine promise and an empty tomb in Jerusalem many centuries ago. Even on the human plane there is little doubt that the faith will survive though the community in which it is enshrined will be much smaller than in the past and less blighted by the nominalism of conventional religion: 'What I suspect we shall see . . . as we enter the millennium is a smaller number of increasingly conservative Churches serving a dwindling minority of highly committed members.'[12] However, a church does not exist solely for the benefit of its members but to worship God and be a sacrament of His presence in the world. That means that the missionary task of the Welsh churches during the new century will be immense. They will need an empathy with the people of this nation in all their dazzling diversity. They will have to earn their right to be heard and will only do that by embodying the gospel message in a corporate life of love, sympathy and care. Evangelism divorced from radical and wholehearted social responsibility will fail and will deserve to fail. All our faith communities whether Catholic or Anglican, mainline or independent, will be called to incarnate a Christian presence which is both pastoral and prophetic.

Yet solidarity with the world cannot be achieved on the world's terms; Christian distinctives will only thrive if they conform to the biblical revelation and remain rooted in sound doctrine. If the dominant theology capitulates to humanism and the non-miraculous (which it did in the case of Nonconformist liberalism in the 1920s and again in the mid-1960s) the church will shrivel and die. The reformation of worship in line with an orthodox appreciation of creation, incarnation, atonement and redemption is not an historical curio but the precondition for life and a viable future. Neither must this knowledge of God through the doctrines of the faith be the preserve of the theologians but the lifeblood of all of God's people.

What are the signs of transcendence in contemporary Wales? Some observers have seen significance in the folk religion which has survived the post-modern breakdown of the Enlightenment ideal. Though alienated from the churches and ignorant of specific Christian truth, the hunger for the mysterious, the spiritual and the arcane which is apparent in many people's lives is a perpetual witness to the fact that humankind cannot live by bread alone. Spiritual credulity may go hand in hand with secular sophistication but it does at least point to the fact that the supernatural can be an accepted reality once more. Others have put great store by the way in which the ecological concerns of the day express an intuitive grasp of ancient Celtic creation spirituality. The lives of the sixth-century saints, their names preserved in Wales's innumerable *llannau*, speak strongly to a restless generation which is uniquely sensitive to the harm which human greed continues to do to the planet. These may be flimsy foundations on which to build a natural theology, but what is incontrovertible is that the Christian verities will abide whatever the fashions of the age and that the church is called to be faithful to its divine calling.

In bringing the story to a close we can, I think, say that Christian witness has been at its best during the twentieth century when it has displayed an evangelical commitment to the gospel in all its scandalous particularity and individual challenge; an ecumenical openness to all that is new and exciting in God's vast creation, and a catholic breadth which embraces the local and the universal, Wales and the world. It is in continuity with this, our Christian past, that we shall find our future.

Notes

NLW   National Library of Wales
UWB   University of Wales Bangor

Introduction: a faith for the third millennium

1 R. Tudur Jones, *Ffydd ac Argyfwng Cenedl: Cristionogaeth a Diwylliant yng Nghymru, 1890–1914*, 2 vols (Abertawe, 1981, 1982), maps this crisis with exceptional perceptiveness and clarity.
2 For recent short assessments of Christianity's future in the new Wales, see D. P. Davies, *Against the Tide: Christianity in Wales on the Threshold of a New Millennium* (Llandysul, 1995) and Noel A. Davies, *Wales: Language, Nation, Faith and Witness* (Geneva, 1996).

1 The state of religion in 1914

1 Statistics taken from *The Catholic Directory* (1914); cf. *The Report of the Royal Commission on the Church of England and other Religious Bodies in Wales and Monmouthshire* (London, 1910), Vol.1, appendix L, pp.127–9.
2 *Report*, Vol.4, pp.275–9.
3 Ibid., Vol.2, q.4796, p.169; for denominational information and statistics see idem. q.4781, p.168, q.7841, pp.246–7 and Vol.7, appendix XV, p.89.
4 Ibid., Vol.1, p.126, appendix K, cf. p.39.
5 Ibid., Vol.2, p.401, q.13315.
6 Ibid., p.402, q.13334, Revd James Whittock.
7 Ibid., p.394, q.13063–7, cf. Vol.7, pp.166–8, appendix XLIII.
8 Ibid., Vol.6, pp.118–48; cf. R. Tudur Jones, *Ffydd ac Argyfwng Cenedl* (Abertawe, 1981), Vol.1, p.50.
9 *Report*, Vol.1, p.41; cf. Vol.2, q.13423, p.406, Vol.4, q.42721, 42726, p.292.
10 Ibid., q.46562–46583, p.443–5; Vol.7, p.76, Appendix XIII.
11 Ibid., Vol.6, p.274, listed as 'undenominational'.
12 Ibid., Vol.7, p.422 *passim* for the Salvation Army, Christadelphians and smaller groups; Vol 1, p.40 for Presbyterian Church of England.

13 Henry Richard, *Letters on the Social and Political Condition of Wales* (London, n.d. [1867]), p.2.

14 K. O. Morgan (ed.), *Lloyd George Family Letters, 1885–1936* (Oxford, 1973), p.12.

15 John Williams, *Digest of Welsh Statistics* (Cardiff, 1985) Vol.2, p.294; for the statistics of the foreign missions see the Church's annual yearbook or *Blwyddiadur,* and for their histories see J. H. Morris, *The History of the Welsh Calvinistic Methodists' Foreign Mission* (Caernarfon, 1910), also Ednyfed Thomas, *Bryniau'r Glaw: Cenhadaeth Casia* (Caernarfon, 1988).

16 *Report,* Vol.1, p.31.

17 Ibid., p.50.

18 Ibid., Vol.2, q.11328, p.340.

19 R. Tudur Jones, *Yr Undeb: Hanes Undeb yr Annibynwyr Cymraeg, 1872–1972* (Abertawe, 1972), p.199; cf. W. Eifion Powell, 'Cyfraniad diwinyddol David Adams', *Y Traethodydd* 134 (1979), pp.162–70.

20 *Digest of Welsh Statistics,* Vol.2, pp.272–3.

21 *Report*, Vol.1, p.214.

22 Ibid., p.49.

23 Eric Edwards (ed.), *Yr Eglwys Fethodistaidd, Hanes Ystadegol* (Llandysul, 1980), *passim*; cf. *Digest of Welsh Statistics,* Vol.2, p.324.

24 The only denomination to list its adherents was the Calvinistic Methodists: it had 335,000. On the basis of the statistical pattern listed above, the churches had perhaps as many as 950,000 adherents in 1914.

25 *Report*, Vol.2, q.2125, p.88.

26 Quoted in Roger L. Brown, *The Welsh Evangelicals* (Tongwynlais, 1986), p.78.

27 C. Dunkley (ed.), *Official Report of the Church Congress held at Swansea, 1909* (London, 1909), p.83.

28 Ibid., p.88.

29 The statistics provided in *The Report of the Royal Commission,* Vol.1, pp.26–8, published in 1910, augmented by the lists published annually by each individual diocese as well as the tables for 1914 included in the *Digest of Welsh Statistics,* Vol.2, pp.258–63, serve as a basis for the following computation.

30 See D. T. W. Price, 'The contribution of St David's College, Lampeter, to the Church in Wales', *Journal of Welsh Ecclesiastical History* 1 (1984), pp.63–83.

31 Owain W. Jones, *Saint Michael's College, Llandaff, 1892–1992* (Llandaff, 1992), p.37.

[32]   Henry Richard, *Letters and Essays on Wales* (London, 1884), p.99.

[33]   The situation in north Wales differed in that most of the incumbents of the Bangor diocese were Oxbridge or Durham graduates while many from St Asaph were educated at St Aidan's College, Birkenhead, and St Bees in Cumberland. Yet whereas Bangor tended towards 'High' Churchmanship, St David's remained either evangelical or 'Broad Church'. Lampeter men did not begin to serve in north Wales parishes to any significant degree until the end of the century.

[34]   See Brown, *The Welsh Evangelicals, passim*; cf. E. T. Davies, *A New History of Wales: Religion and Society in the Nineteenth Century* (Llandybïe, 1981), ch.5.

[35]   A. G. Edwards, *Memories* (London, 1927), pp.86–7.

[36]   See A. Tudno Williams, *Mudiad Rhydychen a Chymru* (Dinbych, 1983), ch.3.

[37]   *Report*, Vol.2, qq.14274–14288, pp.429–30.

[38]   During the late nineteenth century the movement's strongest supporters in those dioceses included George Huntington in Tenby and Bulkeley Owen Jones (Ruthin), T. R. Lloyd (Hope) and Stephen Gladstone (Hawarden).

[39]   *Report*, Vol.2, q.3170, p.119.

[40]   Ibid., Vol.3, q.20252, 20481, pp.71,75.

[41]   Ibid.

[42]   Lambert Rees, *Timothy Rees of Mirfield and Llandaff* (London, 1945), p.12.

[43]   Dunkley (ed.), *Report of the Church Congress,* p.77.

[44]   See K. O. Morgan, *Freedom or Sacrilege? A History of the Campaign for Welsh Disestablishment* (Penarth, 1966); cf. P. M. H. Bell, *Disestablishment in Ireland and Wales* (London, 1969), chs 7–9.

[45]   *Memories,* p.122; cf. idem., *Landmarks in the History of the Welsh Church* (London, 1912), p.220.

[46]   *Report*, Vol.2, qq.2460–1, p.97.

[47]   Ibid., q.1968, p.75.

[48]   *Report*, Vol.4, q.47887, p.506.

[49]   Ibid., q.47638, p.499; cf. *Landmarks in the History of the Welsh Church,* pp.80–90.

[50]   See Roger L. Brown, *David Howell: A Pool of Spirituality [A Life of David Howell (Llawdden)]* (Denbigh, 1998), pp.195–238.

[51]   Quoted in Owain W. Jones, *Glyn Simon, His Life and Opinions* (Llandysul, 1981), p.55.

[52]   D. Parry-Jones, *A Welsh Country Parson* (London, 1975), p.83.

53   *Young Wales* 5 (1898), p.7.

54   G. Hartwell Jones's not unbiased diatribe against the 'bigoted antagonism to Wales and the Welsh' displayed by 'the Lampeter gang' of Edwards and Owen whom he calls a 'knot of ambitious clerics, with their headquarters at Lampeter and Llandovery' whose object had been to capture and monopolize 'the highest offices in the Welsh Church for themselves and their friends' (*A Celt Looks at the World* (London, 1946), ch.10), must be counter-balanced by Eluned Owen's two-volume *Life of Bishop Owen* (Llandysul, 1958 and 1961). Yet for all its jaundiced rumbustiousness it does contain an element of truth.

55   Hartwell Jones, *A Celt Looks at the World*, p.70.

56   R. M. Jones, 'The roots of Welsh inferiority', *Planet* 22 (1974), pp.53–72.

57   George Lerry, *Alfred George Edwards: Archbishop of Wales* (Oswestry, 1939), p.54.

58   A. H. Grey-Edwards, *Reminiscences of an Unknown Man* (Bangor, n.d.), p.40.

59   Dunkley (ed.), *Report of the Church Congress*, p.74.

60   R. R. Hughes, *John Williams Brynsiencyn* (Caernarfon, 1929), p.225.

61   *Llais Llafur*, 13 January 1912, p.7.

62   Robert Pope, *Building Jerusalem: Nonconformity, Labour and the Social Question in Wales, 1906–39* (Cardiff, 1998), p.164.

2   *Christianity and the First World War, 1914–1918*

1   *Llandaff Diocesan Magazine*, January 1914, p.88.

2   The best account of Welsh Christianity's response to the First World War is Dewi Eirug Davies, *Byddin y Brenin: Cymru a'i Chrefydd yn y Rhyfel Mawr* (Llandysul, 1988).

3   UWB MS 16265, 17 October 1914.

4   *Llandaff Diocesan Magazine*, October 1914, p.173.

5   *The Times*, 11 November 1914, p.3.

6   *Y Goleuad,* 11 September 1914, p.4.

7   'Llais y wlad', *Y Genedl Gymreig*, 6 January 1915, p.7.

8   *Y Tyst,* 17 March 1915, p.6.

9   Thomas Rees, 'Y rhyfel a'r eglwysi', *Y Tyst*, 30 September 1914, p.2, 'Y rhyfel a'i phedair ffiloreg', *Y Brython*, 1 October 1914, p.4; J. Puleston Jones, 'Hawl ac ateb', *Y Goleuad*, 11, 18 September 1914, pp.6, 5.

[10] UWB Archives, Bala-Bangor MSS 65, 16 October 1914.

[11] J. Emyr (ed.), *Dyddiadur Milwr a Gweithiau Eraill* (Llandysul, 1988), p.49.

[12] NLW, E. K. Jones Papers.

[13] Ibid., Letter to Revd E. K. Jones, 19 March 1915.

[14] NLW, Minor Deposits, Facsimile 718.

[15] Anglesey County Council, Llangefni Archives, Diary of Tom Owen (1897–1917).

[16] NLW, Diary, p.216; see D. Densil Morgan, 'Ffydd yn y ffosydd: bywyd a gwaith y Caplan D. Cynddelw Williams', *National Library of Wales Journal* 29 (1995), pp.77–100, quotation on p.88.

[17] NLW, Calvinistic Methodist Archive, Owen Prys Papers 22728.

[18] NLW, Lewis Valentine Papers, Diary 23.

[19] NLW, Bishop D. L. Prosser Papers.

[20] Letter to René Hague, 15 July 1973, in *Dai Greatcoat: A Self-Portrait of David Jones in his Letters* (London, 1980), p.249.

[21] NLW Minor Deposits, Facsimile 718.

[22] NLW Calvinistic Methodist Archives, Owen Prys Papers 22683.

[23] Owen Prys Papers 22687.

[24] Stuart Sillars, 'A Welshman in Salonika, 1916–19: Iorwerth Miles Davies', *Llafur* 3 (1983), pp.66–75.

[25] NLW Diary, p.192, Morgan, 'Ffydd yn y ffosydd', pp.89–90.

[26] *From Khaki to Cloth: the Autobiography of the Revd. Morgan Watcyn-Williams MC* (Carnarfon, 1949), p.46.

[27] 'On Active Service: the war diary of a Caernarfonshire quarryman', *Trans. Caernarfonshire Hist. Soc.* 52 (1991–2), pp.98–9; cf. Morgan, 'Ffydd yn y ffosydd', p.94.

[28] From an unidentified newspaper article in NLW Diary, front cover; cf. *From Khaki to Cloth*, p.84.

[29] E. Beynon Davies, *Ar Orwel Pell* (Llandysul, 1965), p.37.

[30] *Up To Mametz* (London, 1931), p.213.

[31] See G. Dewi Roberts, *Witness These Letters: Letters from the Western Front, 1915–18* (Denbigh, 1983), pp.104–5.

[32] UWB Archive, Bangor MS 16265.

[33] NLW, Lewis Valentine Papers, Diary 23, 26 October 1917.

[34] Ibid., Diary 24.

[35] NLW, Calvinistic Methodist Archive, Owen Prys Papers 22648.

[36] *From Khaki to Cloth*, p.117; the contribution of Philip 'Tubby' Clayton, the founder of the Toc H Movement, and G. A. Studdert Kennedy 'Woodbine Willie' is discussed extensively by Alan Wilkinson in *The Church of England and the First World War*, 2nd edn. (London, 1996).

37 According to lists published in the denominational handbooks, 14 Welsh Anglican clergymen, 8 Calvinistic Methodist, 10 Baptist and 14 Congregationalist ministers served in a full-time capacity with the Welsh regiments though a considerably higher number volunteered for occasional service with the YMCA.

38 *From Khaki to Cloth*, pp.54, 75, 109.

39 R. H. Evans, *Cofiant David Williams (1877–1927)* (Caernarfon, 1970), p.105.

40 *Y Goleuad*, 4 August 1916, p.4; Morgan, 'Ffydd yn y ffosydd', p.86.

41 NLW MS 10850C (Frondirion 37), letter to E. Evans, undated.

42 'Croes ai cors?', *Y Drysorfa* 85 (1915), pp.196–200.

43 *Y Drysorfa* 86 (1915), p.319, letter to O. W. Owen 'Alafon', 25 May 1915.

44 David Jenkins, *Thomas Gwynn Jones* (Caernarfon, 1973), p.248.

45 *Y Goleuad*, 25 September 1914, p.9.

46 *Y Llan*, 28 August 1914, p.5.

47 *Y Goleuad*, 11 September 1914, p.8; for Jones's measured response to these and other criticisms see idem., 11 September, p.6, 18 September p.6, 16 October p.9, 23 October, p.5.

48 *Y Llan*, 9 October 1914, p.4.

49 'Principal Rees and the war', *Western Mail*, 7 October 1914, p.4.

50 See Davies, *Byddin y Brenin*, pp.131–8.

51 UWB Archive, Bangor MS 17777, letter to J. T. Rhys, 5 January 1916.

52 Cf. Martin Ceadel, *Pacifism in Britain, 1914–1945: The Defining of a Faith* (Oxford, 1980), ch.1, where he defines *pacificism* as 'no more than being in favour of peace and arbitration and opposed to militarism and settling disputes by war', whereas *pacifism* was 'the personal conviction that it is wrong to take part in war or even . . . to resist evil in any way', pp.3, 4.

53 UWB Archives, Bangor MS 17773.

54 Ibid., Bangor MS 17777, letter to J. T. Rhys, 5 January 1916.

55 *Y Greal* (1916), p.106.

56 *Y Goleuad*, 7 July 1916, p.9.

57 UWB Archive, Bangor MS 15970, J. Williams to E. M. Humphreys, 30 October 1917.

58 For E. Morgan Humphreys's defence of his position see *Y Goleuad*, 27 December 1918, p.4; his endorsement of Asquith appeared in the issue of 26 October 1917.

59 See Aled Eirug, 'Agweddau ar y gwrthwynebiad i'r Rhyfel Byd Cyntaf yng Nghymru', *Llafur* 4 (1986), pp.59–68.

60 NLW, E. K. Jones MSS (Box 12), 24 February 1916.

61 Ibid. (Box 14), B. Meyrick to E. K. Jones, 13 October 1917.

62 UWB Archive, Thomas Jones collection.

63 'P. T. Forsyth ar Ryfel:II', *Y Deyrnas*, April 1917, pp.5, 6.

64 P. T. Forsyth, *The Christian Ethic of War* (London, 1916), p.45.

65 NLW, E. K. Jones MSS, letter from J. B. Hughes, 26 July 1917.

66 NLW, Thomas Rees Papers, 5 July 1918.

67 John Davies, *A History of Wales* (London, 1993), pp.515–16.

68 R. R. Williams, *Breuddwyd Cymro Mewn Dillad Benthyg* (Lerpwl, 1964), pp.4–7.

69 NLW, Diary, p.329; Morgan, 'Ffydd yn y ffosydd', p.81.

70 'The army and religion', *The Welsh Outlook* 4 (1917), pp.441–3, quotation on p.442.

71 *Y Llan*, 1 September 1916, p.7.

72 For the Mission see Wilkinson, *Church of England and the War*, pp.70–9.

73 *Y Cyfaill Eglwysig*, January 1916, p.1; cf. *Y Llan*, 28 January 1916, p.5.

74 *Yr Haul*, June 1916, pp.161, 163.

75 Ibid., May 1916, p.129.

76 Eluned E. Owen, *The Later Life of Bishop Owen* (Llandysul, 1961), p.316; cf. *Y Llan*, 1 December 1916, p.3.

77 NLW, Calvinistic Methodist Archive, Owen Prys Papers 22714.

78 NLW, Bishop D. L. Prosser Papers.

79 NLW, E. K. Jones Papers.

80 Ibid., 17 December 1917.

81 *Blwyddiadur y Methodistiaid Calfinaidd am 1917,* p.29.

82 NLW, Lewis Valentine Papers, Diary 25.

83 Ibid.

84 Owen Prys Papers 22283.

85 Diary 23.

86 Owen Prys Papers 22714, 28 July 1917.

87 Loc. cit.

88 Diary 23.

89 'The army and religion', pp.442, 443.

90 Diary 23.

91 Owen Prys Papers 22649.

92 Ibid., 22283.

93 Watcyn-Williams, *From Khaki to Cloth*, p.71.

94 See R. Tudur Jones, *Ffydd ac Argyfwng Cenedl* (Abertawe, 1982), Vol.2, especially pp.7–86.

95 'Anfarwoldeb yng ngoleuni heddiw', *Seren Gomer* 11 (1917), pp.271–82, quotation on p.272.

96 'Hawl ac ateb', *Y Goleuad*, 14 August 1914, p.5.

[97] 'Dylanwad y rhyfel ar yr eglwysi', *Y Dysgedydd* 96 (1916), pp.37–41, quotation on p.40.

[98] See Thomas Rees, 'Meidroldeb Duw', *Y Dysgedydd* 97 (1917), pp.349–53; D. Miall Edwards, 'Y rhyfel a hollalluogrwydd Duw', *Y Beirniad* 5 (1916), pp.1–15.

[99] NLW, Calvinistic Methodist Archives, D. Morris Jones Papers, Sermons Book C; for more on his wartime experiences see J. E. Wynne Davies, 'Professor David Morris Jones, MC, MA, BD (1887–1957): war diaries', *Cylchgrawn Hanes, Historical Society of the Presbyterian Church of Wales* 22 (1998), pp.35–54.

[100] Ibid.

[101] Ibid., sermon on Matthew 10:29–31.

[102] Ibid.

[103] UWB Archive, Bangor MS 16288, 18 July 1916.

[104] E.g. Hugh Owen (ed.), *Braslun o Hanes Methodistiaeth Galfinaidd Môn, 1880–1935* (Caernarfon, 1937), p.61.

[105] Diary 23.

[106] NLW MS 10938C.

[107] *Y Cyfaill Eglwysig*, December 1917, pp.309–10.

[108] NLW, Bishop D. L. Prosser Papers, 6 October 1916.

[109] 'Ar ôl y rhyfel', *Y Goleuad*, 25 January 1918, p.5.

[110] Owen Prys Papers, 22283.

[111] NLW, Diary p.86; Morgan, 'Ffydd yn y ffosydd', p.93.

[112] Diary 25.

3   *Anglicanism and Catholicism, 1920–1945*

[1] NLW MS 10938C.

[2] *Llandaff Diocesan Magazine*, January 1914, p.88.

[3] Quoted by T. I. Ellis, *Ym Mêr Fy Esgyrn* (Lerpwl, 1955), p. 41.

[4] *Report of the Royal Commission on the Church of England and Other Religious Bodies in Wales and Monmouthshire*, Vol.2 (London, 1910), q.8216, p.336.

[5] A. J. Edwards, *Archbishop Green, His Life and Opinions* (Llandysul, 1986), pp.74–5.

[6] Ibid., p.61.

[7] See John S. Peart-Binns, *Edwin Morris: Archbishop of Wales* (Llandysul, 1991), especially pp.49–62.

[8] Owain W. Jones, *Glyn Simon: His Life and Opinions* (Llandysul, 1982), p.32.

9   Edwards, *Archbishop Green,* p.87.
10 D. T. W. Price, *A History of the Church in Wales in the Twentieth Century* (Penarth, 1990), p.19.
11 See W. Ambrose Bebb, *Dydd-lyfr Pythefnos neu Ddawns Angau* (Bangor, 1939).
12 J. Lambert Rees, *Timothy Rees of Mirfield and Llandaff: A Biography* (London, 1945), p.25.
13 See Alan Wilkinson, *The Community of the Resurrection: A Centenary History* (London, 1992), pp.135, 168–9.
14 Rees, *Timothy Rees*, p.101.
15 J. G. James in E. T. Davies (ed.), *The Story of the Church in Glamorgan, 560–1960* (London, 1962), p.96.
16 J. Lambert Rees, *Sermons and Hymns of Timothy Rees, Bishop of Llandaff* (London, 1946), pp.8, 12.
17 For his part in 'the Macnaughten case', see Edwards, *Archbishop Green,* pp.98–102.
18 D. T. W. Price, *A History of Saint David's University College Lampeter*, Vol.2 (Cardiff, 1990), p.122; cf. n.6 above.
19 Owain Jones, *Saint Michael's College, Llandaff, 1892–1992* (Cardiff, 1992), pp.61–77.
20 Rees, *Sermons and Hymns of Timothy Rees,* pp.99, 107.
21 Menevia Diocesan Archive, Wrexham; quoted by Trystan Hughes in an unpublished paper 'Francis Mostyn, Bishop of Menevia and Archbishop of Wales'.
22 *The Tablet*, 15 June 1935, p.767.
23 John Williams, *A Digest of Welsh Historical Statistics*, Vol.2 (Cardiff, 1985), pp.349–51.
24 *St Peter's (Cardiff) Parish Magazine* (1924), p.37.
25 *Western Mail*, 18 May 1936, p.7.
26 *St Peter's (Cardiff) Parish Magazine* (1921), p.5.
27 Ibid. (1926), p.117.
28 Ibid., p.229.
29 *The Tablet*, 15 August 1925, p.206.
30 *Western Mail,* 15 October 1929, p.10.
31 *Western Mail*, 14 August 1937, p.11.
32 J. Vyrnwy Morgan, *The Welsh Mind in Evolution* (London, 1925), p.190.
33 J. T. F. Williams, *The Month*, 167 (1936), p.260.
34 *Cardiff Advent Pastoral 1927*; cf. *Menevia Advent Pastoral 1927.*
35 *Monmouthshire Beacon,* 17 September 1943, p.5.
36 'Y syniad Catholig am ffydd', in A. Ff. Williams (ed.), *Ffyrdd a Ffydd*

(Dinbych, 1945), pp.11–24, quotation on p.11.

[37]   *Cardiff Lenten Pastoral 1928.*

[38]   *The Welsh Outlook* 14 (1927), p.28.

[39]   Robert Wade, *St Peter's (Cardiff) Parish Magazine* (1924), p.199.

[40]   *Pastoral Letter of the Archbishop of Cardiff . . . 1941.*

[41]   Westminster Diocesan Archives: Bourne Papers; quoted by Trystan Hughes, 'The Catholic Church and Society in Wales, 1916–62', unpublished Ph.D. thesis, University of Wales, Bangor, 1998, p.208; for the 'Sword of the Spirit' see Adrian Hastings, *A History of English Christianity, 1920–90* (London, 1990), pp.393–8.

[42]   *Almanac and Directory for the Archdiocese of Cardiff, 1928*, p.63.

[43]   *Western Mail*, 19 September 1932, p.8; *The Tablet*, 5 December 1936, p.770.

[44]   *Western Mail*, 12 June 1933, p.9.

[45]   *The Tablet*, 5 December 1936, p.770.

[46]   H. W. J. Edwards, *The Good Patch* (London, 1938), p.145.

[47]   Vyrnwy Morgan, *Welsh Mind in Evolution*, p.180.

[48]   D. Winter Lewis in *Western Mail*, 13 February 1930, p.5.

[49]   *Western Mail*, 22 October 1936, p.10.

[50]   *Western Mail*, 8 April 1937, p.8.

[51]   Hughes, 'Catholic Church and Society in Wales', p.128.

[52]   Gwilym Davies, 'Cymru Gyfan a'r Blaid Genedlaethol Gymreig', *Y Traethodydd* 97 (1942), pp.99–111, quotation on p.107.

[53]   *Menevia Advent Pastoral 1937.*

[54]   *The Tablet,* 28 November 1936, p.735.

[55]   Menevia Diocesan Archives; Brecon File; quoted by Hughes, 'Catholic Church and Society in Wales', pp.48, 83.

[56]   *Menevia Lenten Pastoral 1936.*

[57]   *Pastoral Letter of the Archbishop of Cardiff on Mixed Marriages 1941.*

[58]   *The Tablet,* 10 March 1934, p.295.

[59]   T. B. Wills of Merthyr Tydfil in the *Western Mail*, 27 April 1936, p.14.

4   *Nonconformity 1920–1945: confessing the faith*

[1]   Quoted in R. H. Evans, *Y Datganiad Byr ar Ffydd a Buchedd* (Caernarfon, 1971), p.13.

[2]   *Comisiwn Ad-drefnu Cymdeithasfa Methodistiaid Calfinaidd . . . Cymru, Adroddiad 1* (Lerpwl, 1920), p.11.

3   Ibid., p.12.

4   Quoted in Evans, *Datganiad Byr*, pp.58, 59, 61.

5   *Comisiwn Ad-drefnu . . . Adroddiad 1,* p.19.

6   They were Principal Owen Prys, Professor David Phillips of Bala, and the Revds Hywel Harris Hughes and R. R. Hughes, both of whom were based at Liverpool at the time; for the history and background of the Declaratory Statement see R. H. Evans, *Datganiad Byr, passim.*

7   *Comisiwn Ad-drefnu . . . Adroddiad 1,* pp.19–20.

8   Ibid., p.20.

9   D. Francis Roberts, *Llawlyfr ar y Pumllyfr* (Caernarfon, 1920).

10 R. S. Thomas, 'Ysbrydoliaeth llyfrau Moses: adolygiad ar lawlyfr y Parch. D. Francis Roberts ar y Pumllyfr', *Y Drysorfa* 92 (1921), pp.19–24, 46–51; cf. idem. 'Undod awdurol Eseia', *Y Drysorfa* 93 (1923), pp.139–45, 173–8, 222–5, 252–6.

11 *Comisiwn Ad-drefnu . . . Adroddiad 1,* p.55.

12 Ibid., p.20.

13 Ibid., p.21.

14 Ibid., p.54.

15 *Y Geiriadur Beiblaidd*, 2 Vols (Wrecsam, 1926), Thomas Rees, D. Francis Roberts, J. T. Evans and David Williams (eds.), pp.585, 793–4, 780–1, 630–64.

16 G. Wynne Griffith, 'Yr Hen Destament yng ngoleuni Iesu Grist', *Y Traethodydd* 75 (1920), pp.159–60.

17 D. Francis Roberts, 'Ysbrydoliaeth, datguddiad ac awdurdod y Beibl', *Y Traethodydd* 78 (1923), pp.159–60.

18 *Comisiwn Ad-drefnu . . . Adroddiad 1*, p.52.

19 Griffith, 'Yr Hen Destament yng ngoleuni Iesu Grist', p.42.

20 Morgan Watcyn-Williams, 'Things new and old', *The Treasury* 7 (1928), p.23.

21 *Baner ac Amserau Cymru*, 6 September 1923, p.12.

22 D. Francis Roberts, 'Tuedd diwinyddiaeth heddiw', *Baner ac Amserau Cymru,* 27 September 1923, p.8.

23 Saunders Lewis, 'Dogma: ateb i D. Francis Roberts', *Baner ac Amserau Cymru,* 4 October 1923, p.12.

24 Saunders Lewis, 'Llythyr ynghylch Catholigiaeth', *Y Llenor,* 7 (1927), pp.44–7.

25 *Comisiwn Ad-drefnu . . . Adroddiad 1,* p.19.

26 E. O. Davies, 'Our constitution', *The Treasury* 20 (1932), p.124.

27 *Comisiwn Ad-drefnu . . . Adroddiad 1,* p.50.

28 *Y Goleuad*, 24 September 1924, p.1.

29 E. O. Davies, 'Ein Cyffes Ffydd, 1823–1923', in *Ffydd, Trefn a Bywyd*

(Caernarfon, 1930), p.24.

30 *Y Goleuad*, 24 September 1924, p.1.

31 W. Nantlais Williams, *Torri'r Rhaffau* (Caernarfon, 1925), pp.9, 12–13.

32 See *Comisiwn Ad-drefnu y Methodistiaid Calfinaidd, Adroddiad 2* (Lerpwl, 1924), pp.50–6; Davies, *Ffydd, Trefn a Bywyd*, pp.47, 56–7.

33 Williams, *Torri'r Rhaffau*, p.15.

34 *Y Goleuad*, 12 March 1925, p.5.

35 See *The Tom Nefyn Controversy: An Account of the Crisis in Welsh Calvinistic Methodism* (Port Talbot, n.d. but 1930).

36 Tom Nefyn Williams, *Y Ffordd yr Edrychaf ar Bethau* (Dolgellau, 1928), *passim*.

37 See Robert Pope, 'Corwynt gwyllt ynteu tyner awel? Helynt Tom Nefyn yn y Tymbl', *Y Traethodydd* 152 (1997), pp.150–62.

38 *Y Goleuad*, 18 April 1928, p.3.

39 *A Plea and a Protest* (Ebenezer CM Church, Tumble, n.d. but 1928), p.11.

40 See 'Llain y Delyn: Cymdeithas Gristnogol y Tymbl', *Yr Ymofynnydd* (1969).

41 It is virtually ignored in his autobiography *Yr Ymchwil* (Dinbych, 1942); E. H. Griffiths attributes the move to the influence of George M. Ll. Davies, *Seraff yr Efengyl Seml* (Caernarfon, 1968), p.56.

42 A petition organized by Morgan Watcyn-Williams in support of Tom Nefyn and signed by nearly two score of the Connexion's more liberal ministers and laymen was published immediately following the Treherbert association, see *The Tom Nefyn Controversy*, p.8; cf. *From Khaki to Cloth: the Autobiography of Morgan Watcyn-Williams MC* (Caernarfon, 1949), pp.158–9.

43 W. Nantlais Williams, *O Gopa Bryn Nebo: Atgofion Nantlais* (Llandysul, 1967), p.96.

44 Ibid., p.97.

45 Evans, *Y Datganiad Byr*, p.111.

46 E. H. Griffiths, *Heddychwr Mawr Cymru* (Caernarfon, 1967), pp.20–3, 31–3.

47 Evans, *Y Datganiad Byr,* p.114.

48 'Methodistiaeth Galfinaidd' in A. Ff. Williams (ed.), *Ffyrdd a Ffydd* (Dinbych, 1945), p.96.

49 See R. Tudur Jones, *Hanes Annibynwyr Cymru* (Abertawe, 1966), pp.219–38.

50 R. Tudur Jones, *Yr Undeb: Hanes Undeb yr Annibynwyr Cymraeg, 1872–1972* (Abertawe, 1975), p.199.

[51] D. Miall Edwards, *Bannau'r Ffydd* (Wrecsam, 1929), pp.24, 25–6.

[52] Ibid., xiii.

[53] Ibid., pp.39, 372.

[54] Ibid., p.192.

[55] Ibid., p.374.

[56] J. E. Daniel, 'Diwinyddiaeth Cymru', *Yr Efrydydd* 5 (1929), pp.118–22, 173–5, quotations on p.174.

[57] Ibid., pp.197–203, quotations on pp.197, 198, 121.

[58] J. D. Vernon Lewis, 'Diwinyddiaeth Karl Barth', *Yr Efrydydd* 3 (1926–7), pp.254–8.

[59] See H. Martin Rumscheidt, *Theology and Revelation: An Analysis of the Barth–Harnack Correspondence of 1923* (Cambridge, 1972).

[60] For Gruffydd's address see *Adroddiad Undeb Machynlleth* (Abertawe, 1928), pp.783–9; the warm response to its delivery is recorded in *Y Tyst*, 14 June 1928, p.5.

[61] *Adroddiad Undeb Caernarfon* (Abertawe, 1930), p.109.

[62] *Y Tyst*, 3 July 1930, p.3.

[63] Ibid., 21 August–18 September 1930; for an analysis of the controversy in full see D. Densil Morgan, *Torri'r Seiliau Sicr: Detholiad o Ysgrifau J. E. Daniel ynghyd â Rhagymadrodd* (Llandysul, 1993), pp.35–8.

[64] Cf. J. E. Daniel, *Dysgeidiaeth yr Apostol Pawl* (Abertawe, 1933); idem., 'Dyfodol crefydd yng Nghymru' (1933), UCW Bangor Archives, John Morgan Jones Papers.

[65] 'Anghenion crefyddol Cymru', *Y Dysgedydd* 112 (1933), pp.290–4, quotation on p.293.

[66] See Brynmor Pierce Jones, *The Spiritual History of Keswick in Wales, 1903–83* (Cwmbran, 1989), pp.31–55.

[67] See Brynmor Pierce Jones, *The King's Champions* (Cwmbran, 1986), pp.155–61.

[68] Ibid., p.159.

[69] Ibid., pp.151, 184.

[70] R. B. Jones, *Yr Ail-Ddyfodiad yng Ngoleuni'r Epistolau at y Thesaloniaid* (Tonypandy, 1919), p.72.

[71] Cf. D. W. Bebbington, 'Baptists and Fundamentalists in inter-war Britain', *Studies in Church History Subsidia* 7 (1990), pp.297–326.

[72] Noel Gibbard, *Taught to Serve: The History of Barry and Bryntirion Colleges* (Bridgend, 1996), pp.20–6; for Rees Howells (1879–1950) and his college, see Norman Grubb, *Rees Howells Intercessor* (Guildford, 1973).

[73] Cf. Dewi Eirug Davies, *Diwinyddiaeth yng Nghymru, 1927–77*

(Llandysul, 1984), p.87.

[74] Jones, *Keswick in Wales*, p.35.

[75] Gibbard, *Taught to Serve*, p.31.

[76] *The Bible Call* (Journal of the Baptist Bible Union), July–September 1919, p.3, quoted in Bebbington, 'Baptists and Fundamentalists', p.306; Jones, *King's Champions*, p.197.

[77] Jones, *King's Champions*, pp.117–214.

[78] Geraint D. Fielder, *'Excuse me Mr Davies - Hallelujah!': Evangelical Student Witness in Wales, 1923–83* (Bridgend and Leicester, 1983), p.28.

[79] See Geraint D. Fielder, *Lord of the Years: the Story of the Inter-Varsity Fellowship, Universities and Colleges Christian Fellowship, 1928–88* (Leicester, 1988), p.23.

[80] *Yr Efengylydd* 116 (1924), p.125.

[81] Fielder, *'Excuse me Mr Davies'*, pp.78–89.

[82] Jones, *Keswick in Wales*, pp.46–55; Gibbard, *Taught to Serve*, pp.23–36.

[83] See, for instance, Iain Murray, *D. Martyn Lloyd-Jones: the First Forty Years 1899–1939* (Edinburgh, 1982), pp.131–268.

[84] John Morgan Jones, 'Dinistrio'r hen ddiwinyddiaeth', *Yr Efrydydd* 12 (1936), p.270.

[85] Dewi Morgan (ed.), *They Became Anglicans* (London, 1959), p.111.

[86] Ivor Oswy Davies, 'Mudiad Karl Barth', *Y Goleuad*, 22 September 1937, pp.9–11, quotation on p.10.

[87] R. Buick Knox, *Voices from the Past: A History of the English conference of the Presbyterian Church of Wales, 1889–1938* (Llandysul, 1969), p.54.

[88] See Dewi Eirug Davies, *Protest a Thystiolaeth: Agweddau ar y Dystiolaeth Gristionogol yn yr Ail Ryfel Byd* (Llandysul, 1993), pp.117–52.

[89] John Wyn Roberts (ed.), *Sylfeini'r Ffydd* (Llundain, 1942), p.7.

[90] Morgan, *Torri'r Seiliau Sicr*, pp.149–75; for their contemporary effect see Introduction, pp.65–82.

[91] T. Glyn Thomas, *Christ's Handmaid: An Essay on the Church* (Wrexham, 1945), p.56.

5 Nonconformity 1920–1945: responding to the secular challenge

[1] Benjamin Humphreys, *Y Bedyddwyr: eu Hegwyddorion Gwahaniaethol a'u Rhagolygon* (Felin-foel, n.d. but 1926), pp.4, 72, 83.

[2] Hilda Jennings, *Brynmawr: A Study of a Distressed Area* (London, 1934), pp.139–40.

[3] H. W. J. Edwards, *The Good Patch* (London, 1938), p.143.

[4] See R. J. Barker, *Christ in the Valley of the Unemployed* (London, 1936).

[5] Barrie Naylor, *Quakers in the Rhondda, 1926–1986* (Chepstow, 1986), pp.31–59.

[6] NLW, Calvinistic Methodist Archives, Owen Prys Papers 22283.

[7] *Comisiwn Ad-drefnu Cymdeithasfa Methodistiaid Calfinaidd Gogledd Cymru, Adroddiad 5* (Lerpwl, 1921), p.16.

[8] See *Y Goleuad*, 19 March 1924; *Y Tyst*, 27 March 1924; *Seren Cymru* 18 April 1924; *Y Darian*, 21 August 1924; *Yr Efrydydd* 4 (1924), p.105; *The Welsh Outlook* 1924, p.260; *Y Deyrnas* (Llandudno), December 1924, p.4.

[9] See Ieuan Gwynedd Jones (ed.), *Gwilym Davies, A Tribute* (Llandysul, 1981); Robert Pope, 'Lladmerydd y Deyrnas: Herbert Morgan (1875–1945)', *Trafodion Cymdeithas Hanes y Bedyddwyr* (1994), pp.47–65.

[10] Robert Pope, *Building Jerusalem: Nonconformity, Labour and the Social Question in Wales, 1906–39* (Cardiff, 1998), p.157 and *passim*.

[11] *Comisiwn Ad-drefnu . . . Adroddiad 5*, pp.8, 9.

[12] *Cenadwri Gymdeithasol yr Efengyl: Adroddiad is-bwyllgor Gwasanaeth Cymdeithasol i Gyngor Undeb yr Annibynwyr Cymreig* (Abertawe, n.d. but 1923), pp.9, 8, 25, 11.

[13] T. Alban Davies, 'Impressions of life in the Rhondda Valley', in K. S. Hopkins (ed.), *Rhondda Past and Future* (n.d. but 1975), p.15.

[14] R. Tudur Jones, *Yr Undeb: Hanes Undeb yr Annibynwyr Cymraeg, 1872–1972* (Abertawe, 1975), p.212.

[15] Davies, 'Impressions', p.16.

[16] Ibid., pp.16–17; cf. T. Alban Davies, 'Cynrychiolaeth unol eglwysi Cymru at y Prif-Weinidog', *Y Tyst,* 19 August 1937, p.1.

[17] Davies, 'Impressions', p.17.

[18] Saunders Lewis and Lewis Valentine, *Why We Burned the Bombing School* (Caernarfon, 1937).

[19] Jones, *Yr Undeb*, p.215.

[20] See D. Densil Morgan, 'Basel, Bangor a Dyffryn Clwyd: mater y genedl yng ngwaith Karl Barth ac eraill', in Gareth Lloyd Jones (ed.), *Cyfamod a Chenadwri: Cyfrol Deyrnged i'r Athro Gwilym H. Jones* (Dinbych, 1995), pp.149–72.

[21] See D. Densil Morgan, 'Tyst ymhlith y Tystion: profiad Cymro yn Almaen Hitler', *Transactions of the Honourable Society of*

Cymmrodorion, New Series 6 (1995), pp.156–66.

22 *Yr Efrydydd* (1933), p.228; Martin Ceadel, *Pacifism in Britain, 1914–45: The Defining of a Faith* (Oxford, 1980), pp.127–32.

23 E.g. T. Ellis Jones, 'Yn angof ni chant fod', *Seren Cymru,* 18 November 1932, p.1.

24 *Comisiwn Ad-drefnu . . . Adroddiad 5,* p.61.

25 *Adroddiad Undeb Caernarfon* (Abertawe, 1930), pp.32–3.

26 *Seren Cymru,* 23 September 1932, p.8.

27 E. K. Jones, 'Y "Western Mail" a'r Bedyddwyr'; ibid., p.1.

28 E. H. Griffiths, *Heddychwr Mawr Cymru* (Caernarfon, 1967), p.158.

29 Gwilym Davies, *Y Byd – Ddoe a Heddiw* (Llundain, 1938), p.ix.

30 E. H. Griffiths, *Seraff yr Efengyl Seml* (Caernarfon, 1968), p.37.

31 Dewi Eirug Davies, *Protest a Thystiolaeth: Agweddau ar y Dystiolaeth Gristnogol yn yr Ail Ryfel Byd* (Llandysul, 1993), pp.109–15.

32 Gwilym Davies, 'Y byd ar drothwy 1939', *Y Traethodydd* 8 (1939), pp.6–18, quotation on p.16.

33 W. Ambrose Bebb, *Dydd-lyfr Pythefnos neu Ddawns Angau* (Bangor, 1939), pp.64–5.

34 J. P. Davies, 'Tri tasg heddychwr', *Heddiw* 5 (1939), pp.126–30, quotation on p.130.

35 John Williams, *A Digest of Welsh Historical Statistics,* Vol.2 (Cardiff, 1985), pp.286, 294, 325, 328.

36 John Roberts, 'The problems of our Connexion', *The Treasury* 12 (1927), pp.181–2.

37 Lewis Valentine, 'Pregethu', *Y Deyrnas* (Llandudno), June 1930, p.2.

38 Iain Murray, *D. Martyn Lloyd-Jones: The First Forty Years, 1899–1939* (Edinburgh, 1982), pp.153–248.

39 Rhys Davies, *My Wales* (London, 1937), pp.119, 120, 126.

40 John Roberts, *The Calvinistic Methodism of Wales* (Caernarfon, n.d. but 1935), p.77.

41 Diary of Sister Kate Jones, Bryntawel, Bangor, in private possession.

42 Florence Wilson Grey, 'The place of women in the church', *The Treasury* 8 (1920), p.3.

43 Herbert Morgan, 'The churches and labour: a symposium', *The Welsh Outlook* 5 (1918), pp.42, 95–6,127–8,164–6, 198–9.

44 *Comisiwn Ad-drefnu Methodistiaid Calfinaidd Cymru, Adroddiad 4* (Lerpwl, 1921), pp.10, 14.

45 *St Peter's (Cardiff) Parish Magazine* 4 (1924), p.336.

46 *The Tablet,* 15 August 1925, p.206.

47 Ibid., 19 October 1929, p.504.

48 Saunders Lewis, 'The literary man's life in Wales', *The Welsh*

Outlook 16 (1929), pp.294–7, quotation on p.295.

49 J. E. De Hirsch-Davies, 'Wales and Catholicism', *The Welsh Outlook* 13 (1926), pp.54–5, 74–6, quotation on p.76.

50 *The Tablet*, 30 March 1935, p.393.

51 'The Conversion of Wales', *The Month* 167 (1936), pp.242–60, quotations on pp.256–7.

52 *Western Mail*, 7 November 1917.

53 *Western Mail*, 15 November 1917.

54 *Western Mail*, 27 November 1915.

55 *Carmarthen Journal*, April 1915; all the above quotations from John Harris (ed.), *Fury Never Leaves Us: a Miscellany of Caradoc Evans* (Cardiff, 1985).

56 'Crefydd fyw', *Yr Efrydydd* 7 (1930), p.87.

57 E. I. Ellis, *T.J.: A Life of Dr Thomas Jones CH* (Cardiff, 1992), p.183.

58 Goronwy Rees, *A Chapter of Accidents* (London, 1972), pp.34, 252, 236.

59 Rhys Davies, *The Withered Root* (London, 1927), p.53.

60 Rhys Davies, *Print of a Hare's Foot: An Autobiography* (London: 1969), pp.5, 16, 29, 67.

61 Davies, *My Wales*, p.211.

62 See Hywel Francis, *Miners Against Fascism* (London, 1984), p.60.

63 Ibid., pp. 189, 49–55.

64 Dafydd Johnston (ed.), *The Complete Poems of Idris Davies* (Cardiff, 1994), p.xxxvii.

65 Islwyn Jenkins, *Idris Davies of Rhymney* (Llandysul, 1986), p.265.

66 Johnston, *Complete Poems*, p.89.

67 Ibid., p.xii.

68 *Comisiwn Ad-drefnu . . . Adroddiad 4*, p.26.

69 *Y Deyrnas* (Llandudno), June 1929, p.2.

70 Jones, *Yr Undeb*, p.287.

71 Ibid., p.288.

72 Watcyn-Williams, *From Khaki to Cloth*, p.171.

73 Roberts, *Calvinistic Methodism*, p.78.

74 D. Gwenallt Jones, 'Y Meirwon', *Eples* (Aberystwyth, 1951), p.9; translation by Anthony Conran, 'The Dead', in *The Penguin Book of Welsh Verse* (London, 1967), pp.251–2.

75 See Adrian Hastings, *A History of English Christianity, 1920–90* (London, 1990), pp.193–220.

76 D. Gwenallt Jones, 'Ar gyfeiliorn', *Ysgubau'r Awen* (Aberystwyth, 1939), p.28.

77 J. E. Meredith (ed.), *Credaf: Llyfr o Dystiolaeth Gristionogol*

(Aberystwyth, 1943), Gwenallt's essay is on pp.51–75; the quotations above are taken from the translation by Ned Thomas and André Morgan, 'What I Believe', *Planet* 32 (1976), pp.1–10.

78 J. E. Daniel, 'Y syniad seciwlar am ddyn', *Cynllun a Sail* (n.p., 1946), pp.12–20, quotation on p.20.

79 Meredith (ed.), *Credaf,* p.10.

80 Gwenallt, 'Sir Forgannwg a Sir Gaerfyrddin', *Eples*, p.24; 'Glamorganshire and Carmarthenshire', translation by B. S. Johnson and Ned Thomas, *Planet* 29 (1975), p.22.

6 *Reconstruction and Crisis*

1 Ewart Lewis, *The Church in Wales, the Catholic Church and the Future* (Llandybie, 1945), p.5.

2 G. O. Williams, *Welsh Church Congress Handbook* (n.p., 1953), p.103.

3 Moelwyn Merchant, *Fragments of a Life: An Autobiography* (Llandysul, 1990), p.56.

4 Lewis, *The Catholic Church and the Future*, p.10.

5 Roger L. Brown, *The Welsh Evangelicals* (Tongwynlais, 1986), p.168.

6 S. K. Binny, *History of St. Mark's, Gabalfa* (1976); Brown, *Welsh Evangelicals*, p.161.

7 D. T. W. Price, *History of St David's University College, Lampeter*, Vol.2 (Cardiff, 1990), p.149.

8 H. Idris Bell, *The Crisis of Our Time and Other Papers* (Llandybie, 1954), p.42.

9 John S. Peart-Binns, *Edwin Morris: Archbishop of Wales* (Llandysul, 1990), pp.76–7.

10 Edward Lewis, *John Bangor: The People's Bishop* (London, 1962), p.129.

11 Quoted in Peart-Binns, *Edwin Morris,* p.81.

12 Ibid., p.71.

13 Ibid., p.89.

14 Ibid., p.81.

15 *Bangor Diocesan Gazette* 1 (July, 1954), p.4.

16 Peart-Binns, *Edwin Morris,* pp.83–4.

17 Glyn Simon, *A Time of Change* (Penarth, 1966), p.10.

18 Glyn Simon et al., *1662: Three Talks* (Penarth, 1962), pp.7–8.

19 Ibid., p.10.

20 Owain W. Jones, *Glyn Simon: His Life and Opinions* (Llandysul,

1981), p.58.

[21] G. O. Williams, *The Work of the Church* (Caernarfon, 1959), p.44.

[22] H. Idris Bell, *Welsh Church Congress Handbook*, p.84.

[23] John Williams, *Digest of Welsh Statistics*, Vol.2 (Cardiff, 1985), pp.257–8.

[24] Ibid., pp.259–65.

[25] Ewart Lewis, *Prayer Book Revision in the Church in Wales* (Penarth, 1958), p.31.

[26] D. T. W. Price, *A History of the Church in Wales* (Penarth, 1990), p.30.

[27] Lewis, *The Catholic Church and the Future,* p.20.

[28] *Report of the Nation and Prayer Book Commission* (n.p., 1949), p.11.

[29] Ibid., p.42.

[30] Quoted in Peart-Binns, *Edwin Morris*, p.119, and Jones, *Glyn Simon*, p.68.

[31] *Bangor Diocesan Gazette* 4 (January, 1958), p.2.

[32] See D. Gwenallt Jones, *Eples* (Aberystwyth, 1951).

[33] D. Gwenallt Jones, 'Yr Eglwys yng Nghymru', *Y Genhinen* 8 (1958), pp.88, 90–1.

[34] 'Theomemphus', *Bilingual Bishops and All That* (Llandybie, 1958), p.2.

[35] Ibid., p.7.

[36] Ibid., p.16.

[37] Peart-Binns, *Edwin Morris*, p.122.

[38] Ibid., p.127.

[39] Jones, *Glyn Simon*, p.71.

[40] Peart-Binns, *Edwin Morris*, p.136.

[41] Glyn Simon, *Then and Now: A Charge* (Penarth, 1961), p.31.

[42] Ibid., pp.28, 29.

[43] Glyn Simon, *Feeding the Flock* (Derby, 1964), p.55.

[44] Ibid., p.59.

[45] Simon, *Then and Now,* p.30.

[46] *Catholic Herald*, 10 October 1947, p.7.

[47] *Western Mail*, 26 March 1947, p.3.

[48] *Catholic Herald*, 17 March 1948, p.1.

[49] *The Review* 1 (1957), p.11.

[50] *Western Mail*, 15 March 1960, p.4.

[51] Williams, *Digest of Welsh Statistics*, Vol.2, pp.347–50.

[52] A. J. Mills of Cardiff in the *Western Mail,* 22 August 1950, p.4.

[53] NLW, Lewis Valentine Papers 3/26.

[54] See e.g. *Menevia Record* 2 (1955), p.2; 5 (1958), p.11.

55 McGrath and Petit, *Joint Advent Pastoral for Cardiff and Menevia 1950*.
56 *Menevia Record* 2 (1954), p.18.
57 *Cardiff Archdiocese Yearbook 1963*, p.135.
58 *Western Mail*, 9 April 1948, p.3.
59 *Western Mail*, 14 March 1955, p.7.
60 *Pastoral Letter of the Archbishop of Cardiff on 'Mixed Marriages' 1941*.
61 *Cardiff Lenten Pastoral 1951*.
62 *Western Mail*, 9 September 1953, p.5.
63 Petit in the *Western Mail*, 6 September 1949, p.1.
64 *Cardiff Lenten Pastoral 1948*.
65 *Western Mail*, 1 March 1961, p.8.
66 *Western Mail*, 5 July 1954, p.5.
67 McGrath and Petit, *Joint Advent Pastoral for Cardiff and Menevia 1950*.
68 Menevia Diocesan Archive: Aberystwyth file, quoted by Trystan Hughes, 'The Roman Catholic Church and Society in Wales, 1916–62', unpublished Ph.D. thesis, University of Wales, Bangor, 1998, p.211.
69 Adrian Hastings, *A History of English Christianity, 1920–90* (London, 1991), pp.488–9.
70 *Y Tyst*, 31 August 1950, p.2.
71 *Seren Cymru*, 26 January 1951, p.5.
72 *Menevia Record* 1 (1954), p.2.
73 *Menevia Lenten Pastoral 1958*.
74 *Baner ac Amserau Cymru*, 10 January 1951, p.8.
75 Hughes, 'Catholic Church and Society in Wales', p.232.
76 *Western Mail*, 15 March 1960, p.4.
77 *Western Mail*, 20 February 1960, p.6.
78 Etienne Raven, *The Review* 3 (1961), p.10.
79 *The Tablet*, 20 August 1955, p.187.
80 *Western Mail*, 18 December 1952, p.6.
81 *The Tablet*, 21 June 1947, p.319.
82 *Menevia Diocesan Yearbook 1957*, p.102.
83 'A Portrait of South Wales', in Geoffrey Grigson (ed.), *South Wales and the Marches* (London, 1951), p.57.
84 James Griffiths, *Pages From Memory* (London, 1969), pp.204–5.
85 R. Ifor Parry, *Ymneilltuaeth* (Llandysul, 1962), pp.192–3.
86 *South Wales Evening Post*, 10 November 1950.
87 Parry, *Ymneilltuaeth*, p.175.

88 J. E. Hughes, *Y Drysorfa* 121 (1951), p.255.

89 *Y Dysgedydd* 135 (1955), p.239.

90 *Seren Gomer* 46 (1954), p.181.

91 T. Lloyd Evans, *Pris Ein Rhyddid* (Abertawe, 1960), p.66.

92 Islwyn Ffowc Elis in *Y Dysgedydd* 132 (1952), p.99.

93 Parry, *Ymneilltuaeth*, p.194.

94 R. S. Thomas, *Selected Poems, 1946–1968* (London, 1986), p.20.

95 *Hanes Annibynwyr Cymru* (Abertawe, 1966), p.320.

96 E.g. L. Haydn Lewis's series of articles entitled 'Ffwndamentaliaeth' ('Fundamentalism'), *Y Drysorfa* 126 (1956), pp.169–72, 193–5, 217–20, and Iorwerth Jones, *Y Dysgedydd* 137 (1957), pp.66–8.

97 *Seren Gomer* 46 (1954), p.78; cf. D. Densil Morgan, 'Y proffwyd ymhlith y praidd: Lewis Valentine (1893–1986)', *Transactions of the Honourable Society of Cymmrodorion*, New Series 4 (1998), pp.187–215.

98 *Seren Gomer* 45 (1953), pp.175–6.

99 *Y Traethodydd* 150 (1950), p.99.

100 *Y Dysgedydd* 135 (1955), p.28.

101 *Y Traethodydd* 150 (1950), p.101.

102 *Y Dysgedydd* 135 (1955), p.29.

103 *Y Dysgedydd* 142 (1962), p.216.

104 Martyn Lloyd-Jones, *Crefydd Heddiw ac Yfory* (Llandybie, 1947), p.16.

105 For its literary and historical significance, see R. Tudur Jones's introduction, *Cudd Fy Meiau*, 2nd edn. (Abertawe, 1998), pp.7–28.

7   Uncharted waters, 1962–1979

1 Glyn Simon, *Feeding the Flock* (Derby, 1964), p.122.

2 G. O. Williams, *The Work of the Church* (Caernarfon, 1959), p.77.

3 Quoted in Owain W. Jones, *Glyn Simon: His Life and Opinions* (Llandysul, 1981), p.104.

4 J. Peart-Binns, *Edwin Morris: Archbishop of Wales* (Llandysul, 1990), pp.158–9.

5 Glyn Simon, *Then and Now* (Penarth, 1961), pp.31, 32.

6 Glyn Simon, *A Time of Change* (Penarth, 1966), p.17.

7 Ibid., p.29.

8 Vivian Jones (ed.), *The Church in a Mobile Society* (Swansea and Llandybie, 1969), pp.59, 65.

9 Quoted by Noel A. Davies, 'Agweddau ar Hanes Cyngor Eglwysi

Cymru, 1956–90', unpublished Ph.D. thesis, University of Wales, Bangor, 1997, p.131.

[10] *Western Mail*, 28 October 1966.

[11] Jones (ed.), *Church in a Mobile Society,* pp.114, 82.

[12] Simon, *A Time of Change*, p.44.

[13] Ibid., p.41.

[14] Ibid., p.42.

[15] Owain W. Jones, *St Michael's College, Llandaff, 1892–1992* (Llandaff, 1992), p.98.

[16] J. R. Jones, *Yr Argyfwng Gwacter Ystyr* (Llandybïe, 1964), *passim*.

[17] *Barn* 22 (1964), p.283.

[18] *Barn* 27 (1965), p.71.

[19] Ibid., p.72.

[20] D. Z. Phillips, *J. R. Jones*, Writers of Wales Series (Cardiff, 1995), pp.10–11.

[21] Jones, *Yr Argyfwng Gwacter Ystyr*, pp.23–4.

[22] J. R. Jones, *Ac Onide* (Llandybïe, 1970), p.244 (italics in original).

[23] Edward England, *The Mountain that Moved* (London, 1967), p.32.

[24] Jones, *Glyn Simon: His Life and Opinions*, pp.96–7.

[25] Tony Austin, *Aberfan: The Story of a Disaster* (London, 1967), p.60.

[26] England, *The Mountain that Moved*, p.34.

[27] Ibid., p.77.

[28] Austin, *Aberfan: The Story of a Disaster*, p.109.

[29] Lewis Chester in *The Sunday Times*, 4 December 1966.

[30] Austin, *Aberfan: The Story of a Disaster*, p.180.

[31] Joan Miller, *Aberfan: A Disaster and its Aftermath* (London, 1974), p.125.

[32] Erastus Jones and Paul Ballard (eds.), *The Valleys Call* (Ferndale, 1975), p.22.

[33] Ibid., p.495.

[34] Ibid., p.481.

[35] Iain Murray, *D. M. Lloyd-Jones, The Fight of Faith, 1939–81* (Edinburgh, 1990), pp.572–3.

[36] Jones and Ballard (eds.), *The Valleys Call*, p.107.

[37] England, *The Mountain that Moved*, pp.70–1.

[38] For an analysis of this work see D. Densil Morgan, ' "Dagrau tostaf yr ugeinfed ganrif": golwg newydd ar un o gerddi Gwenallt', *Barn* 286 (1986), pp.377–80.

[39] Meirion Lloyd Davies, 'Undeb eglwysig yng Nghymru yn yr ugeinfed ganrif', in O. E. Evans (ed.), *Gwarchod y Gair: Cyfrol Goffa G. T. Roberts* (Dinbych, 1993), p.185.

40   D. Huw Jones, 'The Ecumenical Movement in the Welsh context', in
      D. Huw Jones and Paul Ballard (eds.), *His Land and People: A
      Symposium on Welsh and Christian Identity* (Cardiff, 1979),
      pp.55–71, quotation on p.66.

41   Geraint D. Fielder, *'Excuse Me Mr Davies – Hallelujiah!': Evangelical
      Student Witness in Wales, 1923–83* (Bridgend and Leicester, 1983), p.218.

42   Murray, *Lloyd-Jones, The Fight of Faith*, p.429.

43   J. Elwyn Davies, *Striving Together: The Evangelical Movement of
      Wales, Its Principles and Aims* (Bridgend, 1984), pp.14, 23.

44   John Williams, *Digest of Welsh Statistics*, Vol.2 (Cardiff, 1985),
      pp.271–2, 295; Eric Edwards (ed.), *Yr Eglwys Fethodistaidd, Hanes
      Ystadegol* (Llandysul, 1980), p.34.

45   D. T. W. Price, *A History of the Church in Wales in the Twentieth
      Century* (Penarth, 1990), p.39.

46   J. B. Sinclair and R. W. D. Fenn, *Just the Right Man: J. R. W. Poole-
      Hughes, 1916–88* (Kington, 1992), p.141.

47   Ibid., p.116.

48   Williams, *A Digest of Welsh Statistics*, pp.258–66.

49   Jones, *Glyn Simon: His Life and Opinions*, p.136.

50   Sinclair and Fenn, *Just the Right Man,* p.131.

51   Ibid., p.131.

52   NLW, Lewis Valentine Papers.

53   Quoted by Noel A. Davies, 'Agweddau ar Hanes Cyngor Eglwysi
      Cymru, 1956–90', p.158.

54   The Council's officers were the Revds Huw Wynne Griffith, Erastus
      Jones, M. J. Williams, Alun Francis and the Ven. W. Ungoed Jacob;
      the sub-Commission was represented by Sr Mary Antony, Fr Leo
      Caesar OSB, Fr Langton Fox, auxiliary bishop of Menevia, Dr Harri
      Pritchard Jones and Fr Anselm Putlanevitch.

55   Noel A. Davies, 'Agweddau ar Hanes Cyngor Eglwysi Cymru,
      1956–90', p.193.

56   Jones, *Glyn Simon: His Life and Opinions*, p.124.

57   Ibid.

58   R. Tudur Jones, 'Christian nationalism', in Jones and Ballard (eds.),
      His Land and People, pp.74–97, quotation on p.91. Cf. the essays in
      the symposium edited by D. E. Davies, *Gwinllan a Roddwyd*
      (Llandybïe, 1972), R. Tudur Jones, *Desire of Nations* (Llandybïe,
      1975), and R. M. Jones, *Crist a Chenedlaetholdeb* (Penybont-ar-
      Ogwr, 1994) for this rich theme.

59   Ron Howells, *A Tale of Two Grandmothers: Memoirs of an
      Ecumenist, 1965–85* (Swansea, 1994), p.22.

8   *Towards the new Wales, 1979–2000*

1   Minutes of Industrial Committee, Council of Churches for Wales, 25 January 1980; quoted by Noel A. Davies, 'Agweddau ar Hanes Cyngor Eglwysi Cymru, 1956–90', unpublished Ph.D. thesis, University of Wales, Bangor, 1997, p.258.

2   The diocesan computation extrapolates from the geographical evidence, which is itself only an approximation, in Peter Brierley and Byron Evans, *Prospects for Wales: Results of the Churches Survey for 1982* (Marc Europe, 1983), pp.30–1, 42–62.

3   Information gleaned from *Diocesan Yearbooks* for Cardiff and Menevia; cf. Brierley and Evans, *Prospects*, pp.42–3 for 1982 statistics.

4   Brierley and Evans, *Prospects*, pp.32–9, 45–62.

5   Elfed ap Nefydd Roberts, *Corff ac Ysbryd: Ysgrifau ar Fethodistiaeth* (Caernarfon, 1988), p.135.

6   Brierley and Evans, *Prospects*, pp.40–1.

7   *Privatization: A Dangerous Trend in British Society* (CCW, 1986), p.4.

8   D. P. Davies, *Against the Tide: Christianity in Wales on the Threshold of a New Millennium* (Llandysul, 1995), p.29.

9   *Challenge to Change: Results of the 1995 Welsh Churches Survey* (Cardiff, 1997), *passim*.

10   R. S. Thomas, *Later Poems, 1972–82* (London, 1983), p.123.

11   Glanmor Williams, *The Welsh and their Religion* (Cardiff, 1991), p.72.

12   Davies, *Against the Tide,* p.26.

Index